Yurara

Volume 1

Story & Art by
Chika Shiomi

Contents

Chapter 1 ················· 3

Chapter 2 ················ 59

Chapter 3 ··············· 103

Chapter 4 ··············· 147

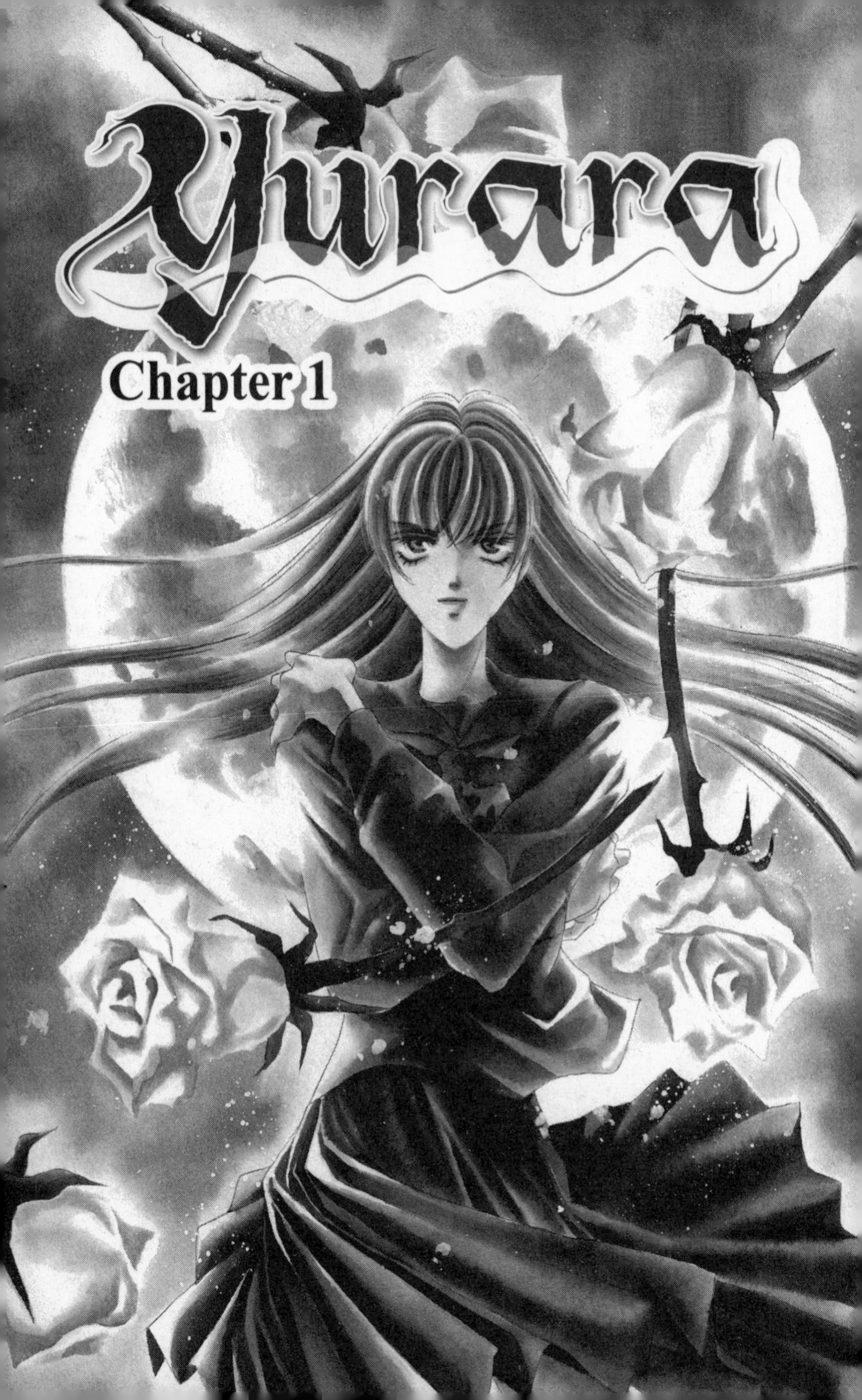
Yurara
Chapter 1

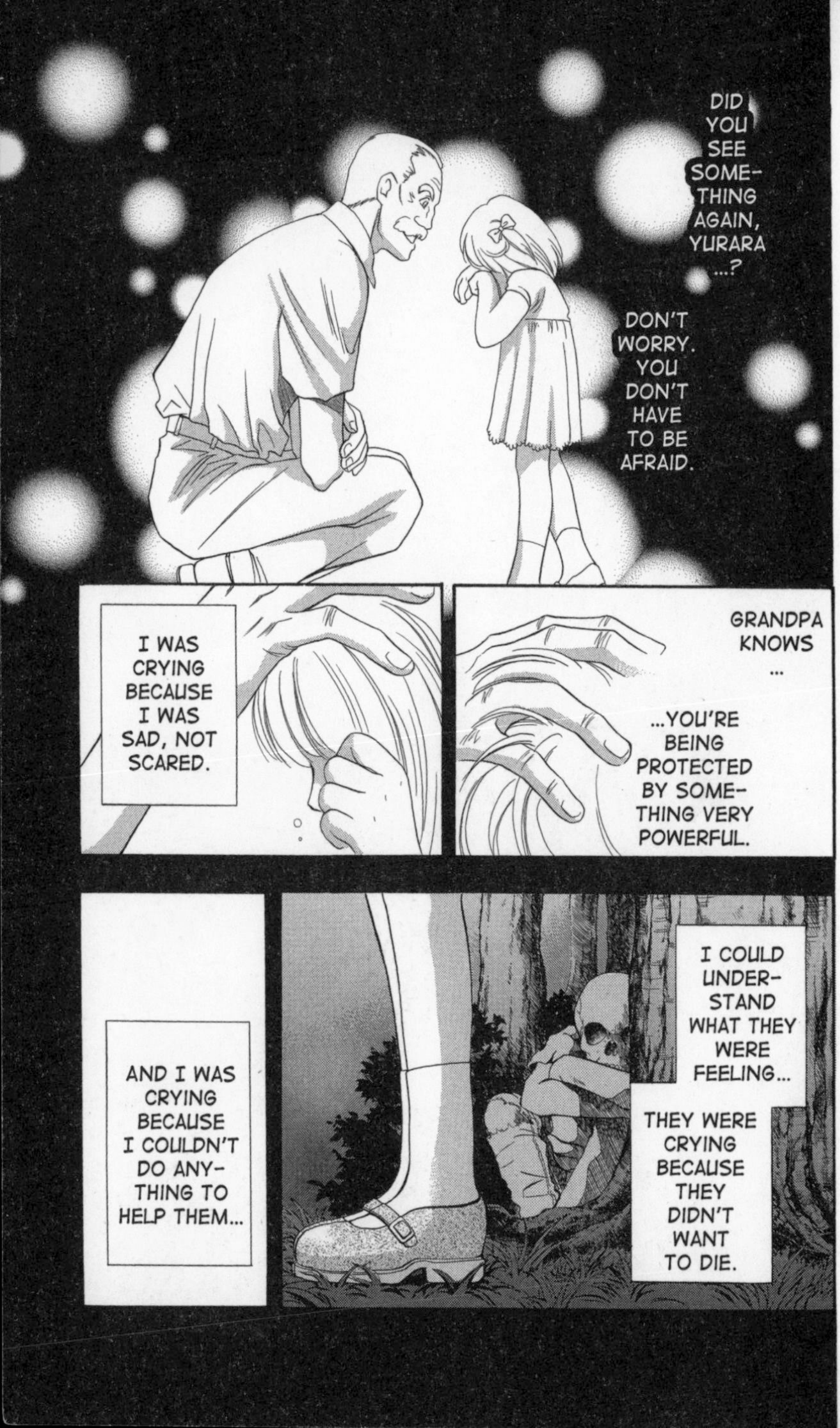
DID YOU SEE SOME-THING AGAIN, YURARA ...?
DON'T WORRY. YOU DON'T HAVE TO BE AFRAID.
GRANDPA KNOWS ...
...YOU'RE BEING PROTECTED BY SOME-THING VERY POWERFUL.
I WAS CRYING BECAUSE I WAS SAD, NOT SCARED.
I COULD UNDER-STAND WHAT THEY WERE FEELING...
THEY WERE CRYING BECAUSE THEY DIDN'T WANT TO DIE.
AND I WAS CRYING BECAUSE I COULDN'T DO ANY-THING TO HELP THEM...

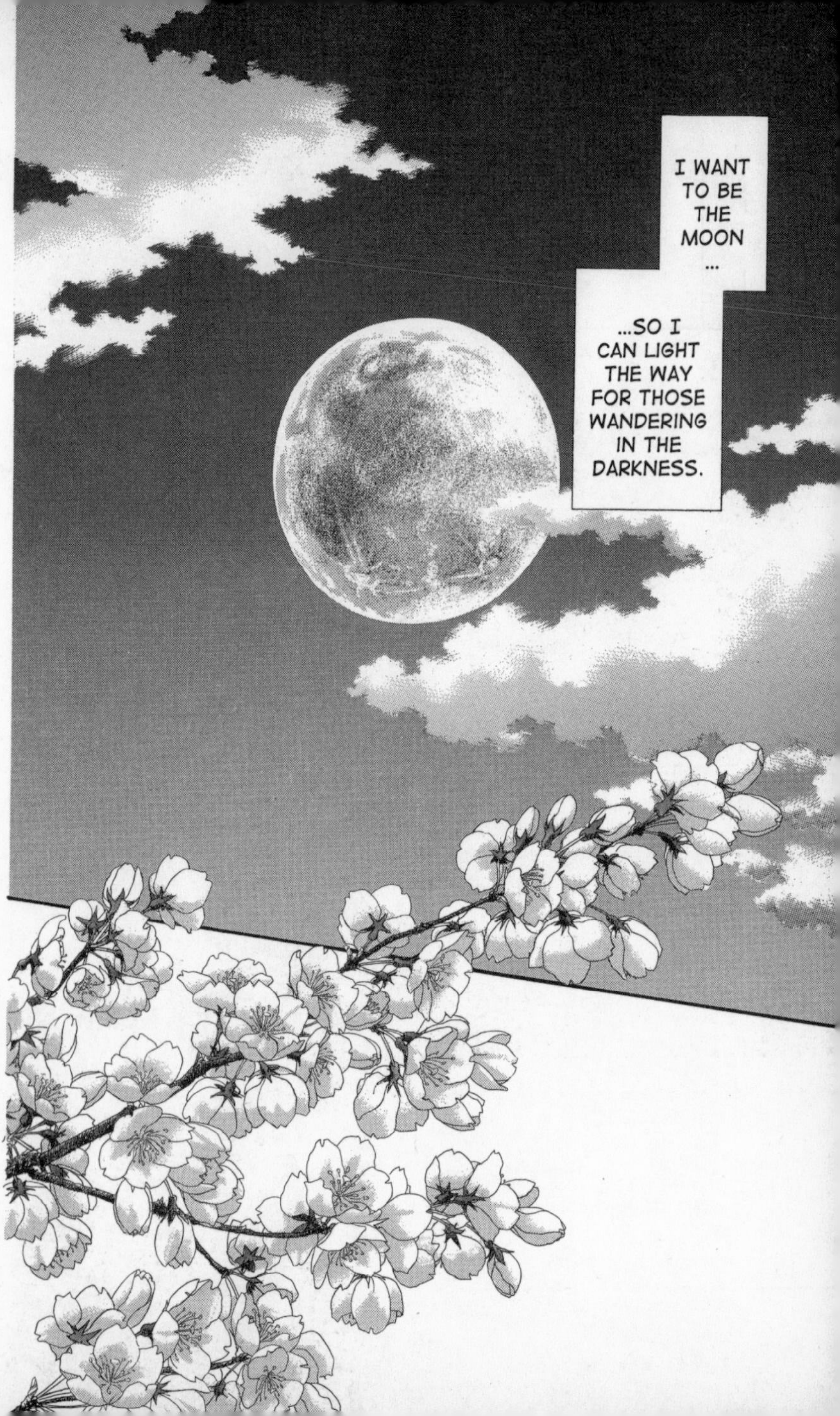
I WANT TO BE THE MOON ...
...SO I CAN LIGHT THE WAY FOR THOSE WANDERING IN THE DARKNESS.

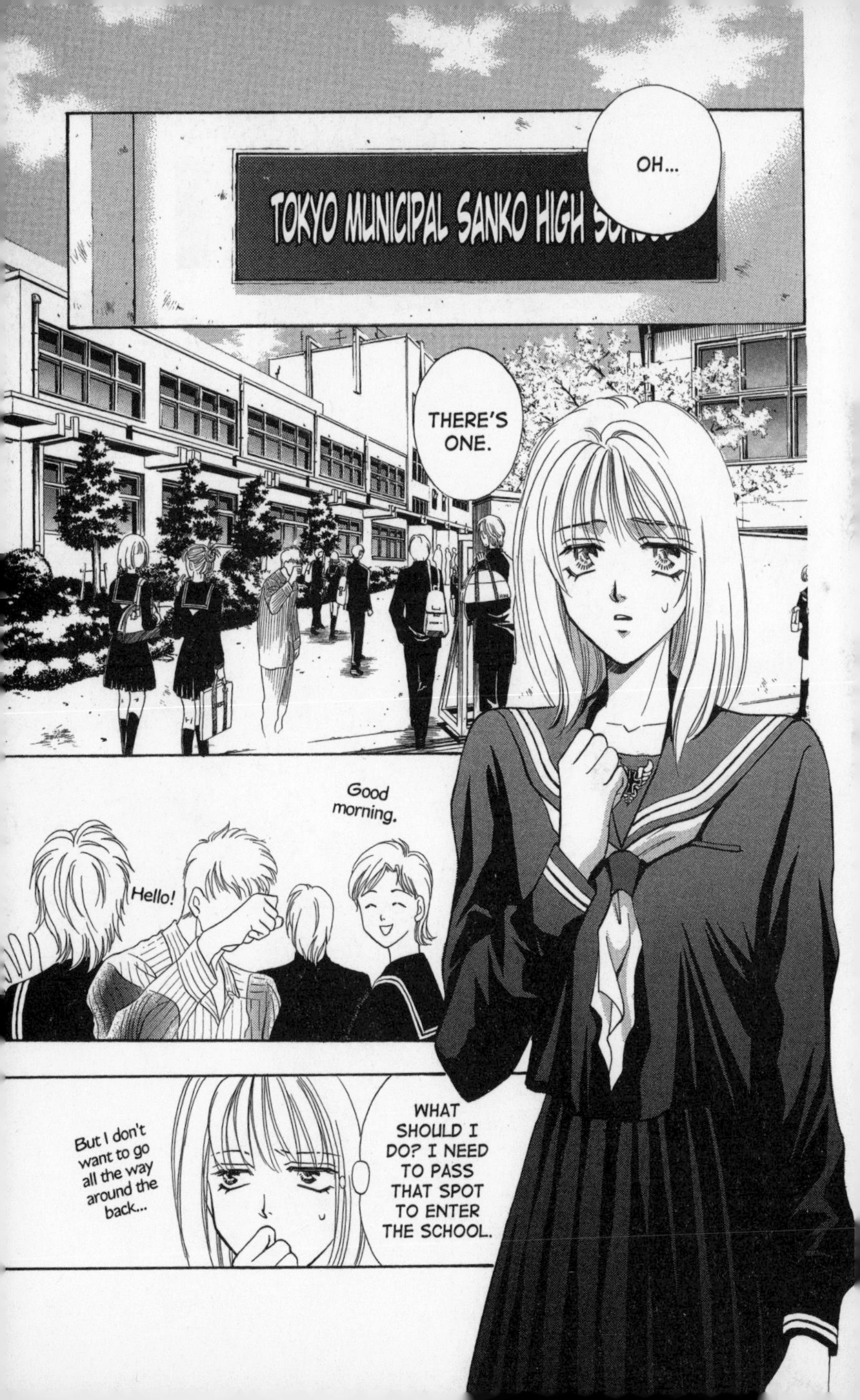
OH...
TOKYO MUNICIPAL SANKO HIGH
THERE'S ONE.
Good morning.
Hello!
WHAT SHOULD I DO? I NEED TO PASS THAT SPOT TO ENTER THE SCHOOL.
But I don't want to go all the way around the back...

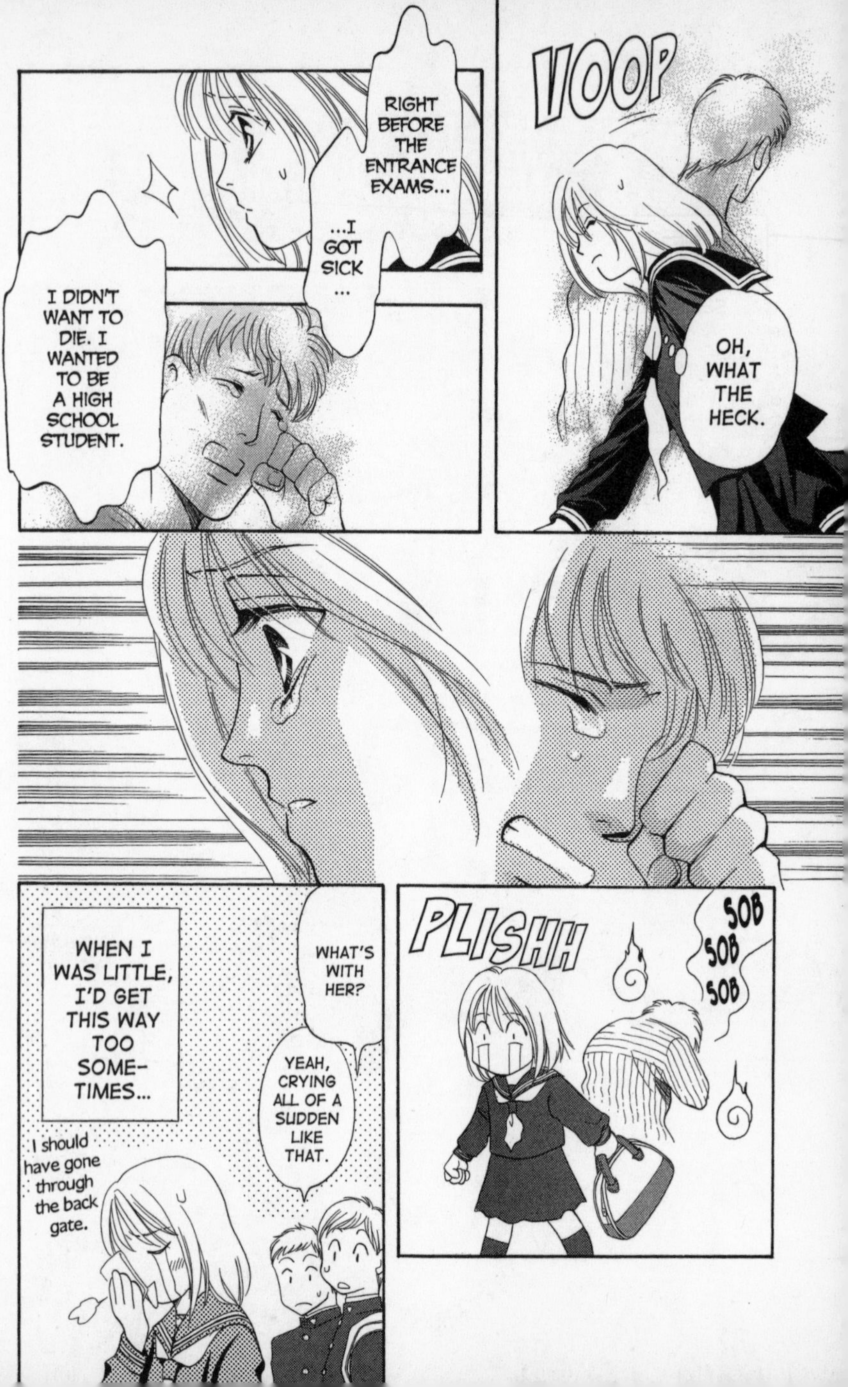
VOOP
OH, WHAT THE HECK.
RIGHT BEFORE THE ENTRANCE EXAMS...
...I GOT SICK...
I DIDN'T WANT TO DIE. I WANTED TO BE A HIGH SCHOOL STUDENT.
PLISHH
SOB SOB SOB
WHAT'S WITH HER?
WHEN I WAS LITTLE, I'D GET THIS WAY TOO SOME-TIMES...
YEAH, CRYING ALL OF A SUDDEN LIKE THAT.
I should have gone through the back gate.

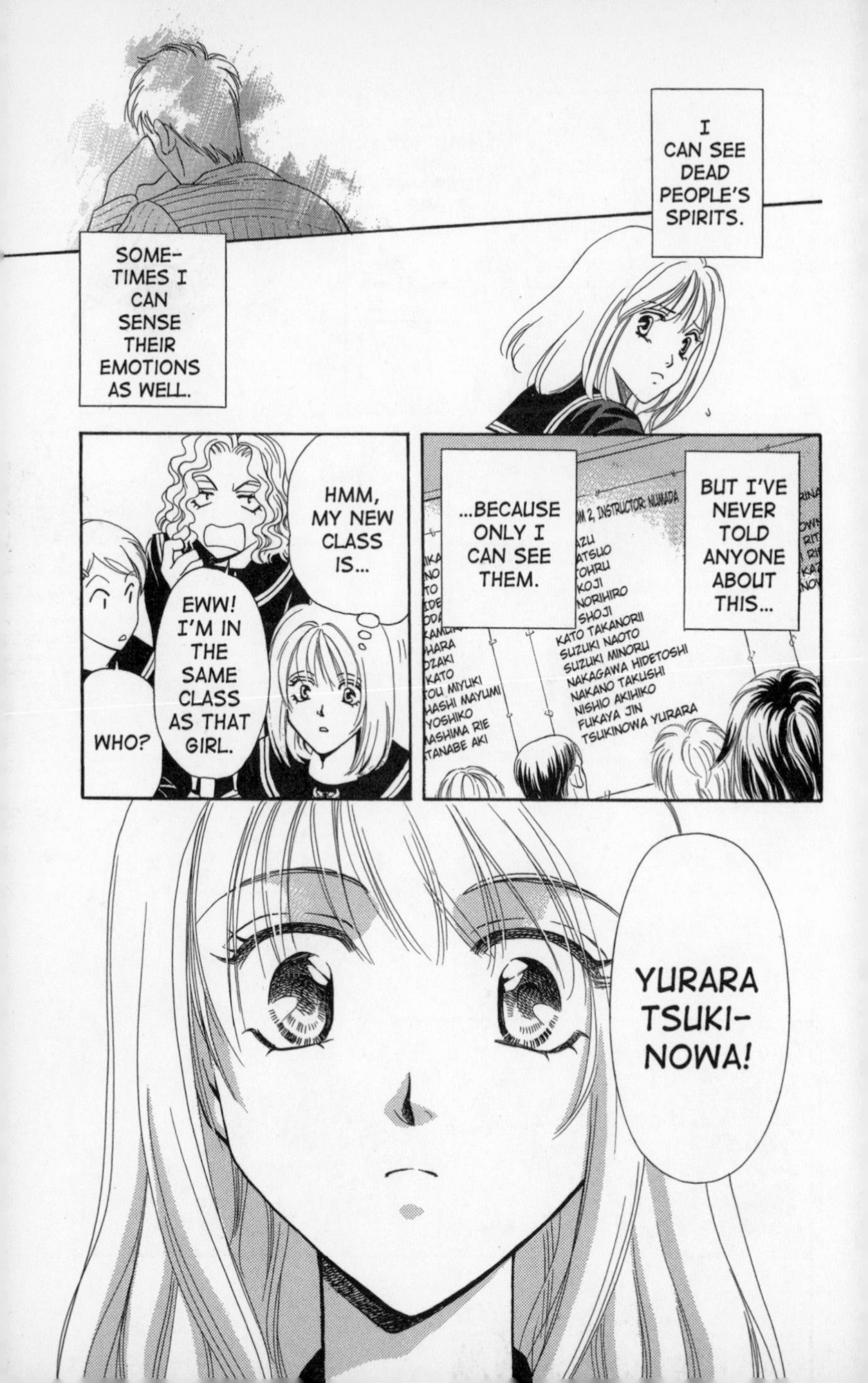
I CAN SEE DEAD PEOPLE'S SPIRITS.
SOME-TIMES I CAN SENSE THEIR EMOTIONS AS WELL.
BUT I'VE NEVER TOLD ANYONE ABOUT THIS...
...BECAUSE ONLY I CAN SEE THEM.
KATO TAKANORII
SUZUKI NAOTO
SUZUKI MINORU
NAKAGAWA HIDETOSHI
NAKANO TAKUSHI
NISHIO AKIHIKO
FUKAYA JIN
TSUKINOWA YURARA
HMM, MY NEW CLASS IS...
EWW! I'M IN THE SAME CLASS AS THAT GIRL.
WHO?
YURARA TSUKI-NOWA!

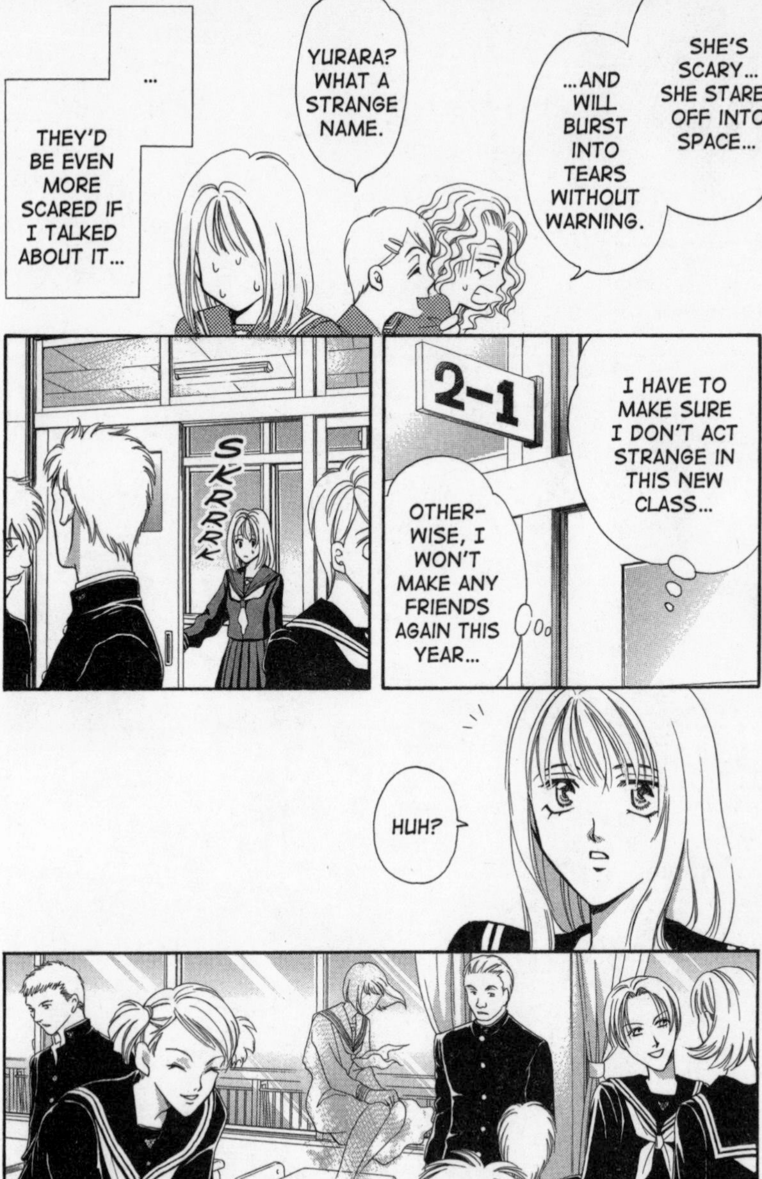
SHE'S SCARY... SHE STARES OFF INTO SPACE...
...AND WILL BURST INTO TEARS WITHOUT WARNING.
YURARA? WHAT A STRANGE NAME.
...
THEY'D BE EVEN MORE SCARED IF I TALKED ABOUT IT...
2-1
I HAVE TO MAKE SURE I DON'T ACT STRANGE IN THIS NEW CLASS...
OTHER-WISE, I WON'T MAKE ANY FRIENDS AGAIN THIS YEAR...
SKRRRR
HUH?

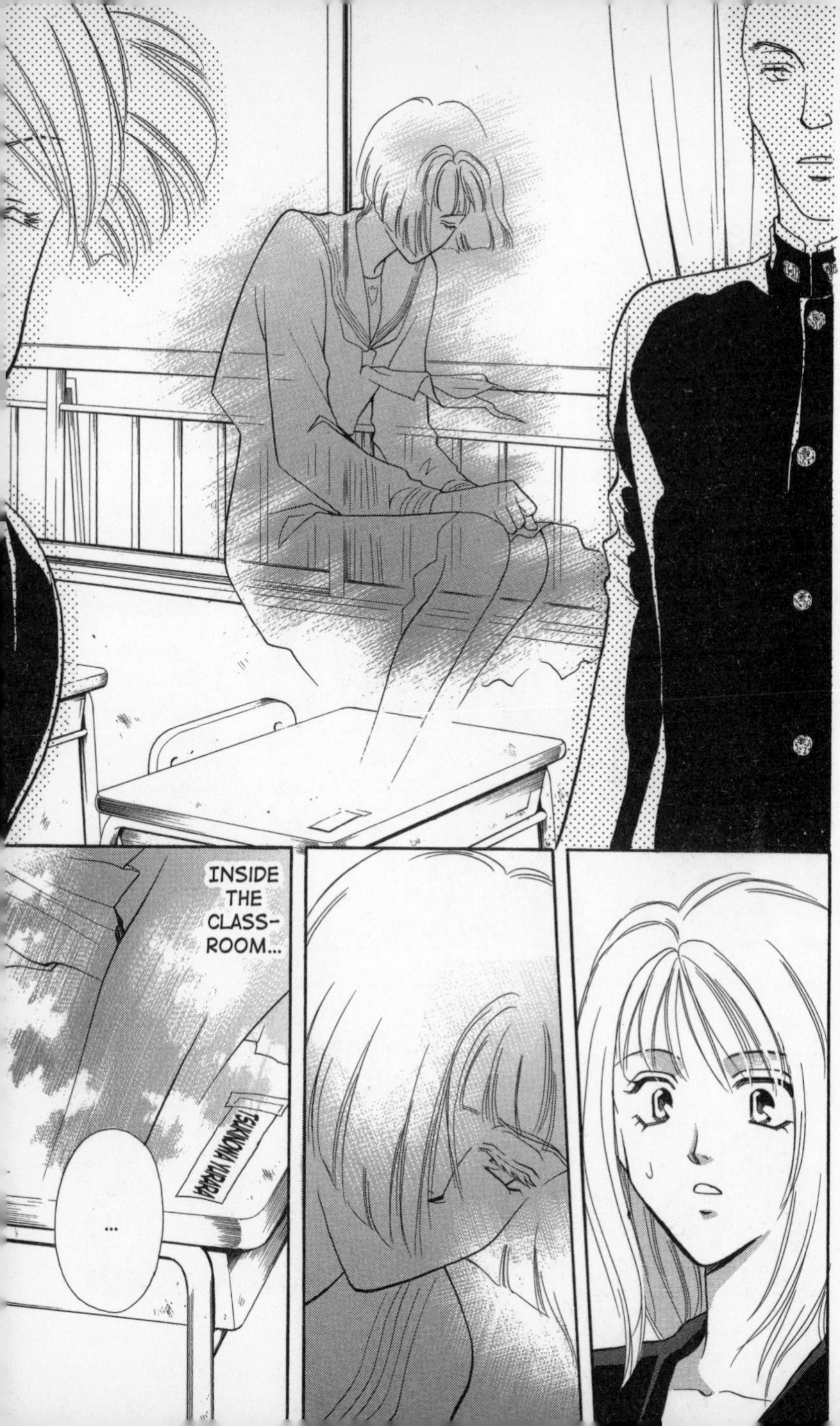
INSIDE THE CLASS-ROOM...
TSUKINOWA YURARA
...

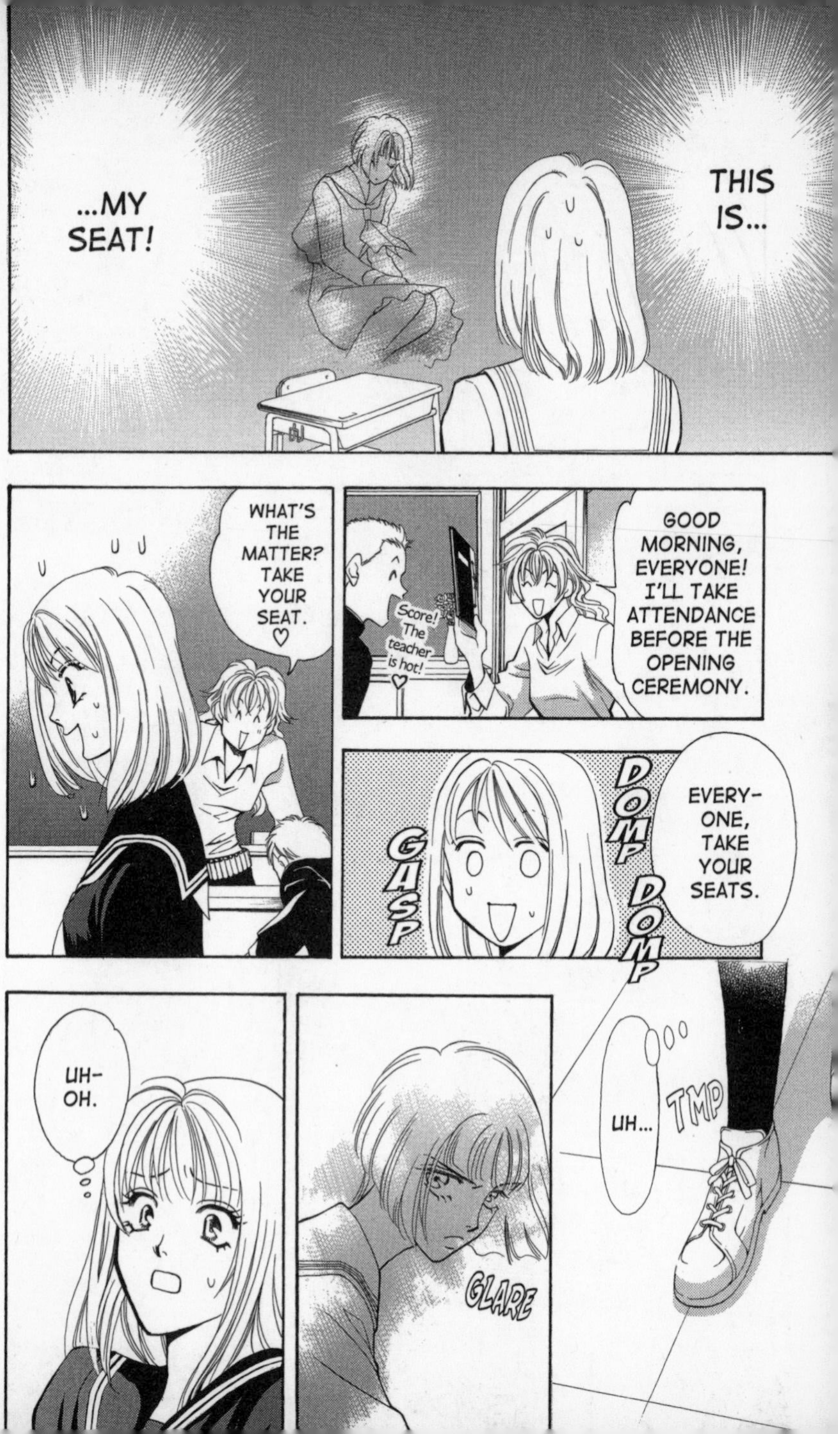
THIS IS...
...MY SEAT!
GOOD MORNING, EVERYONE! I'LL TAKE ATTENDANCE BEFORE THE OPENING CEREMONY.
Score! The teacher is hot! ♡
EVERY-ONE, TAKE YOUR SEATS.
DOMP DOMP
GASP
WHAT'S THE MATTER? TAKE YOUR SEAT. ♡
TMP
UH...
GLARE
UH-OH.

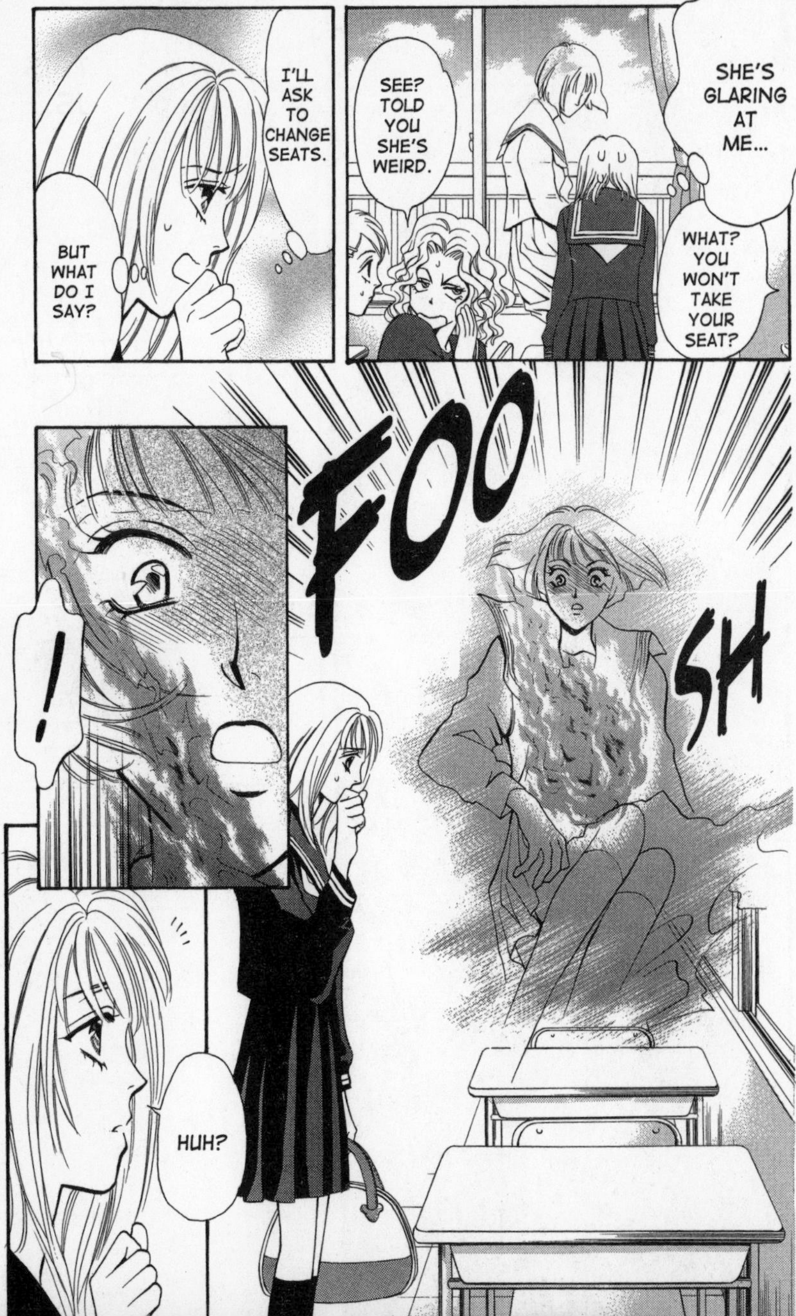
SHE'S GLARING AT ME...
WHAT? YOU WON'T TAKE YOUR SEAT?
SEE? TOLD YOU SHE'S WEIRD.
I'LL ASK TO CHANGE SEATS.
BUT WHAT DO I SAY?
FOOSH
!
HUH?

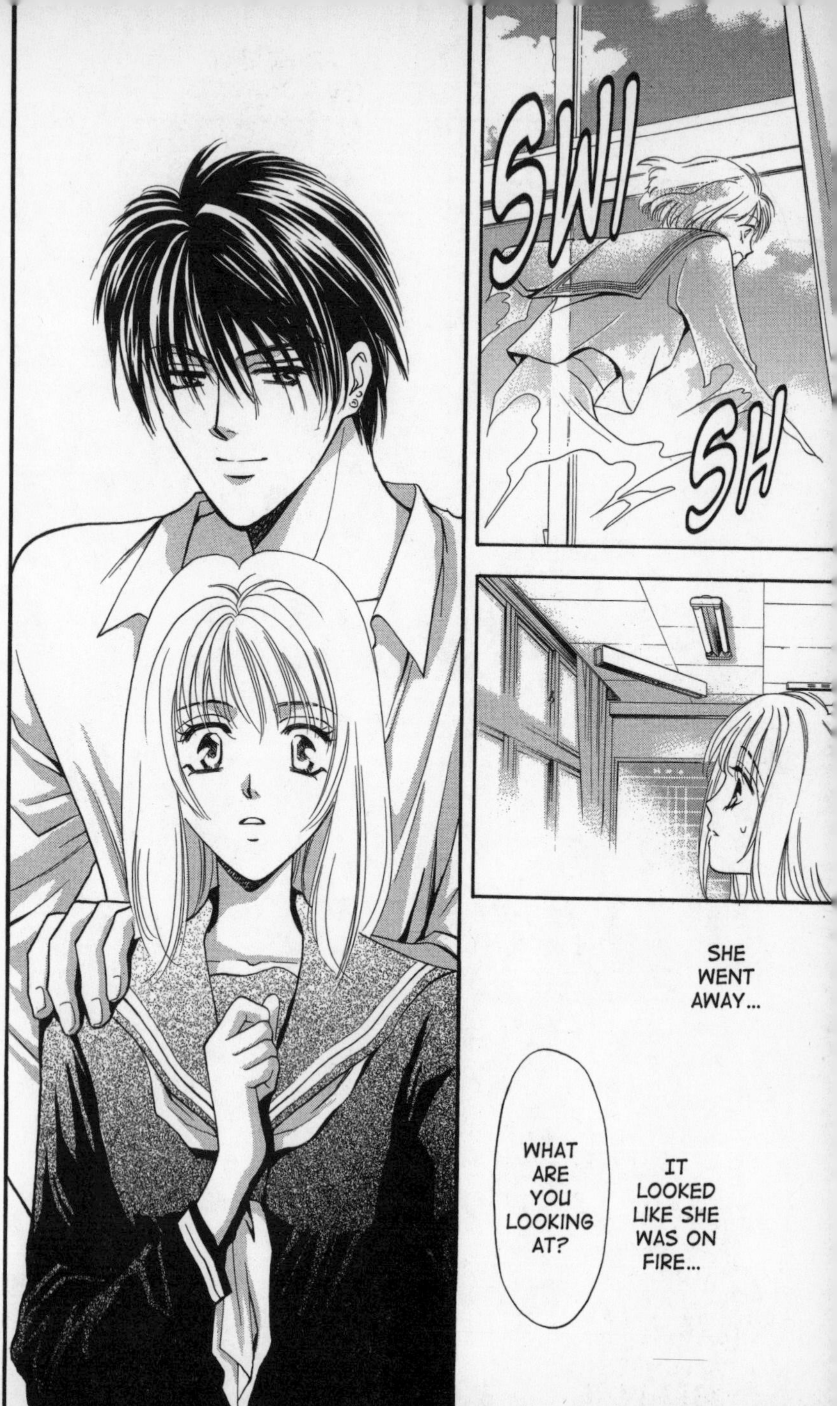
SWISH
SHE WENT AWAY...
IT LOOKED LIKE SHE WAS ON FIRE...
WHAT ARE YOU LOOKING AT?

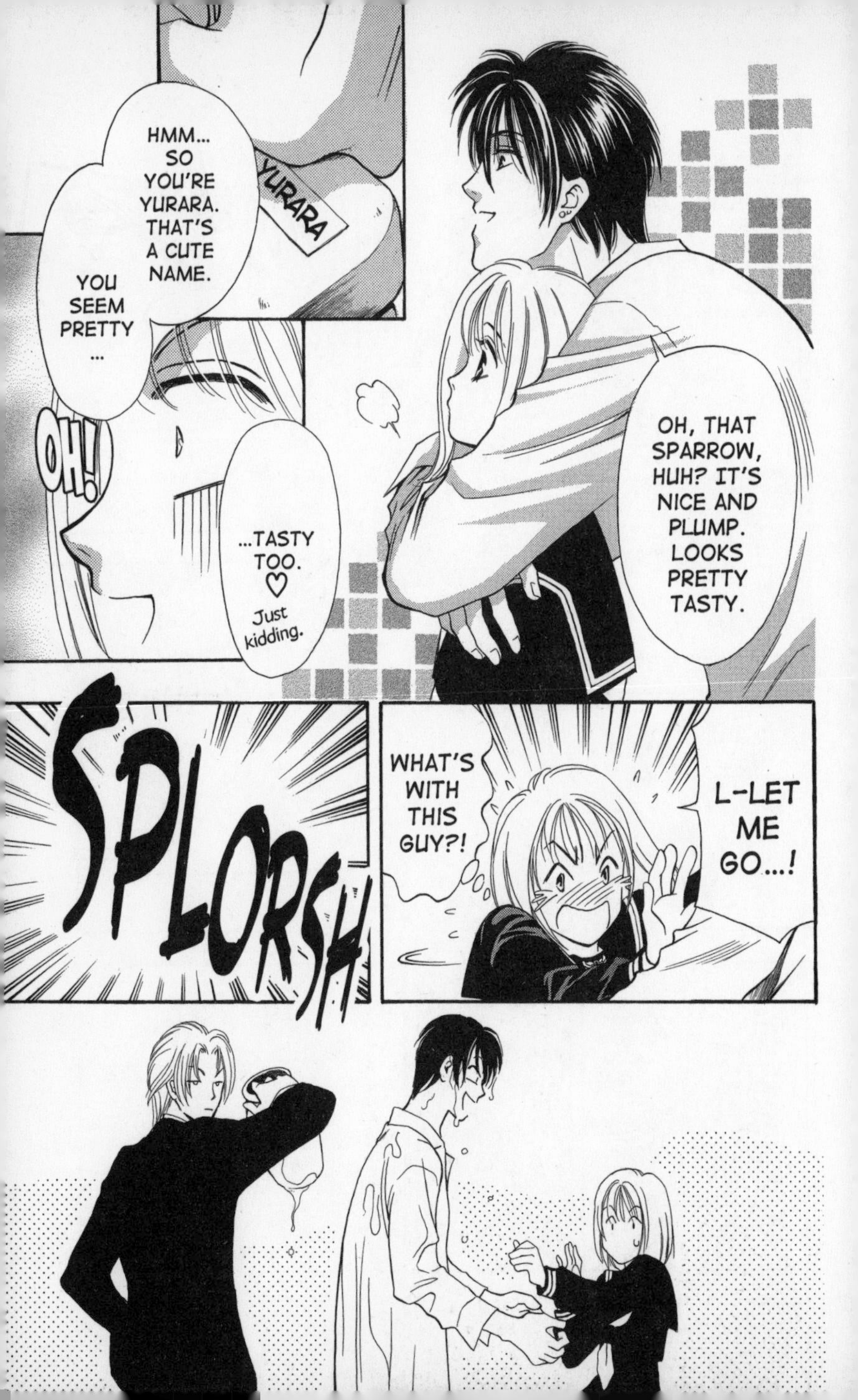
OH, THAT SPARROW, HUH? IT'S NICE AND PLUMP. LOOKS PRETTY TASTY.
HMM... SO YOU'RE YURARA. THAT'S A CUTE NAME.
YURARA
YOU SEEM PRETTY ...
OH!
...TASTY TOO. ♡
Just kidding.
L-LET ME GO...!
WHAT'S WITH THIS GUY?!
SPLORSH

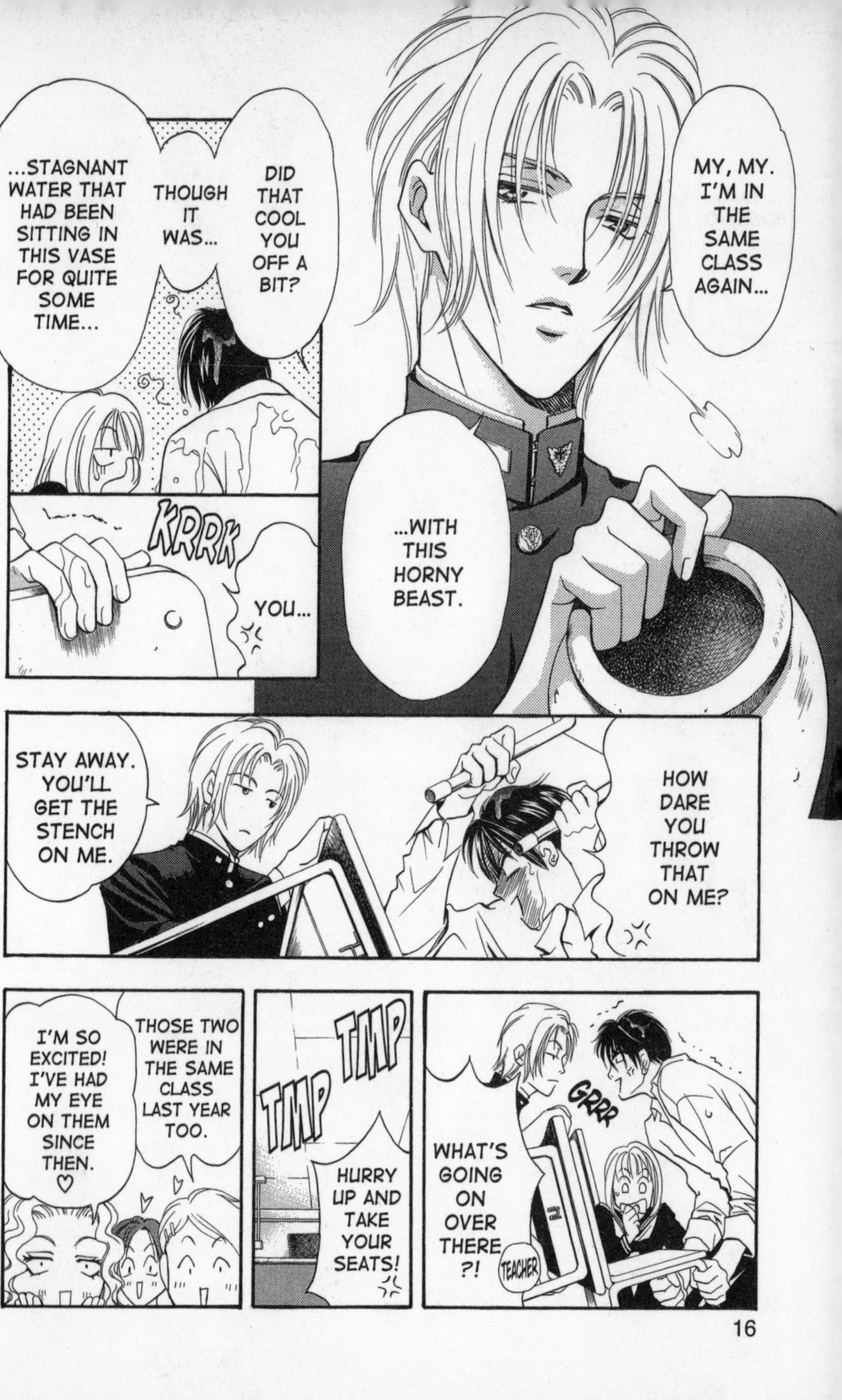
MY, MY. I'M IN THE SAME CLASS AGAIN...
...WITH THIS HORNY BEAST.
DID THAT COOL YOU OFF A BIT?
THOUGH IT WAS...
...STAGNANT WATER THAT HAD BEEN SITTING IN THIS VASE FOR QUITE SOME TIME...
KRRK
YOU...
HOW DARE YOU THROW THAT ON ME?
STAY AWAY. YOU'LL GET THE STENCH ON ME.
GRRR
WHAT'S GOING ON OVER THERE?!
TEACHER
TMP
TMP
HURRY UP AND TAKE YOUR SEATS!
THOSE TWO WERE IN THE SAME CLASS LAST YEAR TOO.
I'M SO EXCITED! I'VE HAD MY EYE ON THEM SINCE THEN. ♡

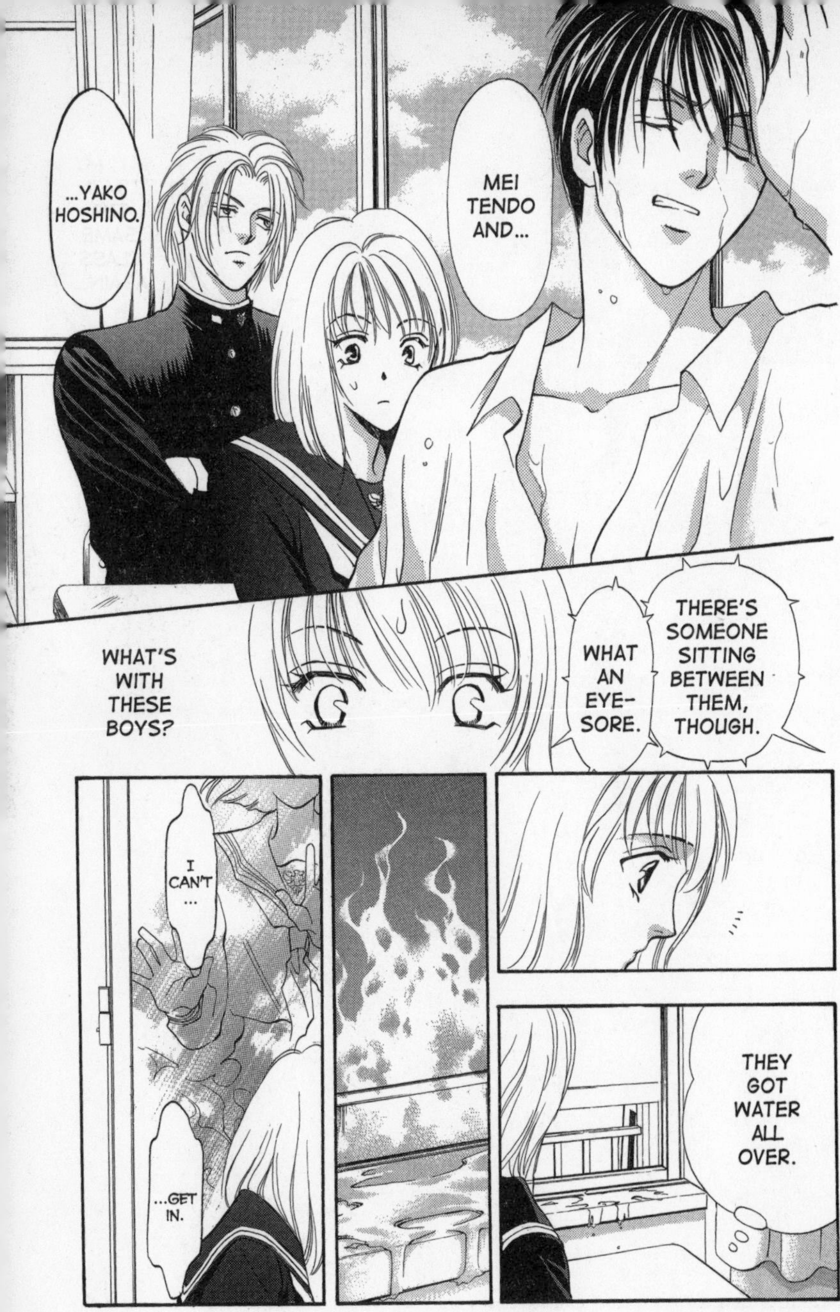
MEI TENDO AND...
...YAKO HOSHINO.
THERE'S SOMEONE SITTING BETWEEN THEM, THOUGH.
WHAT AN EYE-SORE.
WHAT'S WITH THESE BOYS?
...
THEY GOT WATER ALL OVER.
I CAN'T ...
...GET IN.

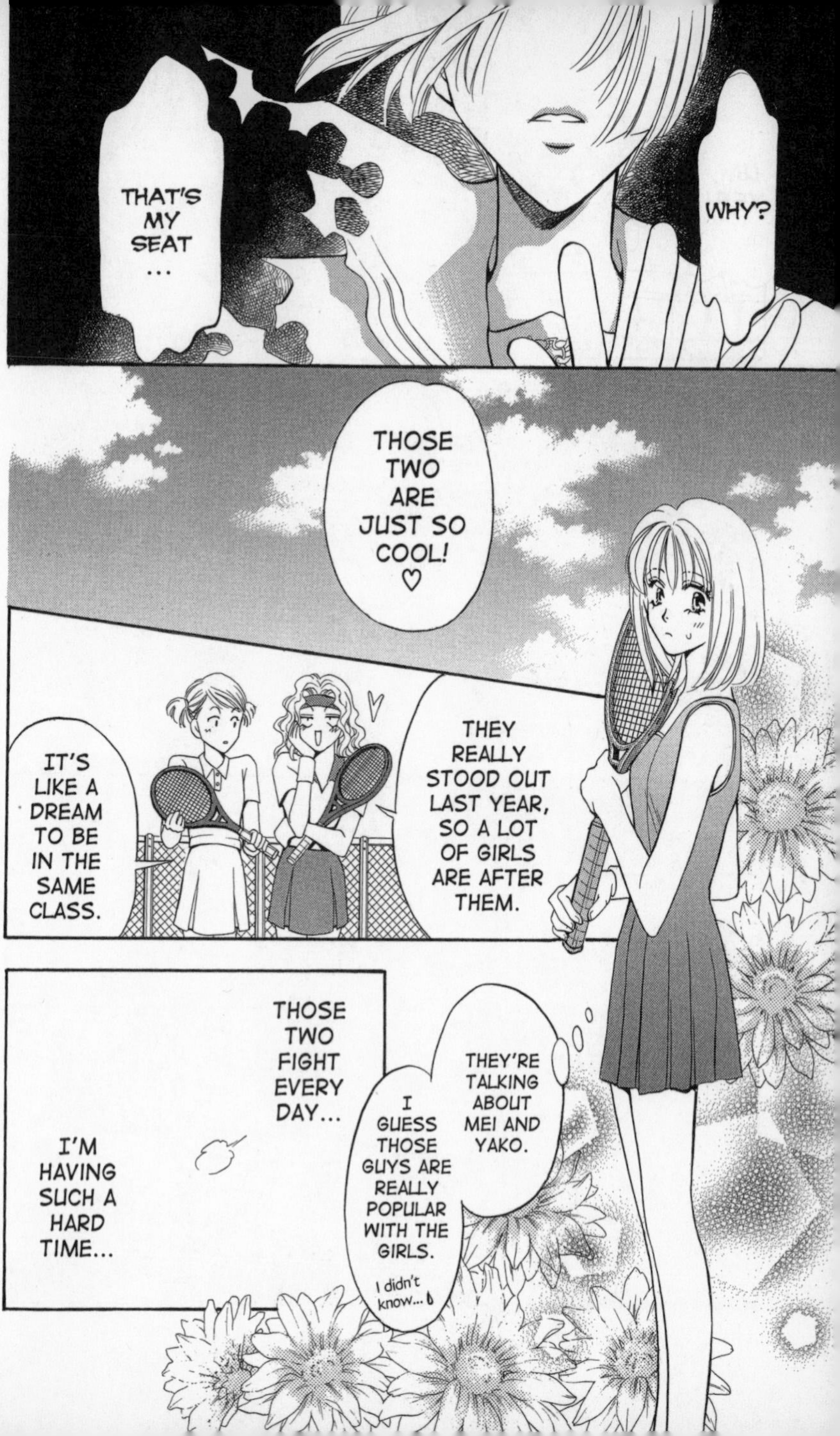
WHY?
THAT'S MY SEAT ...
THOSE TWO ARE JUST SO COOL! ♡
THEY REALLY STOOD OUT LAST YEAR, SO A LOT OF GIRLS ARE AFTER THEM.
IT'S LIKE A DREAM TO BE IN THE SAME CLASS.
THEY'RE TALKING ABOUT MEI AND YAKO.
I GUESS THOSE GUYS ARE REALLY POPULAR WITH THE GIRLS.
I didn't know...
THOSE TWO FIGHT EVERY DAY...
I'M HAVING SUCH A HARD TIME...

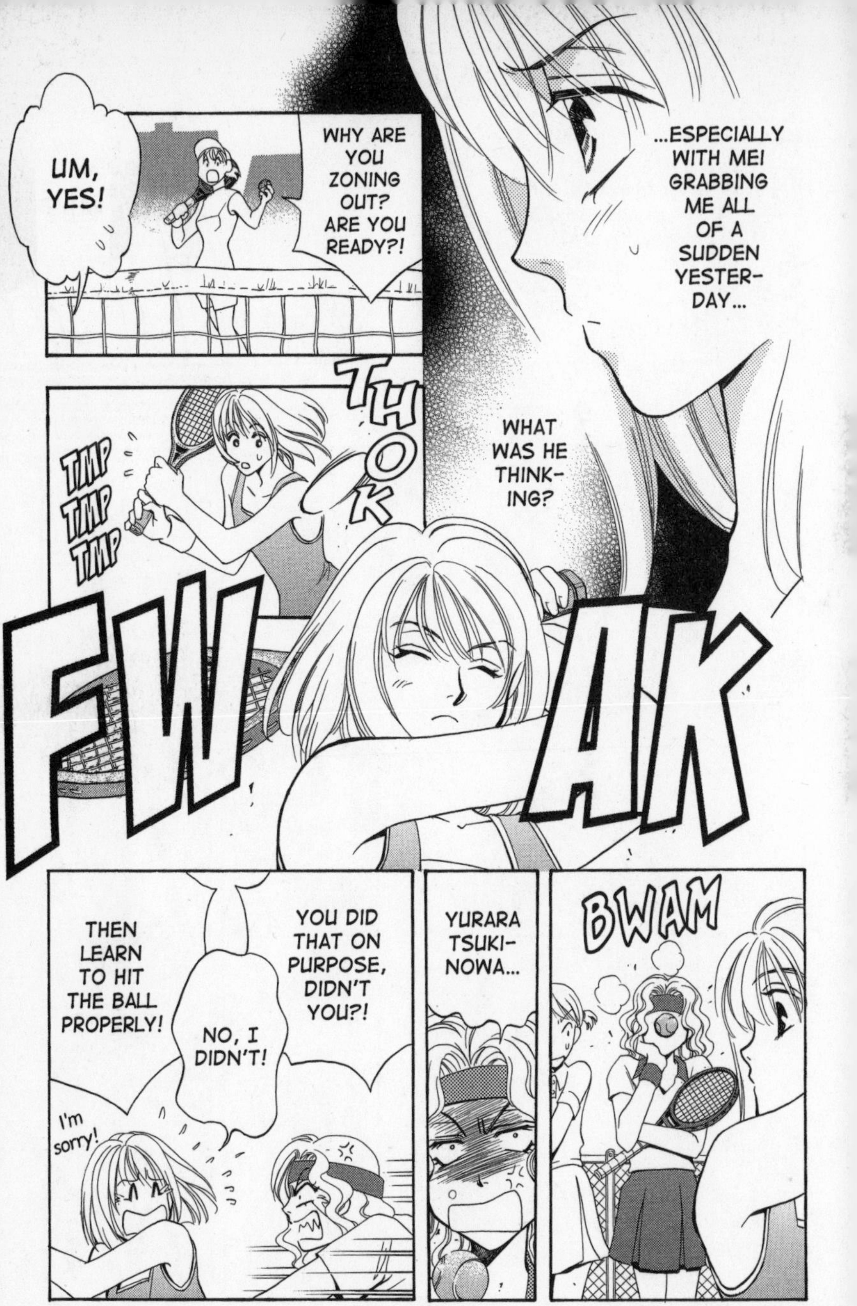
...ESPECIALLY WITH MEI GRABBING ME ALL OF A SUDDEN YESTER-DAY...
WHAT WAS HE THINK-ING?
WHY ARE YOU ZONING OUT? ARE YOU READY?!
UM, YES!
THOK
TMP TMP TMP
FWAK
BWAM
YURARA TSUKI-NOWA...
YOU DID THAT ON PURPOSE, DIDN'T YOU?!
NO, I DIDN'T!
THEN LEARN TO HIT THE BALL PROPERLY!
I'm sorry!

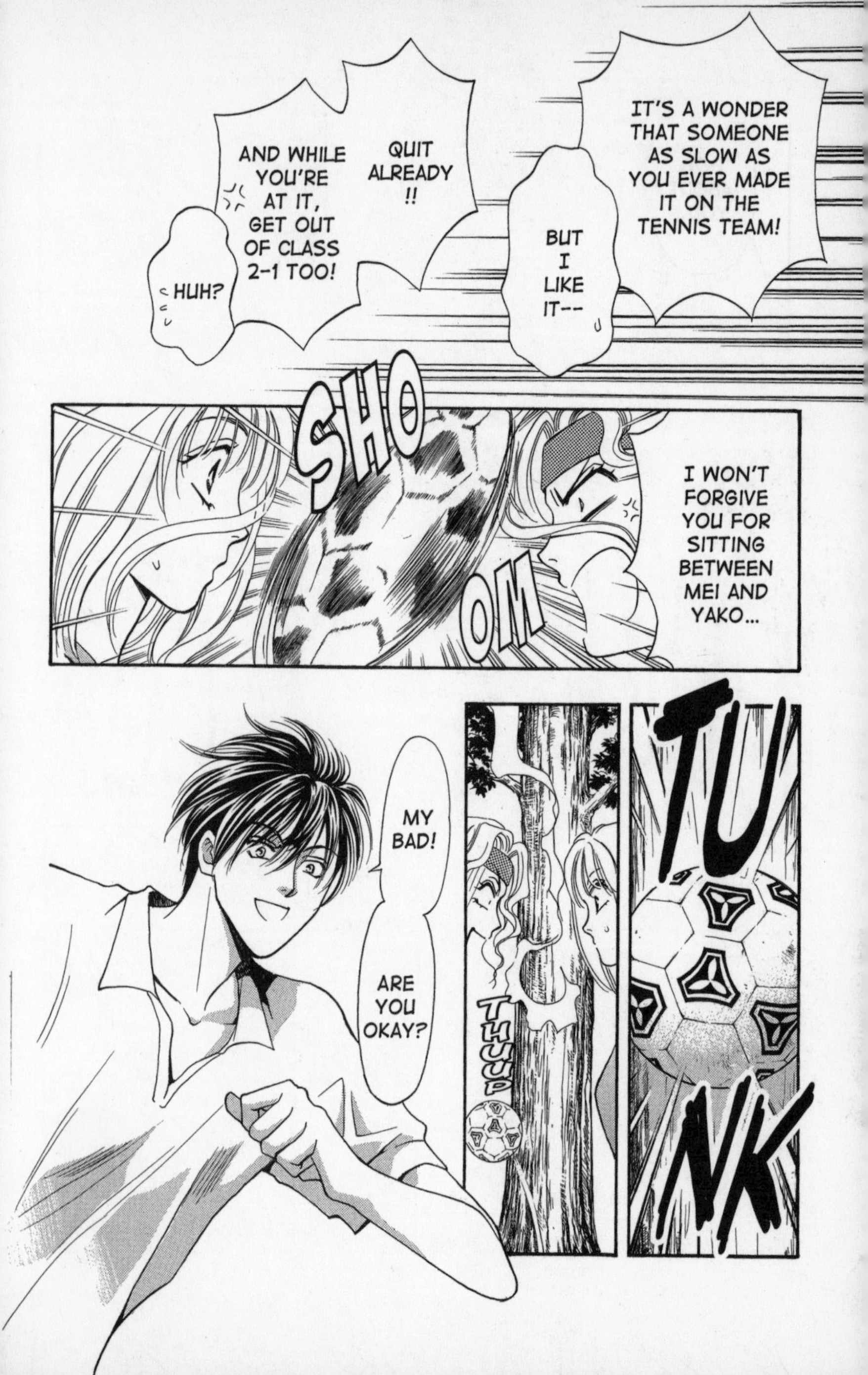
IT'S A WONDER THAT SOMEONE AS SLOW AS YOU EVER MADE IT ON THE TENNIS TEAM!
BUT I LIKE IT--
QUIT ALREADY!!
AND WHILE YOU'RE AT IT, GET OUT OF CLASS 2-1 TOO!
HUH?
I WON'T FORGIVE YOU FOR SITTING BETWEEN MEI AND YAKO...
SHOOM
TUNK
THUUP
MY BAD!
ARE YOU OKAY?

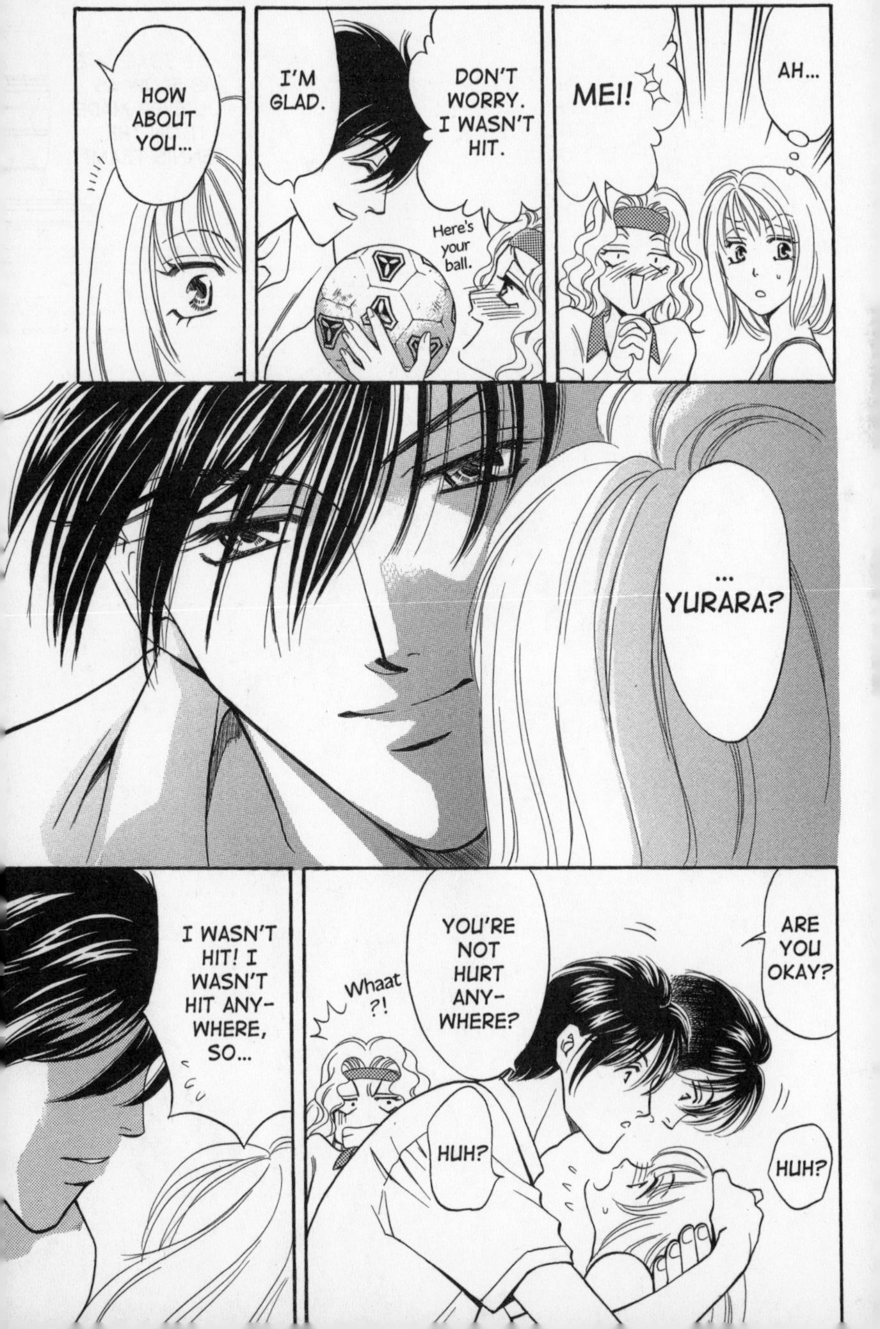
AH...
MEI!
DON'T WORRY. I WASN'T HIT.
I'M GLAD.
Here's your ball.
HOW ABOUT YOU...
... YURARA?
ARE YOU OKAY?
YOU'RE NOT HURT ANY-WHERE?
Whaat?!
HUH?
HUH?
I WASN'T HIT! I WASN'T HIT ANY-WHERE, SO...

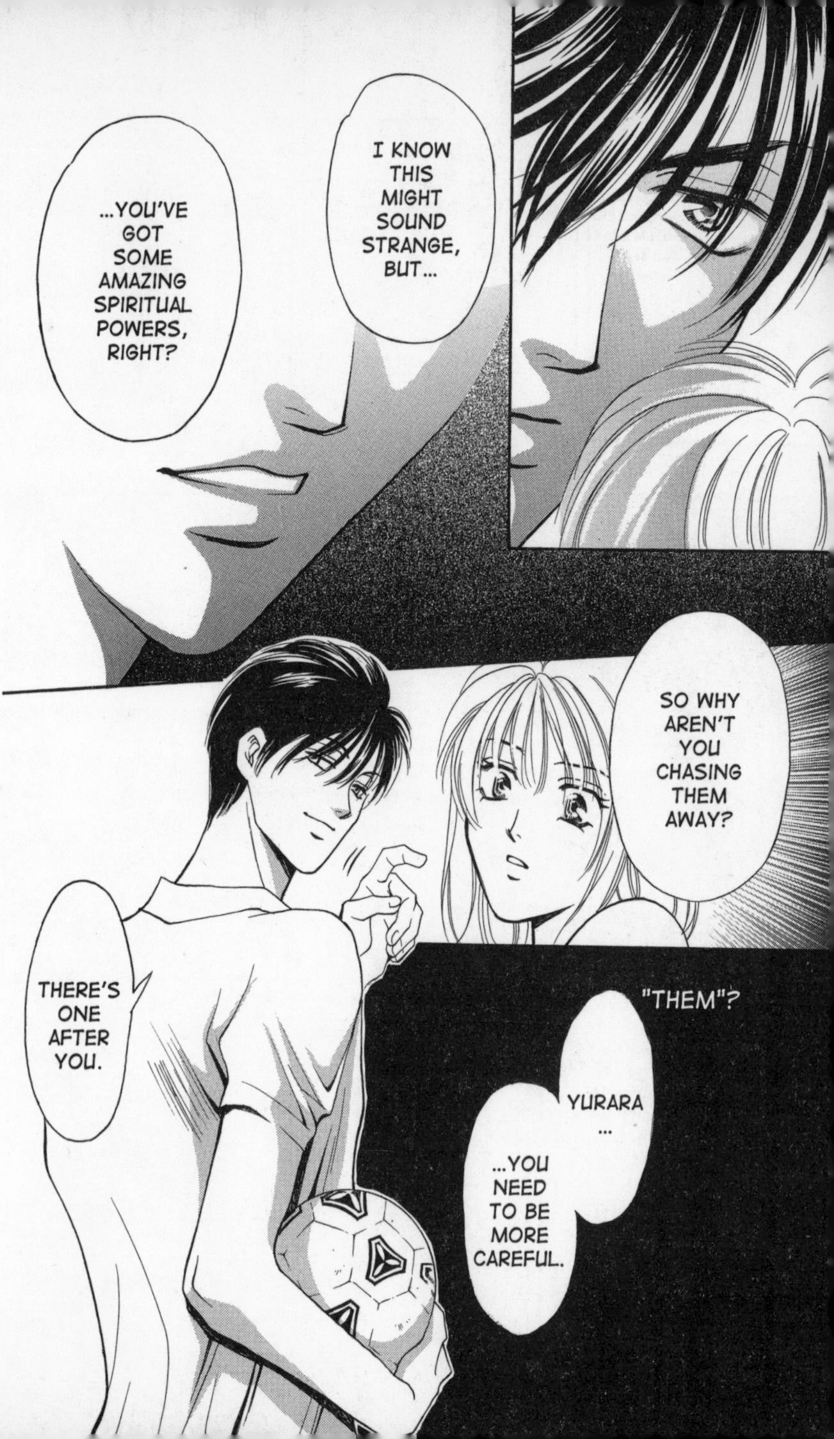
I KNOW THIS MIGHT SOUND STRANGE, BUT...
...YOU'VE GOT SOME AMAZING SPIRITUAL POWERS, RIGHT?
SO WHY AREN'T YOU CHASING THEM AWAY?
"THEM"?
YURARA ...
...YOU NEED TO BE MORE CAREFUL.
THERE'S ONE AFTER YOU.

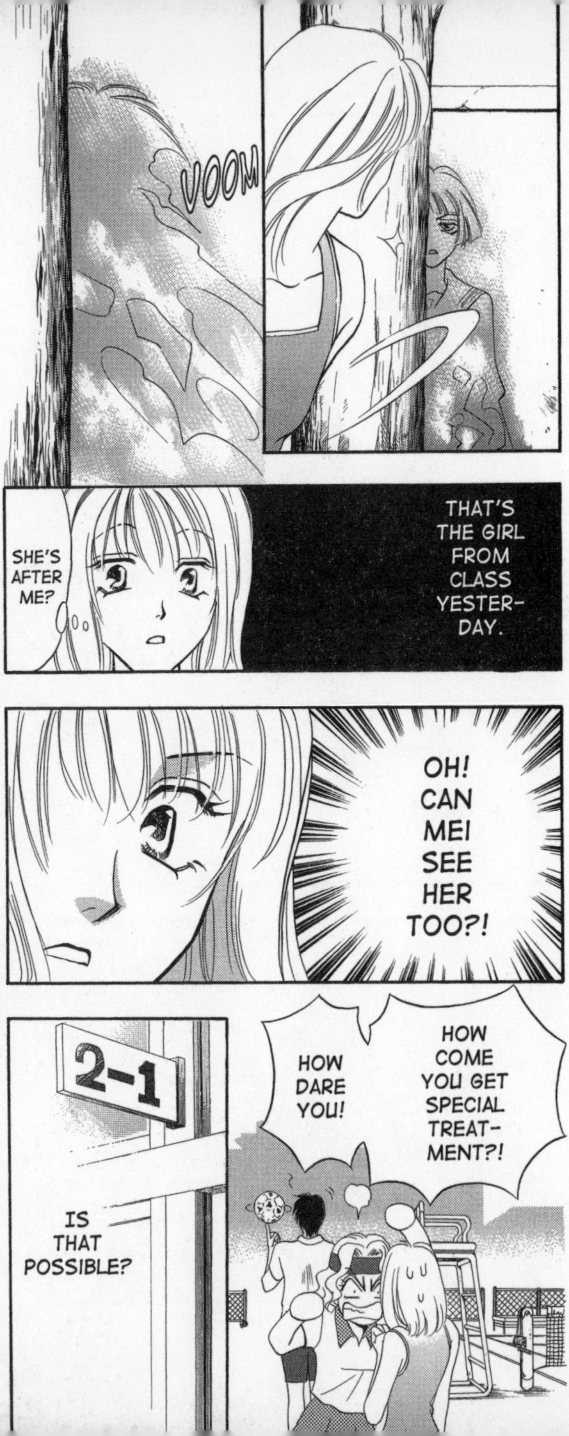
VOOM
THAT'S THE GIRL FROM CLASS YESTERDAY.
SHE'S AFTER ME?
OH! CAN MEI SEE HER TOO?!
HOW COME YOU GET SPECIAL TREATMENT?!
HOW DARE YOU!
2-1
IS THAT POSSIBLE?

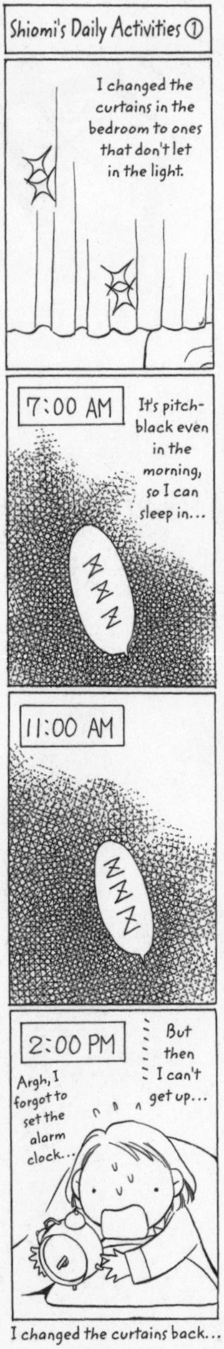
Shiomi's Daily Activities ①
I changed the curtains in the bedroom to ones that don't let in the light.
7:00 AM
It's pitch-black even in the morning, so I can sleep in...
ZZZ
11:00 AM
ZZZ
2:00 PM
But then I can't get up...
Argh, I forgot to set the alarm clock...
I changed the curtains back...

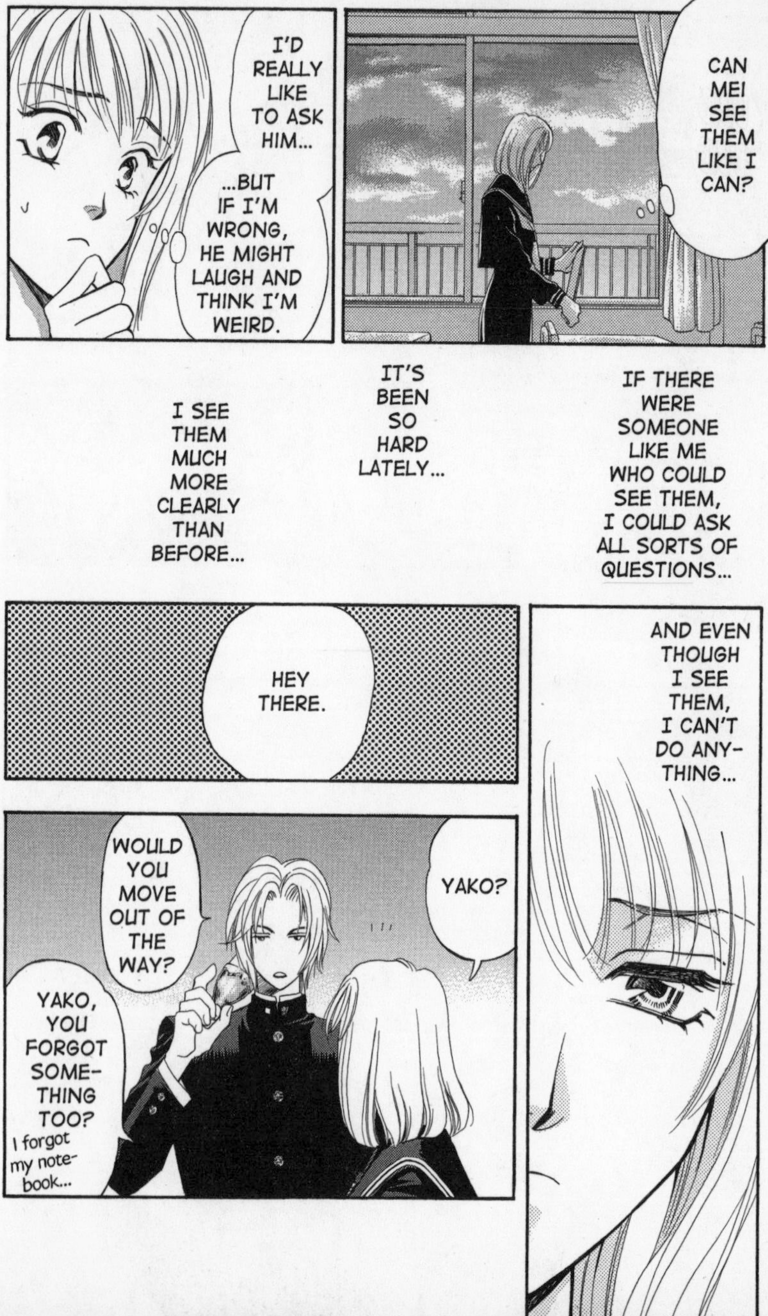
CAN MEI SEE THEM LIKE I CAN?
I'D REALLY LIKE TO ASK HIM...
...BUT IF I'M WRONG, HE MIGHT LAUGH AND THINK I'M WEIRD.
IF THERE WERE SOMEONE LIKE ME WHO COULD SEE THEM, I COULD ASK ALL SORTS OF QUESTIONS...
IT'S BEEN SO HARD LATELY...
I SEE THEM MUCH MORE CLEARLY THAN BEFORE...
AND EVEN THOUGH I SEE THEM, I CAN'T DO ANY-THING...
HEY THERE.
YAKO?
WOULD YOU MOVE OUT OF THE WAY?
YAKO, YOU FORGOT SOME-THING TOO?
I forgot my note-book...

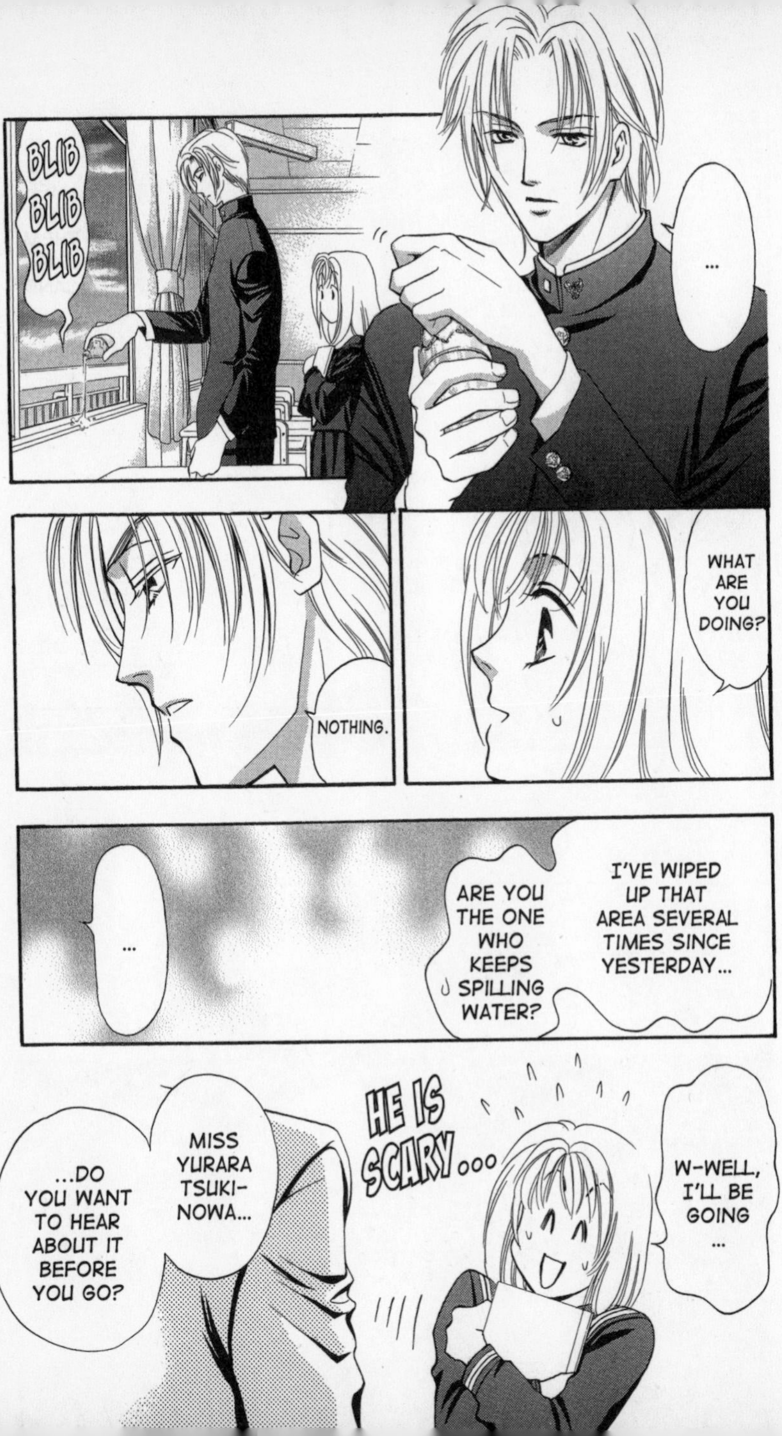
...
BLIB BLIB BLIB
WHAT ARE YOU DOING?
NOTHING.
I'VE WIPED UP THAT AREA SEVERAL TIMES SINCE YESTERDAY...
ARE YOU THE ONE WHO KEEPS SPILLING WATER?
...
W-WELL, I'LL BE GOING ...
HE IS SCARY...
MISS YURARA TSUKI-NOWA...
...DO YOU WANT TO HEAR ABOUT IT BEFORE YOU GO?

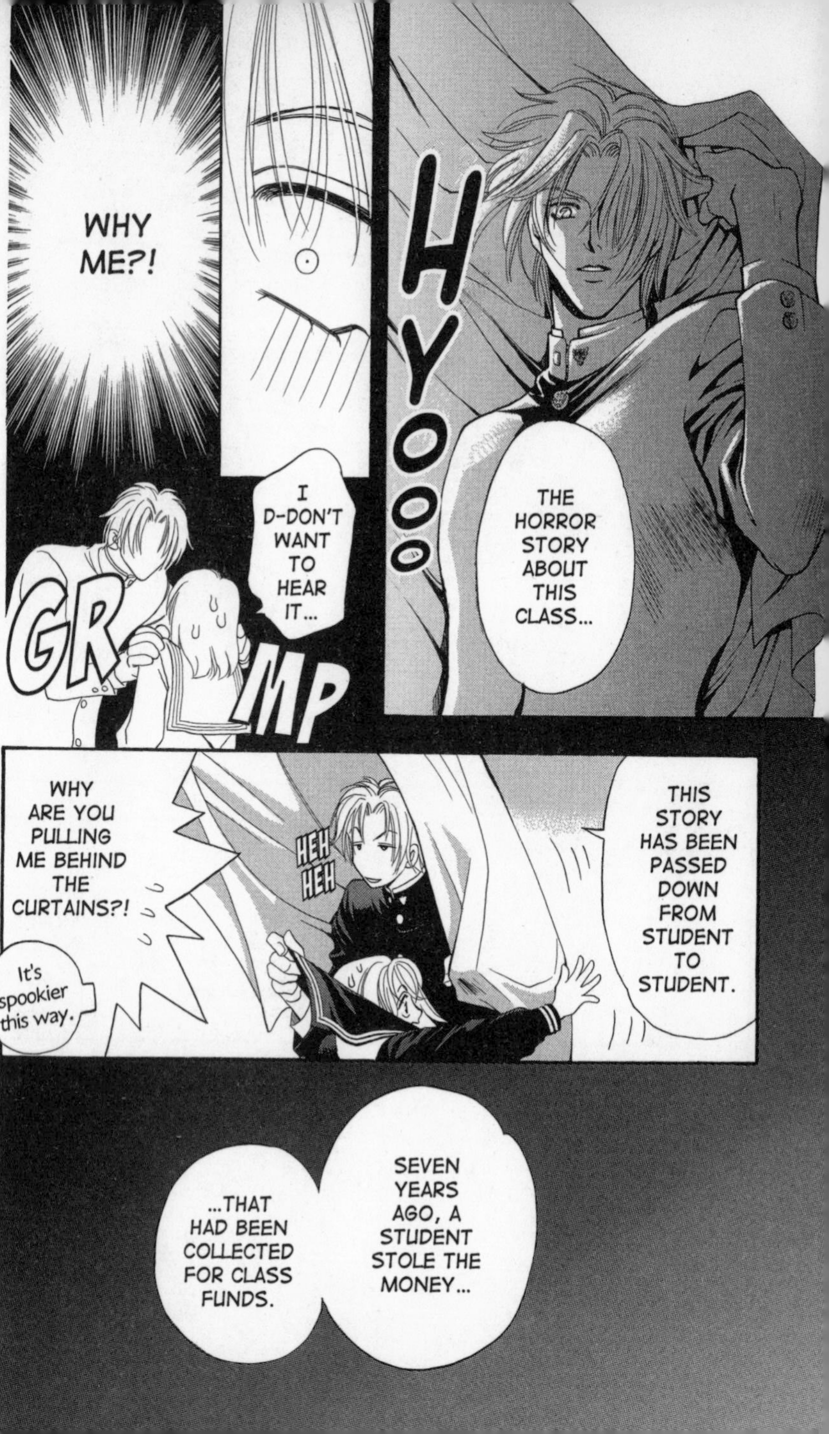
HYOOO
THE HORROR STORY ABOUT THIS CLASS...
WHY ME?!
I D-DON'T WANT TO HEAR IT...
GRMP
THIS STORY HAS BEEN PASSED DOWN FROM STUDENT TO STUDENT.
HEH HEH
WHY ARE YOU PULLING ME BEHIND THE CURTAINS?!
It's spookier this way.
SEVEN YEARS AGO, A STUDENT STOLE THE MONEY...
...THAT HAD BEEN COLLECTED FOR CLASS FUNDS.

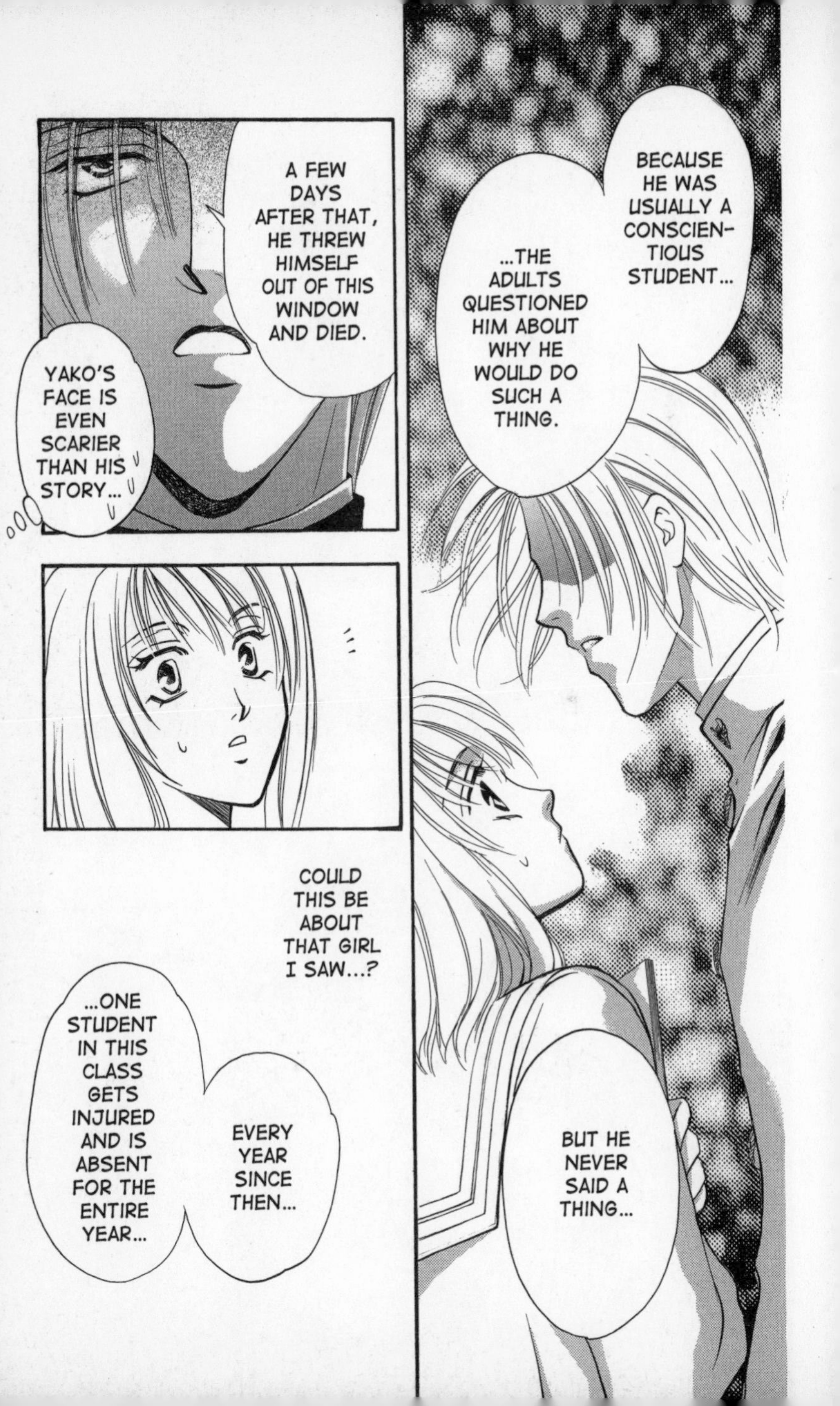
BECAUSE HE WAS USUALLY A CONSCIEN-TIOUS STUDENT...
...THE ADULTS QUESTIONED HIM ABOUT WHY HE WOULD DO SUCH A THING.
BUT HE NEVER SAID A THING...
A FEW DAYS AFTER THAT, HE THREW HIMSELF OUT OF THIS WINDOW AND DIED.
YAKO'S FACE IS EVEN SCARIER THAN HIS STORY...
COULD THIS BE ABOUT THAT GIRL I SAW...?
EVERY YEAR SINCE THEN...
...ONE STUDENT IN THIS CLASS GETS INJURED AND IS ABSENT FOR THE ENTIRE YEAR...

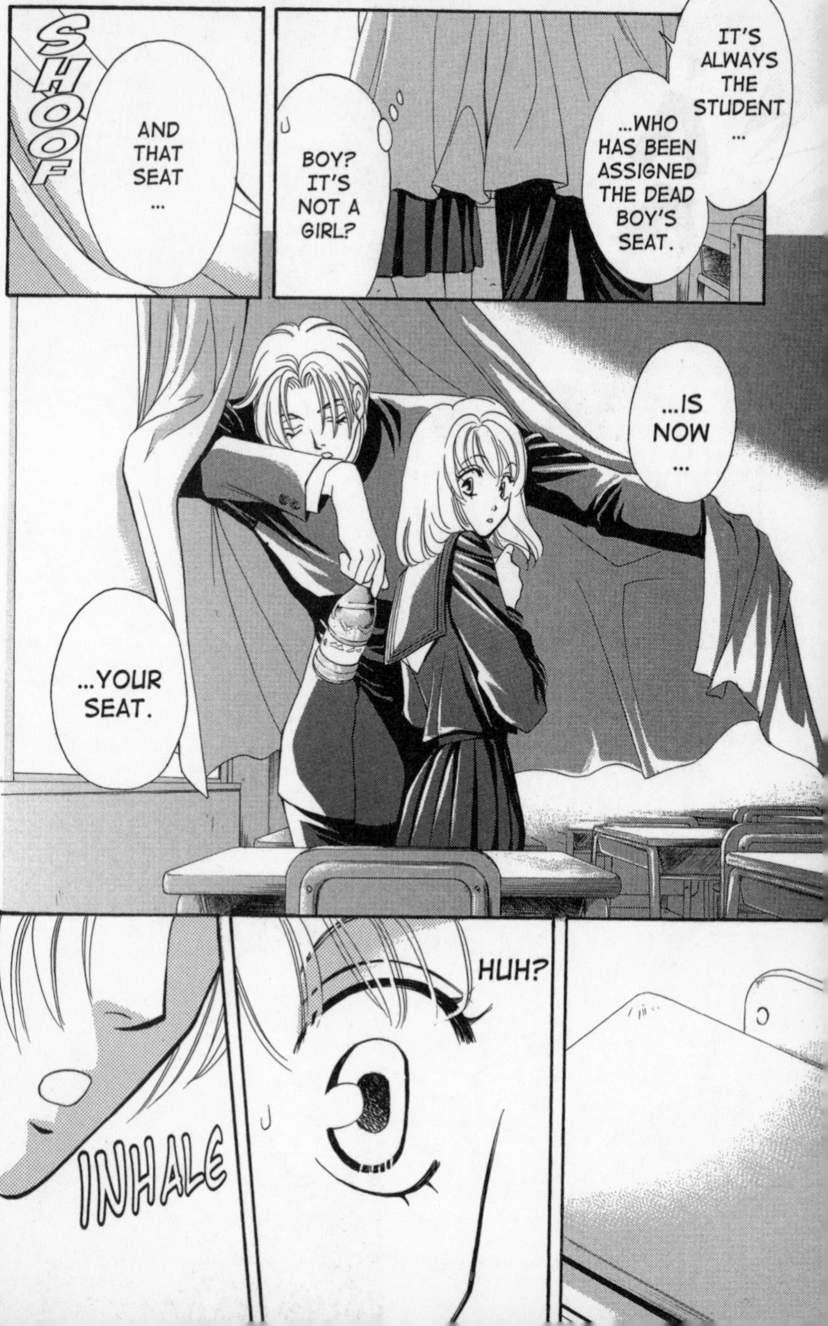
IT'S ALWAYS THE STUDENT ...
...WHO HAS BEEN ASSIGNED THE DEAD BOY'S SEAT.
BOY? IT'S NOT A GIRL?
SHOOF
AND THAT SEAT ...
...IS NOW ...
...YOUR SEAT.
HUH?
INHALE

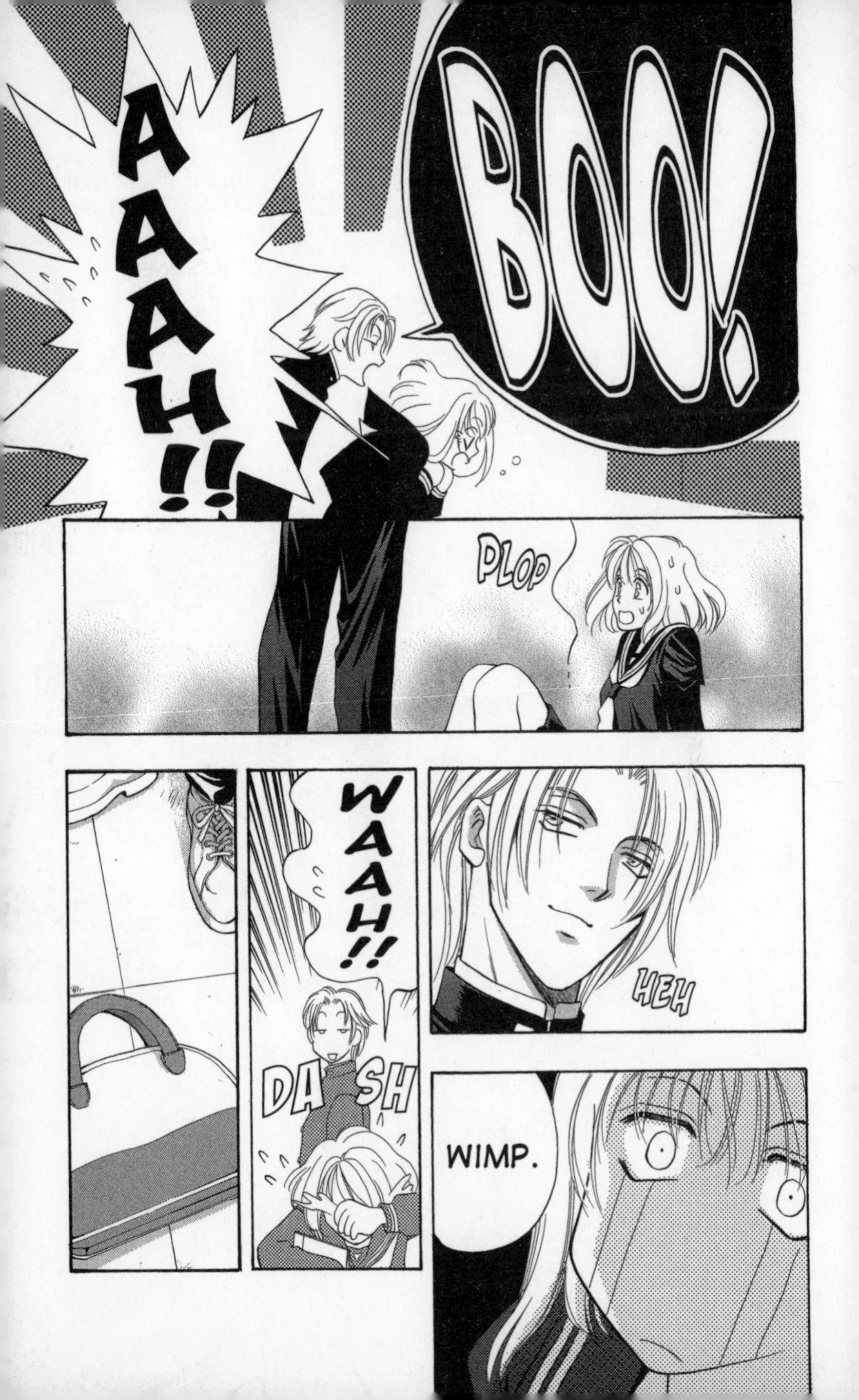
BOO!
AAAH!!
PLOP
HEH
WIMP.
WAAAH!!
DASH

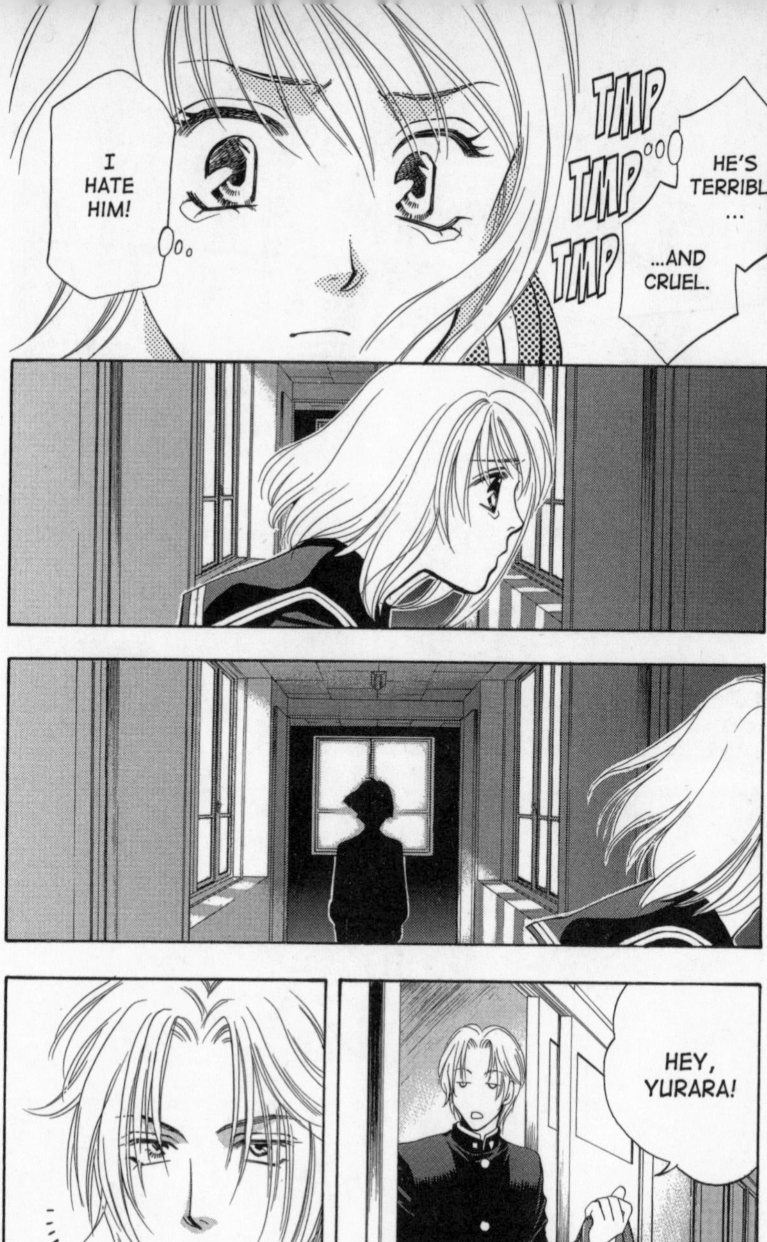
HE'S TERRIBLE ... ...AND CRUEL.
TMP TMP TMP
I HATE HIM!
HEY, YURARA!
...

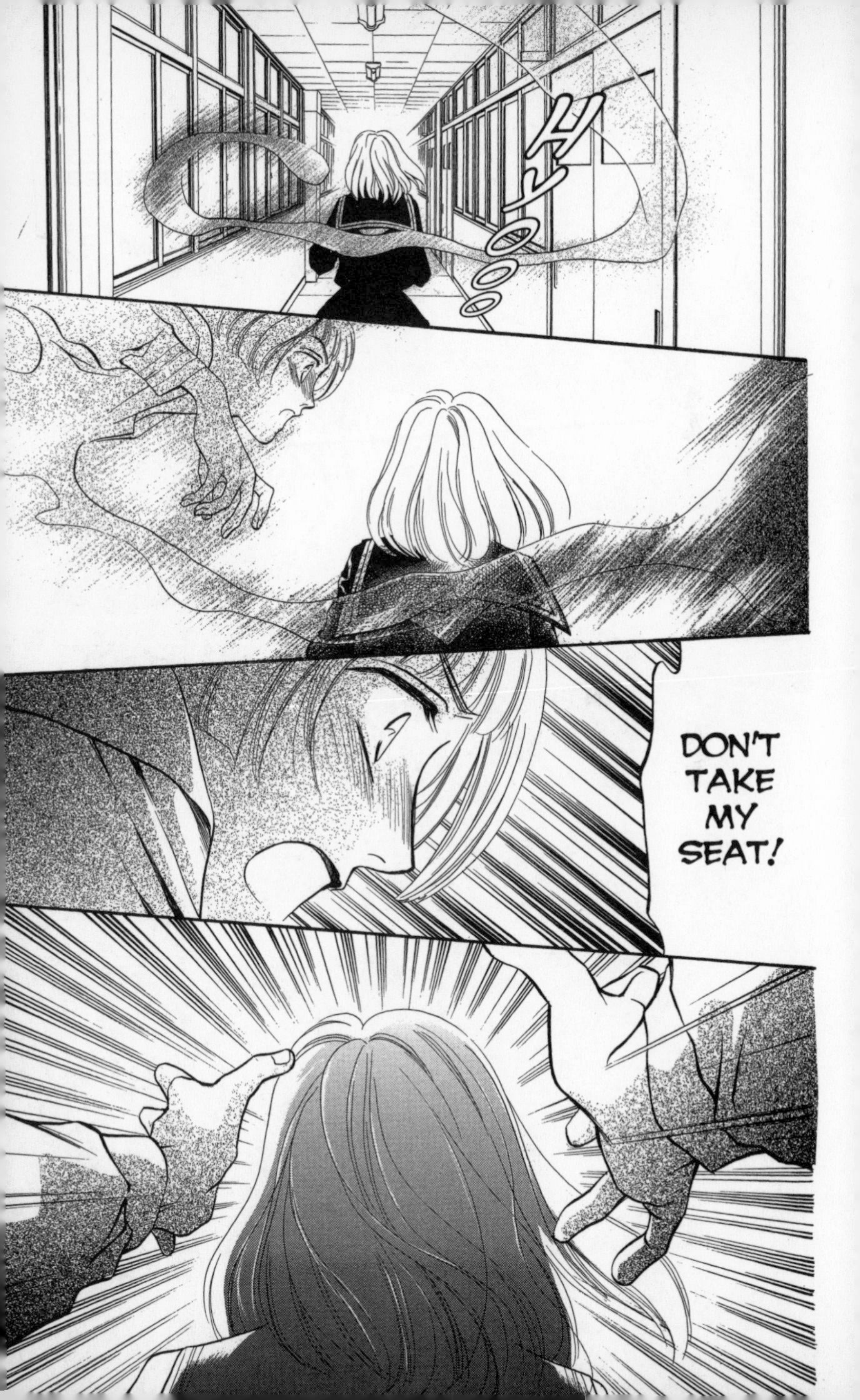
HUOOOO
DON'T TAKE MY SEAT!

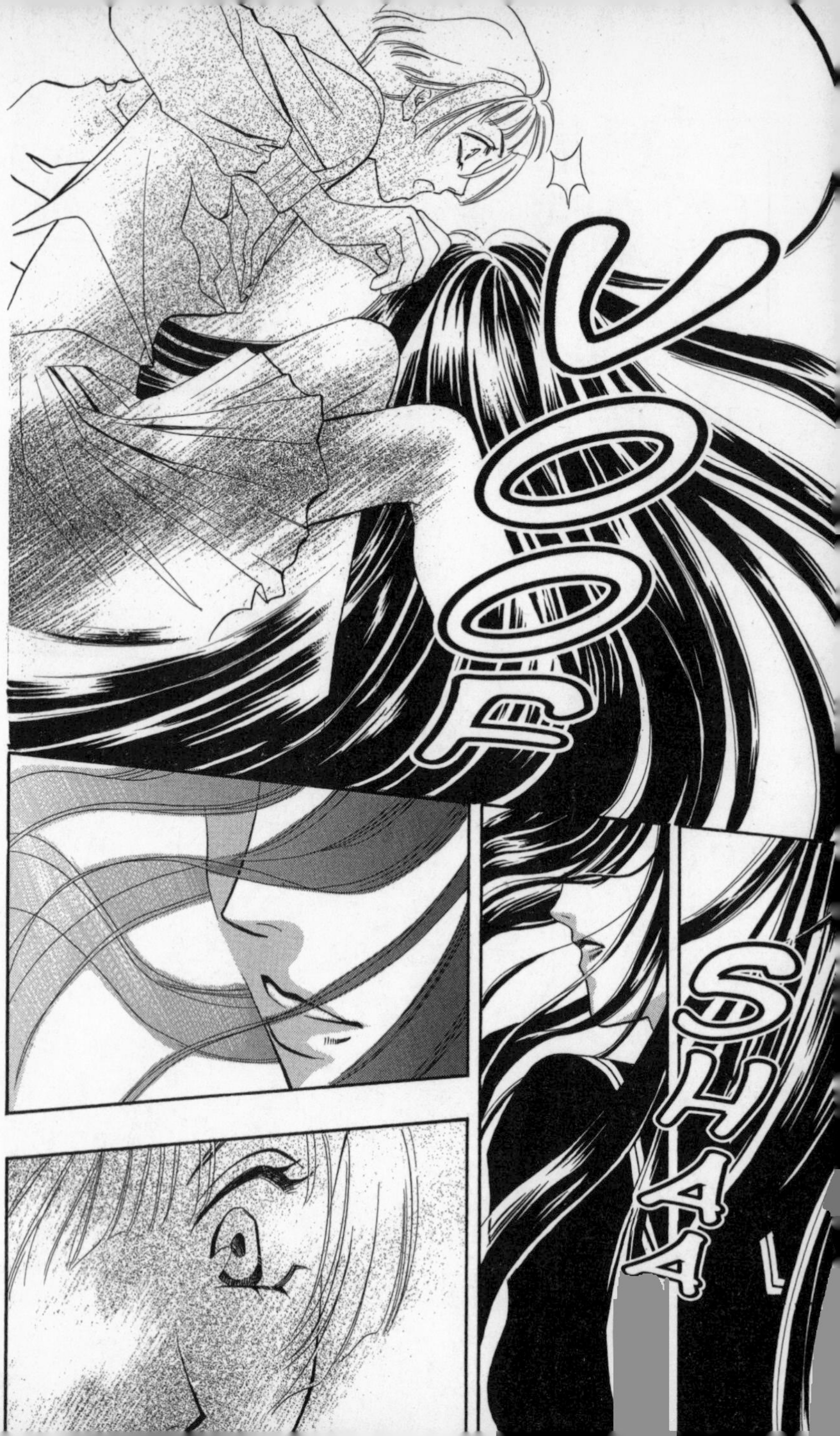
VOOF
SHHAA

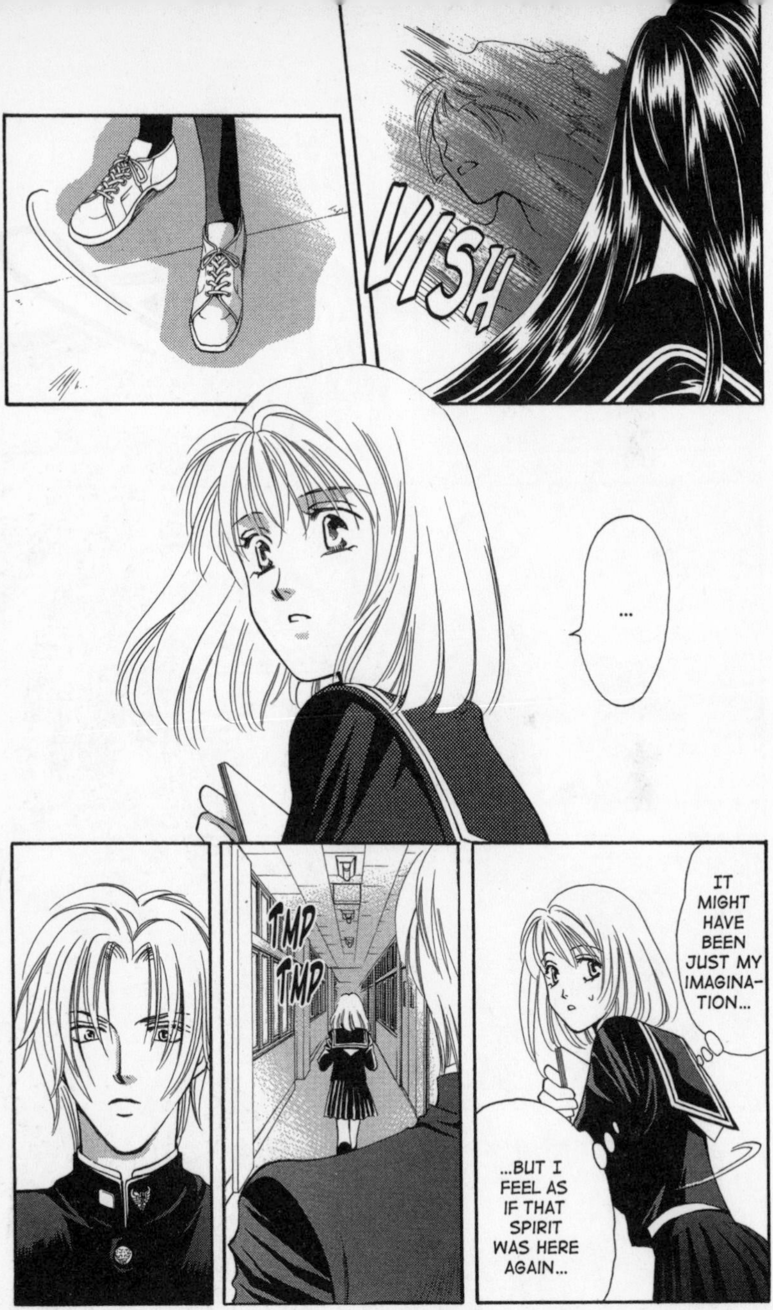
VISH
...
IT MIGHT HAVE BEEN JUST MY IMAGINA-TION...
...BUT I FEEL AS IF THAT SPIRIT WAS HERE AGAIN...
TMP TMP

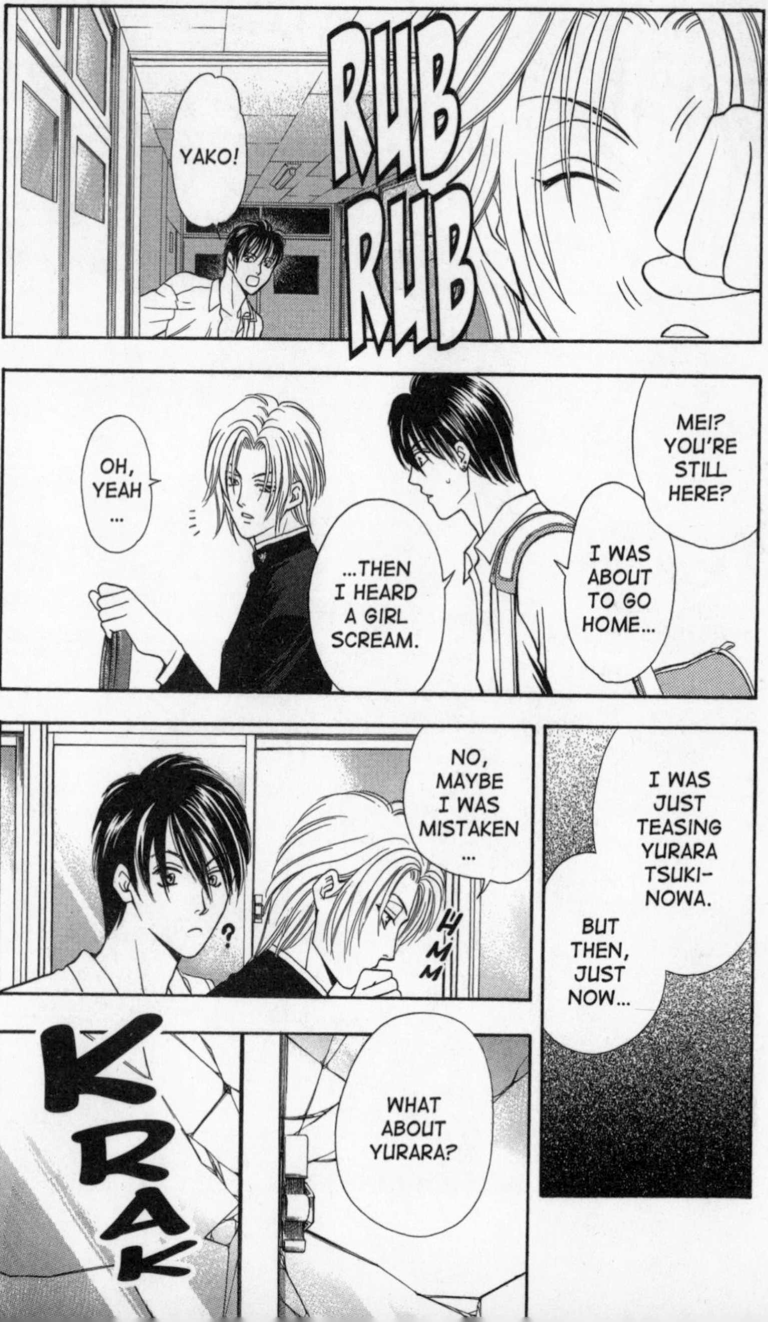
RUB RUB
YAKO!
MEI? YOU'RE STILL HERE?
I WAS ABOUT TO GO HOME...
...THEN I HEARD A GIRL SCREAM.
OH, YEAH ...
I WAS JUST TEASING YURARA TSUKI-NOWA.
BUT THEN, JUST NOW...
NO, MAYBE I WAS MISTAKEN ...
HMMM
KRAK
WHAT ABOUT YURARA?

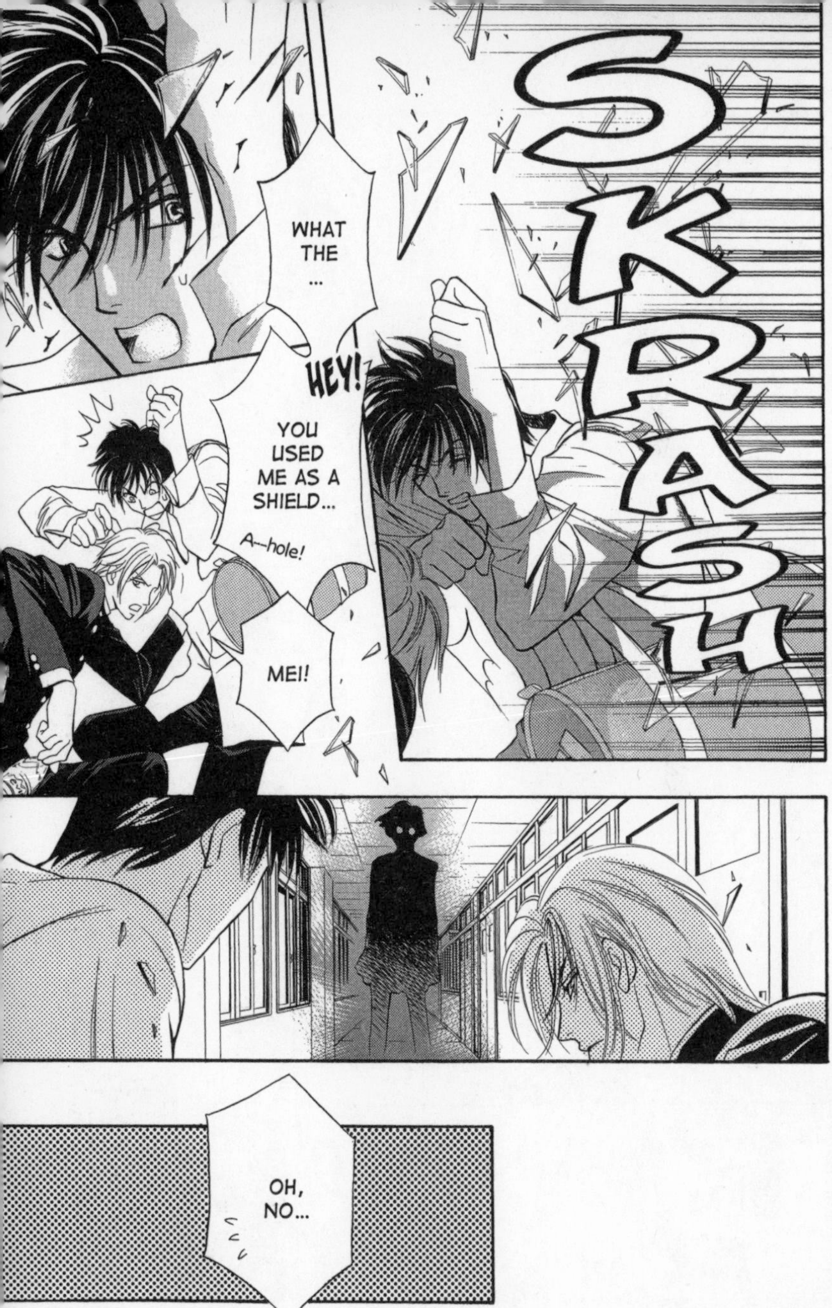
SKRASH
WHAT THE ...
HEY!
YOU USED ME AS A SHIELD...
A--hole!
MEI!
OH, NO...

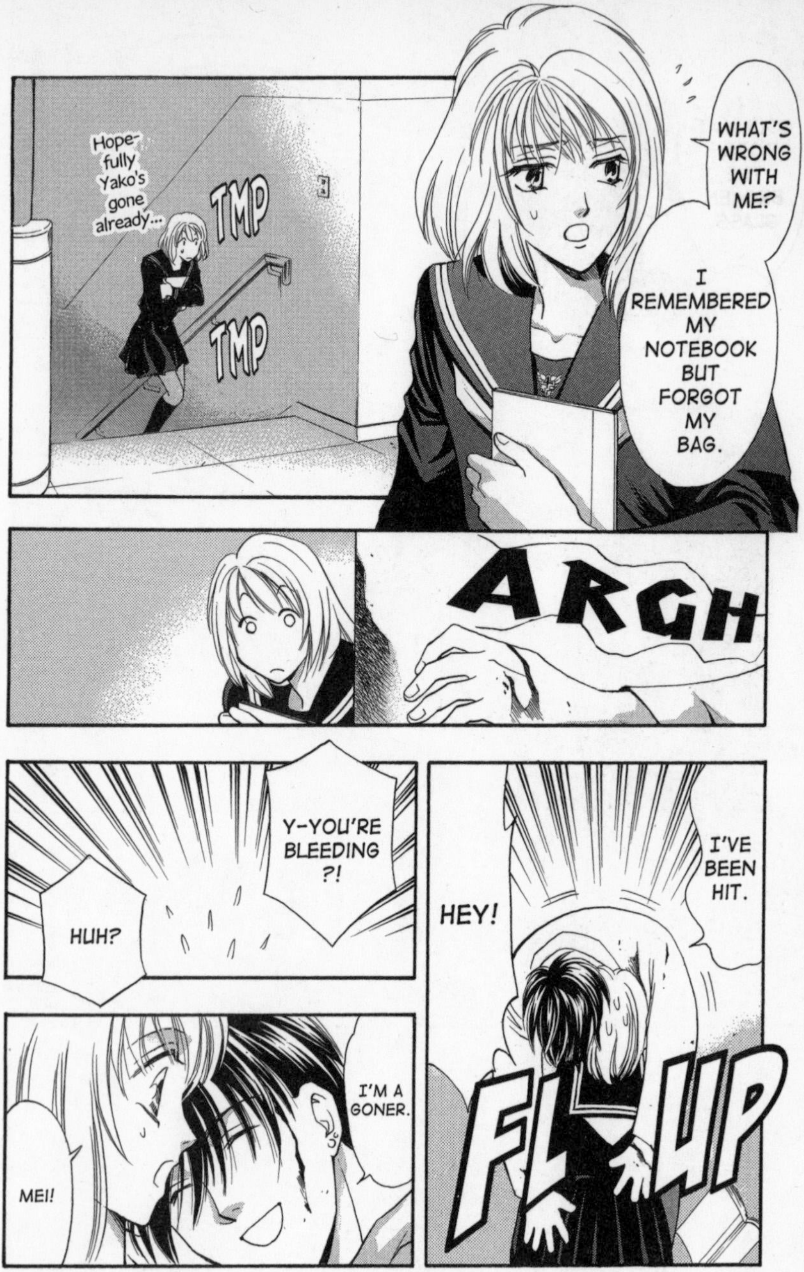
WHAT'S WRONG WITH ME?
I REMEMBERED MY NOTEBOOK BUT FORGOT MY BAG.
Hope-fully Yako's gone already...
TMP
TMP
ARGH
I'VE BEEN HIT.
HEY!
FL UP
Y-YOU'RE BLEEDING ?!
HUH?
I'M A GONER.
MEI!

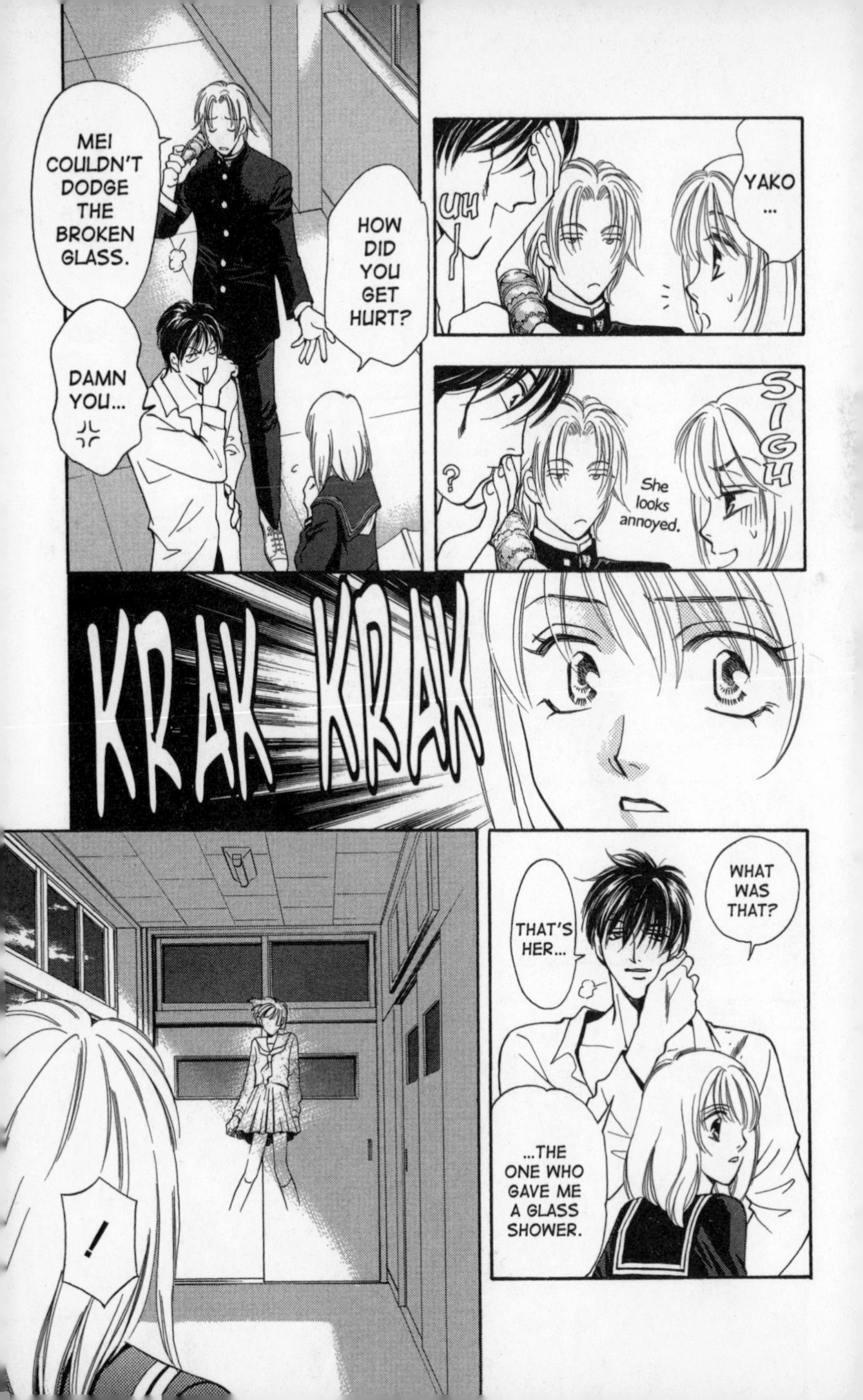
YAKO ...
UH
SIGH
?
She looks annoyed.
HOW DID YOU GET HURT?
MEI COULDN'T DODGE THE BROKEN GLASS.
DAMN YOU...
KRAK KRAK
WHAT WAS THAT?
THAT'S HER...
...THE ONE WHO GAVE ME A GLASS SHOWER.
!

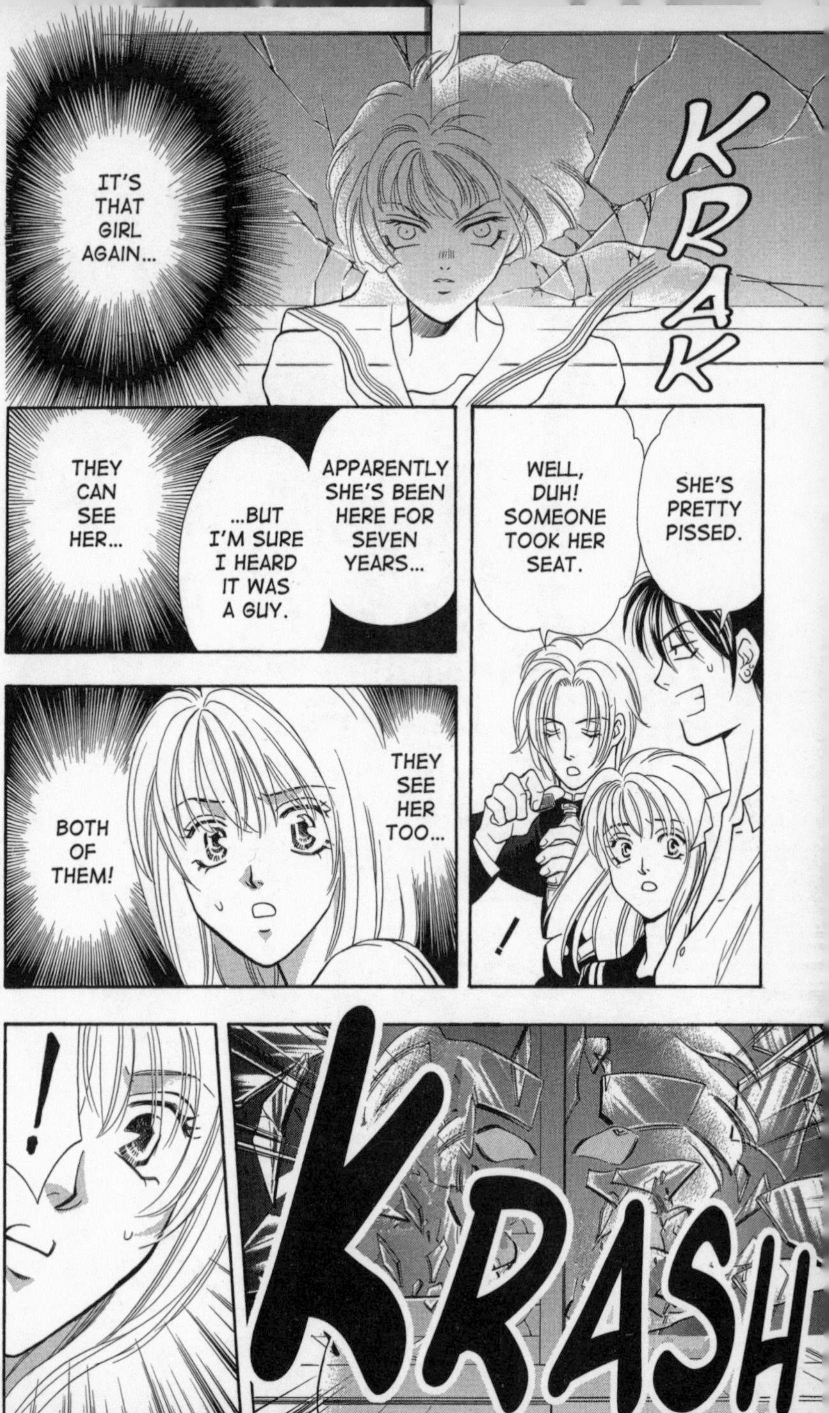
KRAK
IT'S THAT GIRL AGAIN...
SHE'S PRETTY PISSED.
WELL, DUH! SOMEONE TOOK HER SEAT.
!
APPARENTLY SHE'S BEEN HERE FOR SEVEN YEARS...
...BUT I'M SURE I HEARD IT WAS A GUY.
THEY CAN SEE HER...
THEY SEE HER TOO...
BOTH OF THEM!
KRASH
!

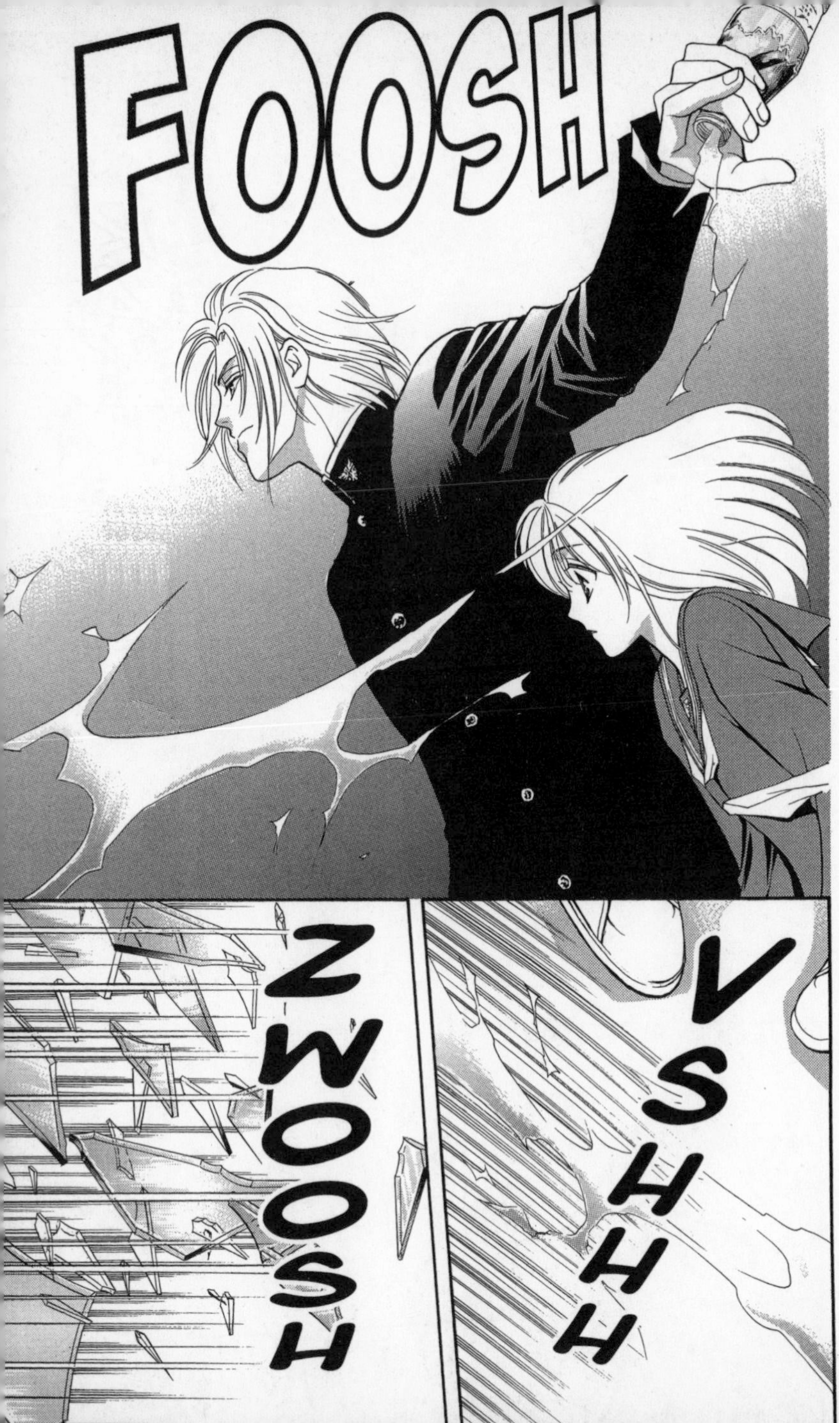
FOOSH
VSHHHH
ZWOOSH

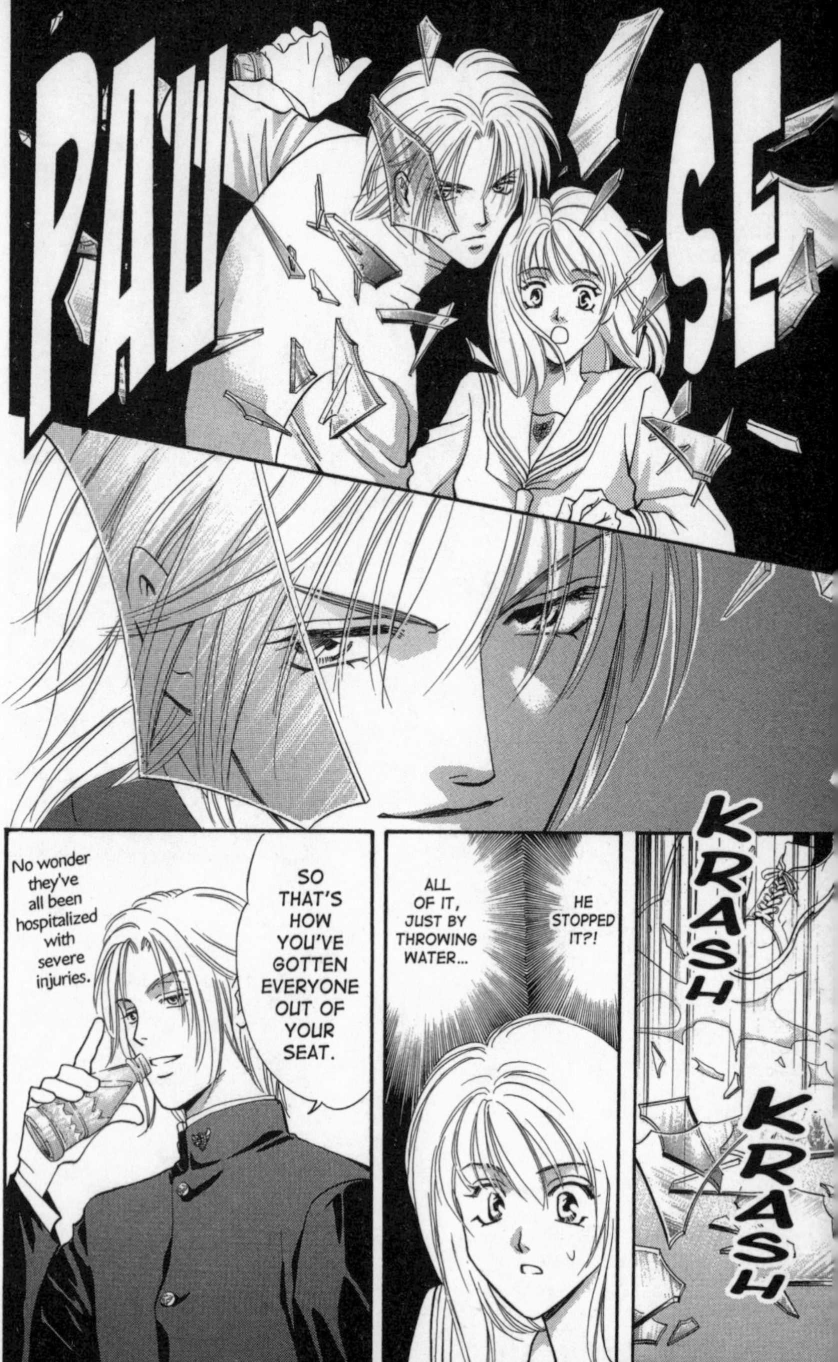
PAUSE
KRASH
KRASH
HE STOPPED IT?!
ALL OF IT, JUST BY THROWING WATER...
SO THAT'S HOW YOU'VE GOTTEN EVERYONE OUT OF YOUR SEAT.
No wonder they've all been hospitalized with severe injuries.

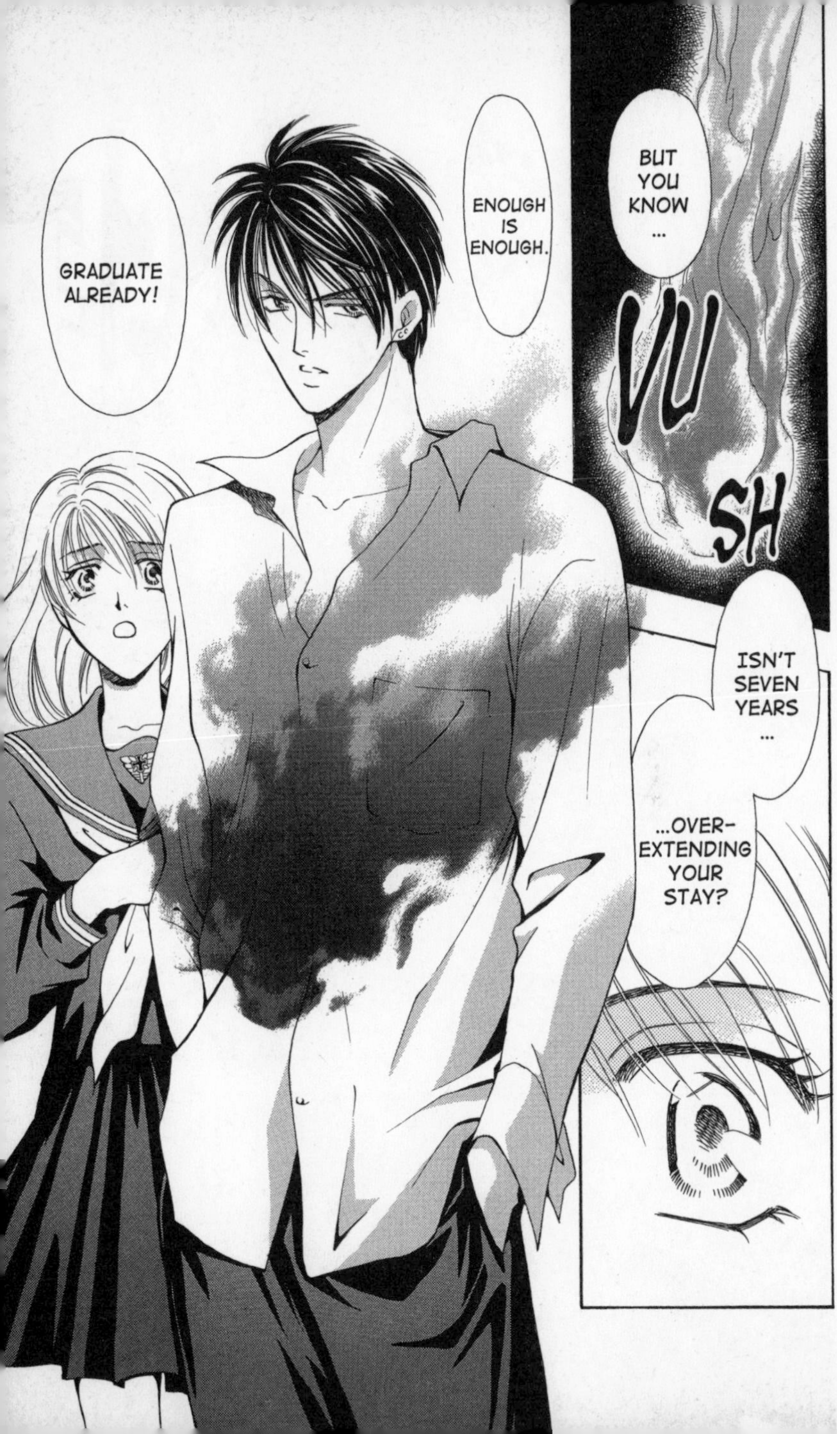
BUT YOU KNOW ...
VUSH
ISN'T SEVEN YEARS ...
...OVER-EXTENDING YOUR STAY?
ENOUGH IS ENOUGH.
GRADUATE ALREADY!

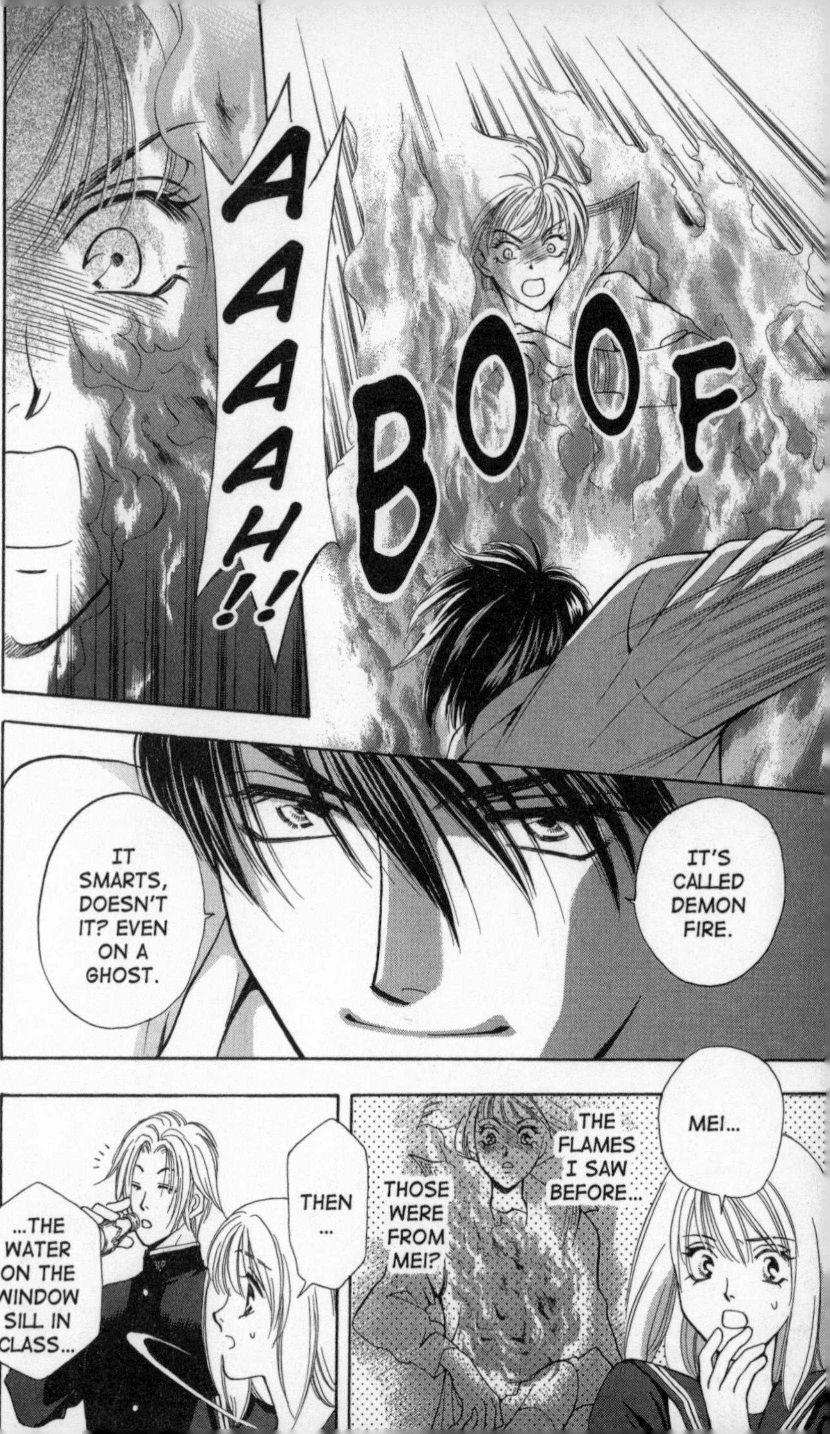
BOOF
AAAAH!!
IT'S CALLED DEMON FIRE.
IT SMARTS, DOESN'T IT? EVEN ON A GHOST.
MEI...
THE FLAMES I SAW BEFORE...
THOSE WERE FROM MEI?
THEN...
...THE WATER ON THE WINDOW SILL IN CLASS...

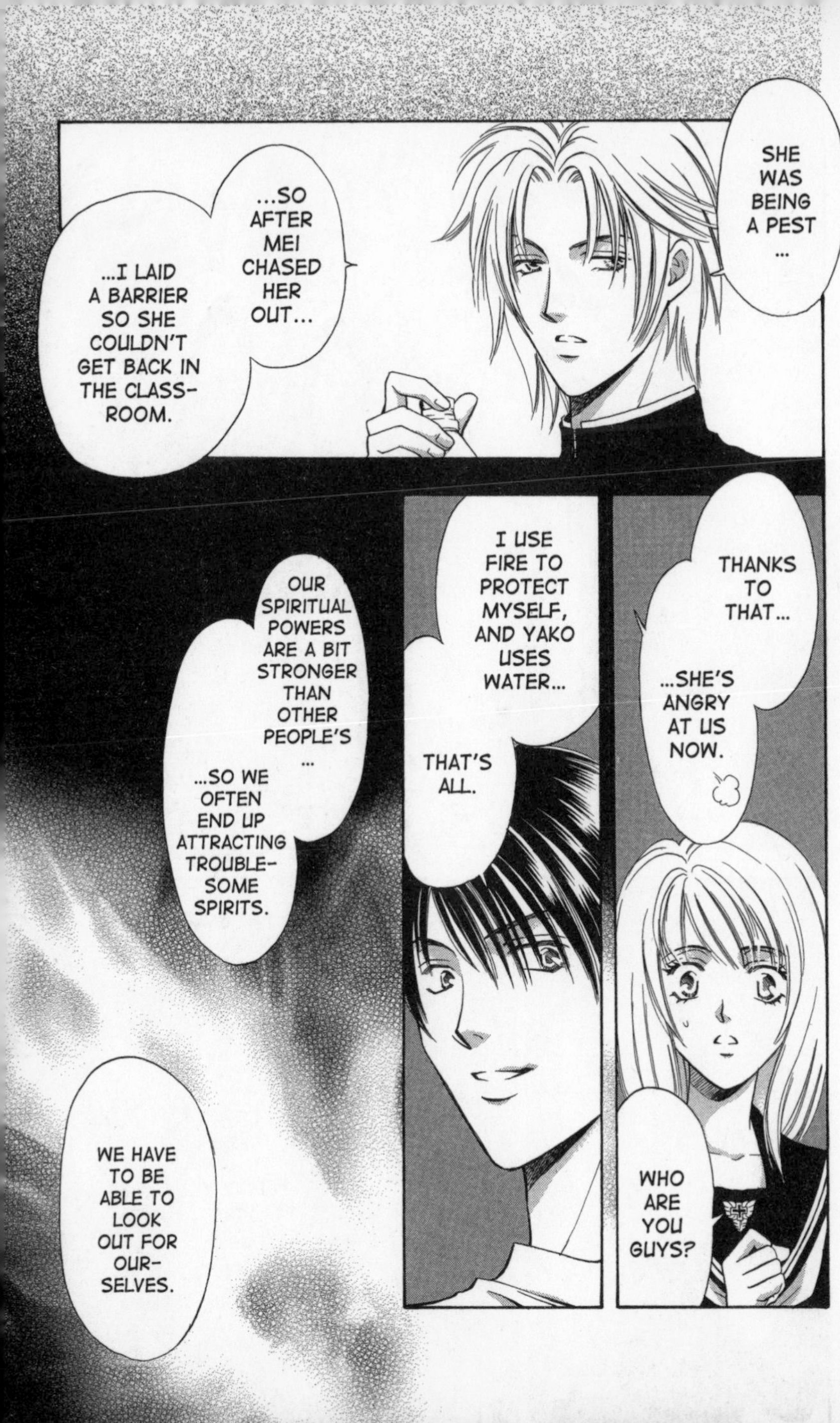
SHE WAS BEING A PEST ...
...SO AFTER MEI CHASED HER OUT...
...I LAID A BARRIER SO SHE COULDN'T GET BACK IN THE CLASS-ROOM.
THANKS TO THAT...
...SHE'S ANGRY AT US NOW.
WHO ARE YOU GUYS?
I USE FIRE TO PROTECT MYSELF, AND YAKO USES WATER...
THAT'S ALL.
OUR SPIRITUAL POWERS ARE A BIT STRONGER THAN OTHER PEOPLE'S ...
...SO WE OFTEN END UP ATTRACTING TROUBLE-SOME SPIRITS.
WE HAVE TO BE ABLE TO LOOK OUT FOR OUR-SELVES.

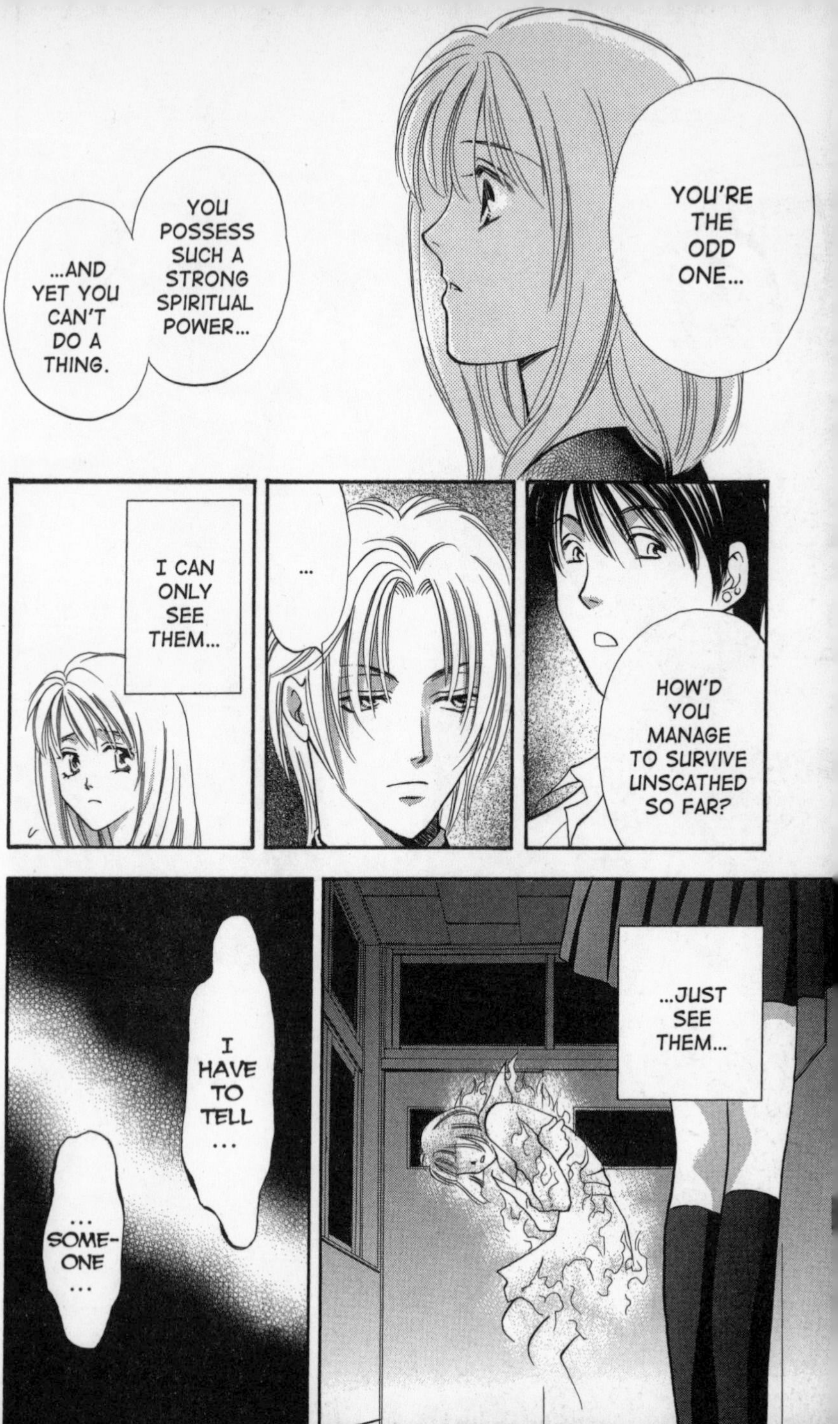
YOU'RE THE ODD ONE...
YOU POSSESS SUCH A STRONG SPIRITUAL POWER...
...AND YET YOU CAN'T DO A THING.
HOW'D YOU MANAGE TO SURVIVE UNSCATHED SO FAR?
...
I CAN ONLY SEE THEM...
...JUST SEE THEM...
I HAVE TO TELL ...
... SOME-ONE ...

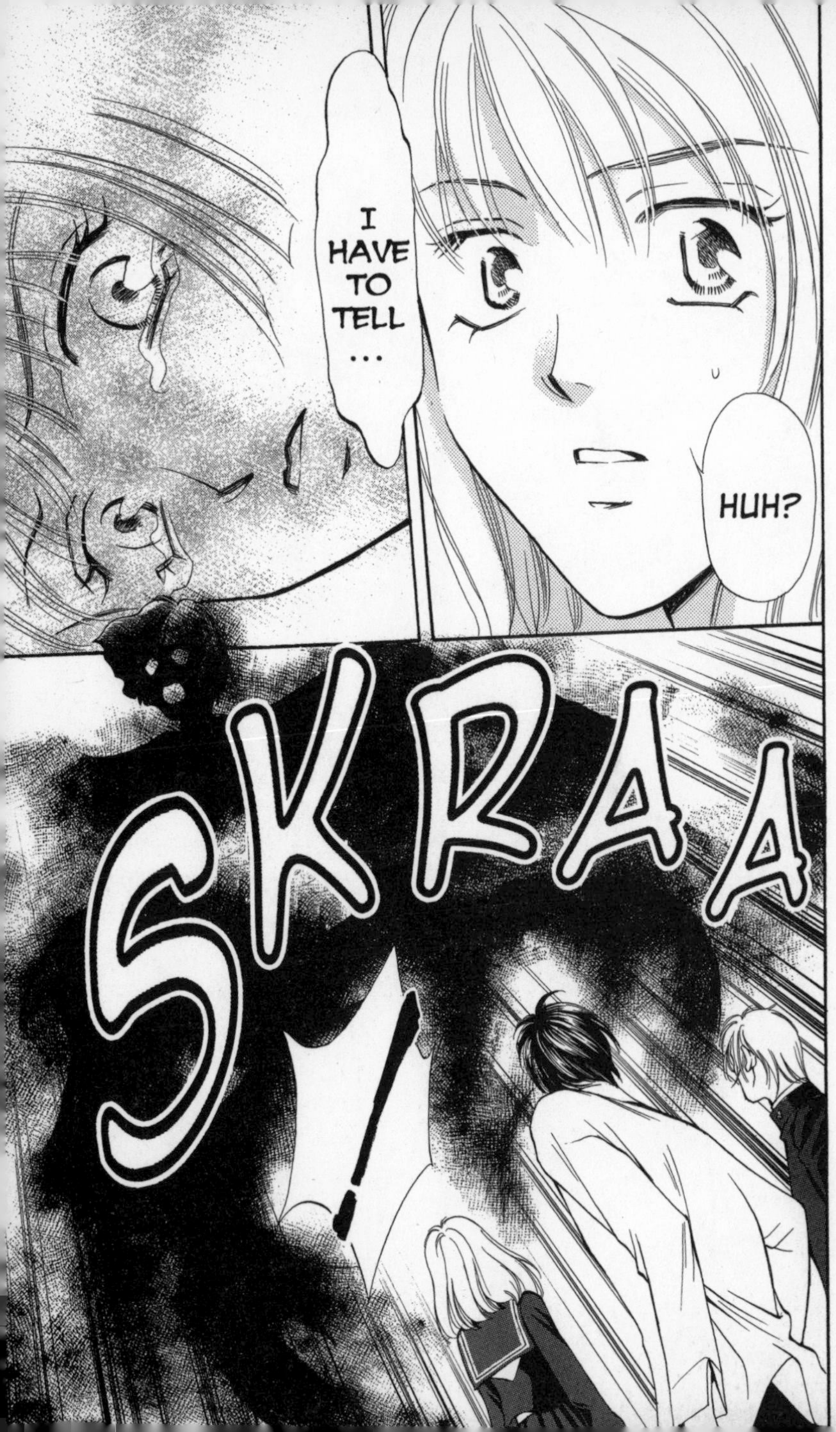
HUH?
I HAVE TO TELL ...
SKRAA

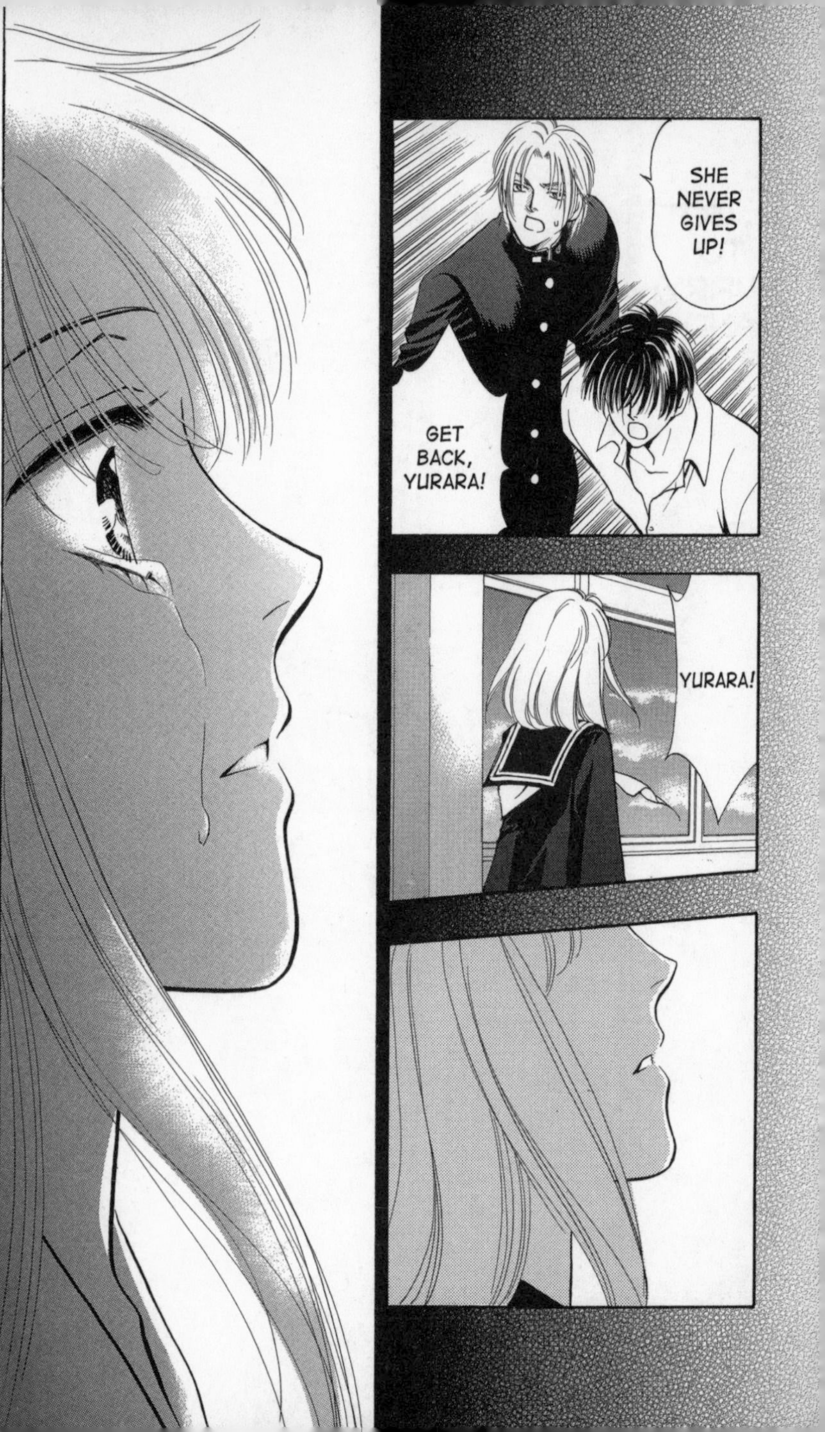
SHE NEVER GIVES UP!
GET BACK, YURARA!
YURARA!

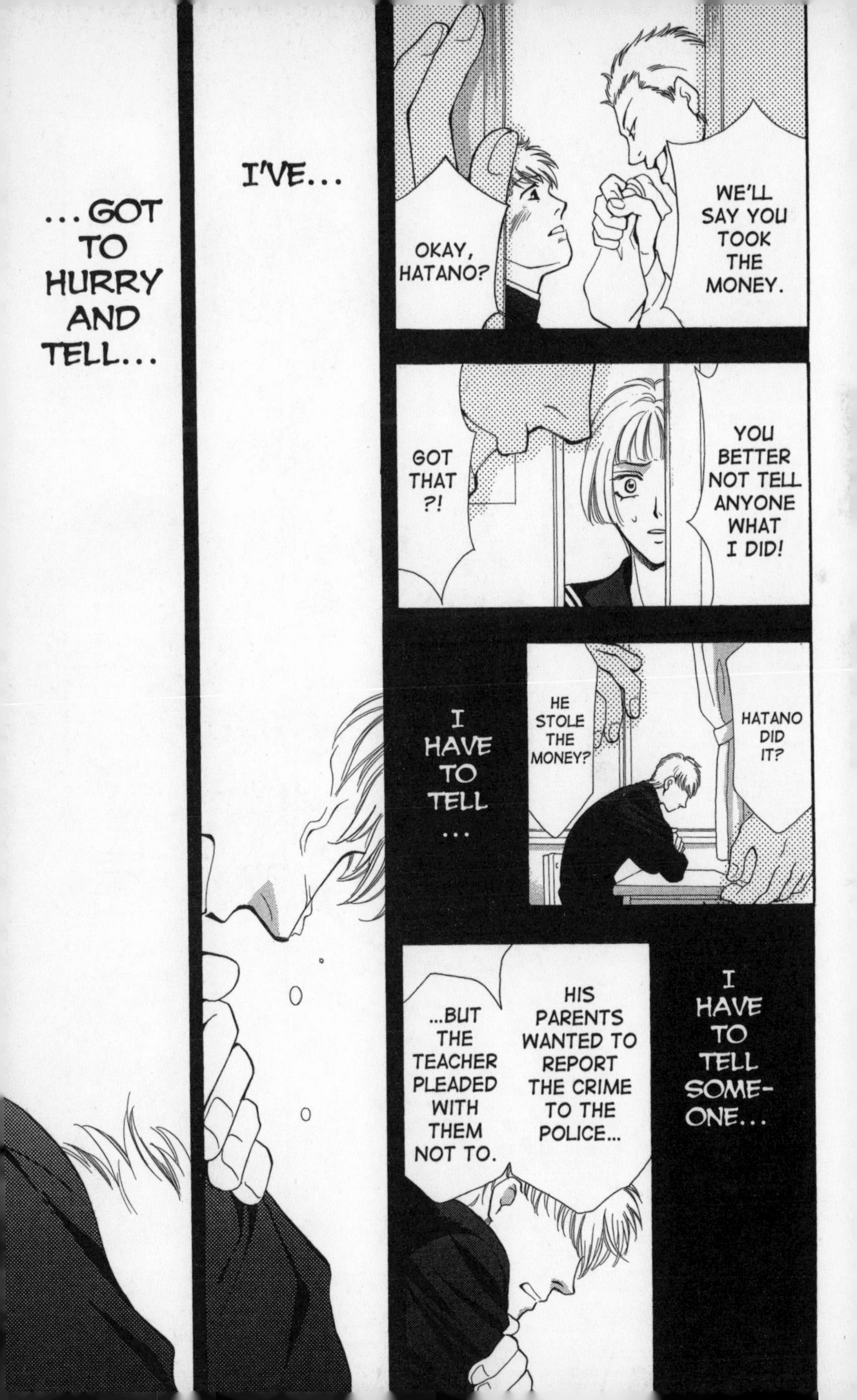
WE'LL SAY YOU TOOK THE MONEY.
OKAY, HATANO?
YOU BETTER NOT TELL ANYONE WHAT I DID!
GOT THAT?!
HATANO DID IT?
HE STOLE THE MONEY?
I HAVE TO TELL...
I HAVE TO TELL SOME-ONE...
HIS PARENTS WANTED TO REPORT THE CRIME TO THE POLICE...
...BUT THE TEACHER PLEADED WITH THEM NOT TO.
I'VE...
...GOT TO HURRY AND TELL...

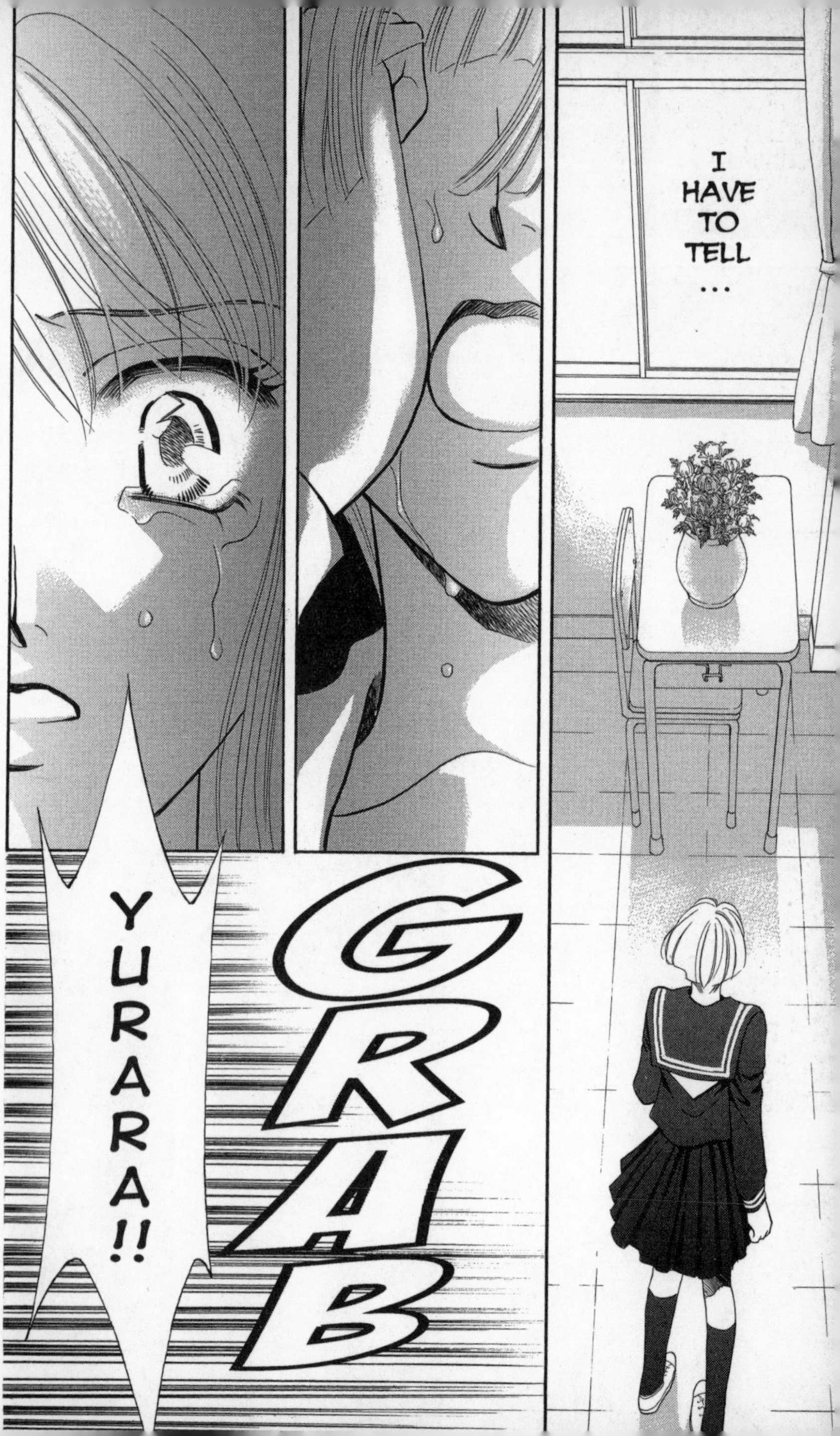
I HAVE TO TELL ...
GRAB
YURARA!!

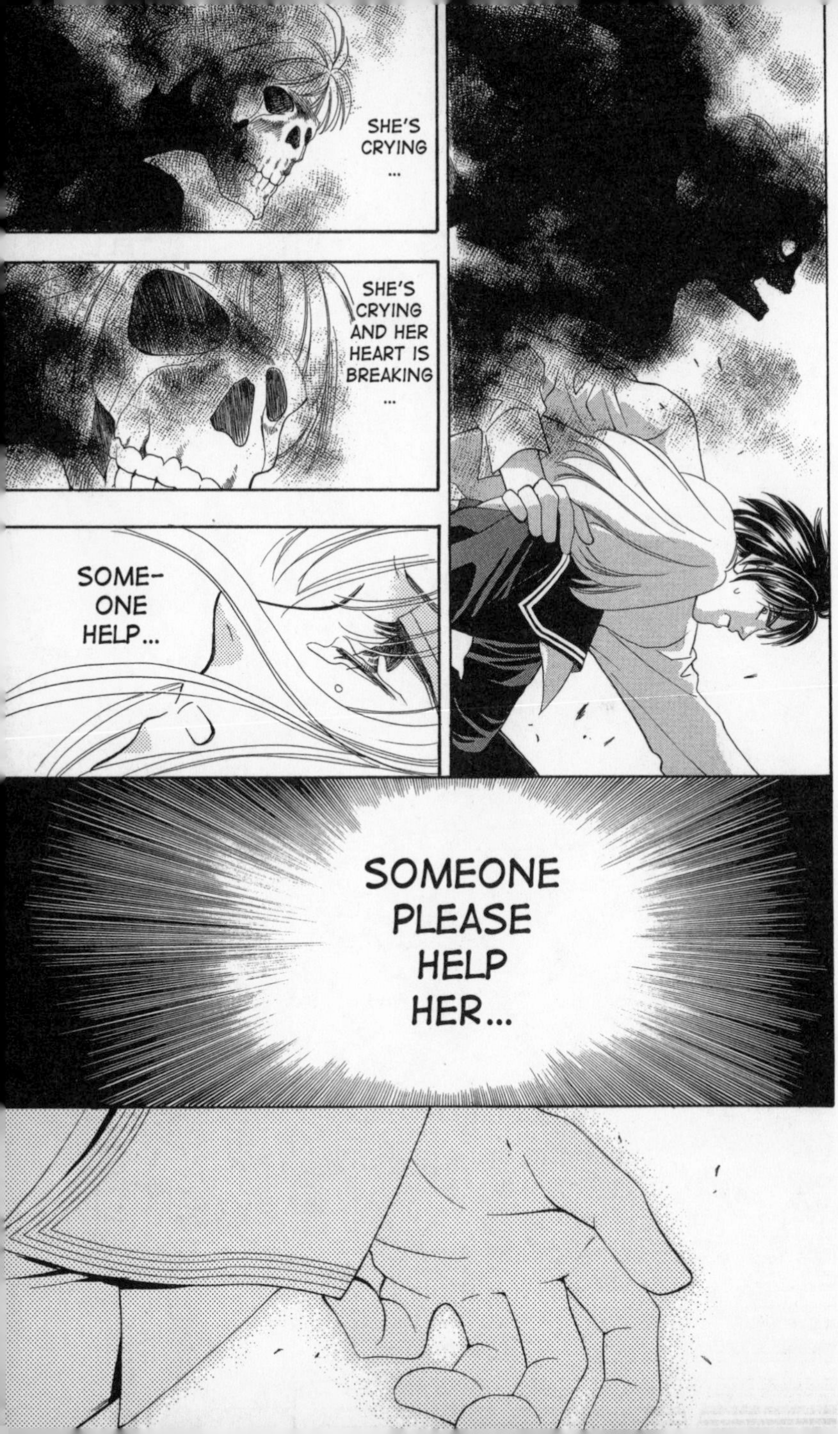
SHE'S CRYING ...
SHE'S CRYING AND HER HEART IS BREAKING ...
SOME-ONE HELP...
SOMEONE PLEASE HELP HER...

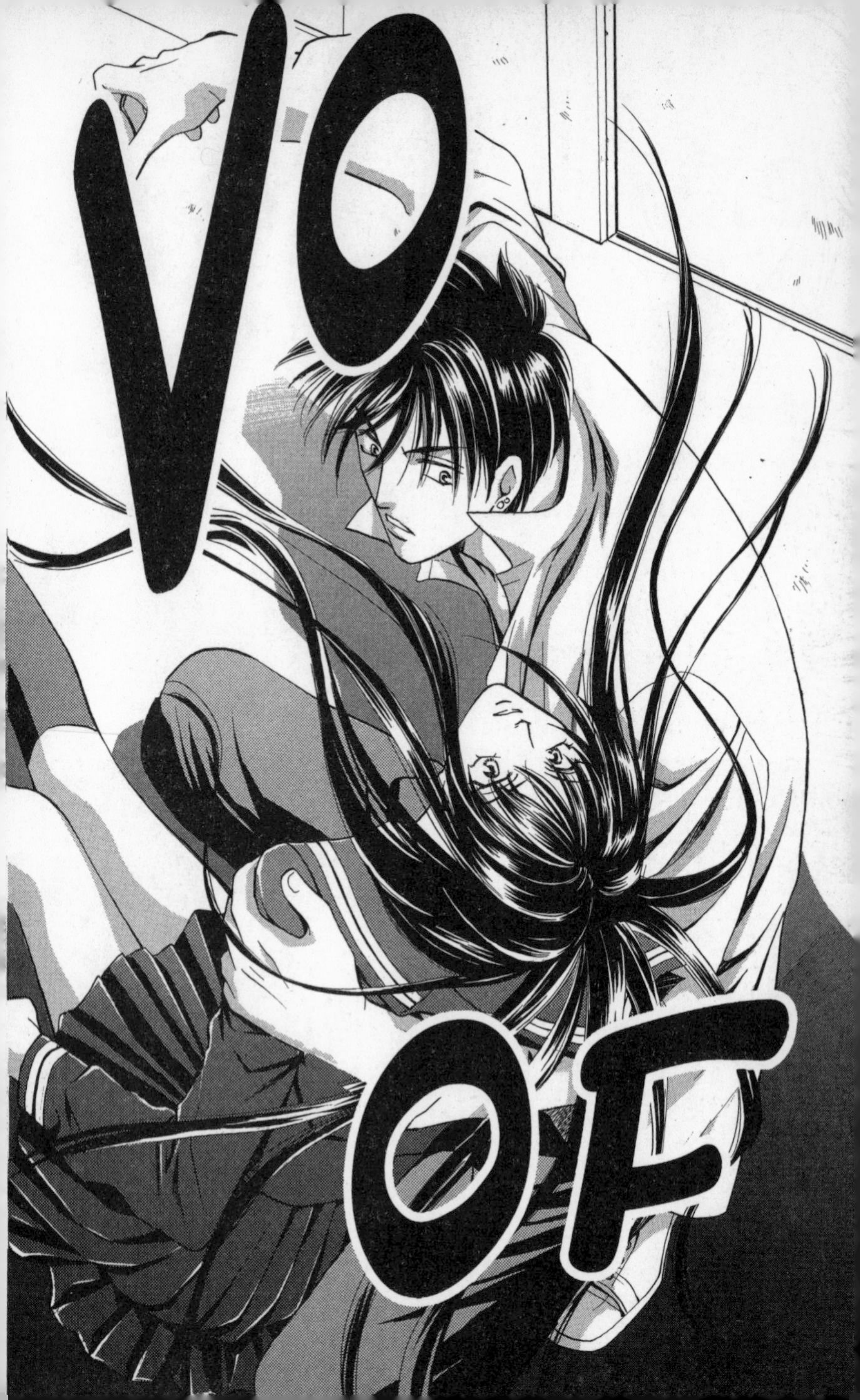
VOOF

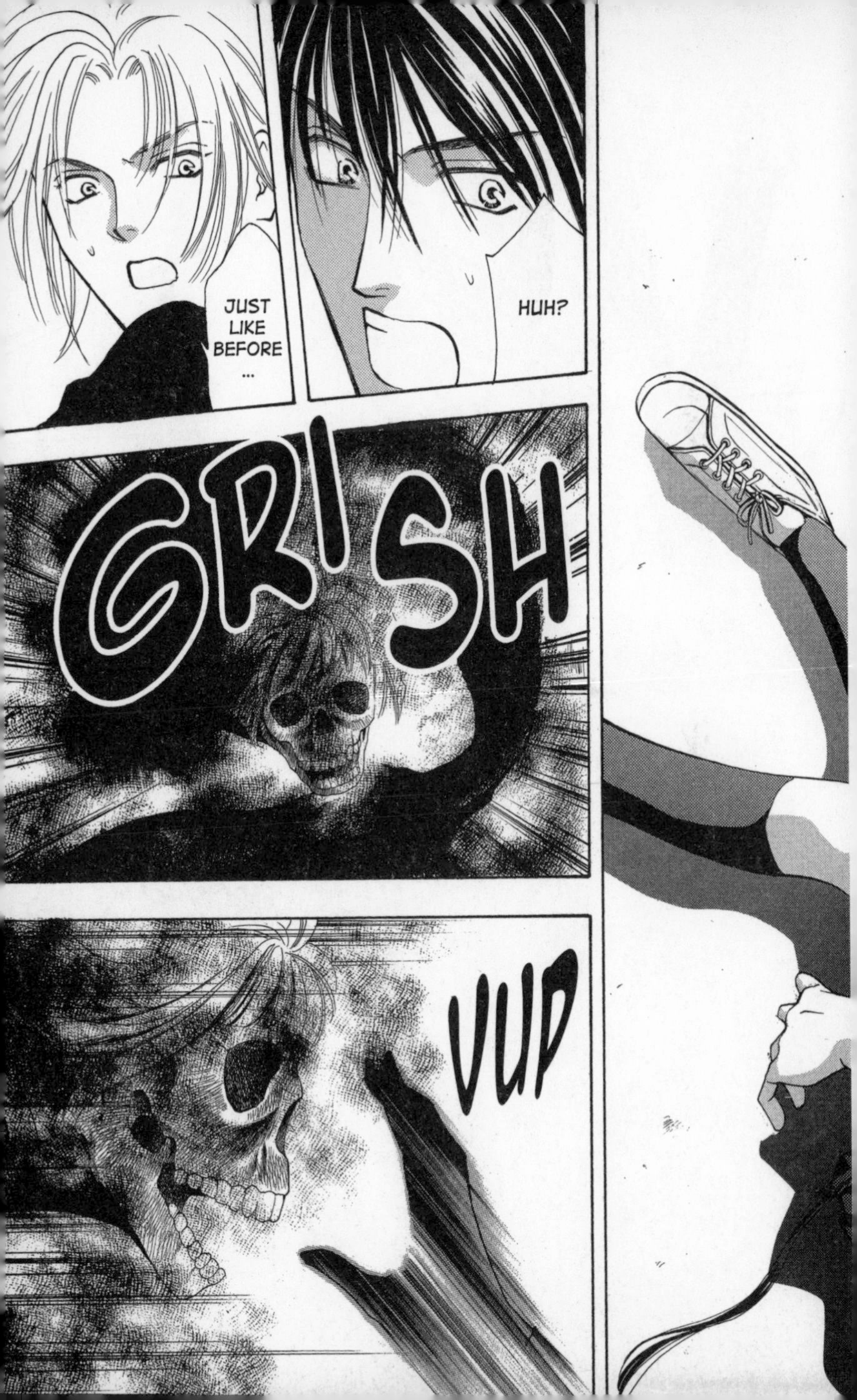
HUH?
JUST LIKE BEFORE ...
GRISH
VUP

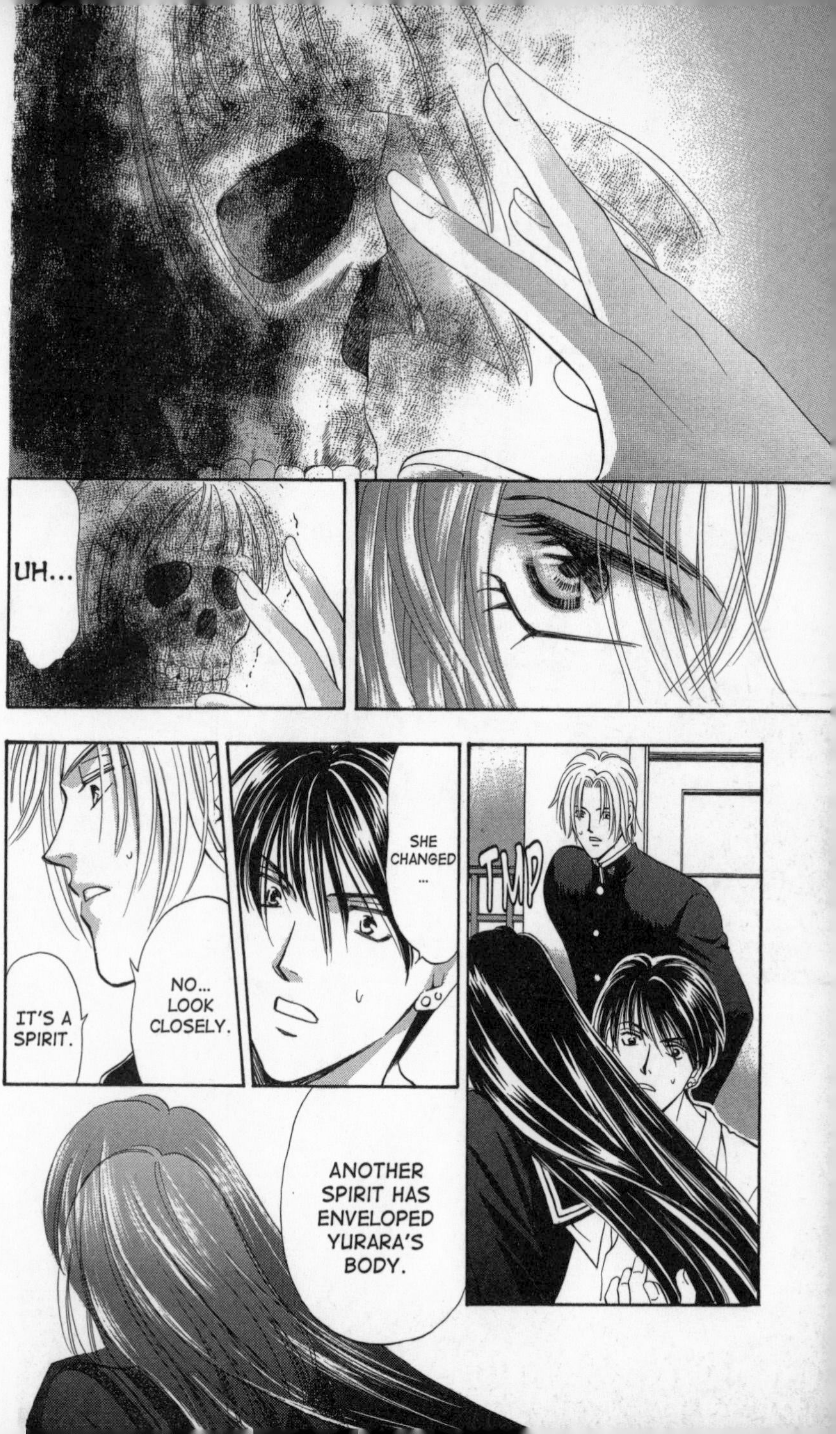
UH...
TMP
SHE CHANGED ...
NO... LOOK CLOSELY.
IT'S A SPIRIT.
ANOTHER SPIRIT HAS ENVELOPED YURARA'S BODY.

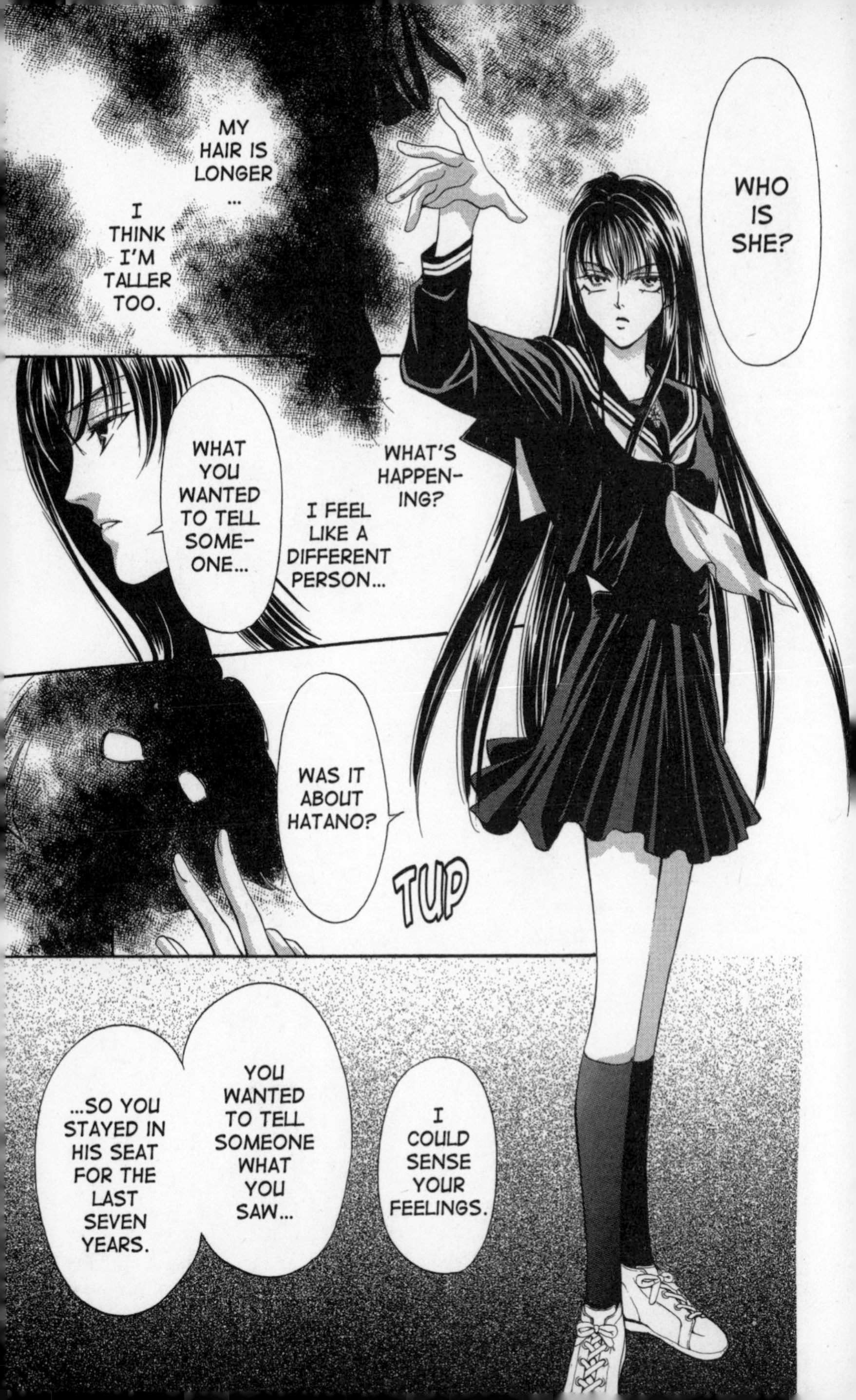

WHO IS SHE?
MY HAIR IS LONGER ...
I THINK I'M TALLER TOO.
WHAT'S HAPPENING?
I FEEL LIKE A DIFFERENT PERSON...
WHAT YOU WANTED TO TELL SOMEONE...
WAS IT ABOUT HATANO?
TUP
I COULD SENSE YOUR FEELINGS.
YOU WANTED TO TELL SOMEONE WHAT YOU SAW...
...SO YOU STAYED IN HIS SEAT FOR THE LAST SEVEN YEARS.

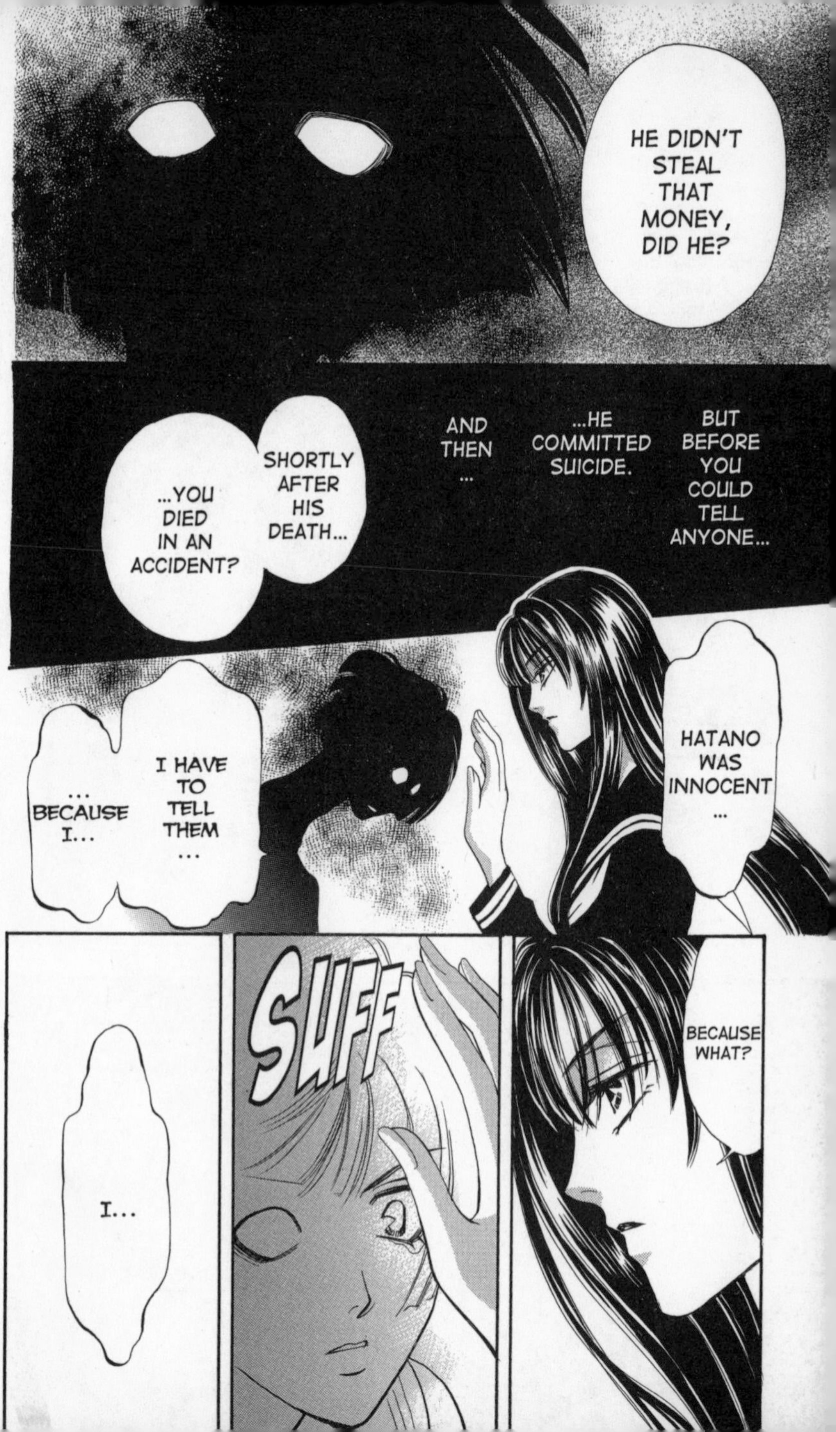
HE DIDN'T STEAL THAT MONEY, DID HE?
BUT BEFORE YOU COULD TELL ANYONE...
...HE COMMITTED SUICIDE.
AND THEN ...
SHORTLY AFTER HIS DEATH...
...YOU DIED IN AN ACCIDENT?
HATANO WAS INNOCENT ...
I HAVE TO TELL THEM ...
... BECAUSE I...
BECAUSE WHAT?
SUFF
I...

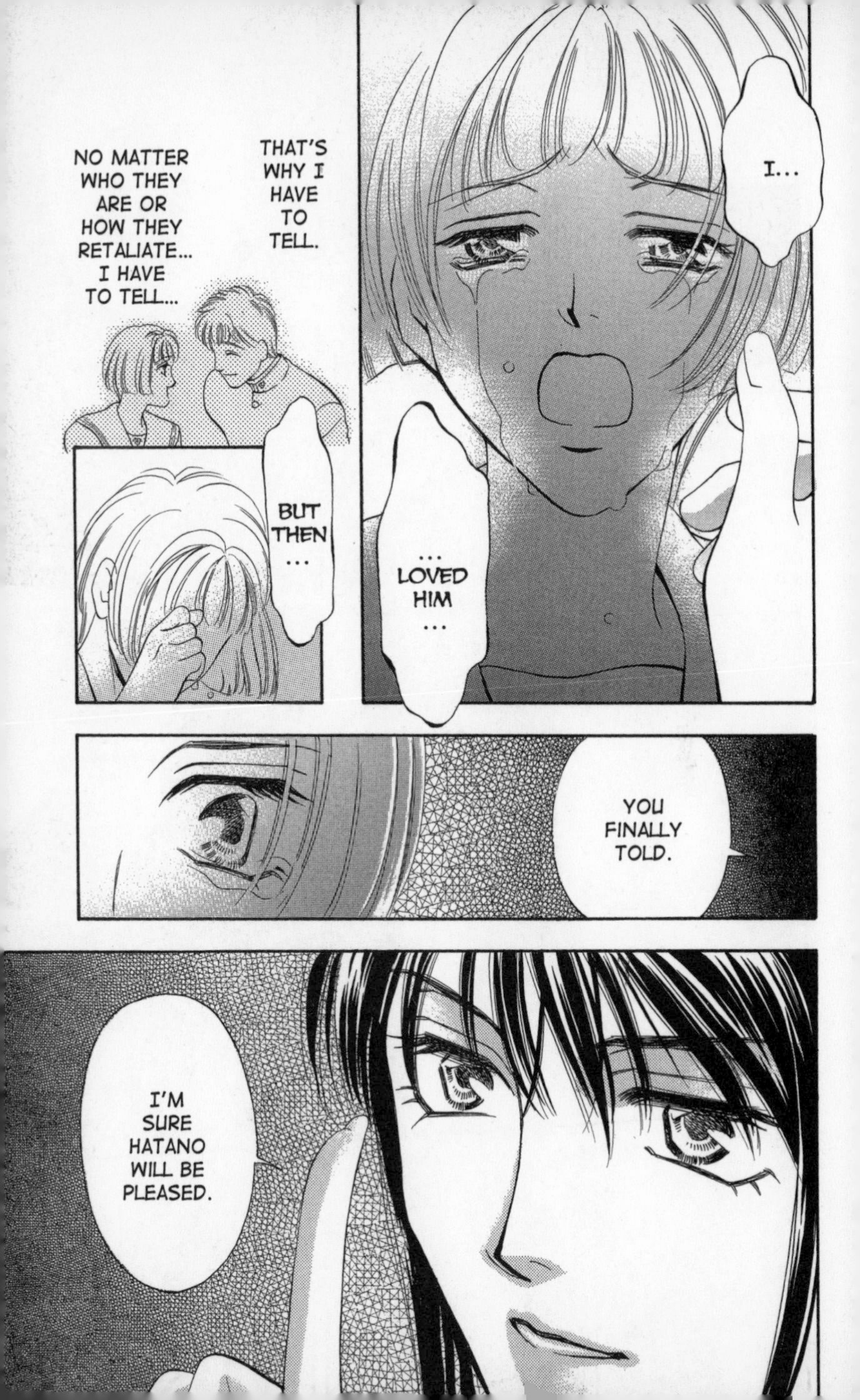
I...
...LOVED HIM...
THAT'S WHY I HAVE TO TELL.
NO MATTER WHO THEY ARE OR HOW THEY RETALIATE... I HAVE TO TELL...
BUT THEN...
YOU FINALLY TOLD.
I'M SURE HATANO WILL BE PLEASED.

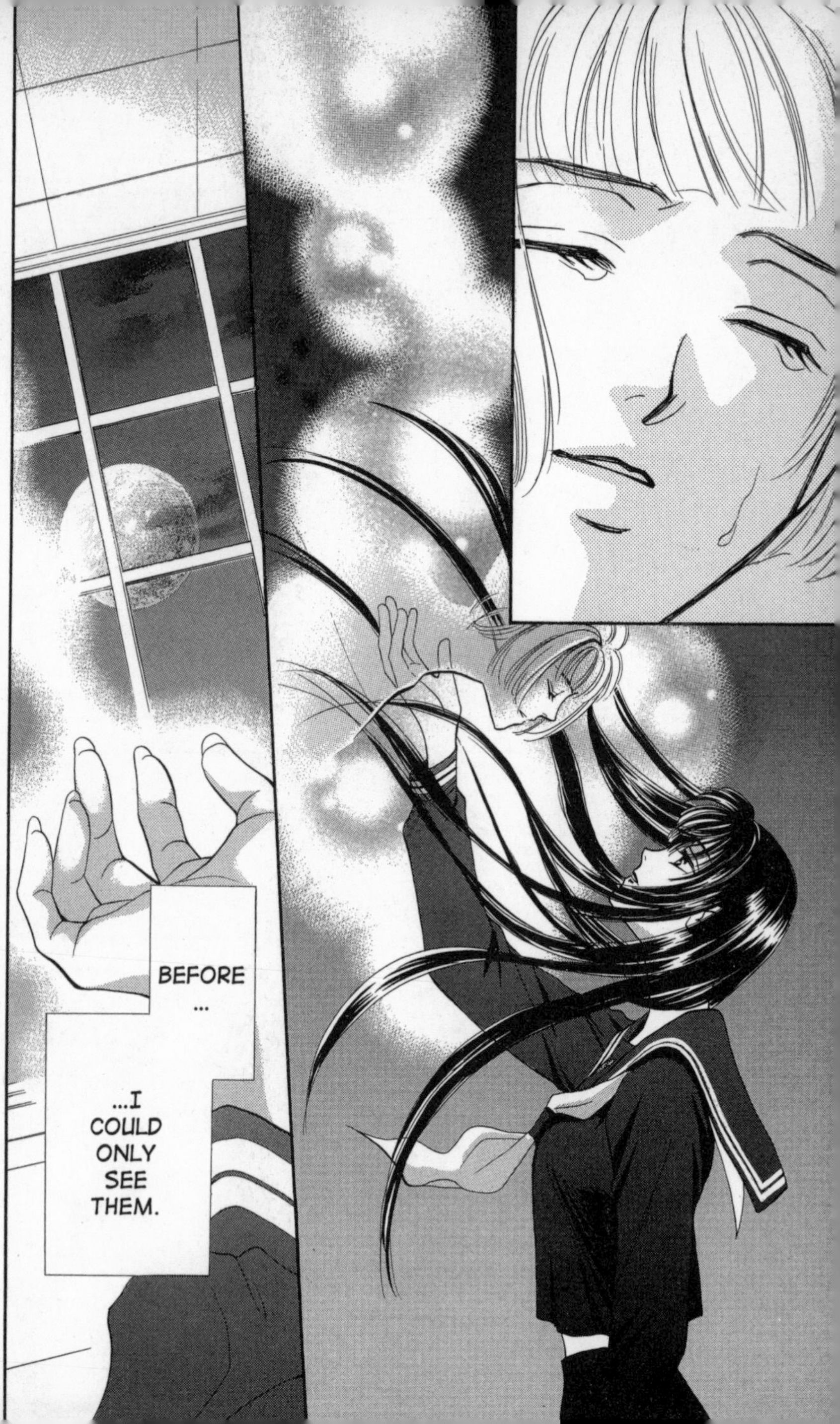
BEFORE ...
...I COULD ONLY SEE THEM.

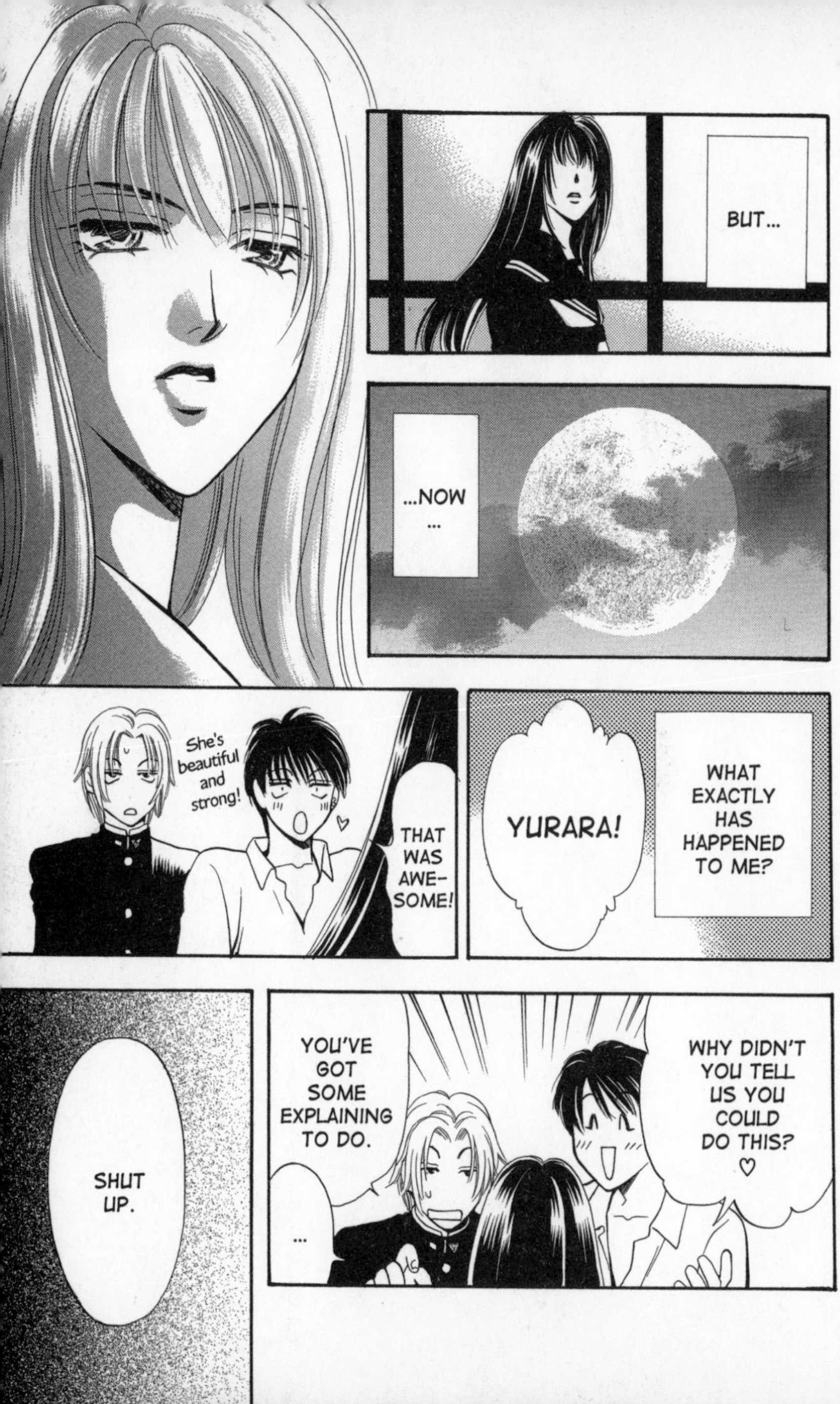
BUT...
...NOW ...
WHAT EXACTLY HAS HAPPENED TO ME?
YURARA!
THAT WAS AWE-SOME!
She's beautiful and strong!
WHY DIDN'T YOU TELL US YOU COULD DO THIS? ♡
YOU'VE GOT SOME EXPLAINING TO DO.
...
SHUT UP.

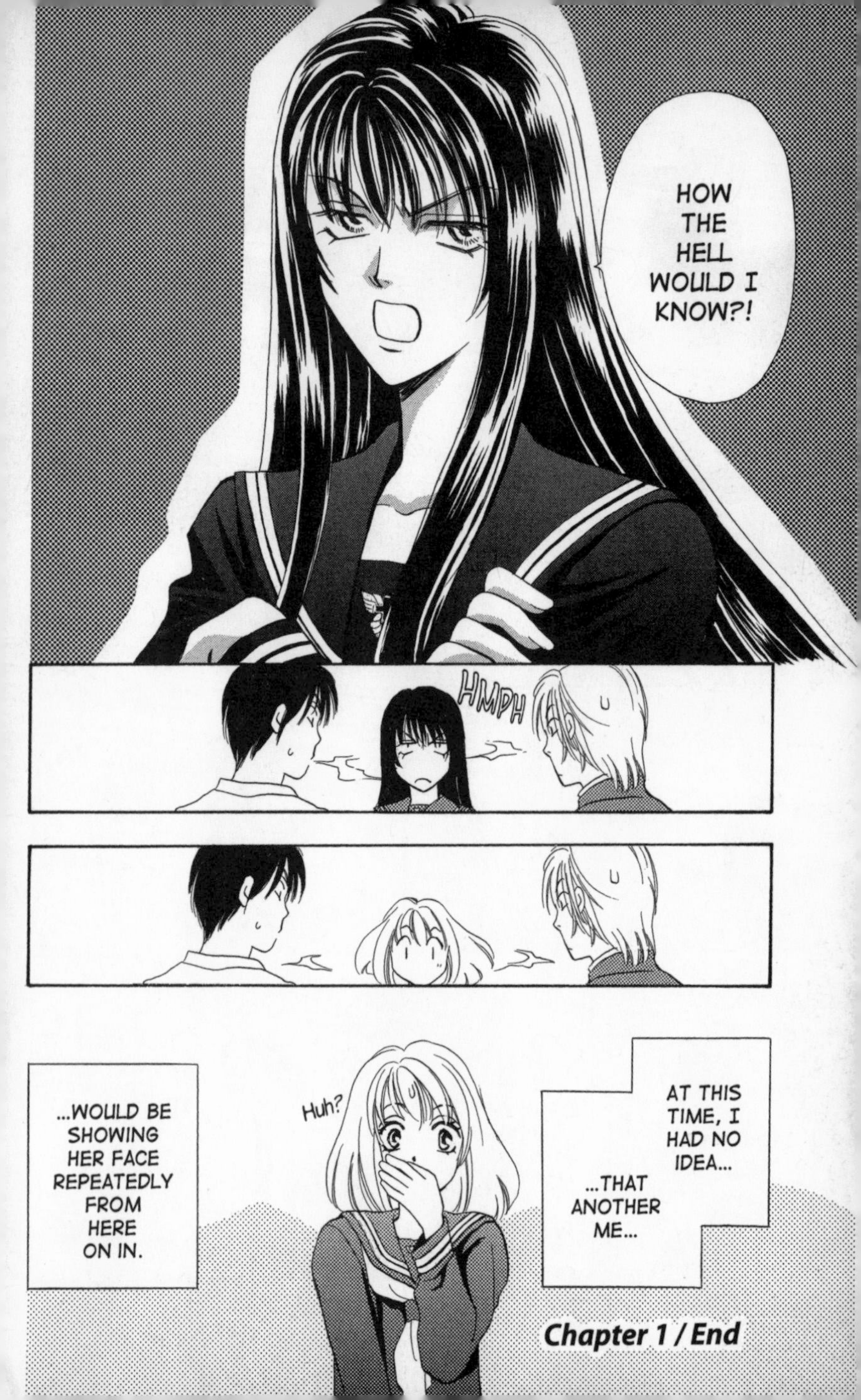
HOW THE HELL WOULD I KNOW?!
HMPH
AT THIS TIME, I HAD NO IDEA...
...THAT ANOTHER ME...
Huh?
...WOULD BE SHOWING HER FACE REPEATEDLY FROM HERE ON IN.
Chapter 1 / End

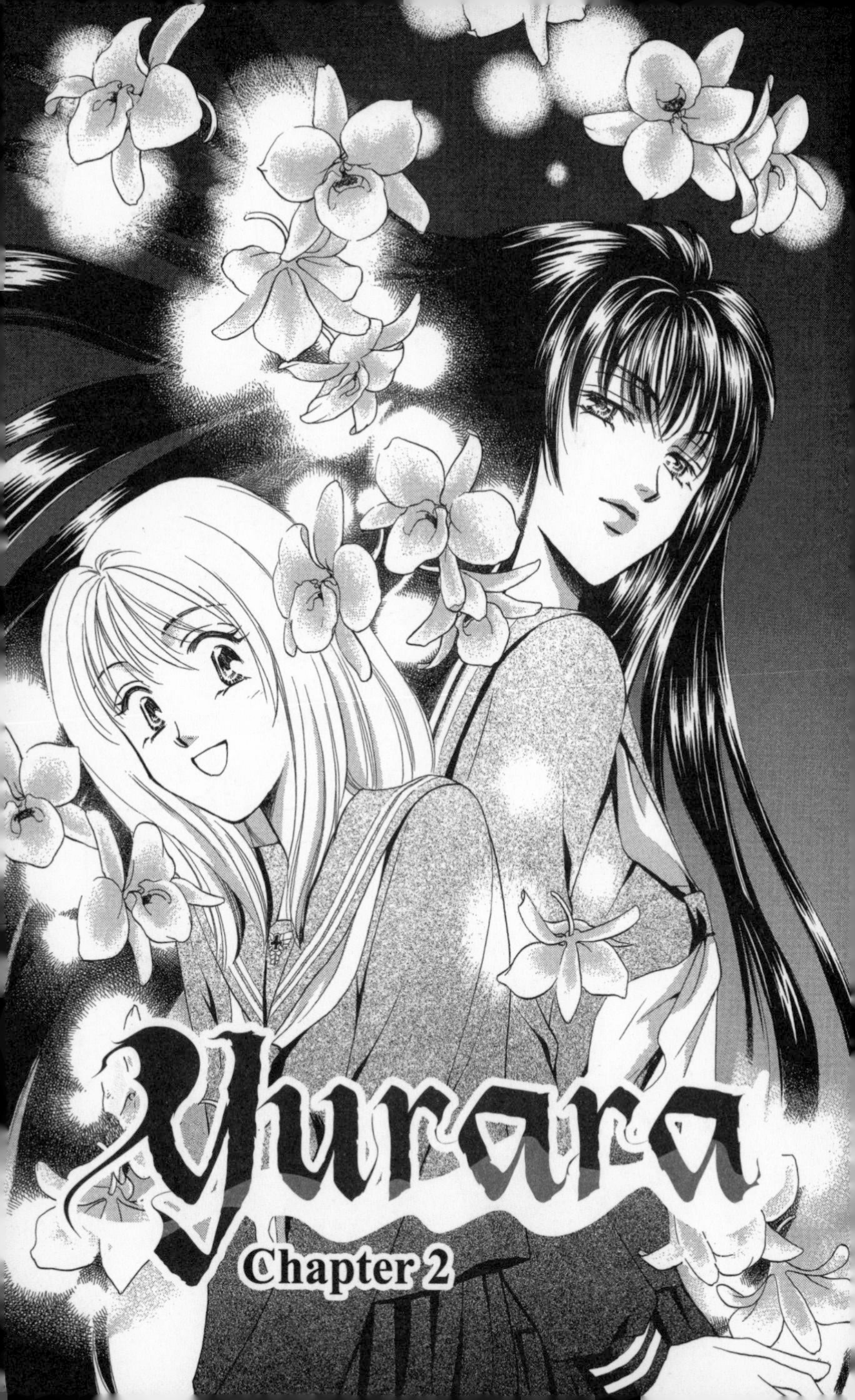
Yurara
Chapter 2

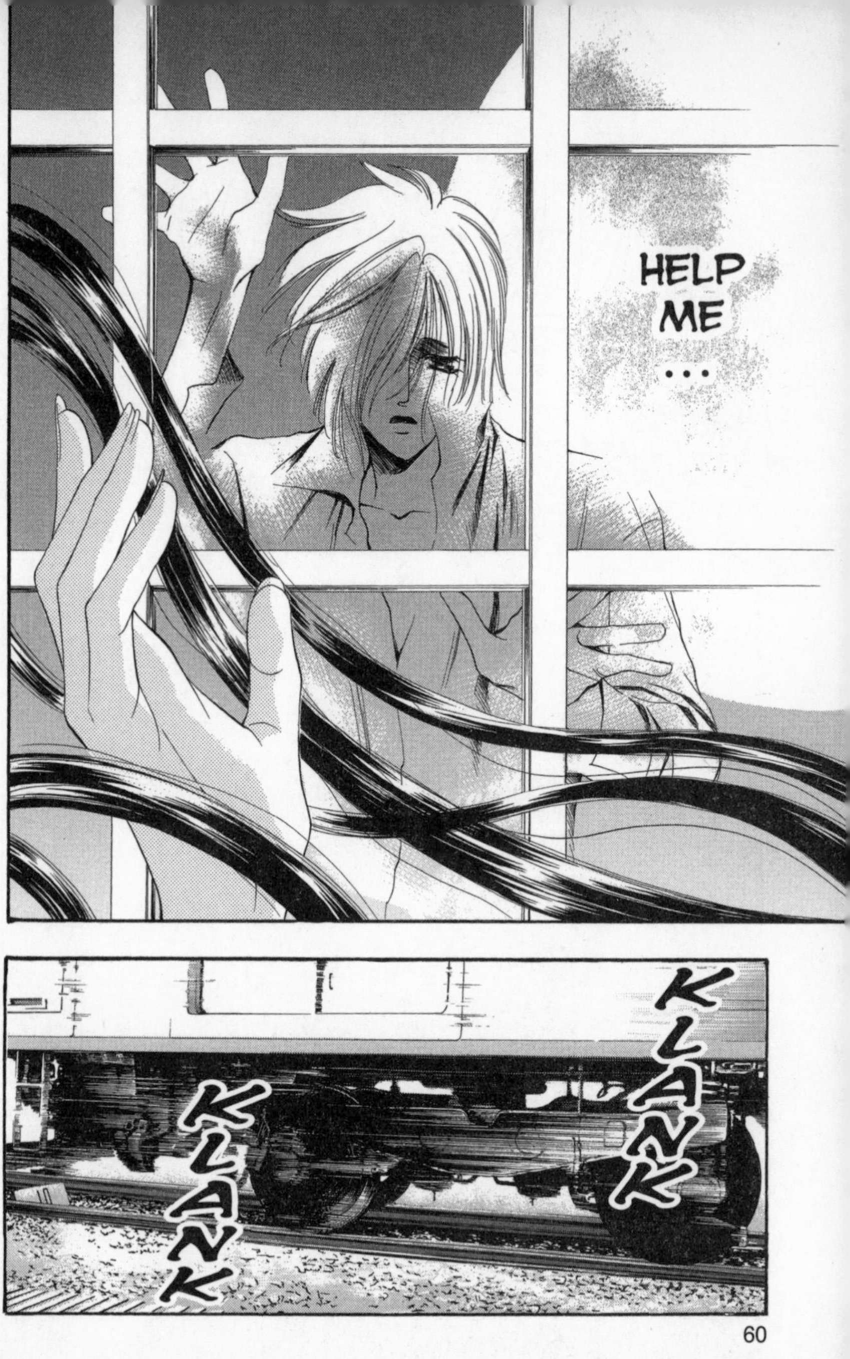
HELP ME ...
KLANK
KLANK

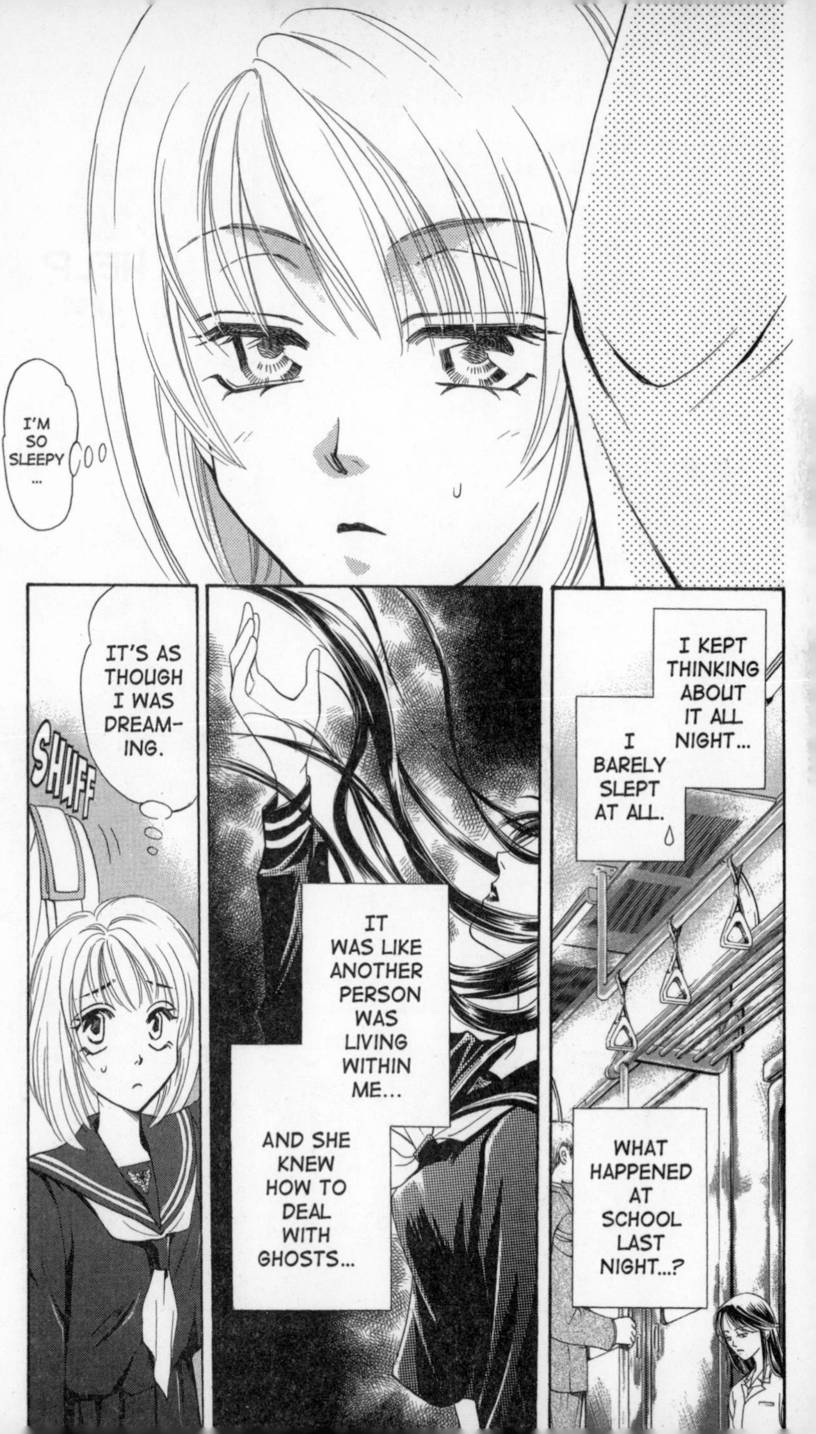
I'M SO SLEEPY...
I KEPT THINKING ABOUT IT ALL NIGHT...
I BARELY SLEPT AT ALL.
WHAT HAPPENED AT SCHOOL LAST NIGHT...?
IT WAS LIKE ANOTHER PERSON WAS LIVING WITHIN ME...
AND SHE KNEW HOW TO DEAL WITH GHOSTS...
IT'S AS THOUGH I WAS DREAMING.
SHUFF

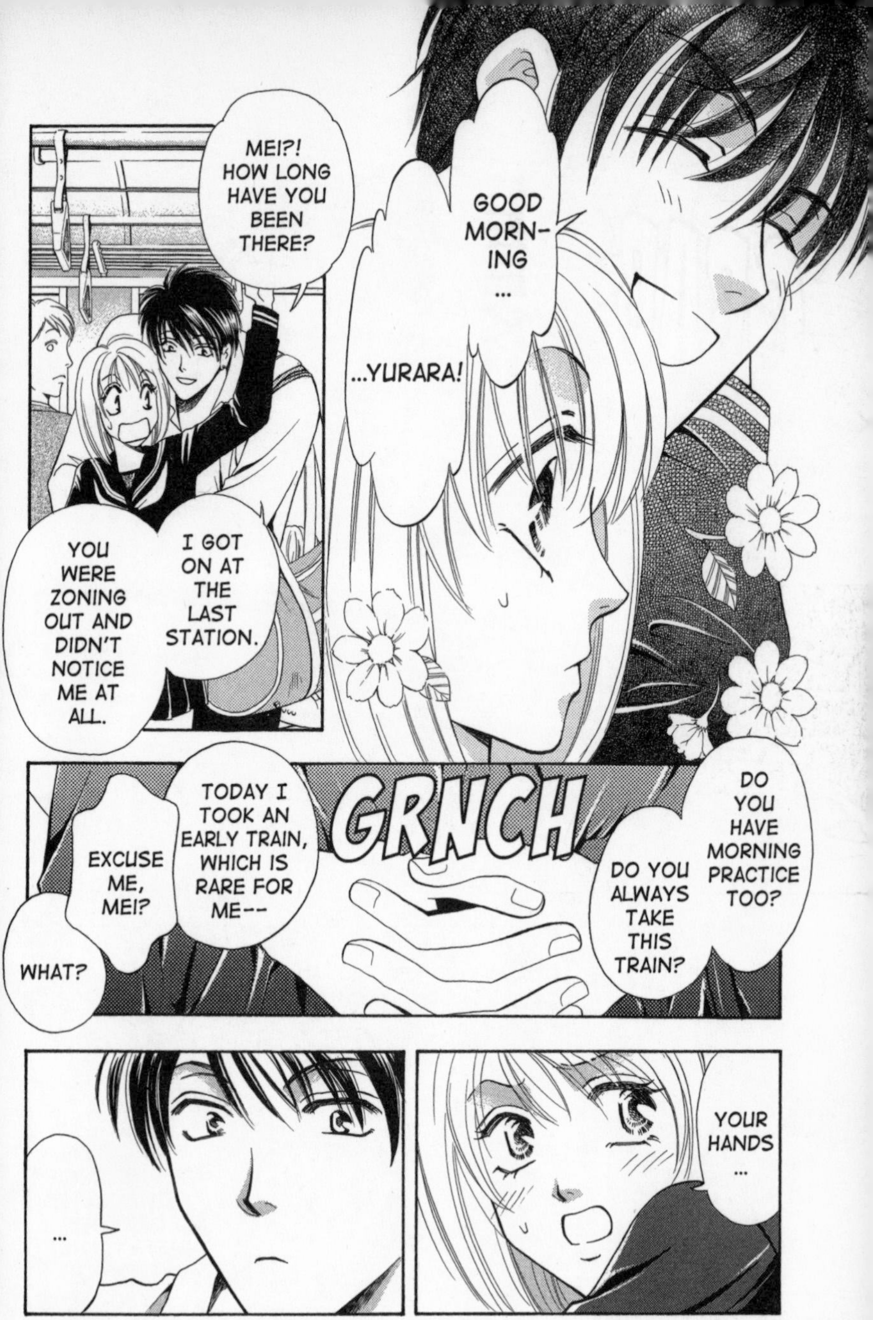
GOOD MORNING...
...YURARA!
MEI?! HOW LONG HAVE YOU BEEN THERE?
I GOT ON AT THE LAST STATION.
YOU WERE ZONING OUT AND DIDN'T NOTICE ME AT ALL.
DO YOU HAVE MORNING PRACTICE TOO?
DO YOU ALWAYS TAKE THIS TRAIN?
GRNCH
TODAY I TOOK AN EARLY TRAIN, WHICH IS RARE FOR ME--
EXCUSE ME, MEI?
WHAT?
YOUR HANDS...
...

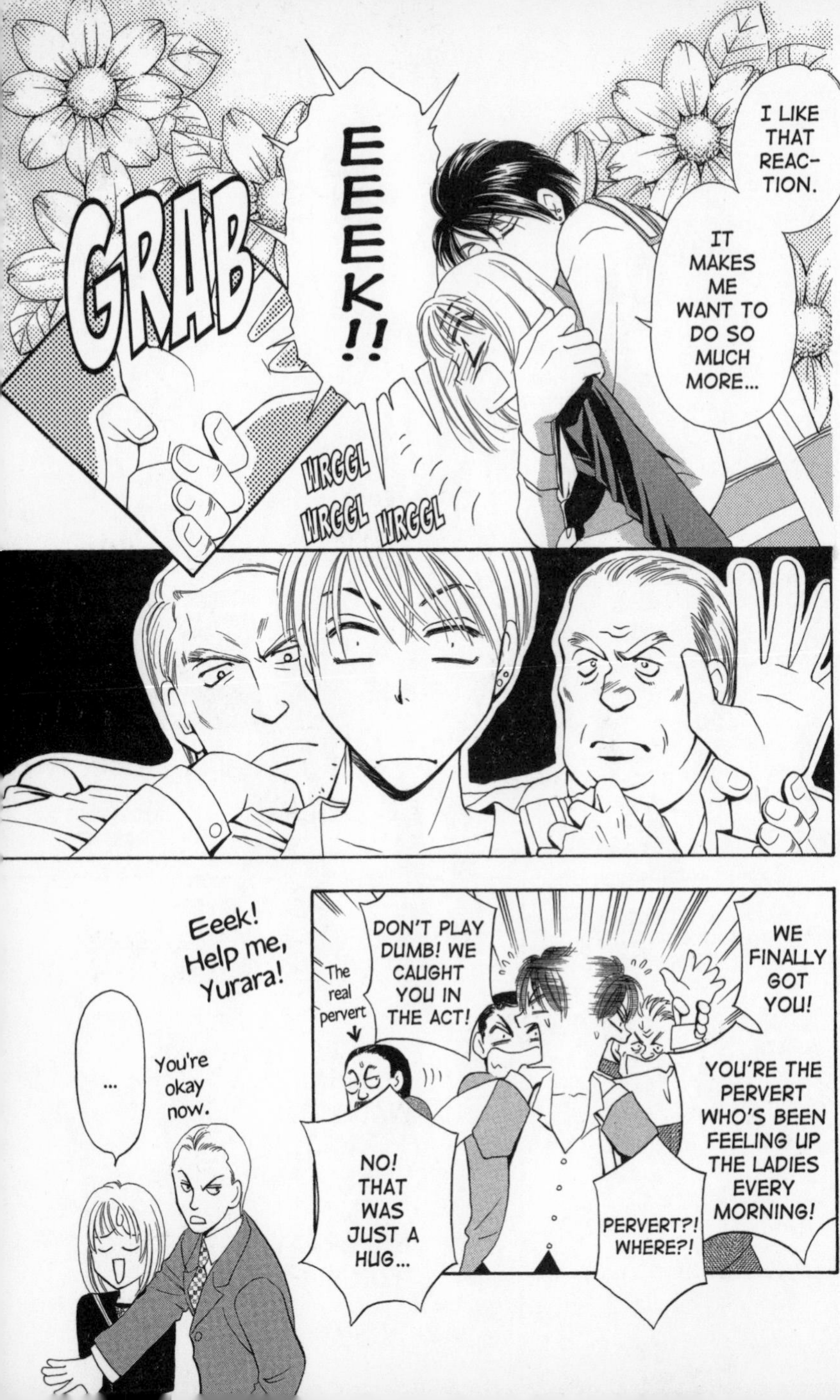
I LIKE THAT REACTION.
IT MAKES ME WANT TO DO SO MUCH MORE...
EEEEK!!
GRAB
WRGGL
WRGGL
WRGGL
WE FINALLY GOT YOU!
DON'T PLAY DUMB! WE CAUGHT YOU IN THE ACT!
The real pervert
YOU'RE THE PERVERT WHO'S BEEN FEELING UP THE LADIES EVERY MORNING!
PERVERT?! WHERE?!
NO! THAT WAS JUST A HUG...
Eeek! Help me, Yurara!
...
You're okay now.

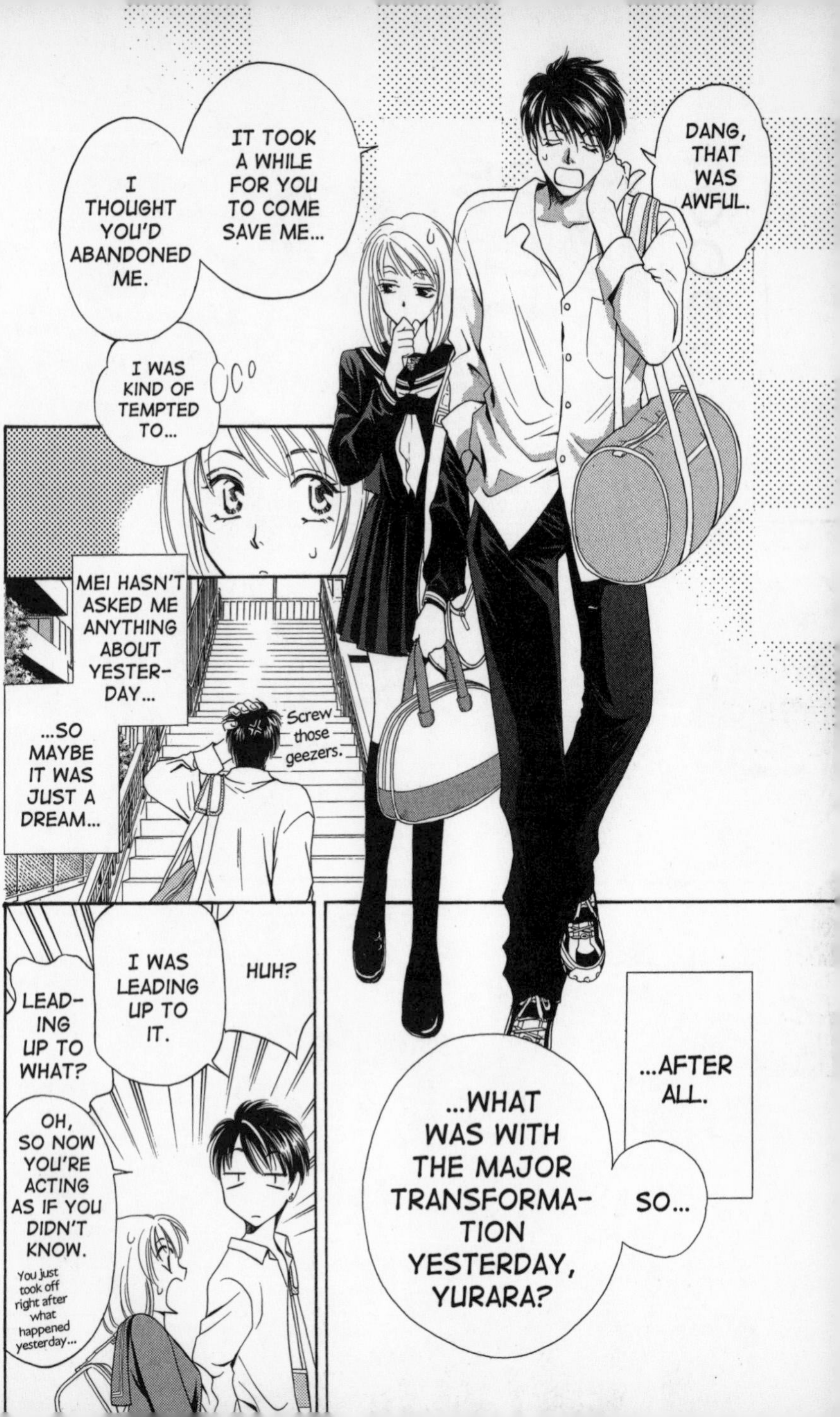
DANG, THAT WAS AWFUL.
IT TOOK A WHILE FOR YOU TO COME SAVE ME...
I THOUGHT YOU'D ABANDONED ME.
I WAS KIND OF TEMPTED TO...
MEI HASN'T ASKED ME ANYTHING ABOUT YESTER-DAY...
Screw those geezers.
...SO MAYBE IT WAS JUST A DREAM...
...AFTER ALL.
SO...
...WHAT WAS WITH THE MAJOR TRANSFORMA-TION YESTERDAY, YURARA?
HUH?
I WAS LEADING UP TO IT.
LEAD-ING UP TO WHAT?
OH, SO NOW YOU'RE ACTING AS IF YOU DIDN'T KNOW.
You just took off right after what happened yesterday...

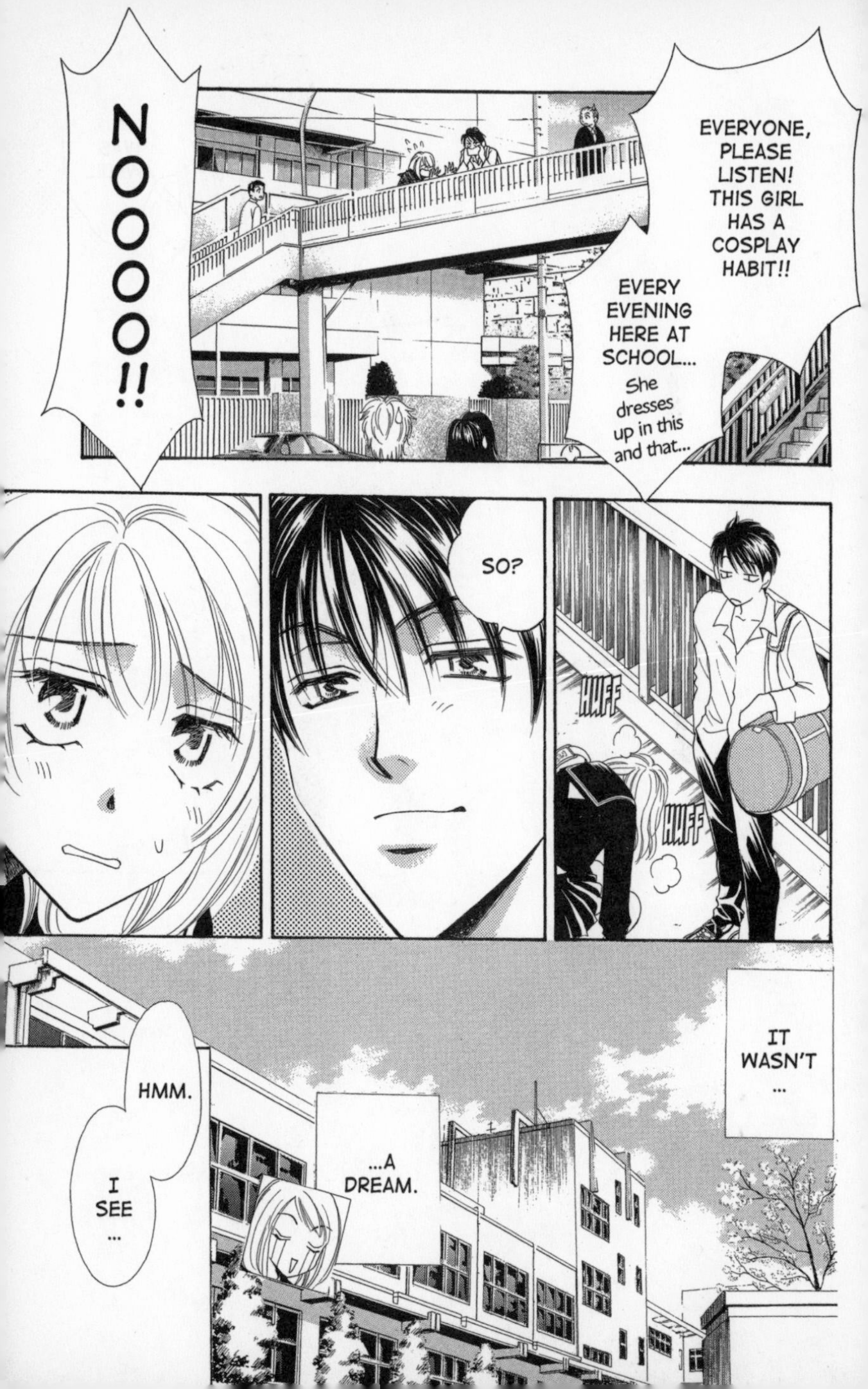
EVERYONE, PLEASE LISTEN! THIS GIRL HAS A COSPLAY HABIT!!
EVERY EVENING HERE AT SCHOOL...
She dresses up in this and that...
NOOOO!!
HUFF
HUFF
SO?
IT WASN'T ...
...A DREAM.
HMM.
I SEE ...

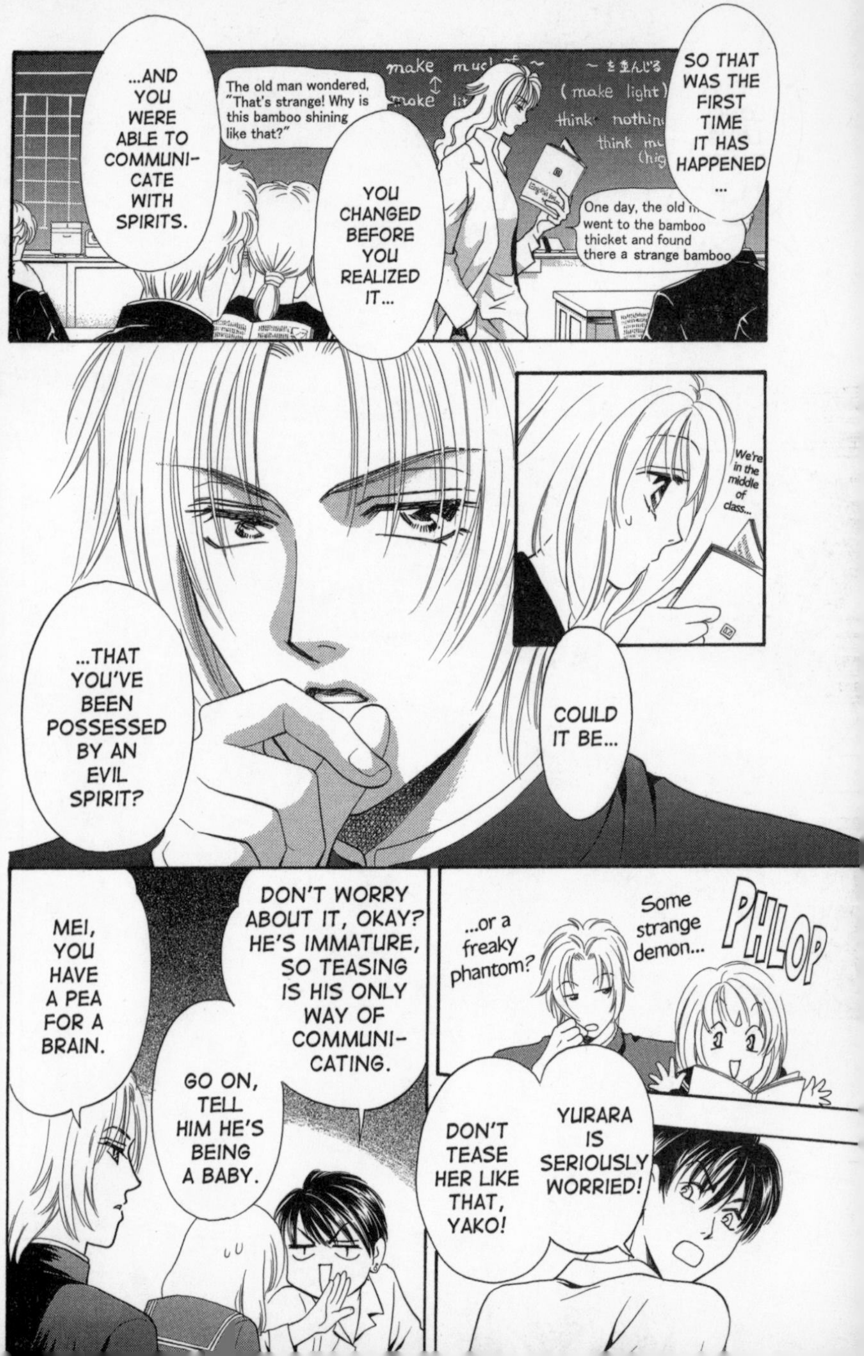
SO THAT WAS THE FIRST TIME IT HAS HAPPENED...
One day, the old m went to the bamboo thicket and found there a strange bamboo
...AND YOU WERE ABLE TO COMMUNICATE WITH SPIRITS.
The old man wondered, "That's strange! Why is this bamboo shining like that?"
YOU CHANGED BEFORE YOU REALIZED IT...
We're in the middle of class...
COULD IT BE...
...THAT YOU'VE BEEN POSSESSED BY AN EVIL SPIRIT?
PHLOP
Some strange demon...
...or a freaky phantom?
YURARA IS SERIOUSLY WORRIED!
DON'T TEASE HER LIKE THAT, YAKO!
DON'T WORRY ABOUT IT, OKAY? HE'S IMMATURE, SO TEASING IS HIS ONLY WAY OF COMMUNICATING.
MEI, YOU HAVE A PEA FOR A BRAIN.
GO ON, TELL HIM HE'S BEING A BABY.

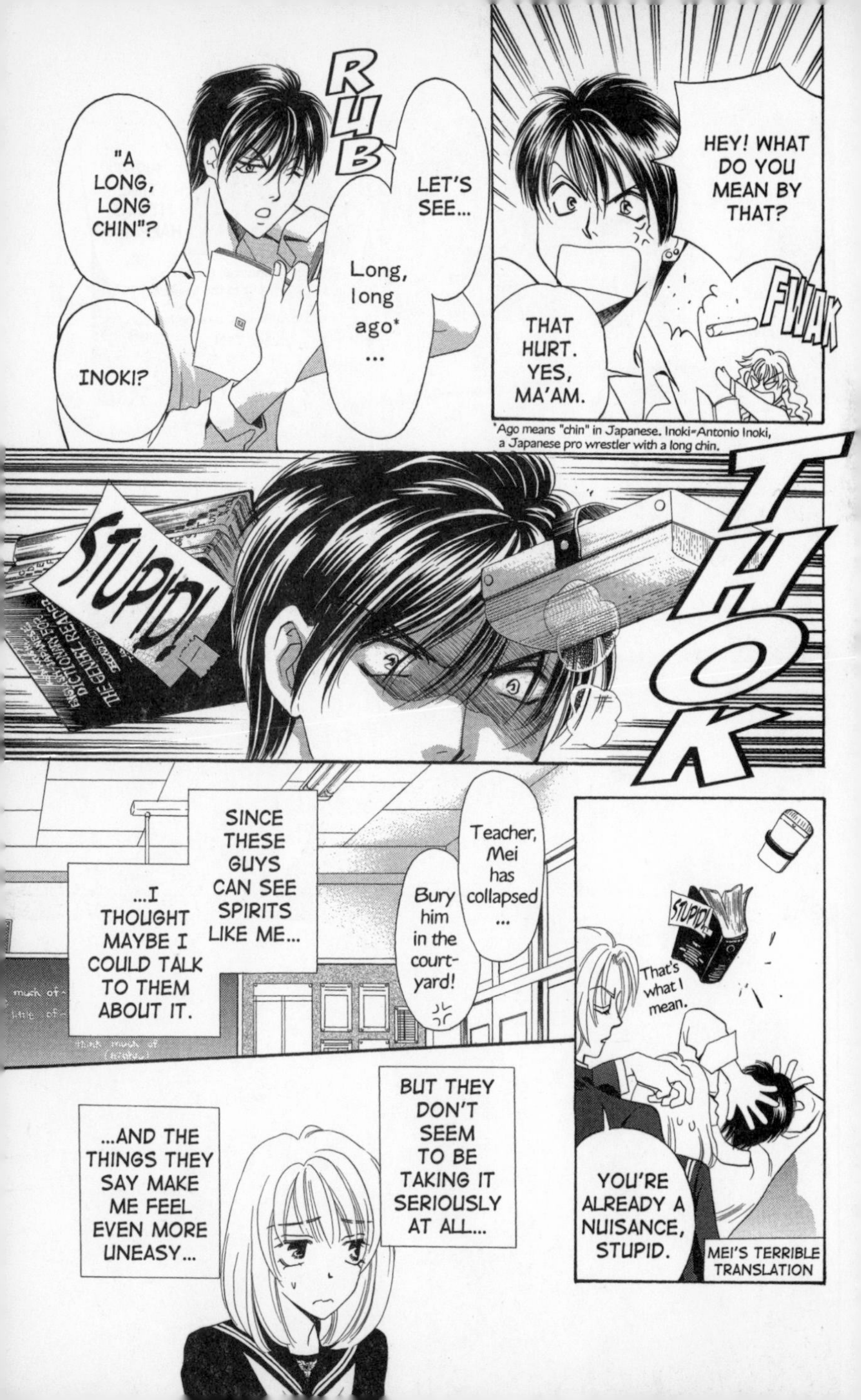
HEY! WHAT DO YOU MEAN BY THAT?
FWAK
THAT HURT. YES, MA'AM.
RUB
LET'S SEE...
Long, long ago* ...
"A LONG, LONG CHIN"?
INOKI?
THOK
STUPID!
STUPID!
That's what I mean.
YOU'RE ALREADY A NUISANCE, STUPID.
MEI'S TERRIBLE TRANSLATION
Teacher, Mei has collapsed ...
Bury him in the court-yard!
SINCE THESE GUYS CAN SEE SPIRITS LIKE ME...
...I THOUGHT MAYBE I COULD TALK TO THEM ABOUT IT.
BUT THEY DON'T SEEM TO BE TAKING IT SERIOUSLY AT ALL...
...AND THE THINGS THEY SAY MAKE ME FEEL EVEN MORE UNEASY...

*Ago means "chin" in Japanese. Inoki=Antonio Inoki, a Japanese pro wrestler with a long chin.

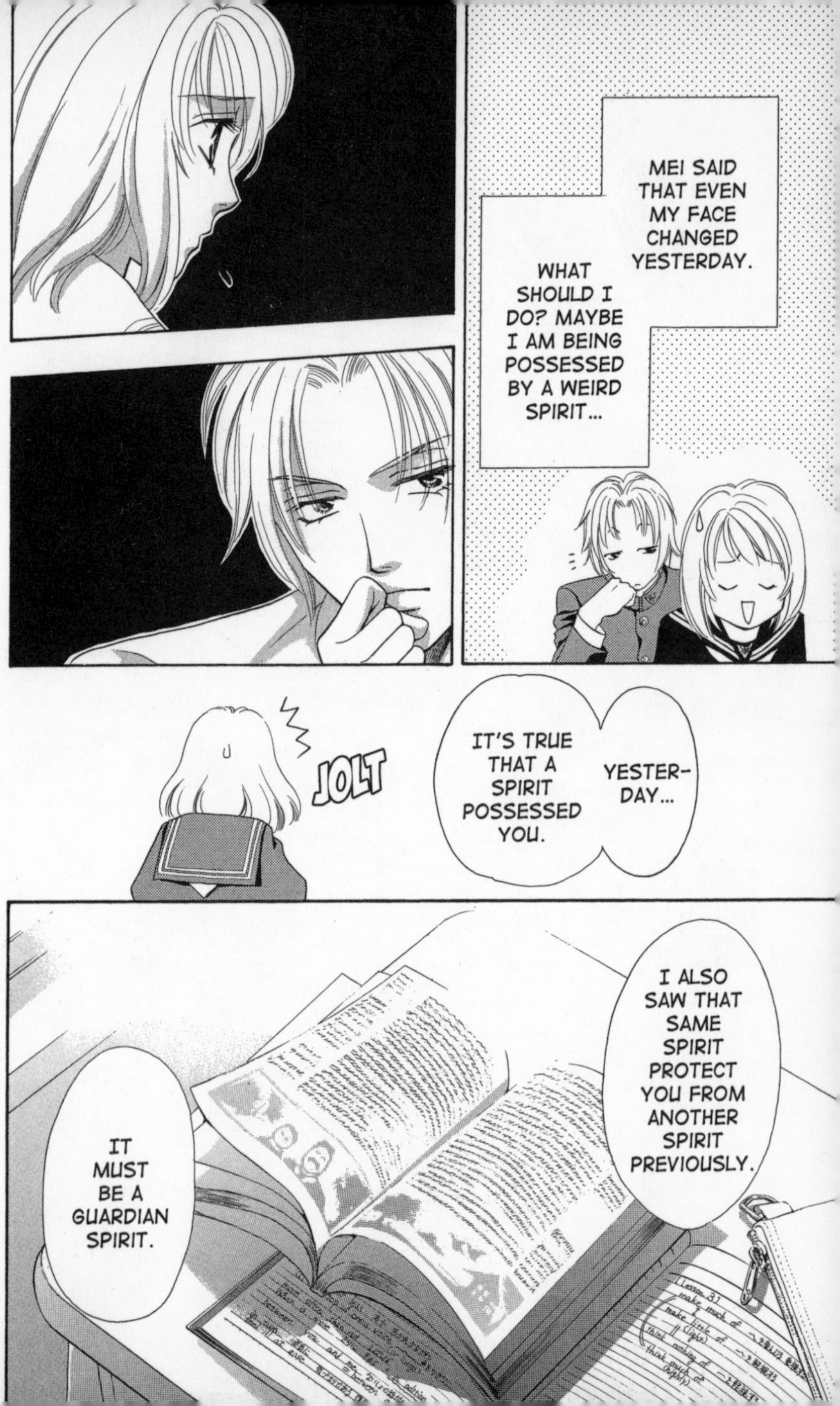
MEI SAID THAT EVEN MY FACE CHANGED YESTERDAY.
WHAT SHOULD I DO? MAYBE I AM BEING POSSESSED BY A WEIRD SPIRIT...
YESTER-DAY...
IT'S TRUE THAT A SPIRIT POSSESSED YOU.
JOLT
I ALSO SAW THAT SAME SPIRIT PROTECT YOU FROM ANOTHER SPIRIT PREVIOUSLY.
IT MUST BE A GUARDIAN SPIRIT.

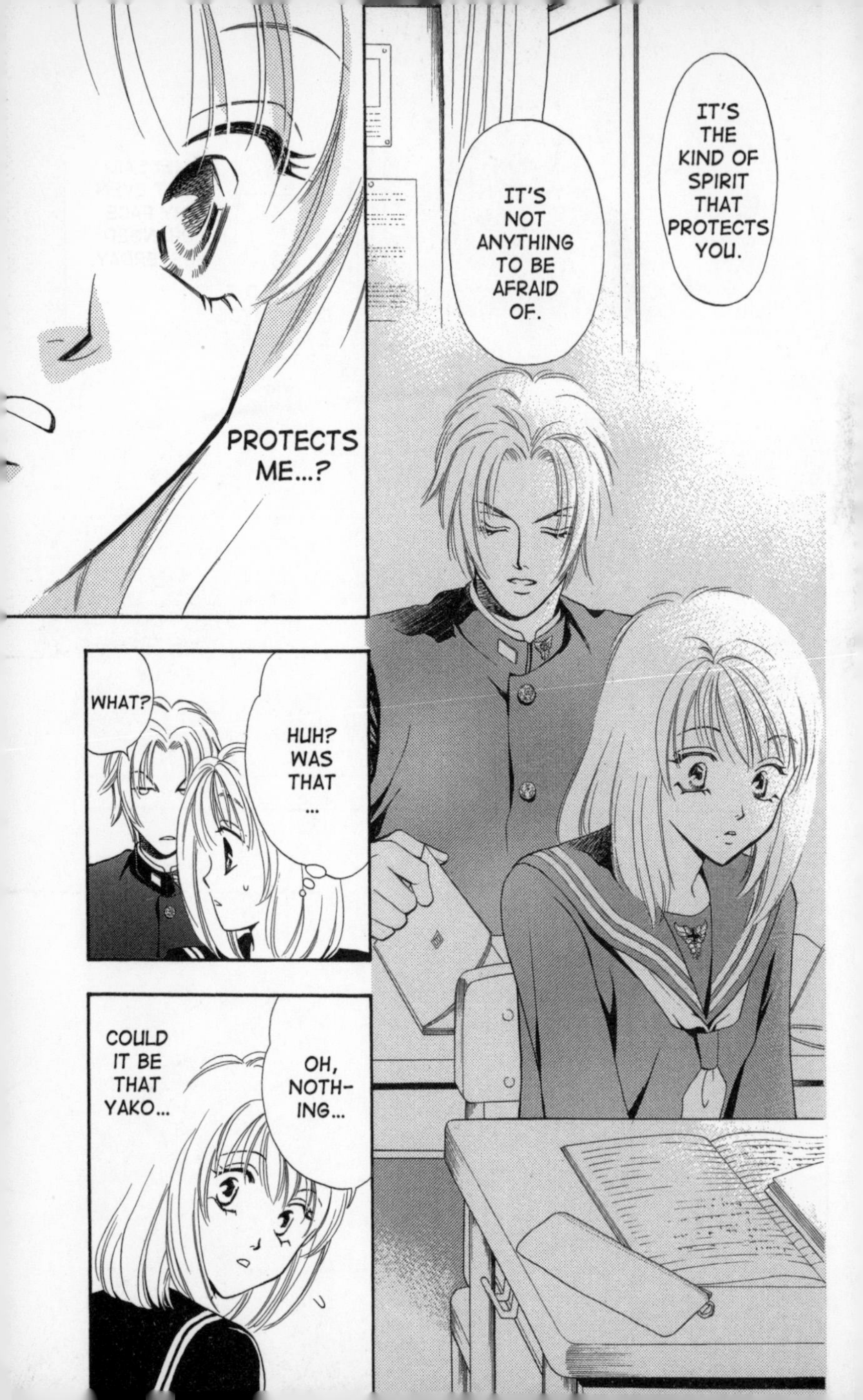
IT'S THE KIND OF SPIRIT THAT PROTECTS YOU.
IT'S NOT ANYTHING TO BE AFRAID OF.
PROTECTS ME...?
HUH? WAS THAT ...
WHAT?
OH, NOTH-ING...
COULD IT BE THAT YAKO...

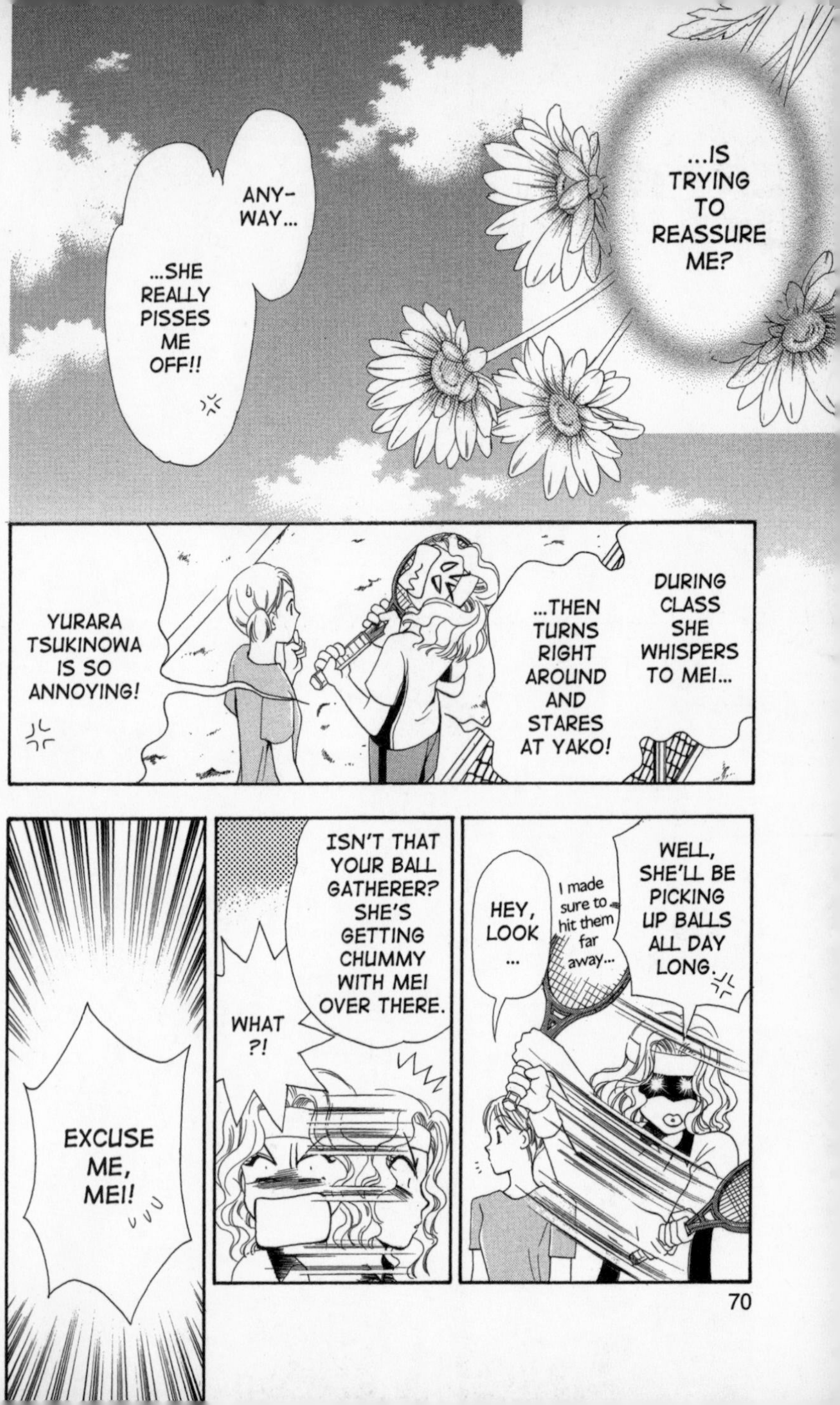
...IS TRYING TO REASSURE ME?
ANY-WAY...
...SHE REALLY PISSES ME OFF!!
DURING CLASS SHE WHISPERS TO MEI...
...THEN TURNS RIGHT AROUND AND STARES AT YAKO!
YURARA TSUKINOWA IS SO ANNOYING!
WELL, SHE'LL BE PICKING UP BALLS ALL DAY LONG.
I made sure to hit them far away...
HEY, LOOK ...
ISN'T THAT YOUR BALL GATHERER? SHE'S GETTING CHUMMY WITH MEI OVER THERE.
WHAT ?!
EXCUSE ME, MEI!

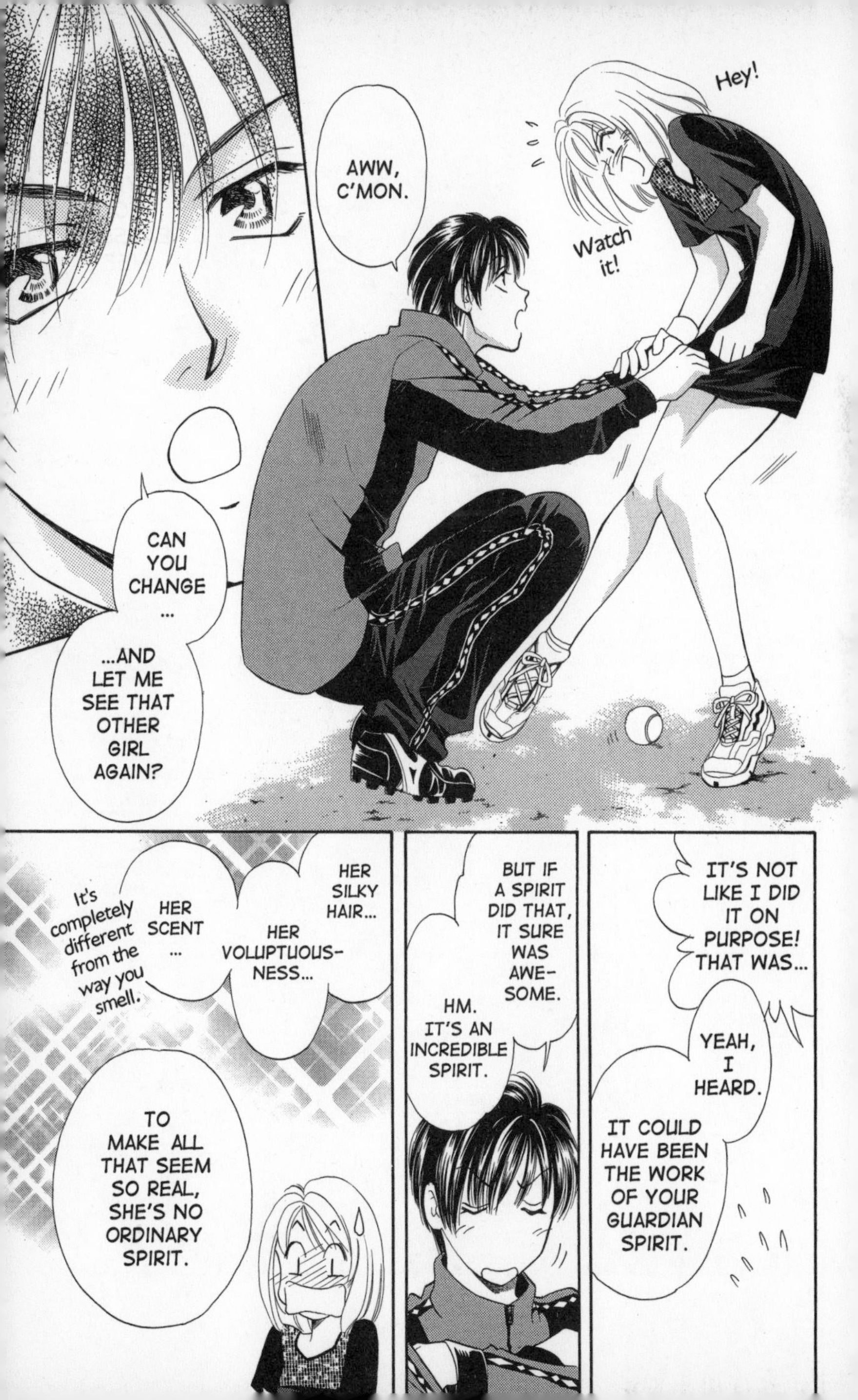
Hey!
Watch it!
AWW, C'MON.
CAN YOU CHANGE ...
...AND LET ME SEE THAT OTHER GIRL AGAIN?
IT'S NOT LIKE I DID IT ON PURPOSE! THAT WAS...
YEAH, I HEARD.
IT COULD HAVE BEEN THE WORK OF YOUR GUARDIAN SPIRIT.
BUT IF A SPIRIT DID THAT, IT SURE WAS AWESOME.
HM. IT'S AN INCREDIBLE SPIRIT.
HER SILKY HAIR...
HER VOLUPTUOUSNESS...
HER SCENT ...
It's completely different from the way you smell.
TO MAKE ALL THAT SEEM SO REAL, SHE'S NO ORDINARY SPIRIT.

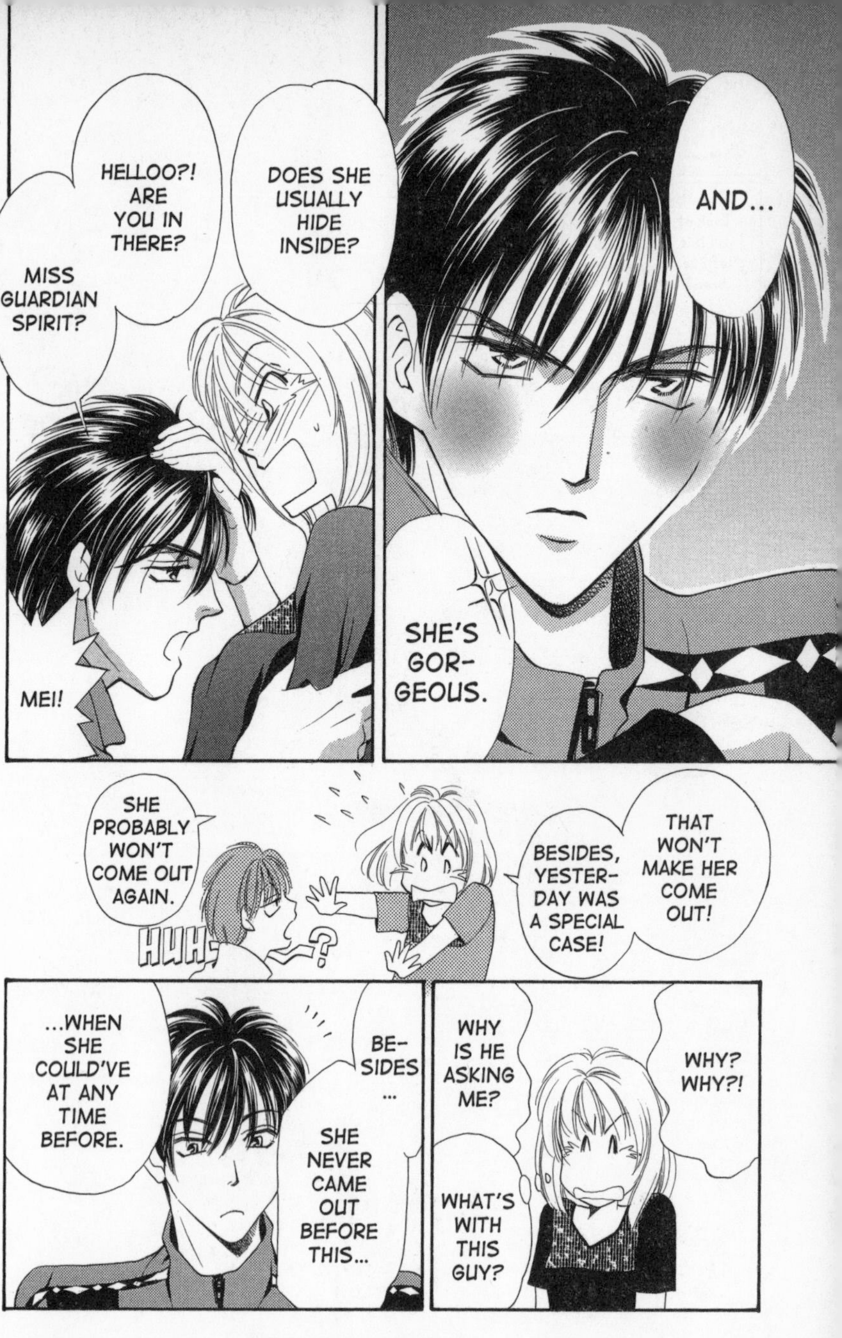
AND...
SHE'S GOR-GEOUS.
DOES SHE USUALLY HIDE INSIDE?
HELLOO?! ARE YOU IN THERE?
MISS GUARDIAN SPIRIT?
MEI!
THAT WON'T MAKE HER COME OUT!
BESIDES, YESTER-DAY WAS A SPECIAL CASE!
SHE PROBABLY WON'T COME OUT AGAIN.
HUH
?
WHY? WHY?!
WHY IS HE ASKING ME?
WHAT'S WITH THIS GUY?
BE-SIDES ...
SHE NEVER CAME OUT BEFORE THIS...
...WHEN SHE COULD'VE AT ANY TIME BEFORE.

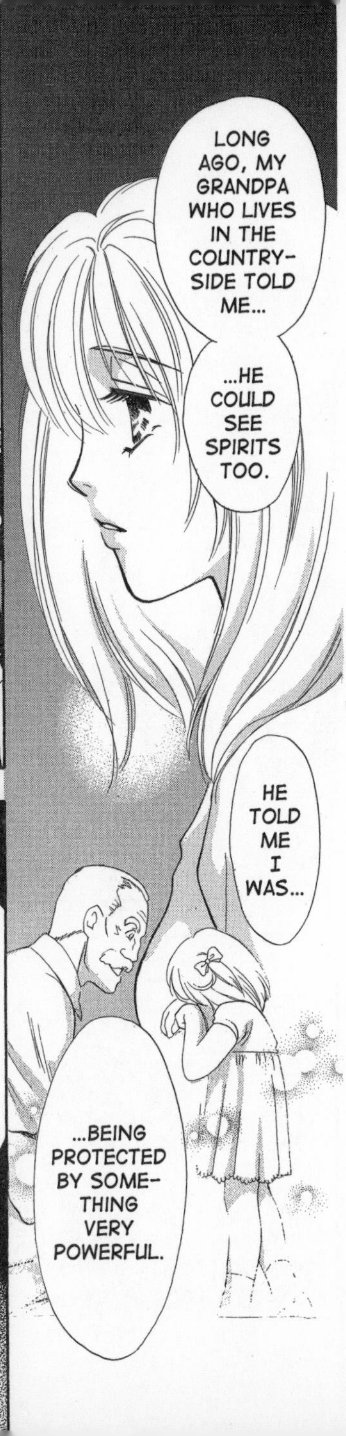
LONG AGO, MY GRANDPA WHO LIVES IN THE COUNTRYSIDE TOLD ME...
...HE COULD SEE SPIRITS TOO.
HE TOLD ME I WAS...
...BEING PROTECTED BY SOMETHING VERY POWERFUL.

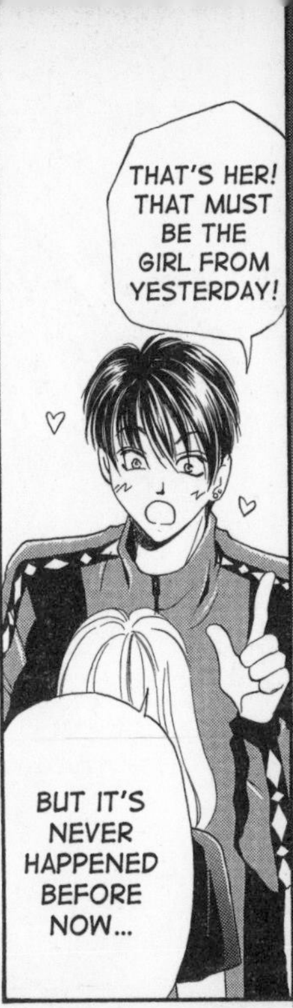
THAT'S HER! THAT MUST BE THE GIRL FROM YESTERDAY!
BUT IT'S NEVER HAPPENED BEFORE NOW...

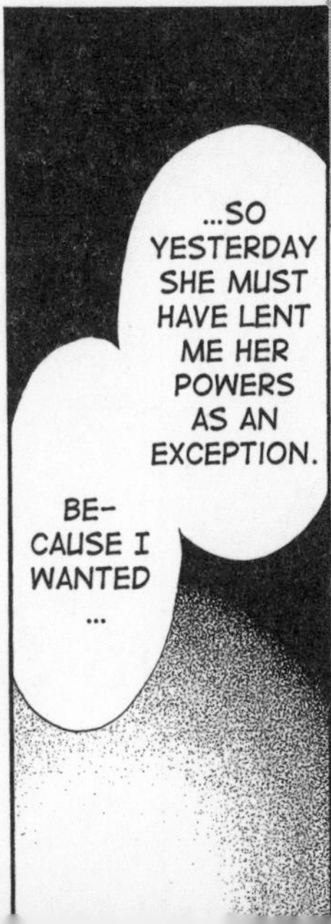
...SO YESTERDAY SHE MUST HAVE LENT ME HER POWERS AS AN EXCEPTION.
BECAUSE I WANTED...

Shiomi's Daily Activities ②

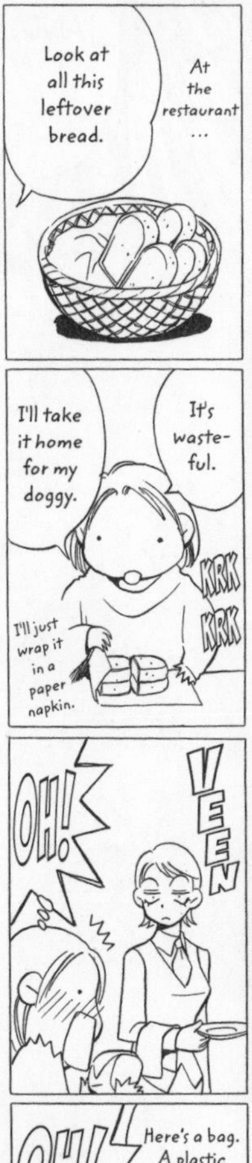
At the restaurant...
Look at all this leftover bread.
It's wasteful.
I'll take it home for my doggy.
KRK KRK
I'll just wrap it in a paper napkin.
OH!
VEEN
OH! OH!
Here's a bag. A plastic bag and a carry-out package.

Please overlook this...

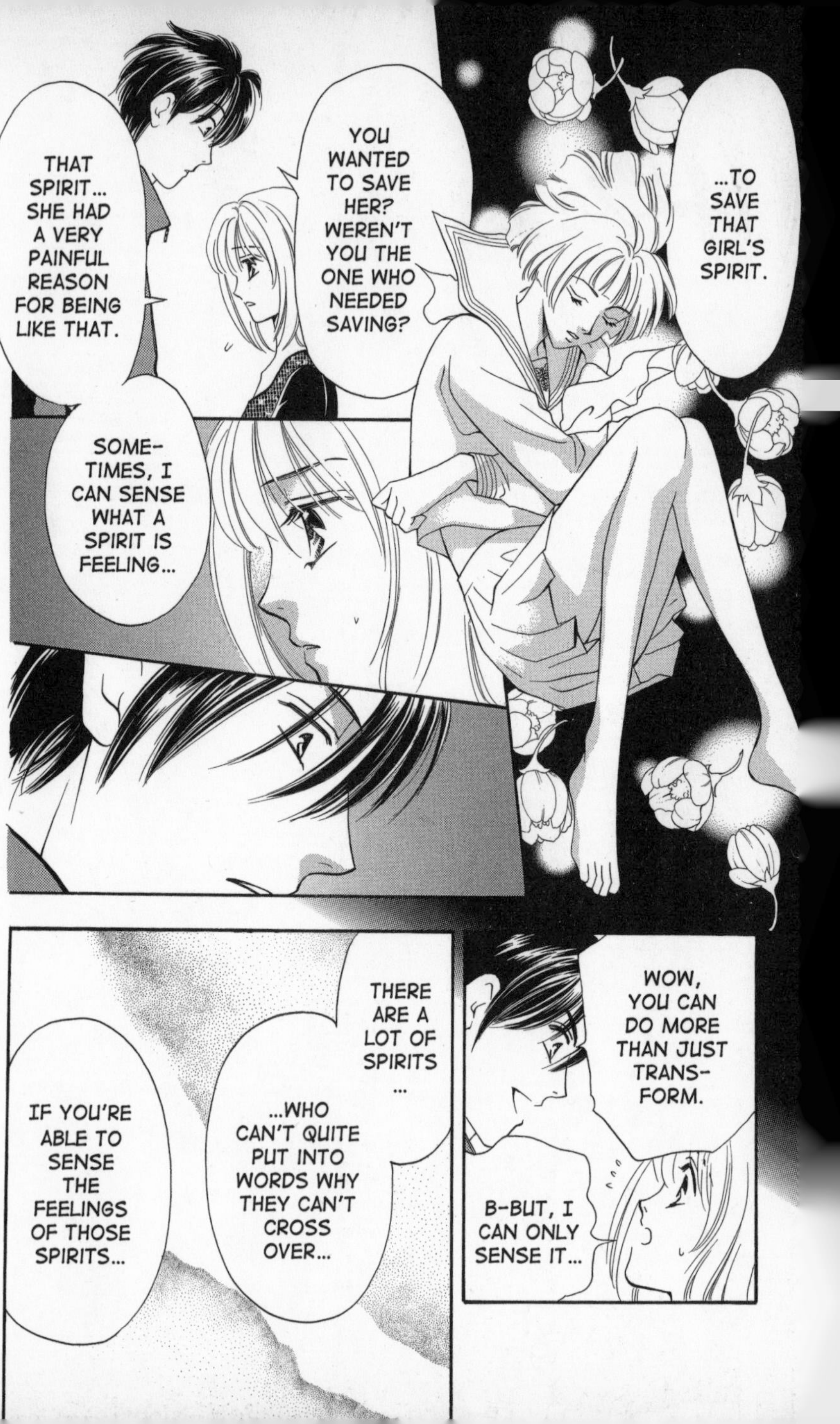
...TO SAVE THAT GIRL'S SPIRIT.
YOU WANTED TO SAVE HER? WEREN'T YOU THE ONE WHO NEEDED SAVING?
THAT SPIRIT... SHE HAD A VERY PAINFUL REASON FOR BEING LIKE THAT.
SOME-TIMES, I CAN SENSE WHAT A SPIRIT IS FEELING...
WOW, YOU CAN DO MORE THAN JUST TRANS-FORM.
B-BUT, I CAN ONLY SENSE IT...
THERE ARE A LOT OF SPIRITS ...
...WHO CAN'T QUITE PUT INTO WORDS WHY THEY CAN'T CROSS OVER...
IF YOU'RE ABLE TO SENSE THE FEELINGS OF THOSE SPIRITS...

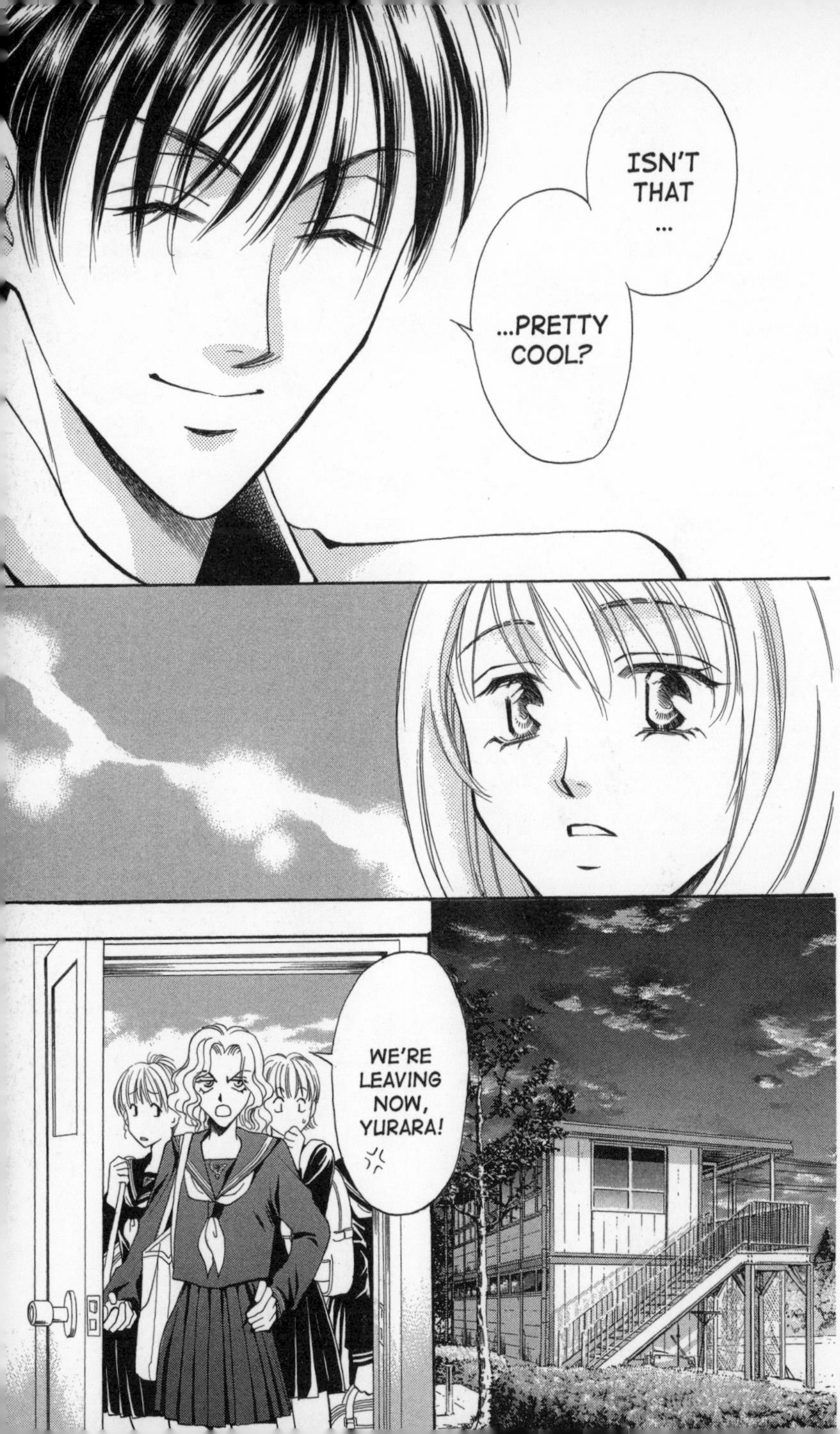
ISN'T THAT ...
...PRETTY COOL?
WE'RE LEAVING NOW, YURARA!

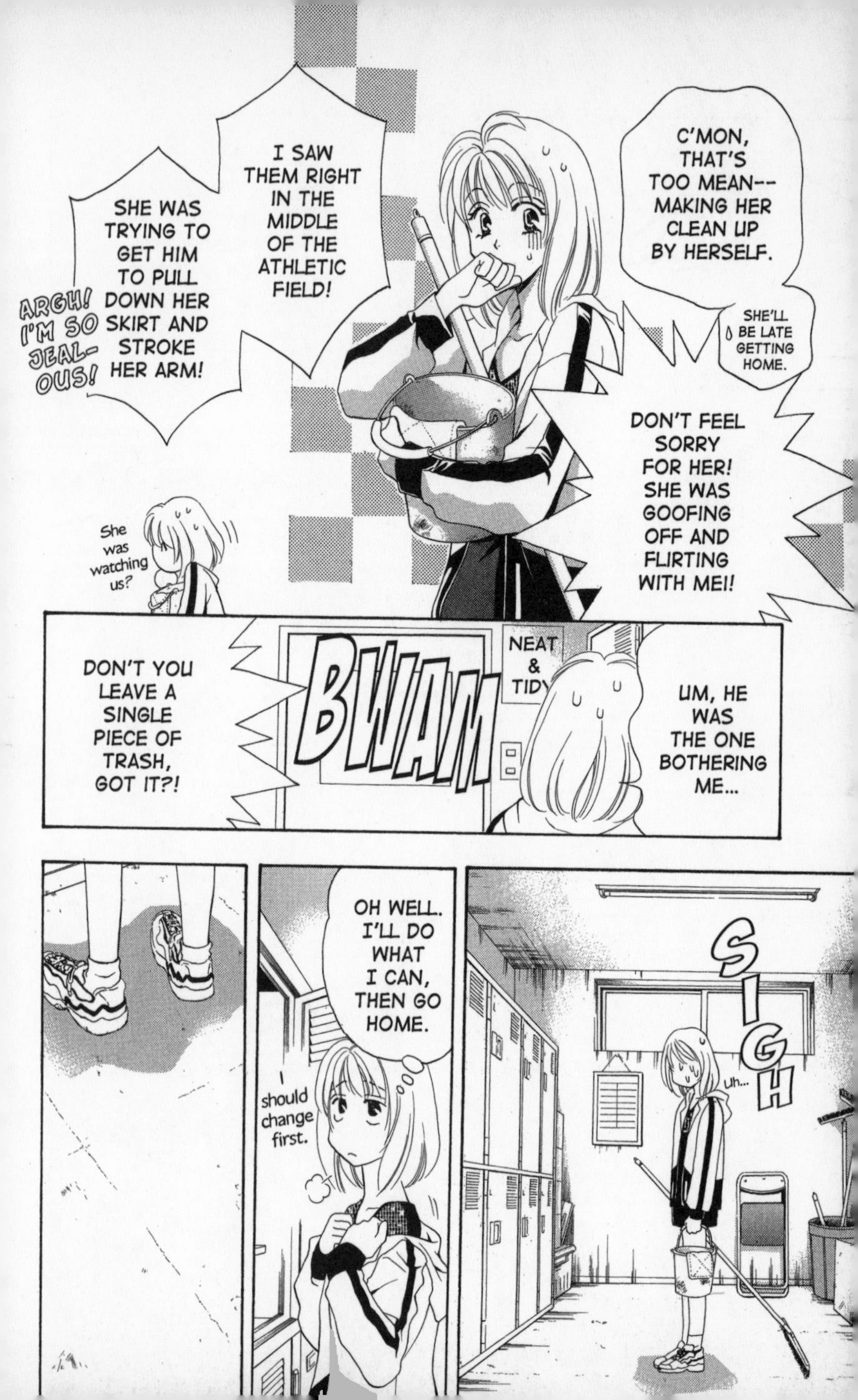
C'MON, THAT'S TOO MEAN-- MAKING HER CLEAN UP BY HERSELF.
SHE'LL BE LATE GETTING HOME.
DON'T FEEL SORRY FOR HER! SHE WAS GOOFING OFF AND FLIRTING WITH MEI!
I SAW THEM RIGHT IN THE MIDDLE OF THE ATHLETIC FIELD!
SHE WAS TRYING TO GET HIM TO PULL DOWN HER SKIRT AND STROKE HER ARM!
ARGH! I'M SO JEAL-OUS!
She was watching us?
UM, HE WAS THE ONE BOTHERING ME...
NEAT & TIDY
BWAM
DON'T YOU LEAVE A SINGLE PIECE OF TRASH, GOT IT?!
SIGH
uh...
OH WELL. I'LL DO WHAT I CAN, THEN GO HOME.
I should change first.

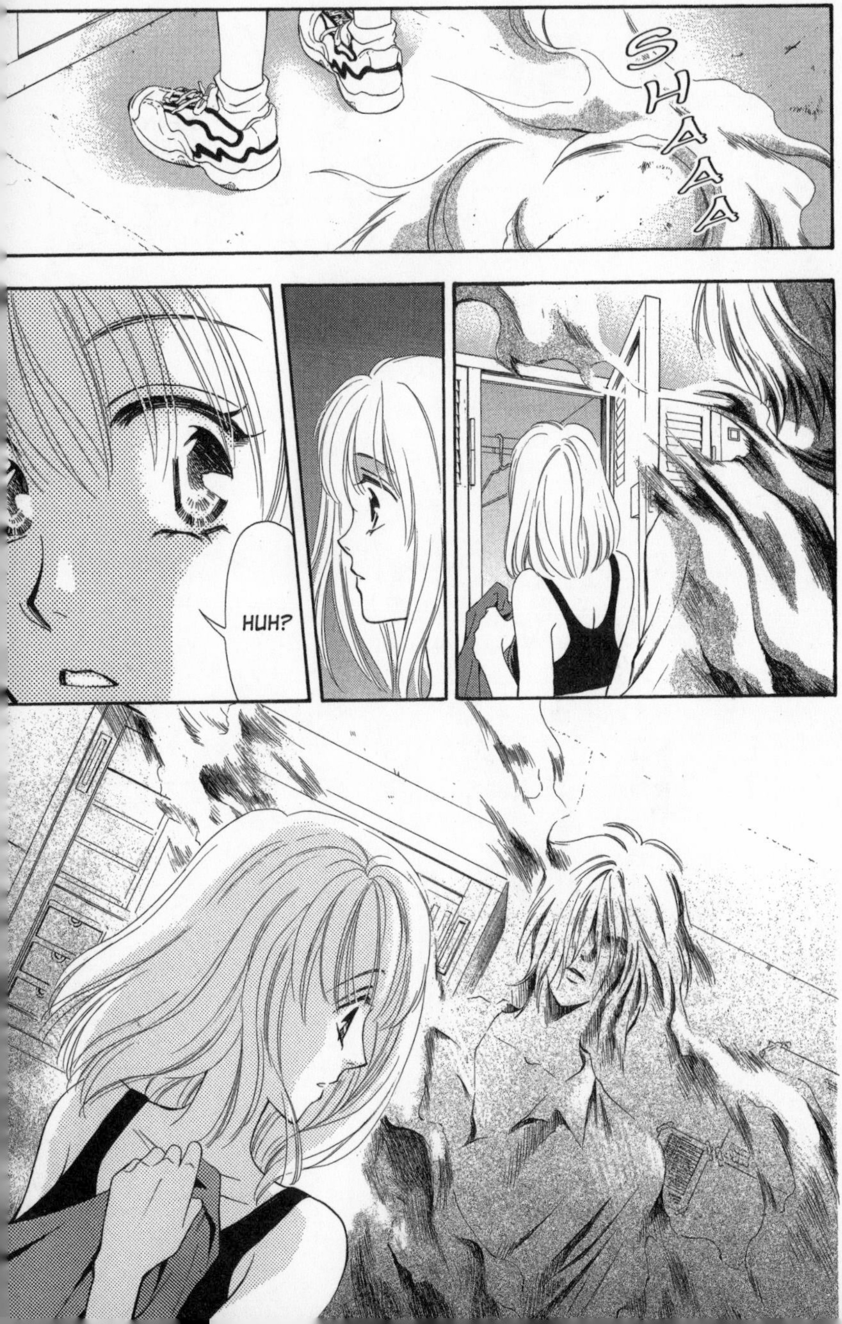
SHAAA
HUH?

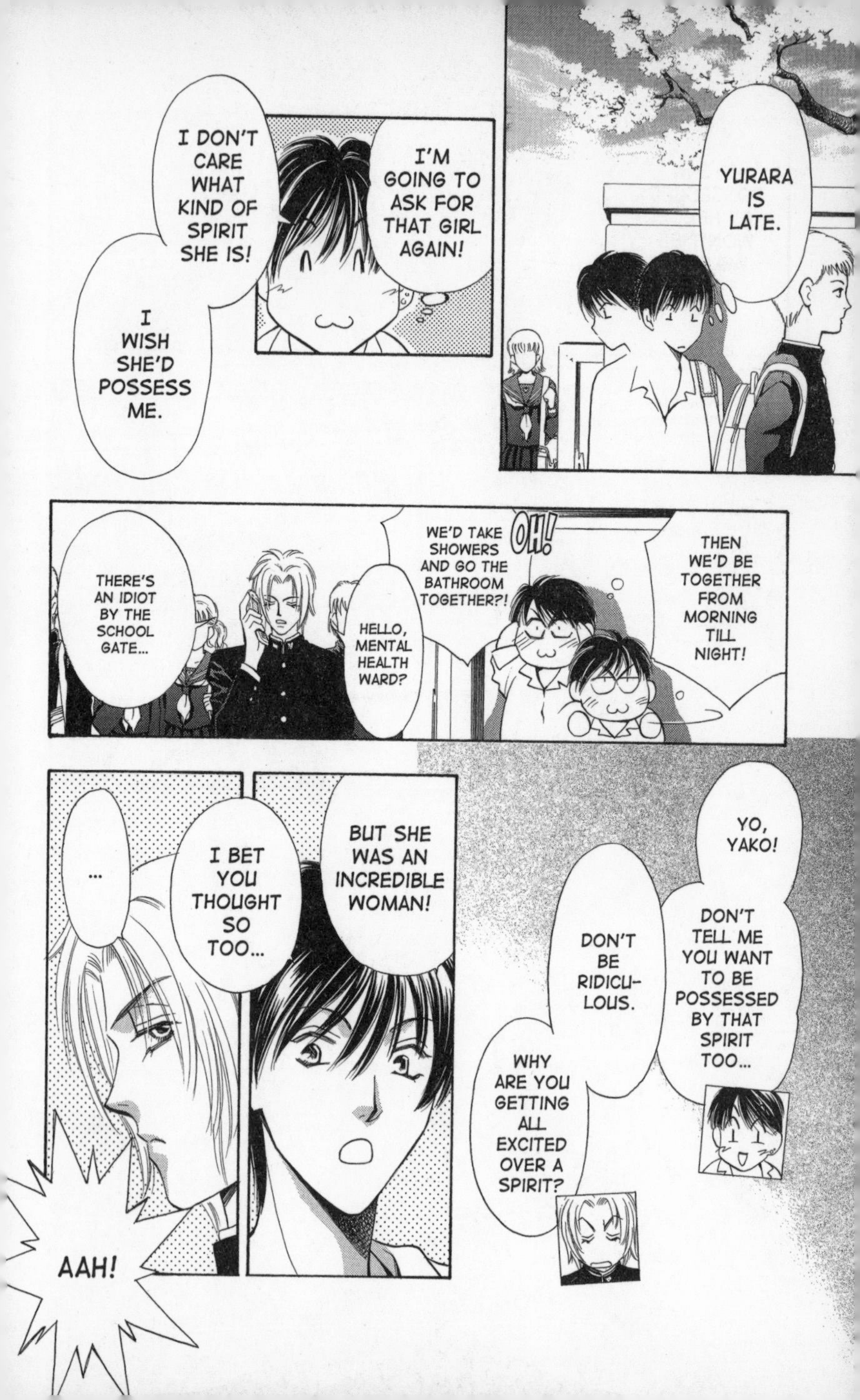
YURARA IS LATE.
I'M GOING TO ASK FOR THAT GIRL AGAIN!
I DON'T CARE WHAT KIND OF SPIRIT SHE IS!
I WISH SHE'D POSSESS ME.
THEN WE'D BE TOGETHER FROM MORNING TILL NIGHT!
OH!
WE'D TAKE SHOWERS AND GO THE BATHROOM TOGETHER?!
HELLO, MENTAL HEALTH WARD?
THERE'S AN IDIOT BY THE SCHOOL GATE...
YO, YAKO!
DON'T TELL ME YOU WANT TO BE POSSESSED BY THAT SPIRIT TOO...
DON'T BE RIDICULOUS.
WHY ARE YOU GETTING ALL EXCITED OVER A SPIRIT?
BUT SHE WAS AN INCREDIBLE WOMAN!
I BET YOU THOUGHT SO TOO...
...
AAH!

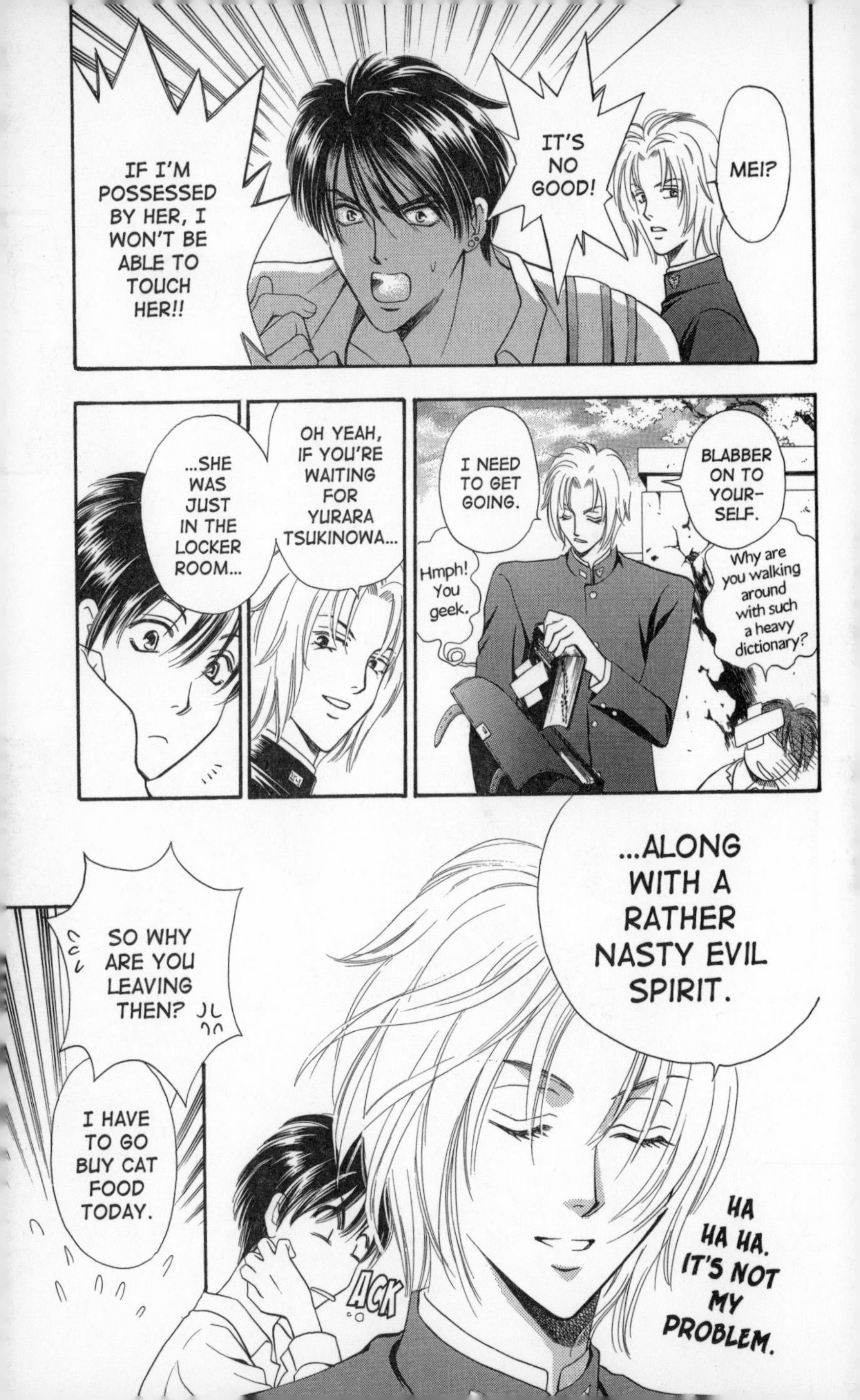
MEI?
IT'S NO GOOD!
IF I'M POSSESSED BY HER, I WON'T BE ABLE TO TOUCH HER!!
BLABBER ON TO YOURSELF.
Why are you walking around with such a heavy dictionary?
I NEED TO GET GOING.
Hmph! You geek.
OH YEAH, IF YOU'RE WAITING FOR YURARA TSUKINOWA...
...SHE WAS JUST IN THE LOCKER ROOM...
...ALONG WITH A RATHER NASTY EVIL SPIRIT.
HA HA HA. IT'S NOT MY PROBLEM.
SO WHY ARE YOU LEAVING THEN?
I HAVE TO GO BUY CAT FOOD TODAY.
ACK

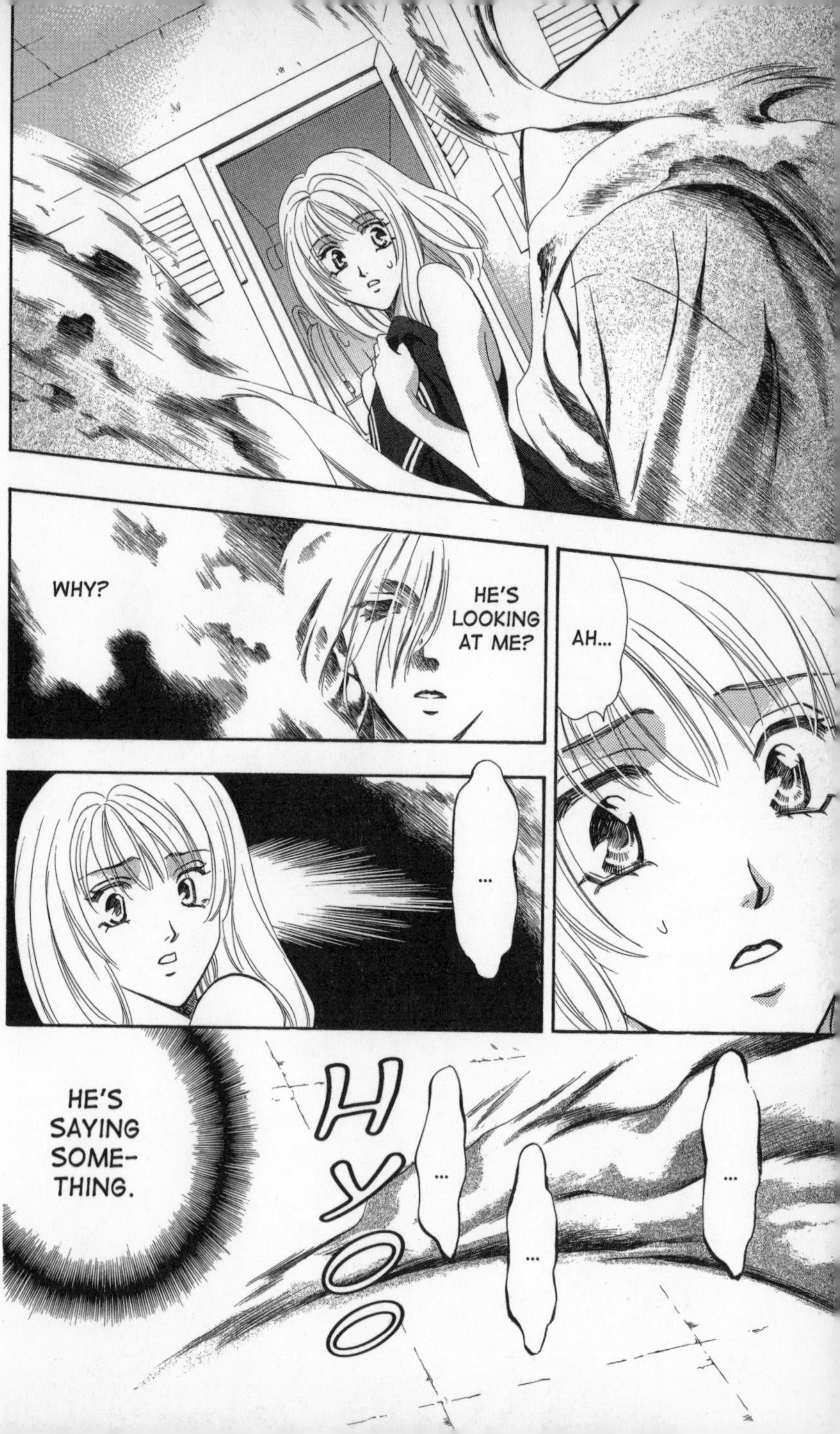
AH...
HE'S LOOKING AT ME?
WHY?
...
...
...
...
HYOO
HE'S SAYING SOMETHING.

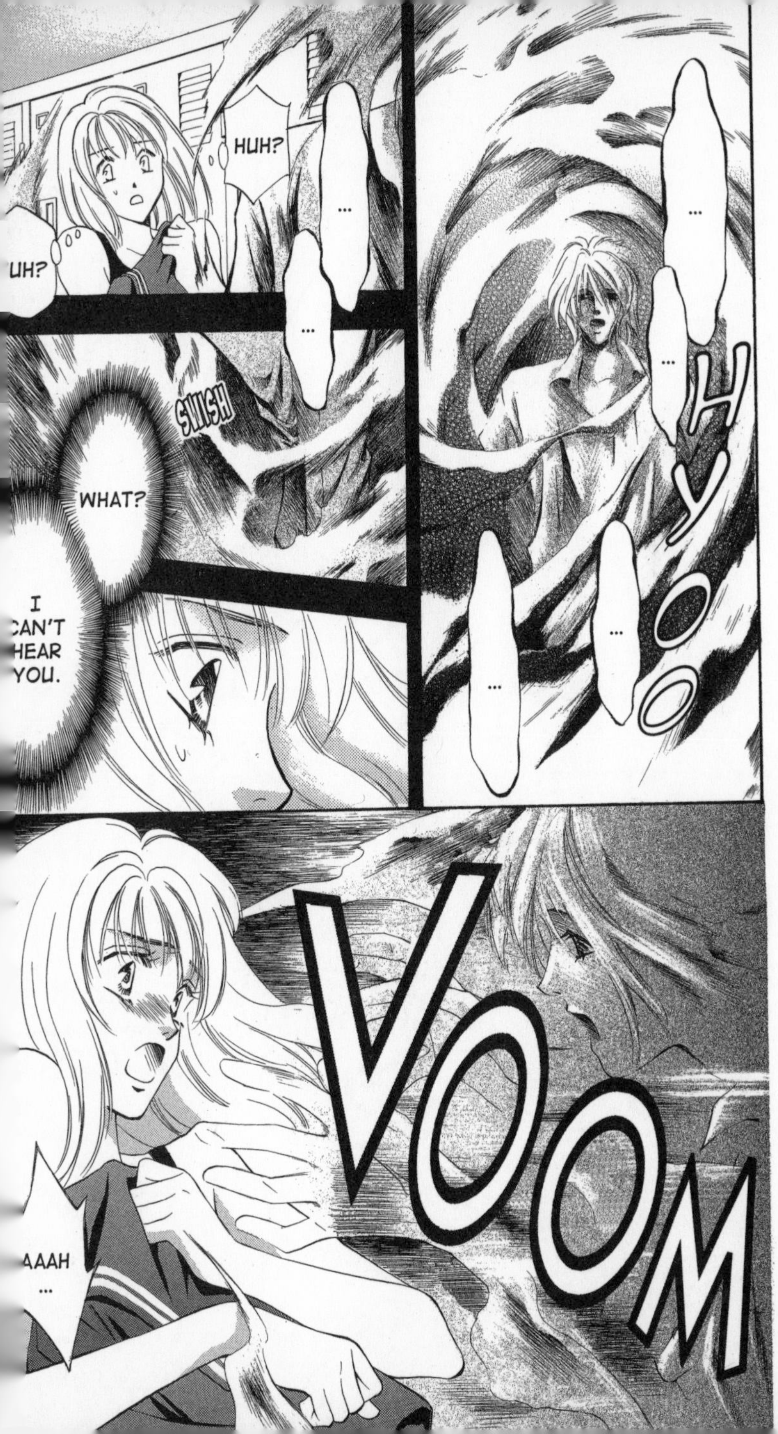

...
...
...
...
HYOOO
HUH?
...
...
HUH?
SWISH
WHAT?
I CAN'T HEAR YOU.
VOOM
AAAH ...

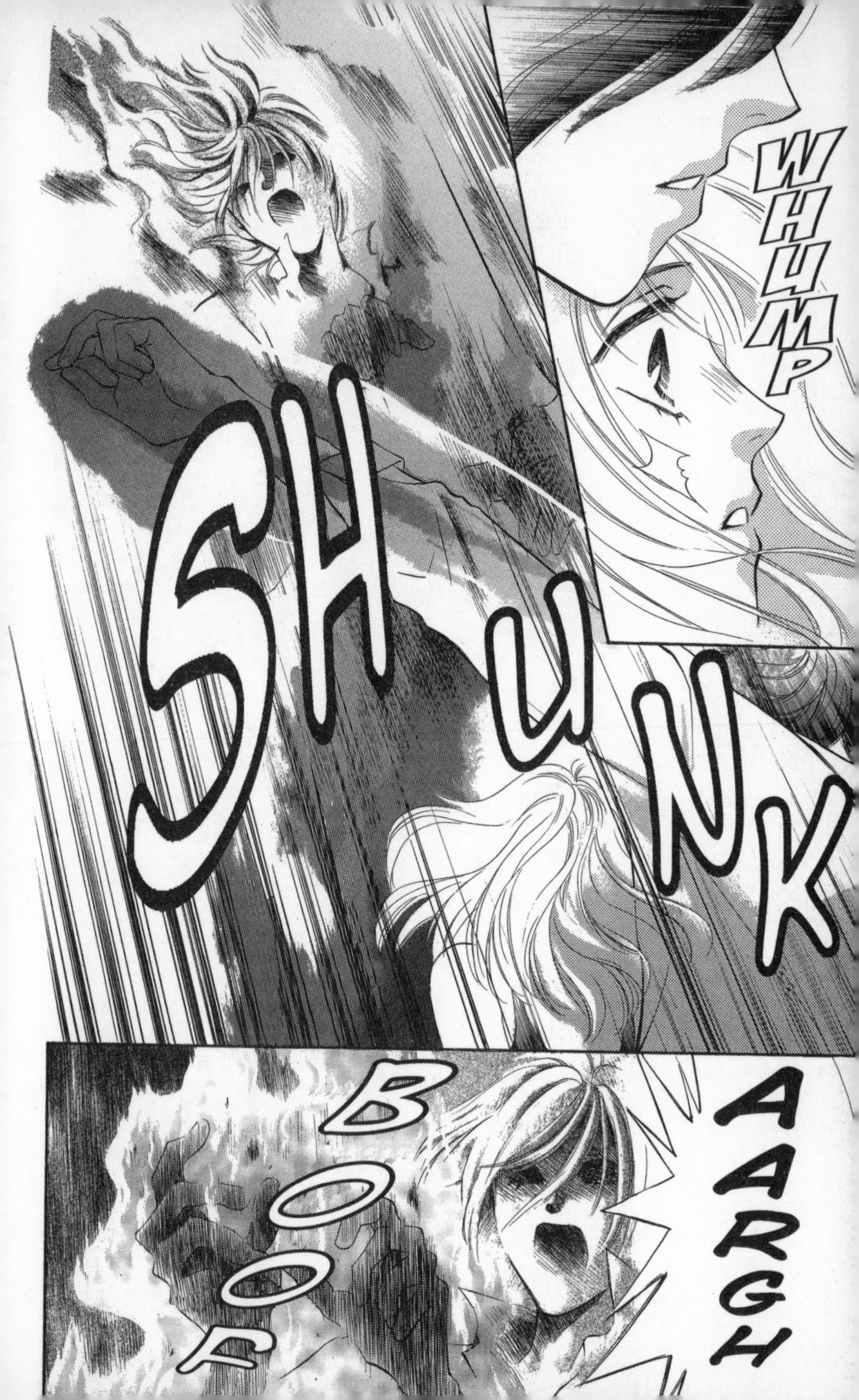
WHUMP
SHUNK
AARGH
BOOOF

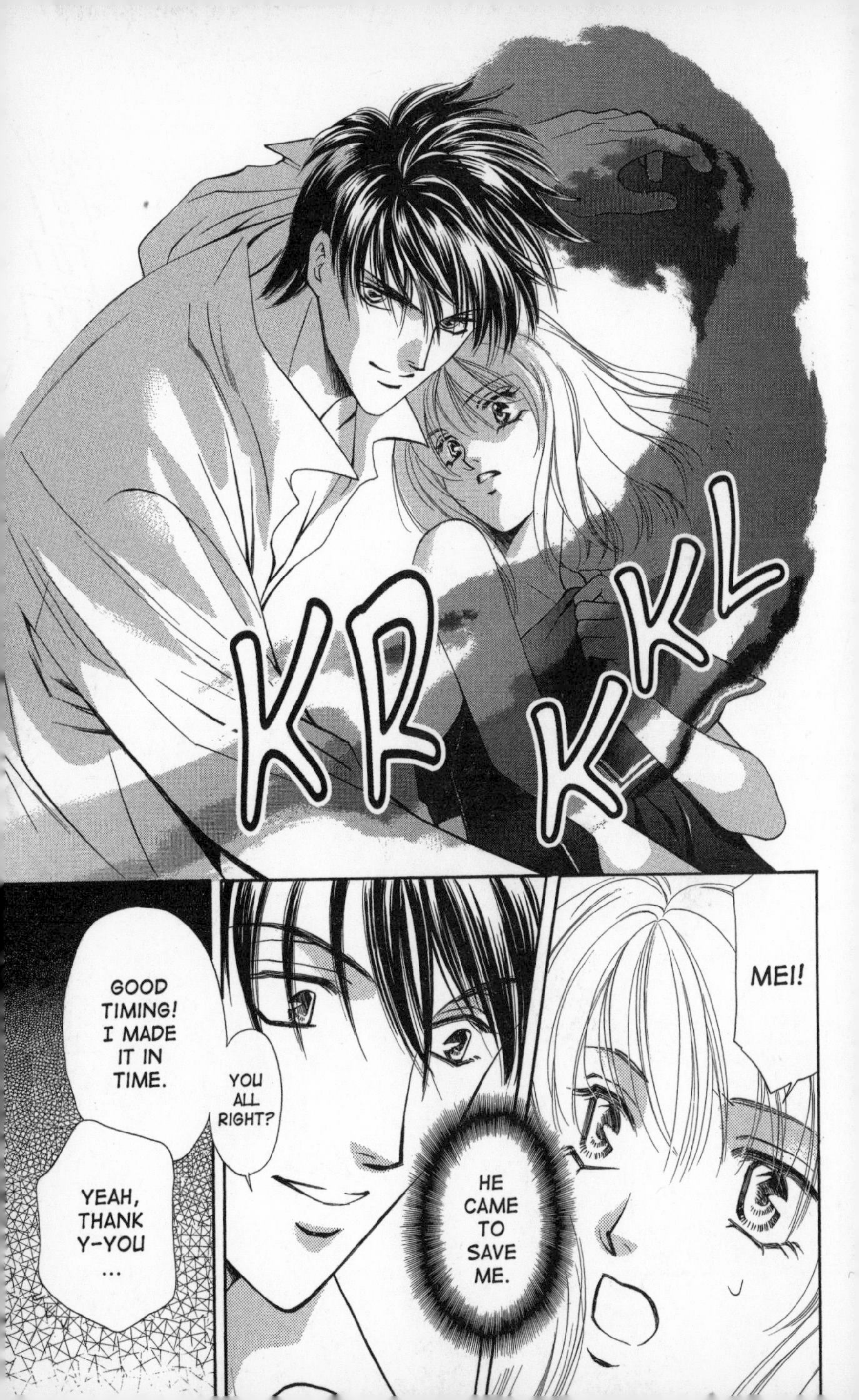
KRKKL
MEI!
GOOD TIMING! I MADE IT IN TIME.
YOU ALL RIGHT?
YEAH, THANK Y-YOU ...
HE CAME TO SAVE ME.

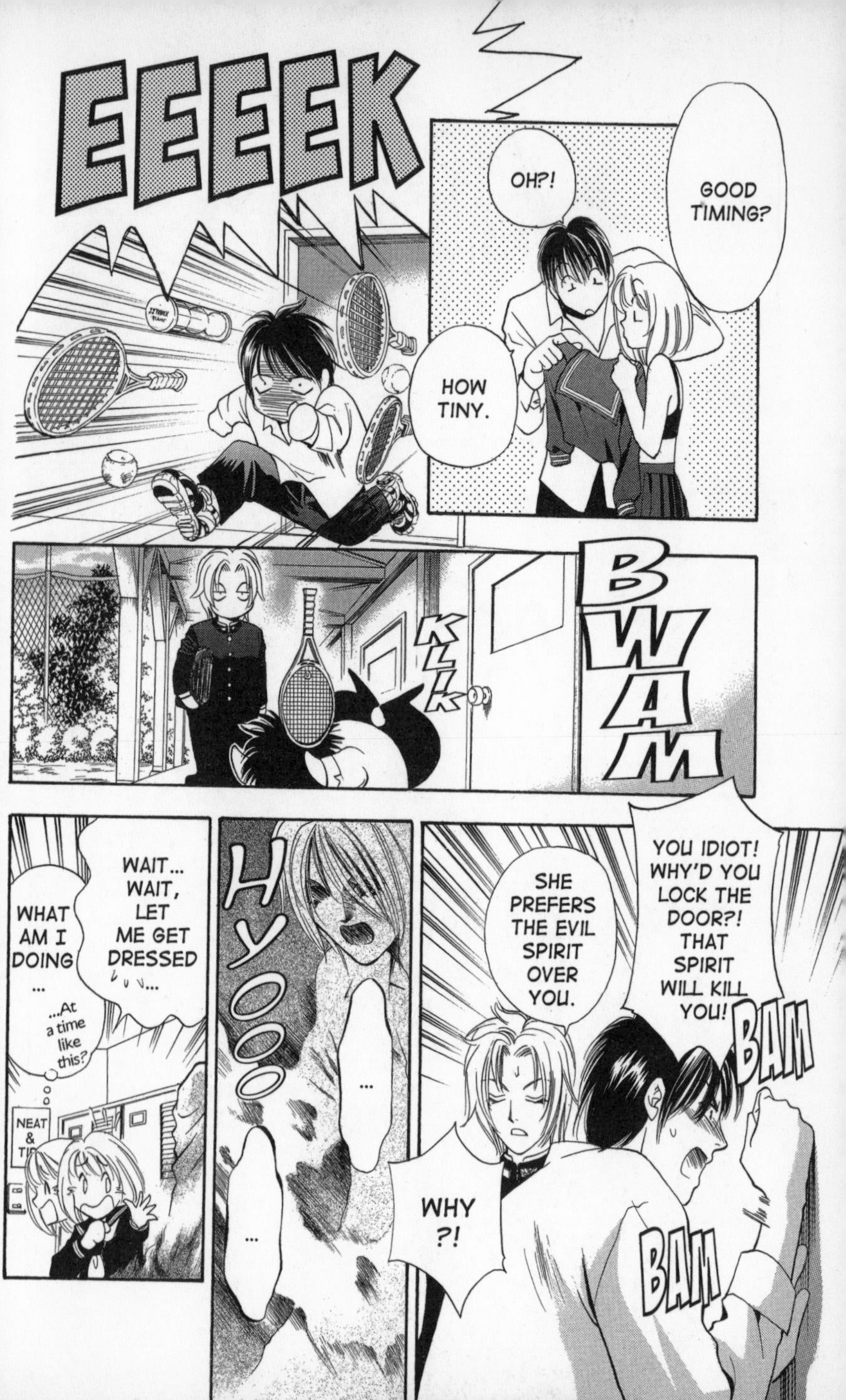
GOOD TIMING?
OH?!
HOW TINY.
EEEEK
BWAM
KLIK
YOU IDIOT! WHY'D YOU LOCK THE DOOR?! THAT SPIRIT WILL KILL YOU!
SHE PREFERS THE EVIL SPIRIT OVER YOU.
BAM
BAM
WHY?!
HYOOOO
...
...
WAIT... WAIT, LET ME GET DRESSED
WHAT AM I DOING ...
...At a time like this?

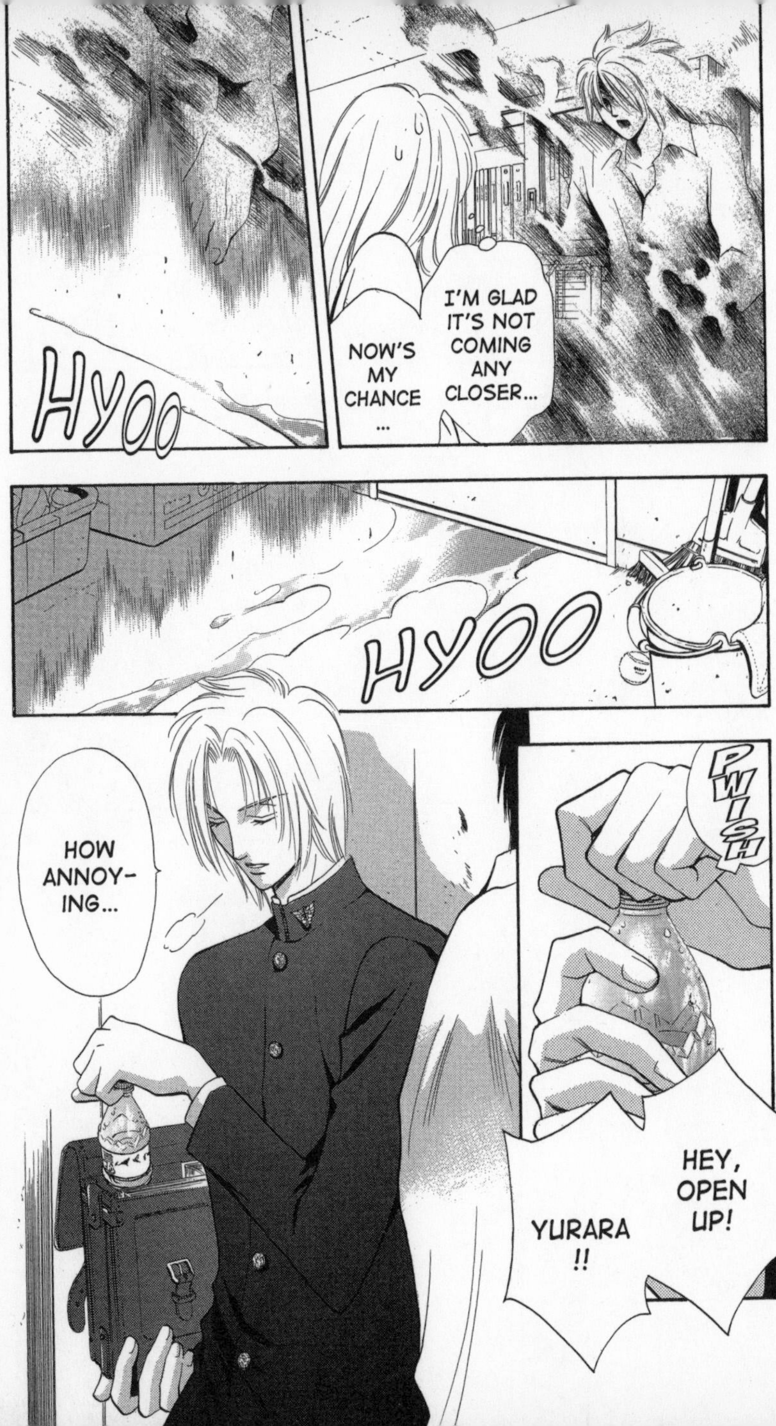
I'M GLAD IT'S NOT COMING ANY CLOSER...
NOW'S MY CHANCE ...
HYOO
HYOO
PWISH
HEY, OPEN UP!
YURARA !!
HOW ANNOY-ING...

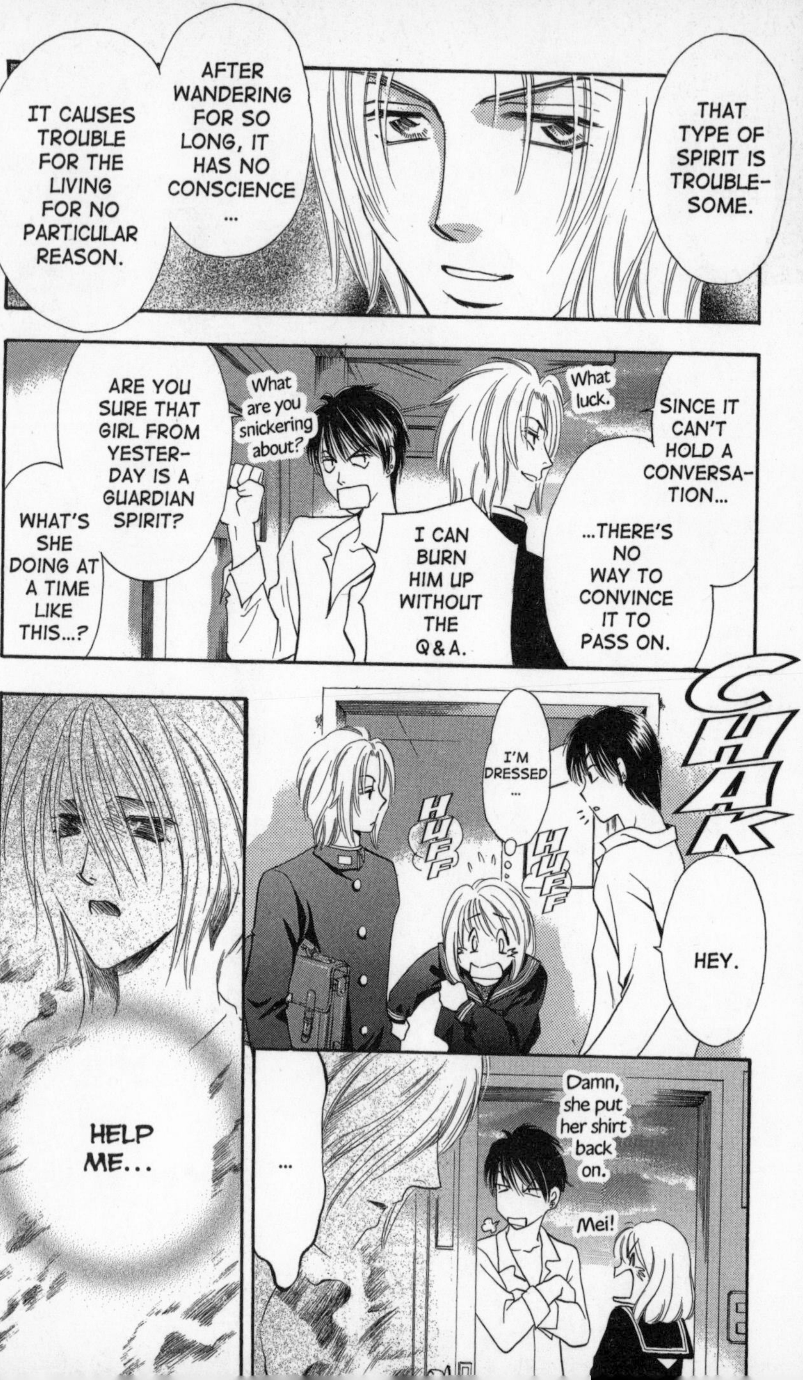
THAT TYPE OF SPIRIT IS TROUBLE-SOME.
AFTER WANDERING FOR SO LONG, IT HAS NO CONSCIENCE ...
IT CAUSES TROUBLE FOR THE LIVING FOR NO PARTICULAR REASON.
What luck.
SINCE IT CAN'T HOLD A CONVERSA-TION...
...THERE'S NO WAY TO CONVINCE IT TO PASS ON.
I CAN BURN HIM UP WITHOUT THE Q&A.
What are you snickering about?
ARE YOU SURE THAT GIRL FROM YESTER-DAY IS A GUARDIAN SPIRIT?
WHAT'S SHE DOING AT A TIME LIKE THIS...?
CHAK
HEY.
I'M DRESSED ...
HUFF
HUFF
Damn, she put her shirt back on.
Mei!
...
HELP ME...

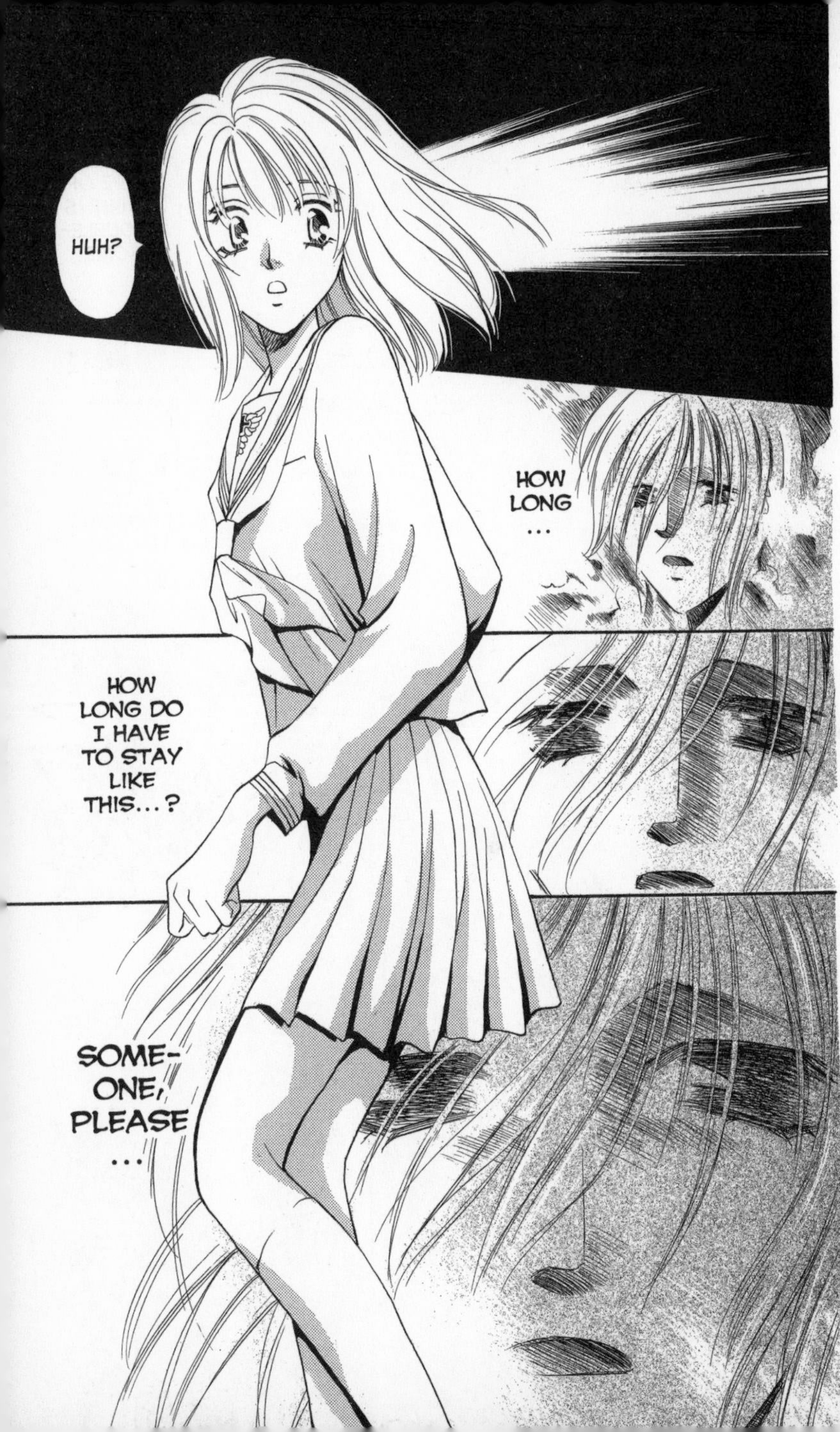
HUH?
HOW LONG …
HOW LONG DO I HAVE TO STAY LIKE THIS…?
SOME-ONE, PLEASE …

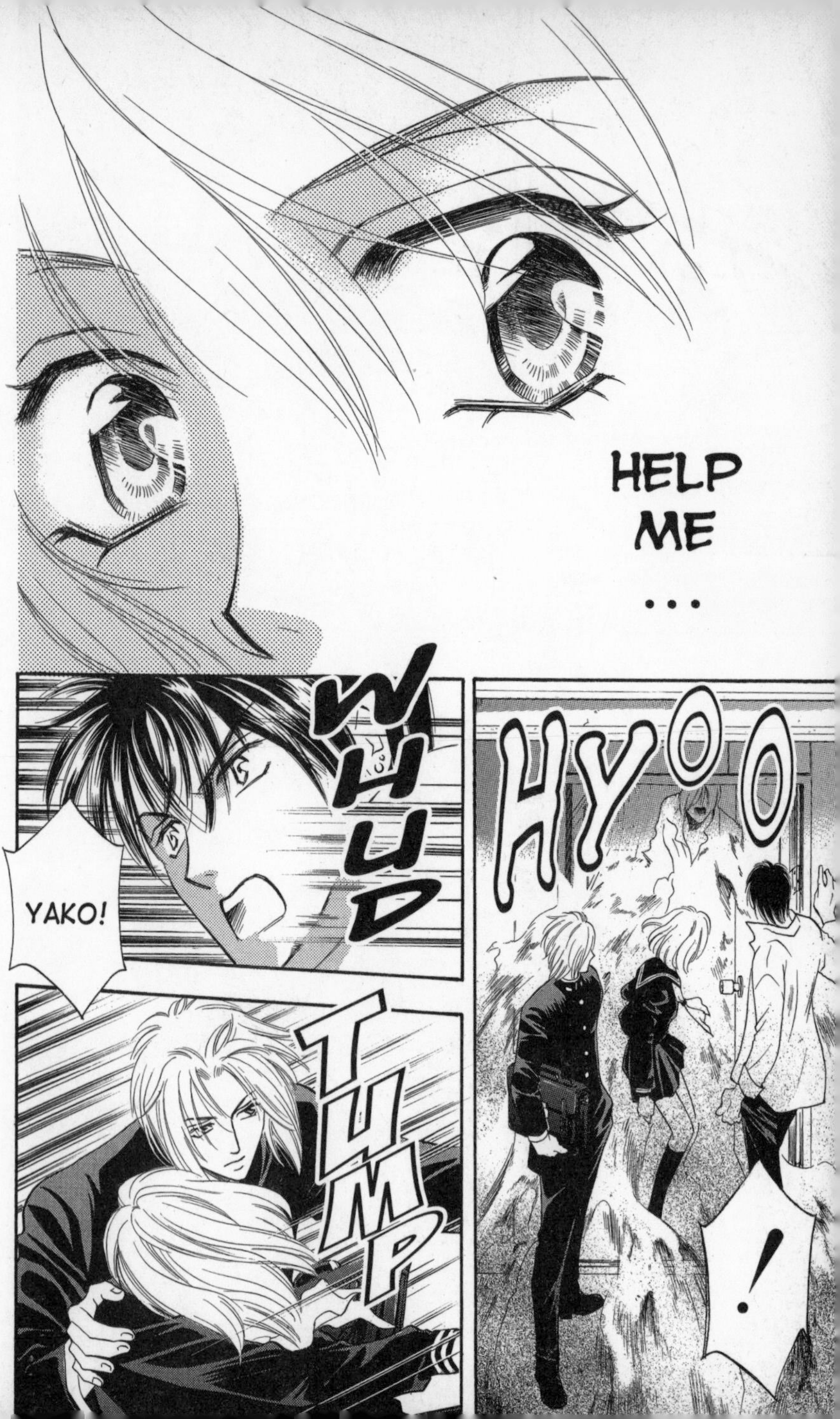
HELP ME
...
HYOO
!
WHUD
YAKO!
TUMP

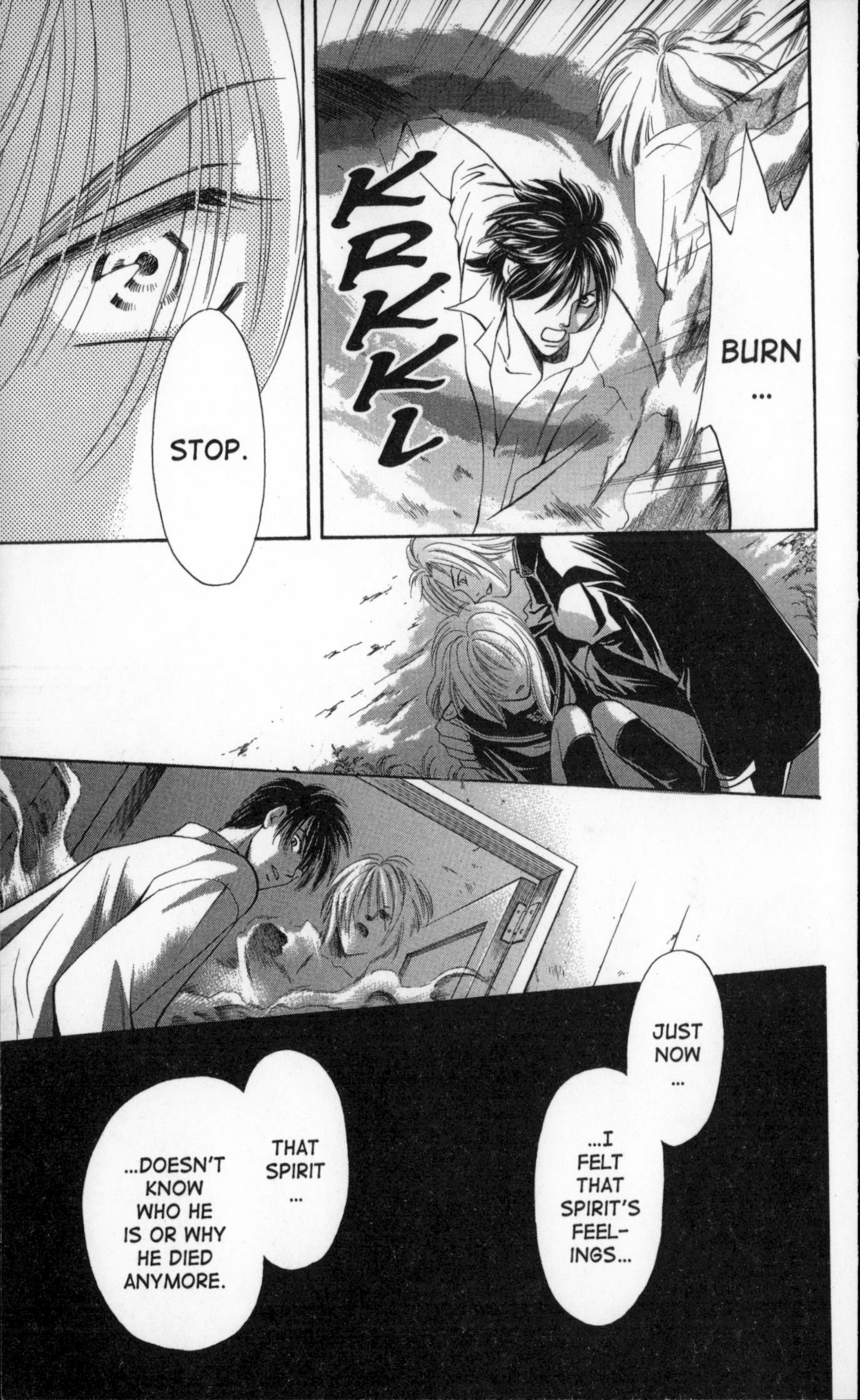
BURN ...
KRKKL
STOP.
JUST NOW ...
...I FELT THAT SPIRIT'S FEEL-INGS...
THAT SPIRIT ...
...DOESN'T KNOW WHO HE IS OR WHY HE DIED ANYMORE.

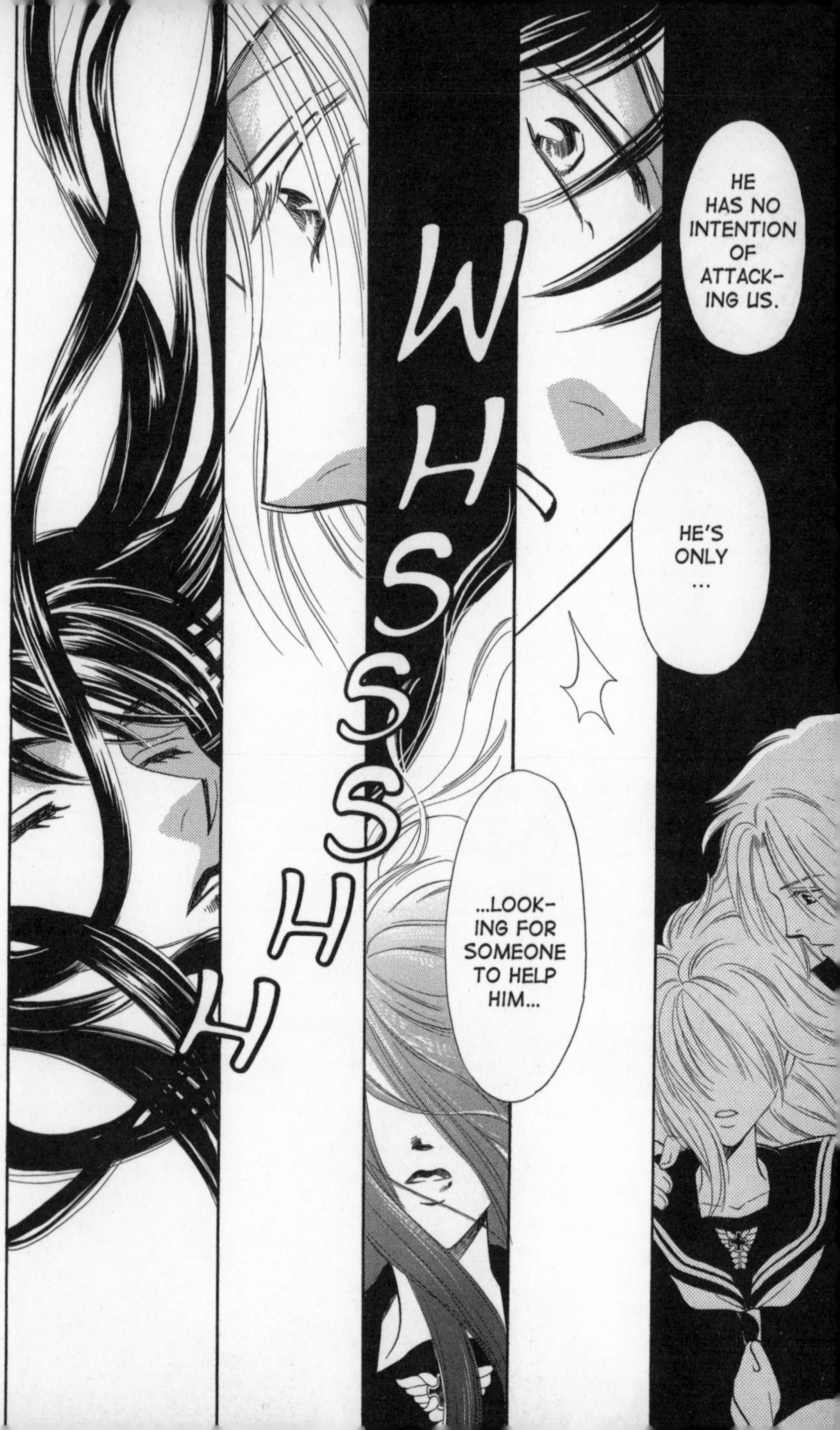
HE HAS NO INTENTION OF ATTACK-ING US.
HE'S ONLY ...
...LOOK-ING FOR SOMEONE TO HELP HIM...
WHSSHH

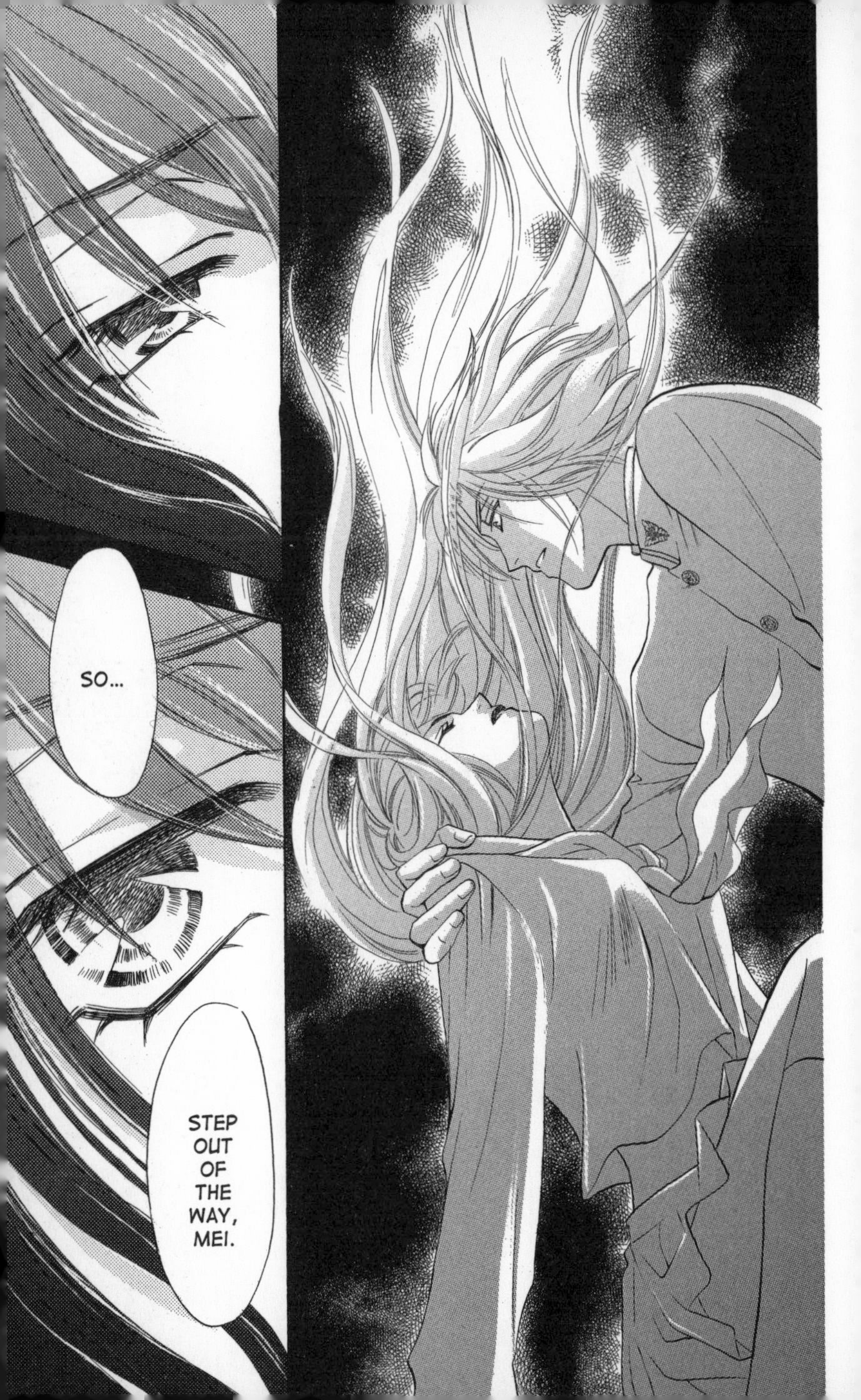
SO...
STEP OUT OF THE WAY, MEI.

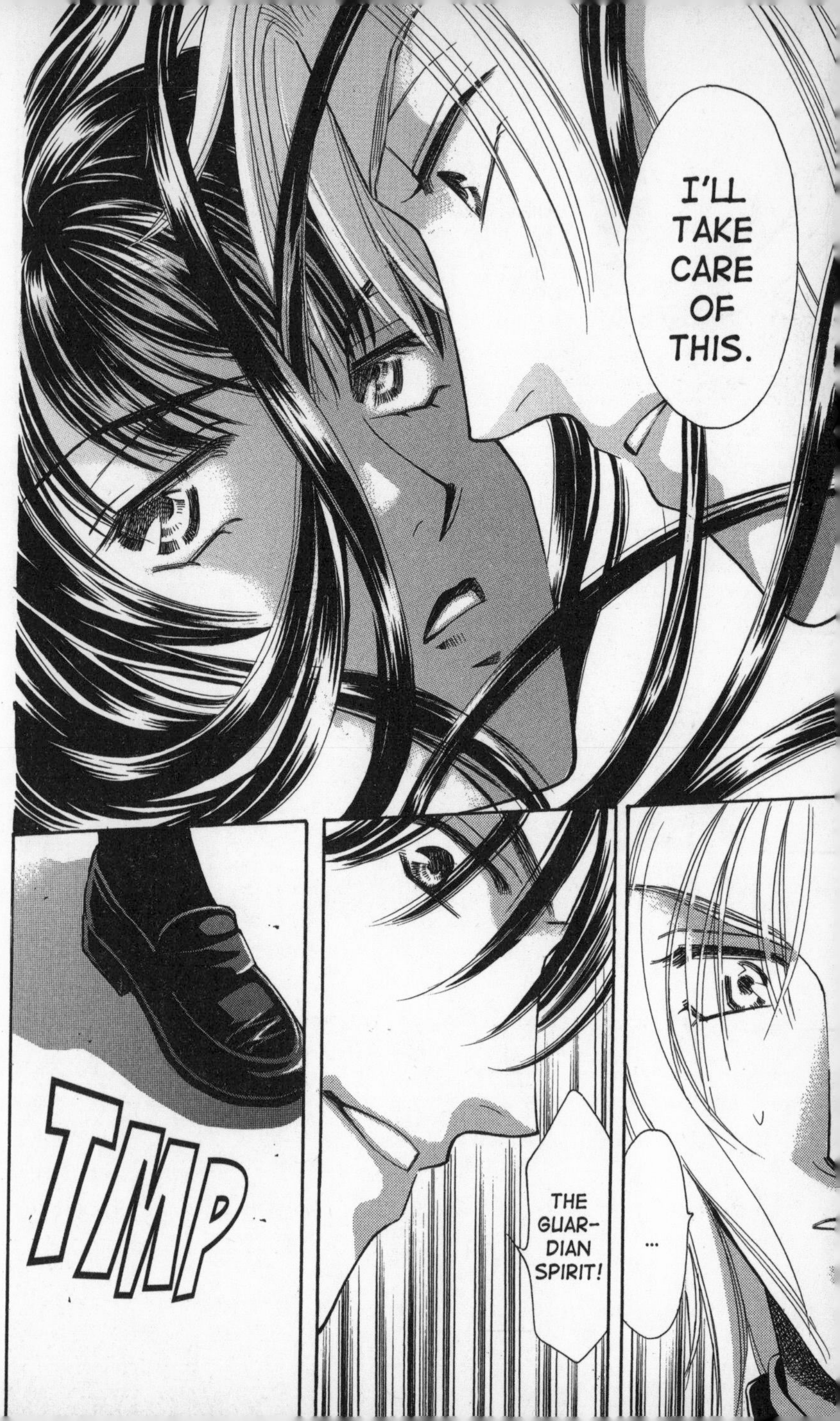
I'LL TAKE CARE OF THIS.
...
THE GUAR-DIAN SPIRIT!
TMP

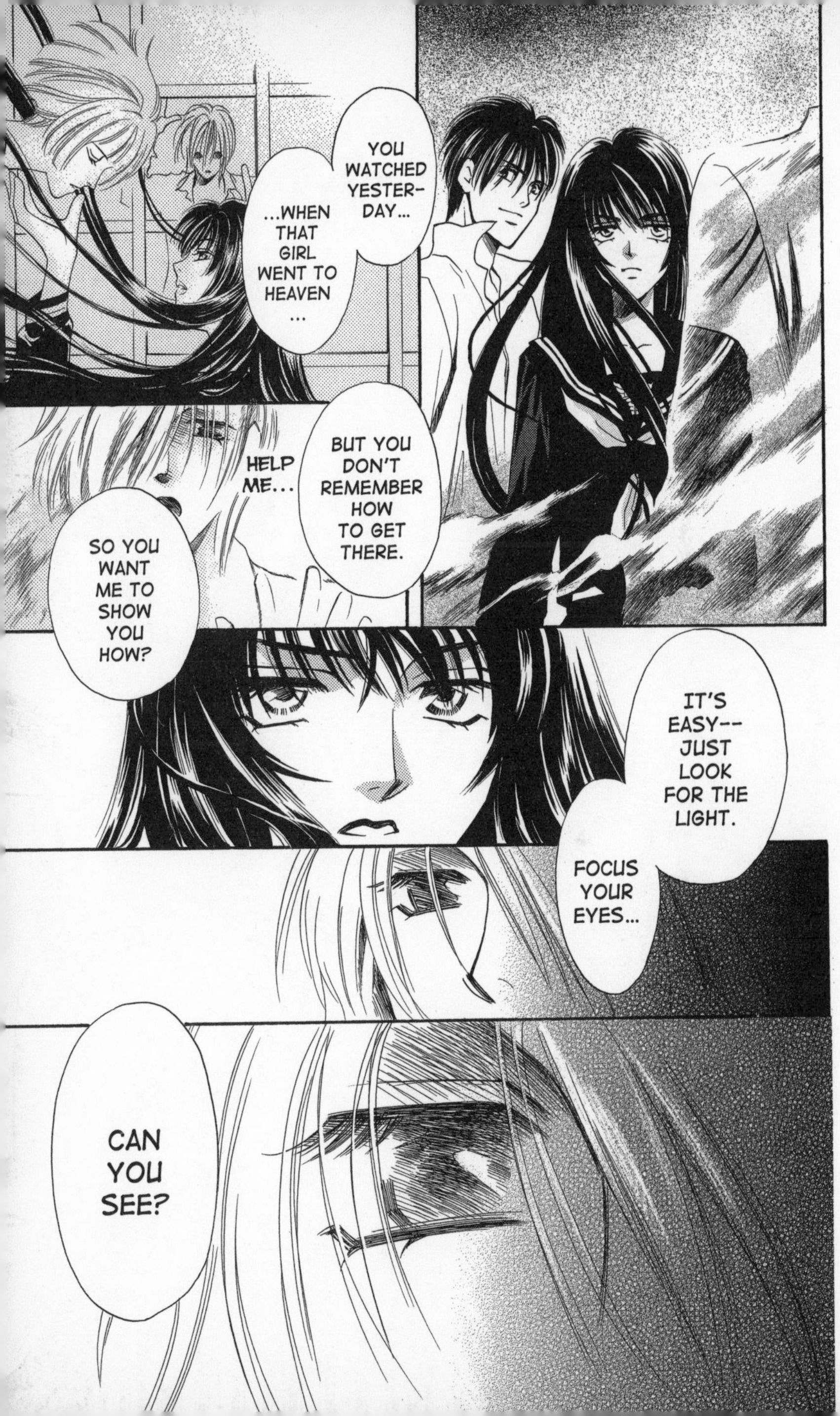
YOU WATCHED YESTER-DAY...
...WHEN THAT GIRL WENT TO HEAVEN ...
BUT YOU DON'T REMEMBER HOW TO GET THERE.
HELP ME...
SO YOU WANT ME TO SHOW YOU HOW?
IT'S EASY-- JUST LOOK FOR THE LIGHT.
FOCUS YOUR EYES...
CAN YOU SEE?

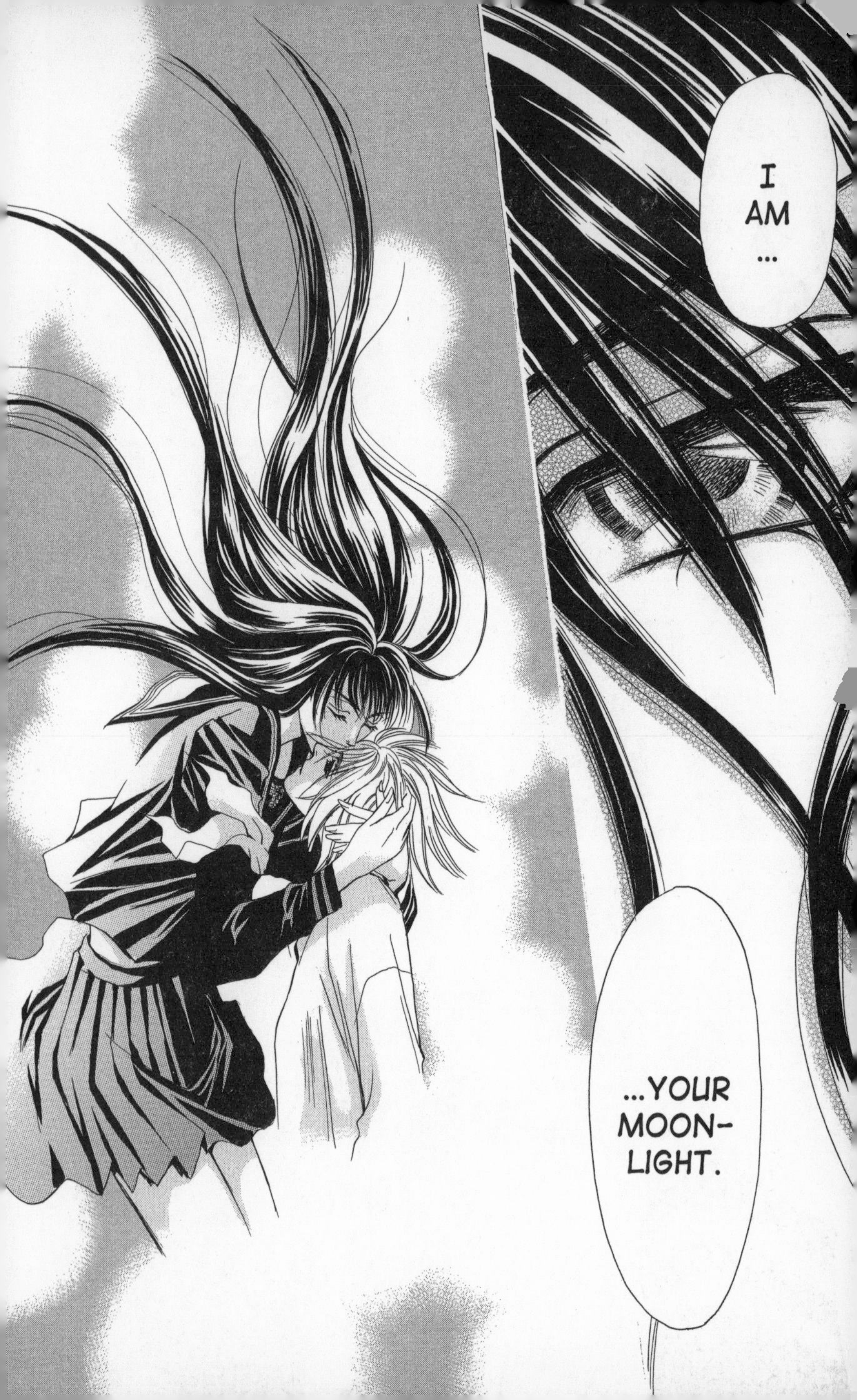
I AM ...
...YOUR MOONLIGHT.

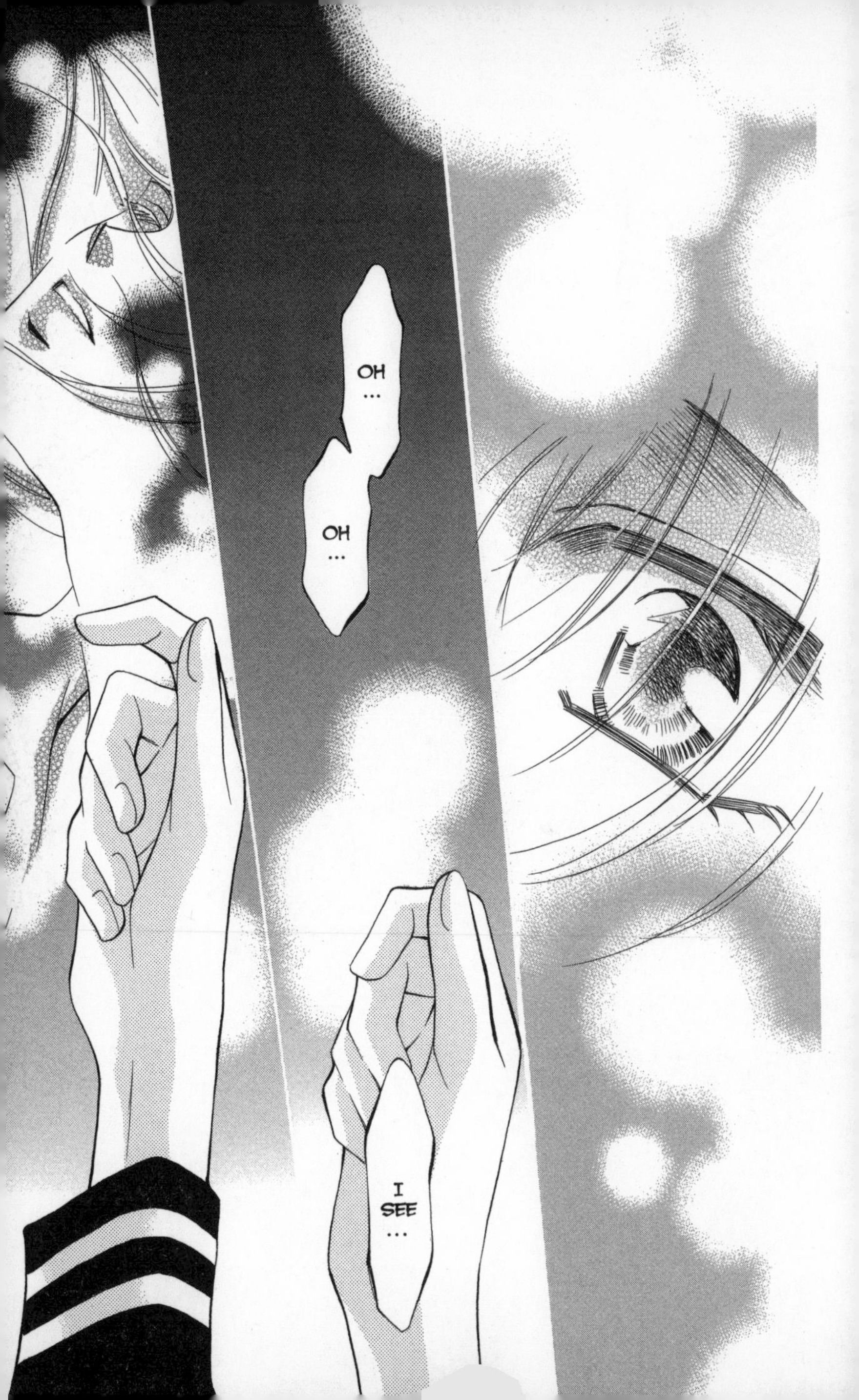
OH ...
OH ...
I SEE ...

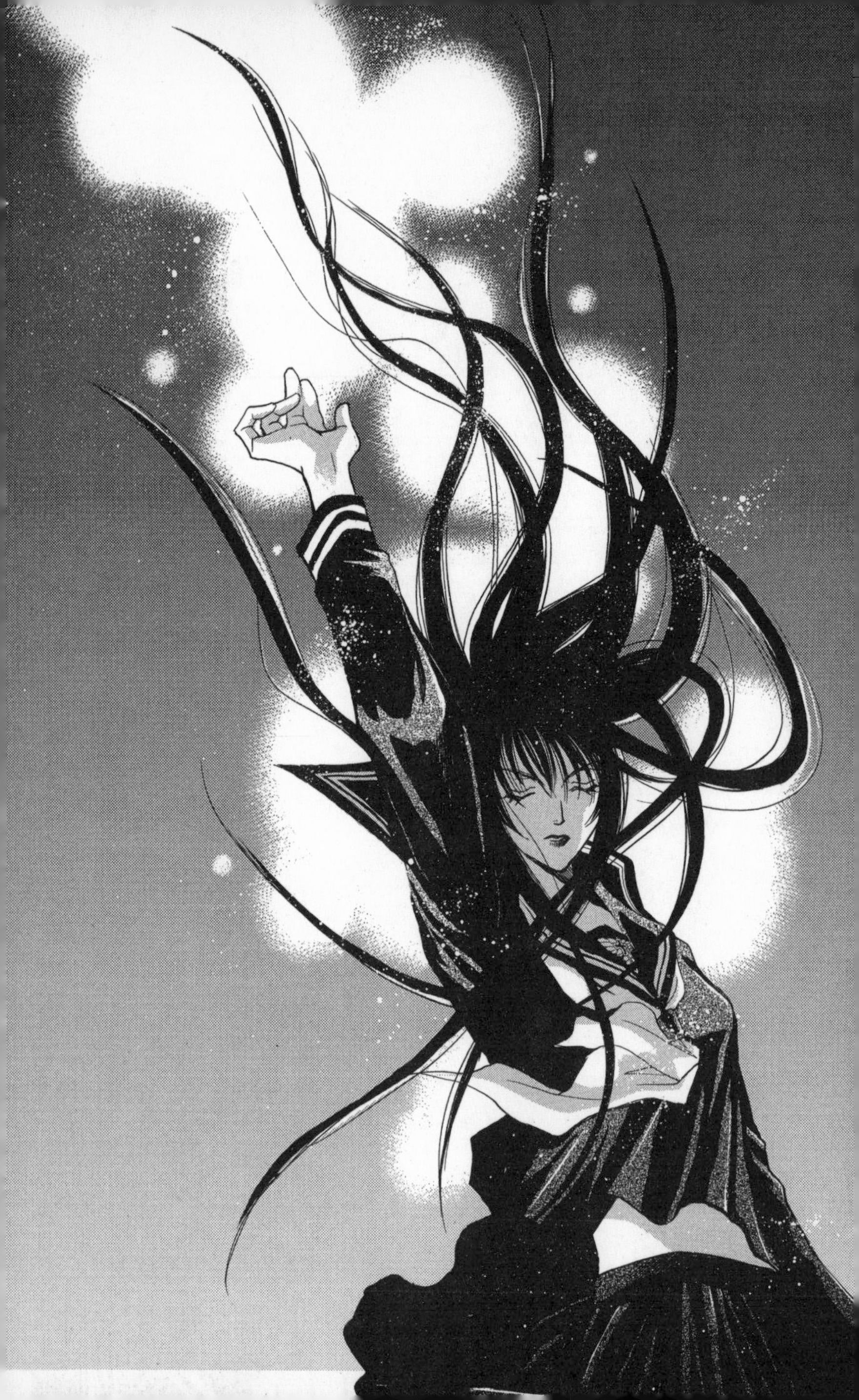

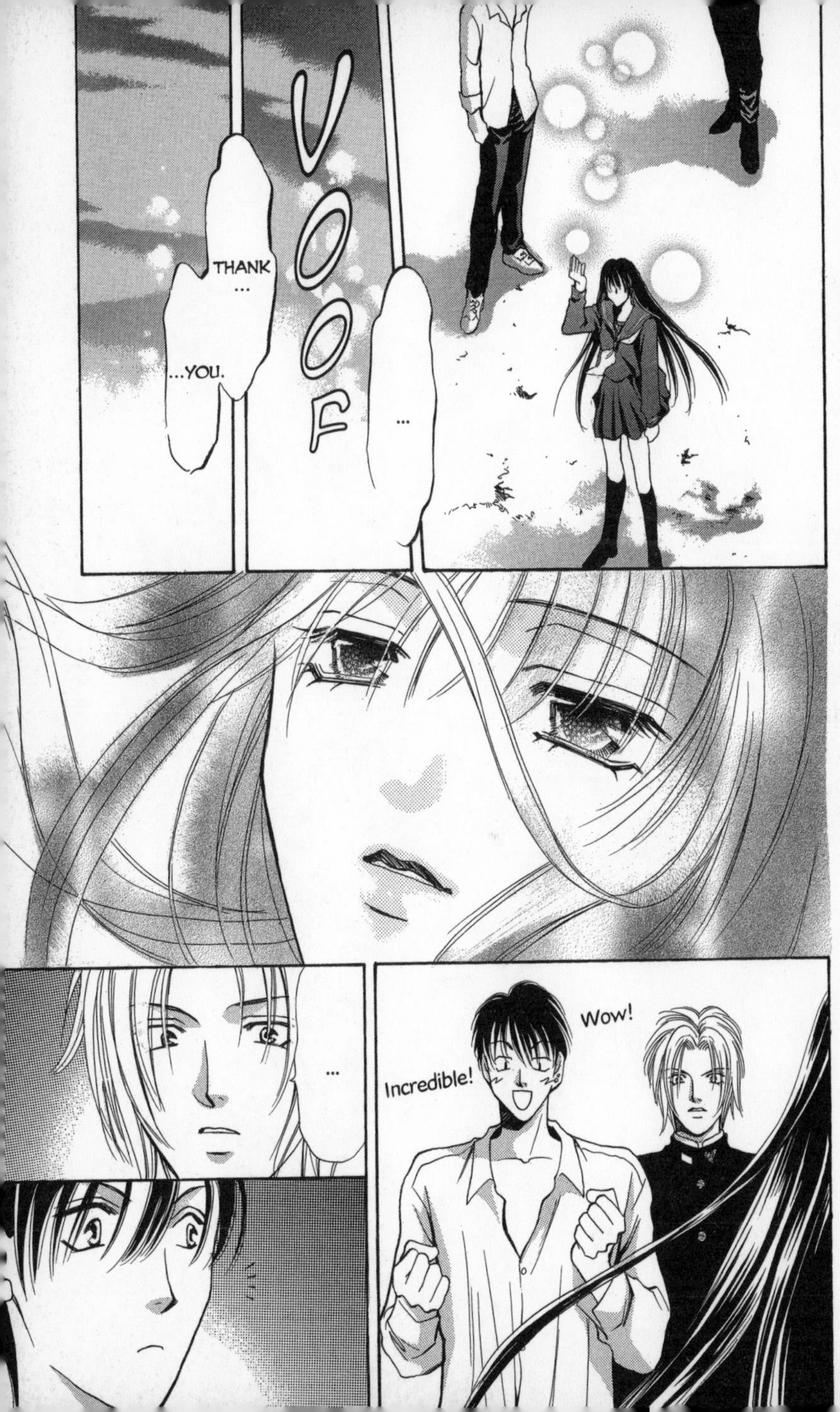
...
VOOOF
THANK
...
...YOU.
Wow!
Incredible!
...

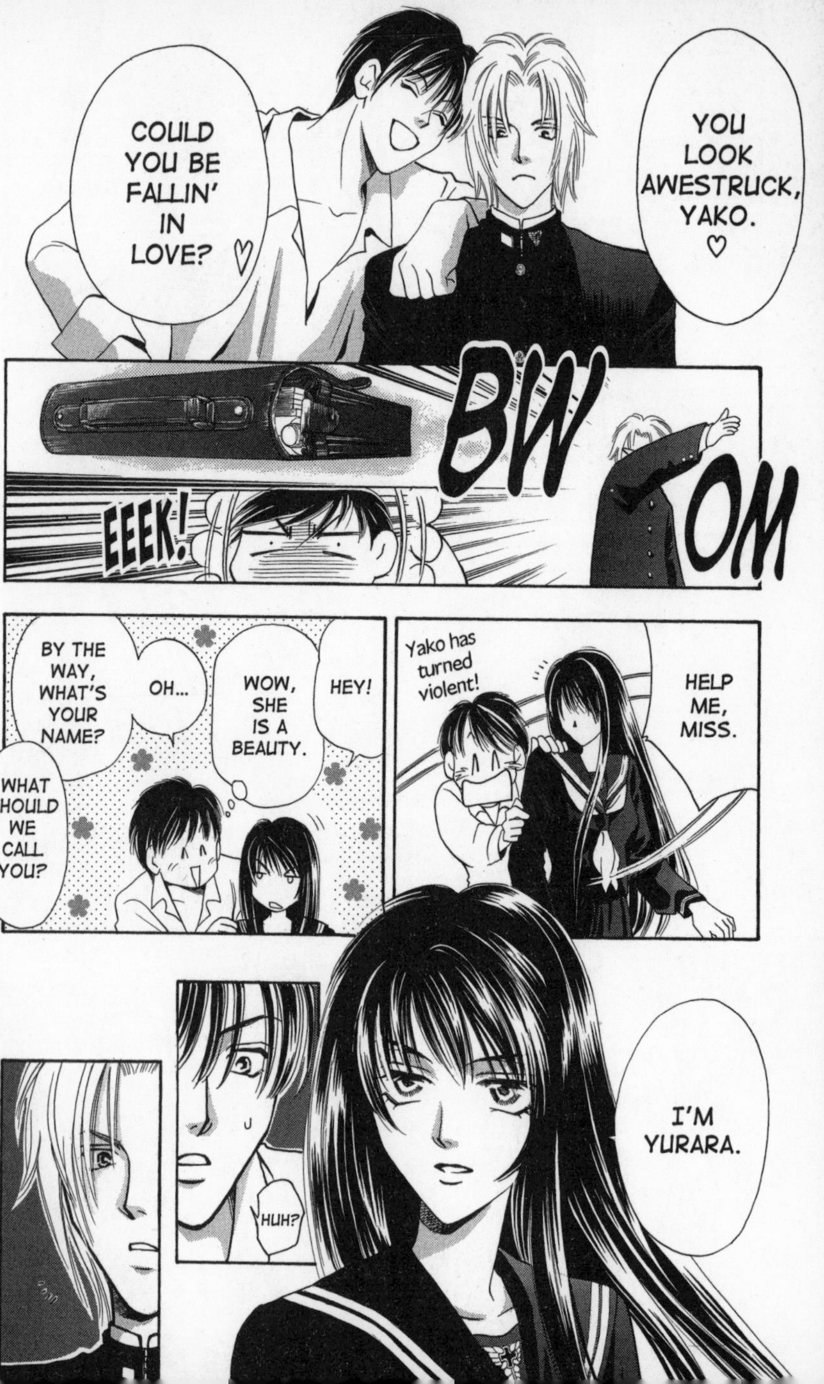
YOU LOOK AWESTRUCK, YAKO. ♡
COULD YOU BE FALLIN' IN LOVE? ♡
BWOOM
EEEK!
HELP ME, MISS.
Yako has turned violent!
HEY!
WOW, SHE IS A BEAUTY.
OH...
BY THE WAY, WHAT'S YOUR NAME?
WHAT SHOULD WE CALL YOU?
I'M YURARA.
HUH?

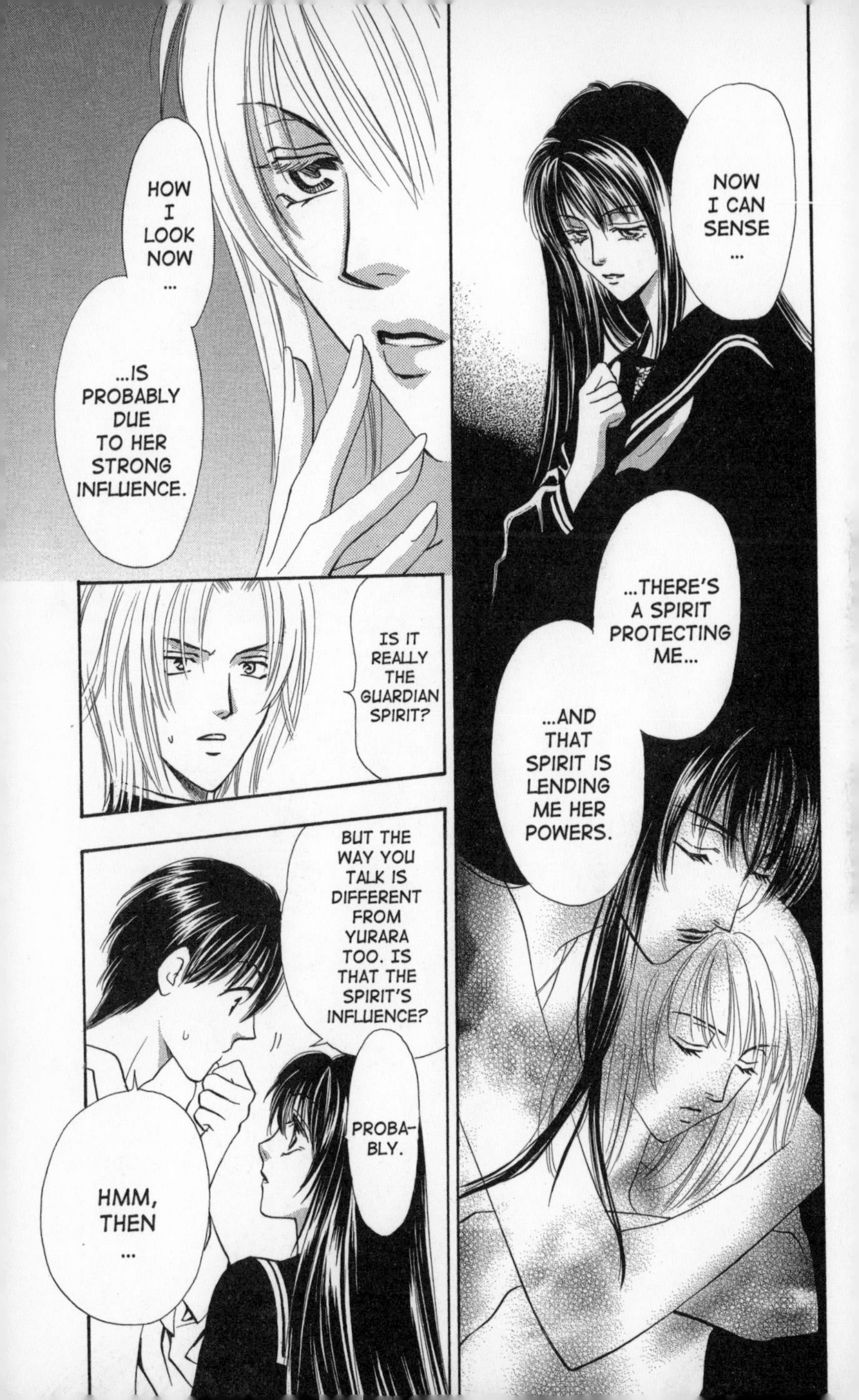
NOW I CAN SENSE ...
...THERE'S A SPIRIT PROTECTING ME...
...AND THAT SPIRIT IS LENDING ME HER POWERS.
HOW I LOOK NOW ...
...IS PROBABLY DUE TO HER STRONG INFLUENCE.
IS IT REALLY THE GUARDIAN SPIRIT?
BUT THE WAY YOU TALK IS DIFFERENT FROM YURARA TOO. IS THAT THE SPIRIT'S INFLUENCE?
PROBA-BLY.
HMM, THEN ...

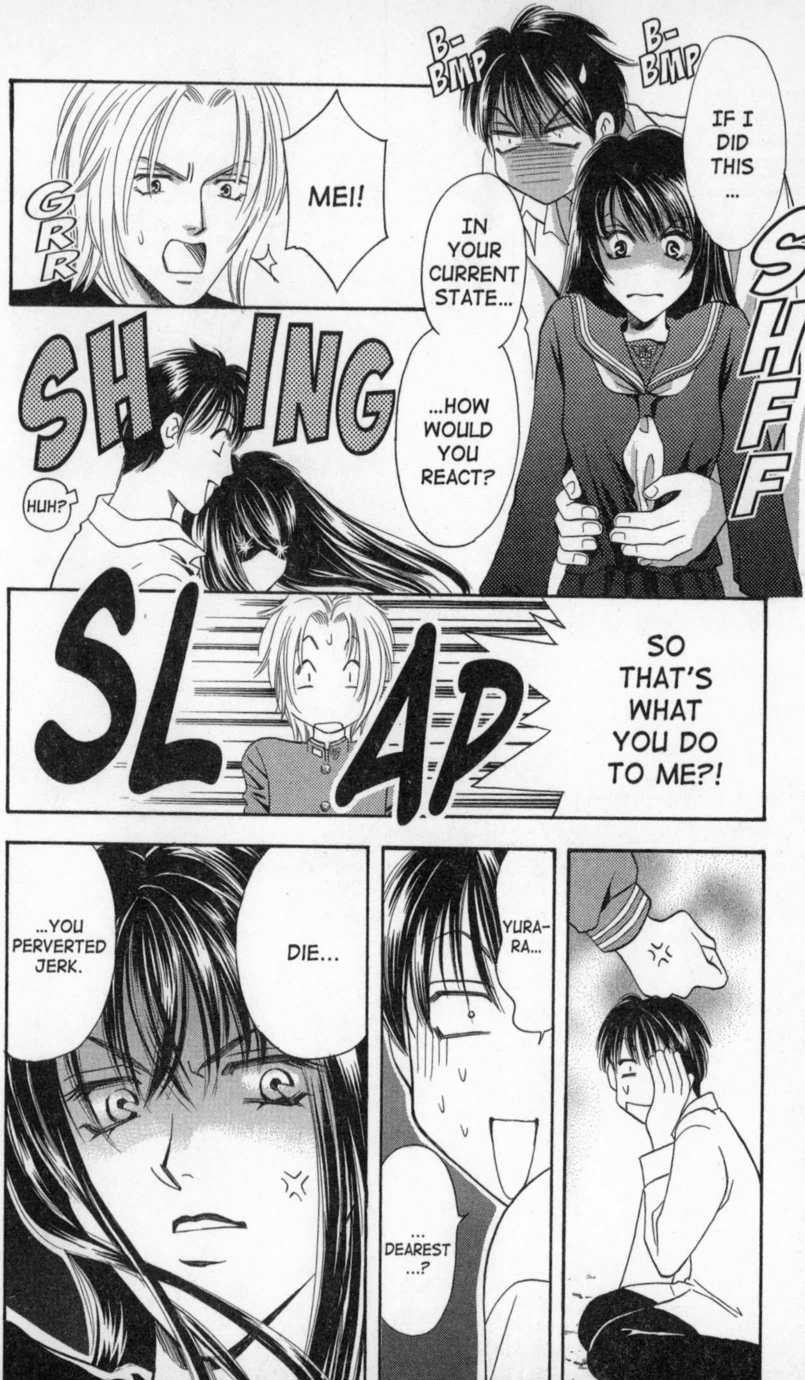
B-BMP
B-BMP
IF I DID THIS ...
IN YOUR CURRENT STATE...
...HOW WOULD YOU REACT?
SHFFF
GRR
MEI!
SHING
HUH?
SO THAT'S WHAT YOU DO TO ME?!
SLAP
YURA-RA...
... DEAREST ...?
DIE...
...YOU PERVERTED JERK.

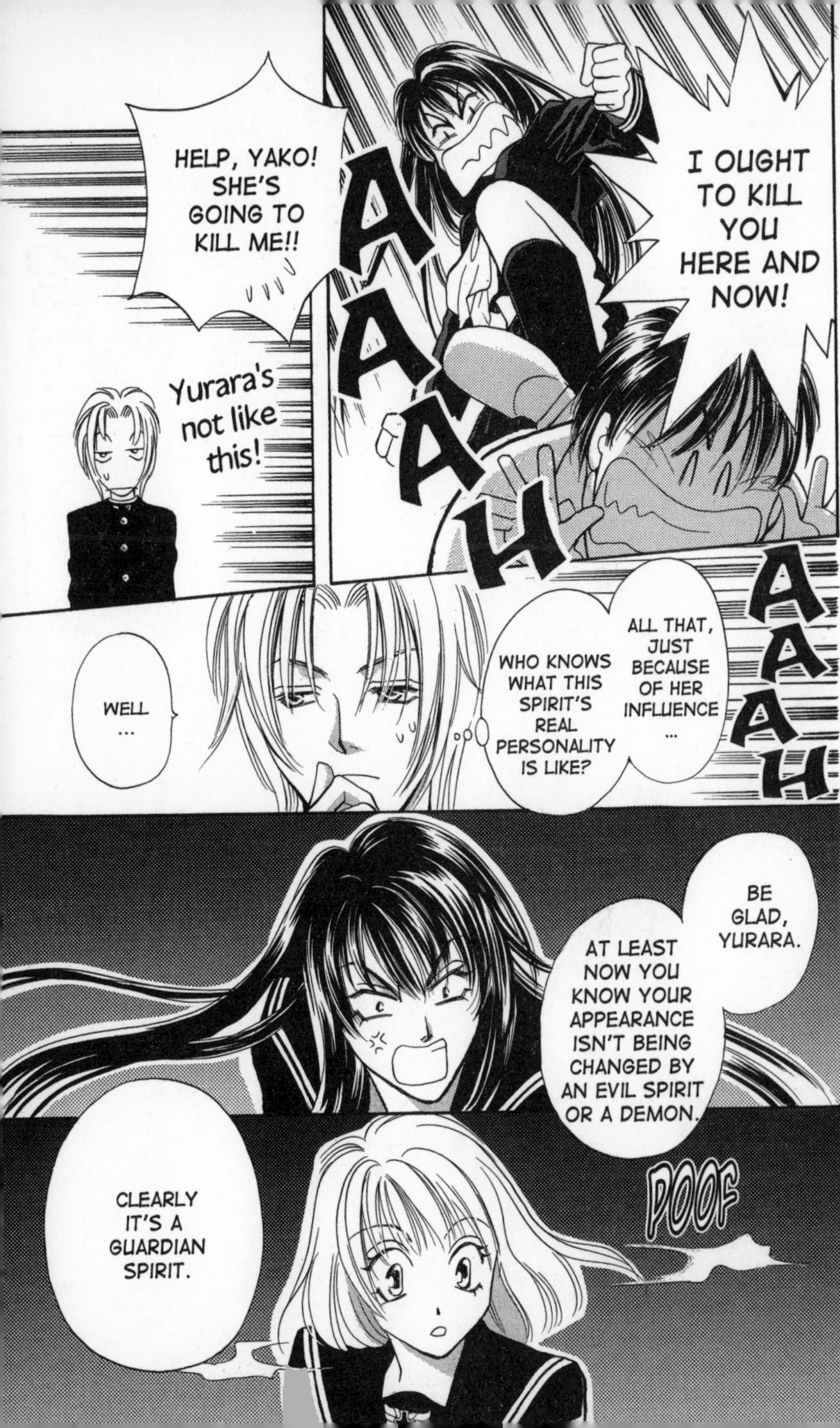
I OUGHT TO KILL YOU HERE AND NOW!
AAAAH
HELP, YAKO! SHE'S GOING TO KILL ME!!
Yurara's not like this!
AAAH
ALL THAT, JUST BECAUSE OF HER INFLUENCE ...
WHO KNOWS WHAT THIS SPIRIT'S REAL PERSONALITY IS LIKE?
WELL ...
BE GLAD, YURARA.
AT LEAST NOW YOU KNOW YOUR APPEARANCE ISN'T BEING CHANGED BY AN EVIL SPIRIT OR A DEMON.
POOF
CLEARLY IT'S A GUARDIAN SPIRIT.

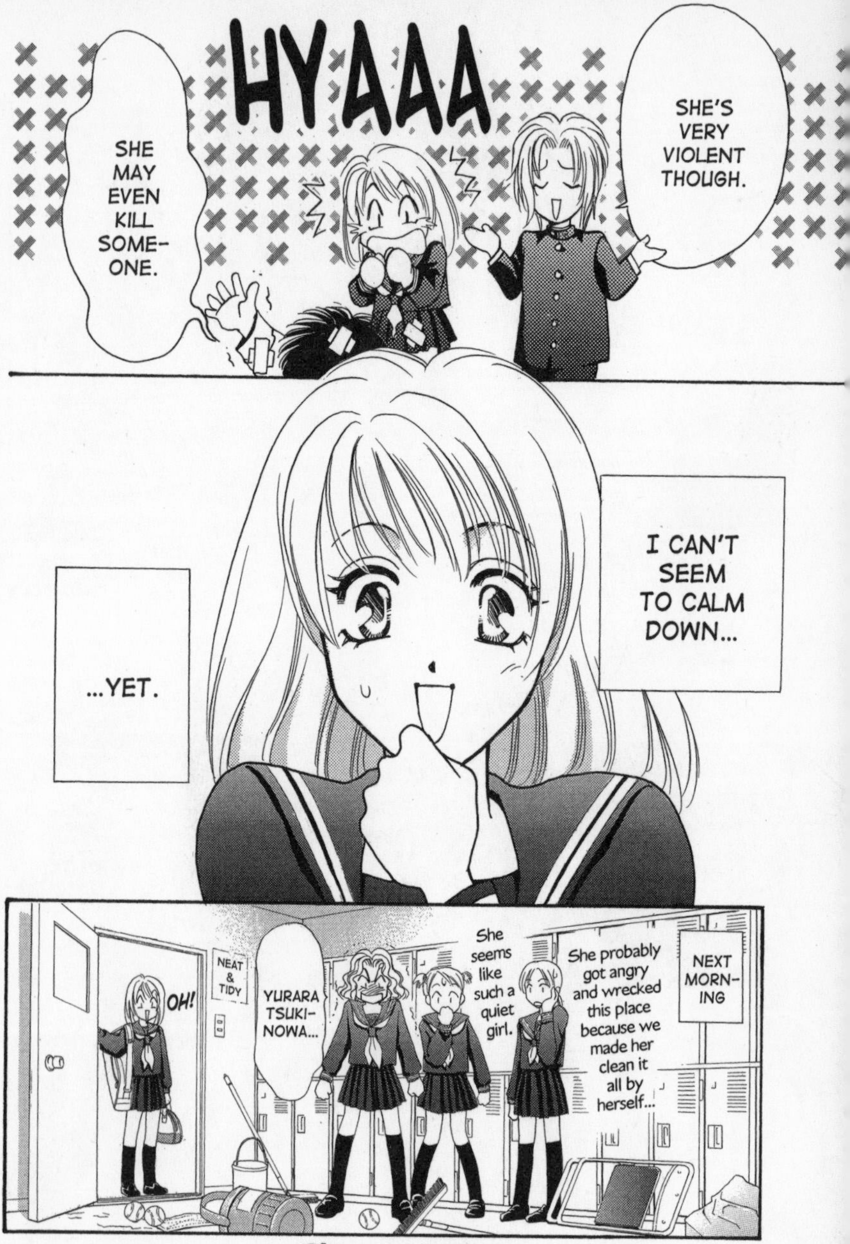
SHE'S VERY VIOLENT THOUGH.
HYAAA
SHE MAY EVEN KILL SOME-ONE.
I CAN'T SEEM TO CALM DOWN...
...YET.
NEXT MORN-ING
She probably got angry and wrecked this place because we made her clean it all by herself...
She seems like such a quiet girl.
YURARA TSUKI-NOWA...
NEAT & TIDY
OH!

Chapter 2/End

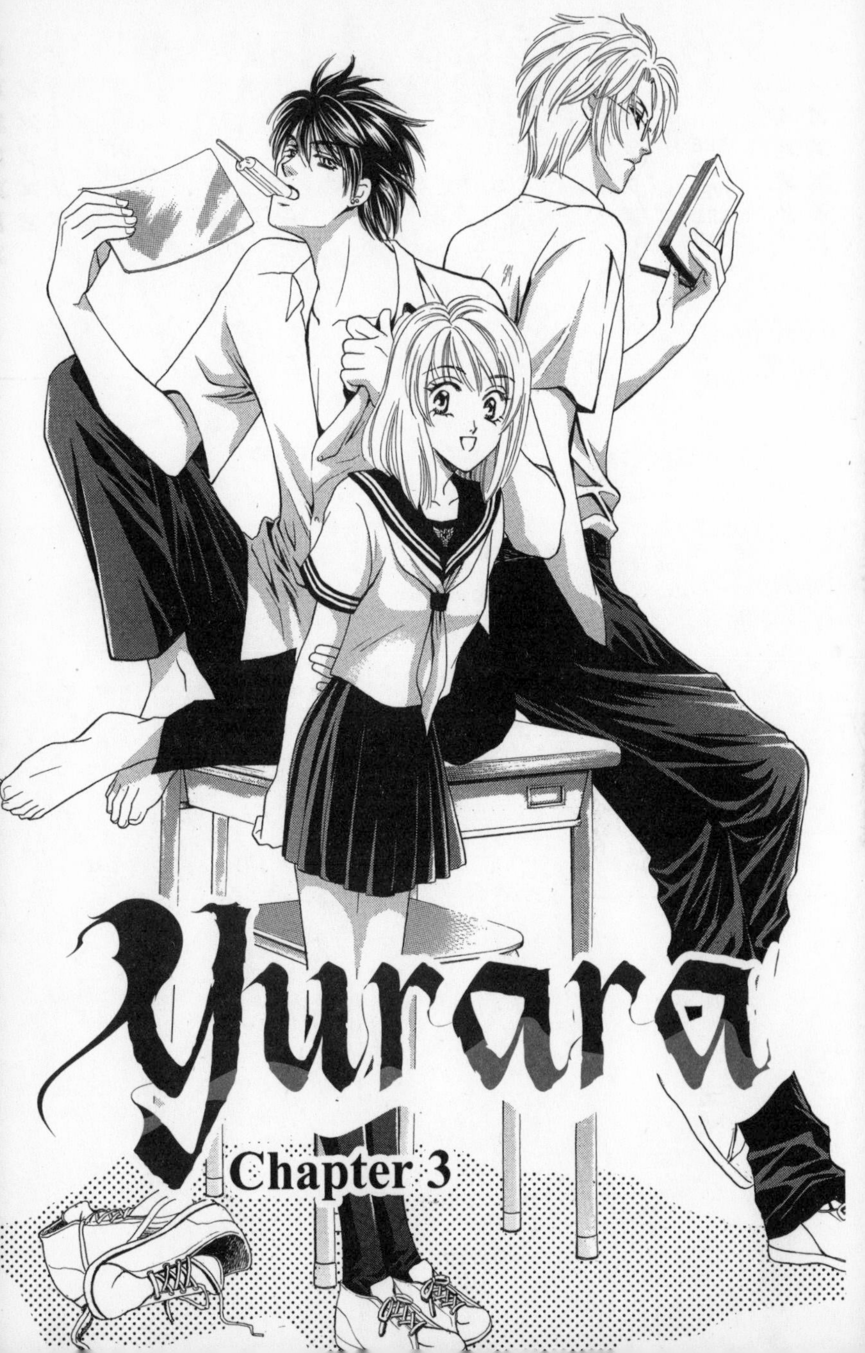
Yurara
Chapter 3

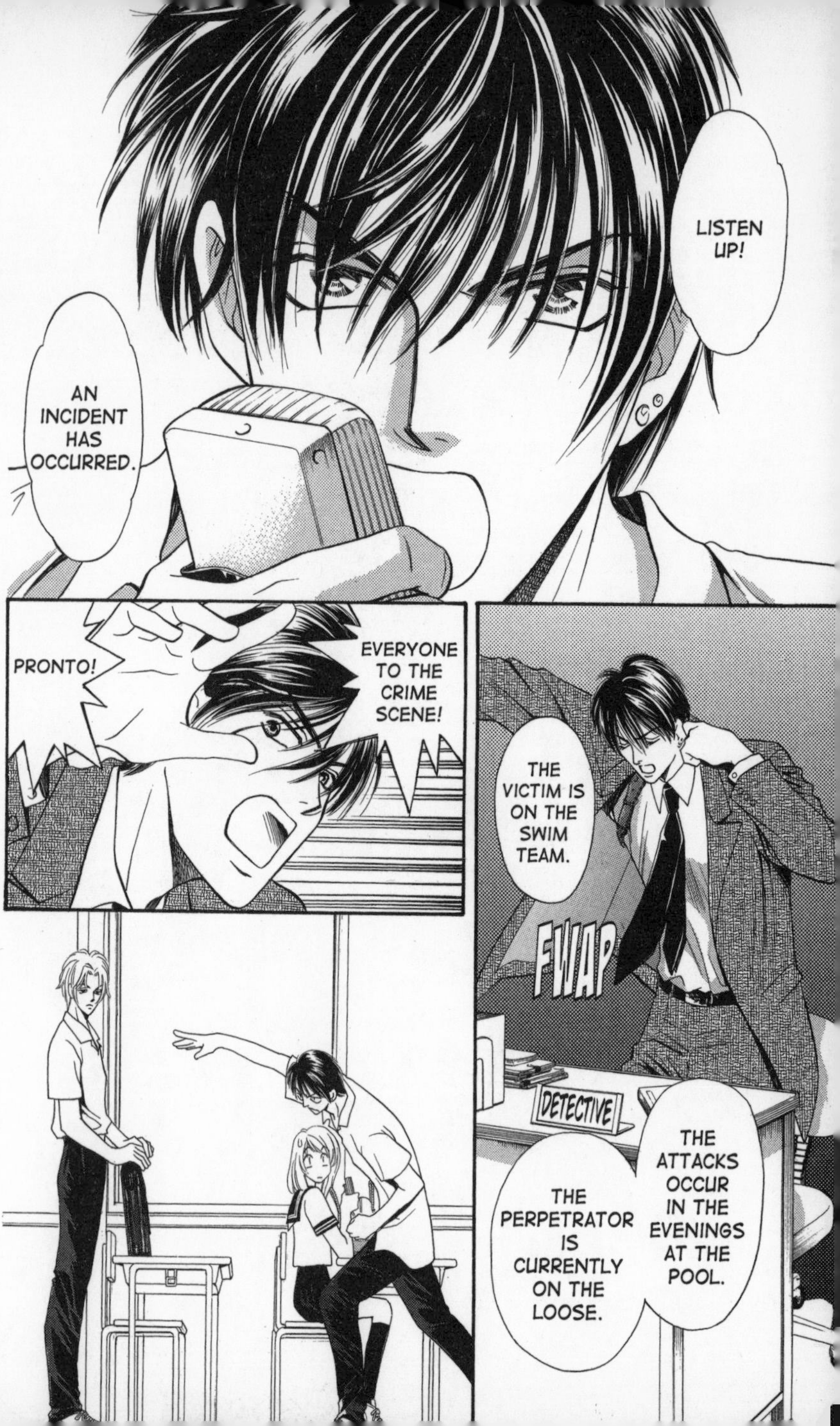
LISTEN UP!
AN INCIDENT HAS OCCURRED.
THE VICTIM IS ON THE SWIM TEAM.
FWAP
DETECTIVE
THE ATTACKS OCCUR IN THE EVENINGS AT THE POOL.
THE PERPETRATOR IS CURRENTLY ON THE LOOSE.
EVERYONE TO THE CRIME SCENE!
PRONTO!

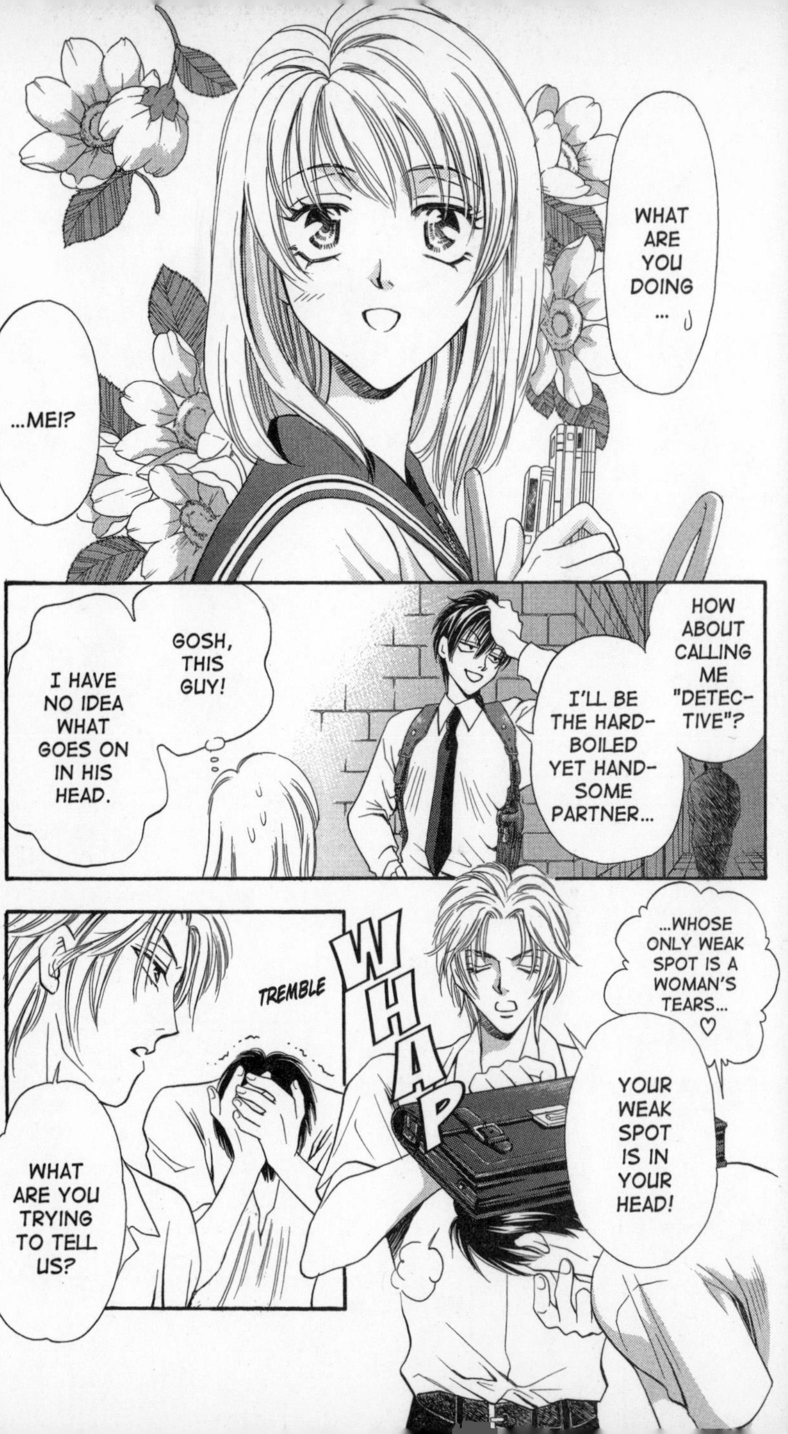
WHAT ARE YOU DOING...
...MEI?
HOW ABOUT CALLING ME "DETECTIVE"?
I'LL BE THE HARD-BOILED YET HANDSOME PARTNER...
GOSH, THIS GUY!
I HAVE NO IDEA WHAT GOES ON IN HIS HEAD.
...WHOSE ONLY WEAK SPOT IS A WOMAN'S TEARS... ♡
WHAP
YOUR WEAK SPOT IS IN YOUR HEAD!
TREMBLE
WHAT ARE YOU TRYING TO TELL US?

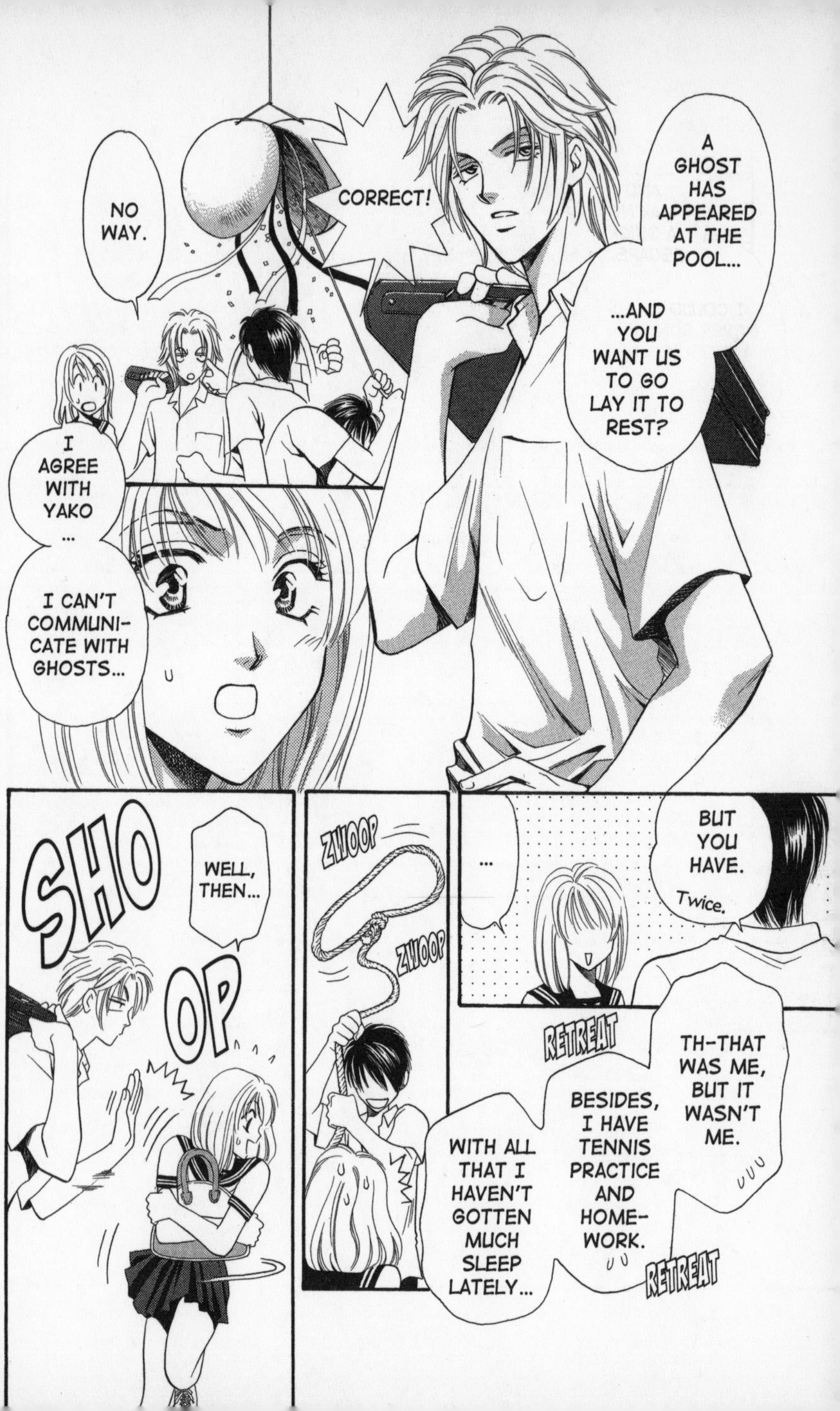
A GHOST HAS APPEARED AT THE POOL...
...AND YOU WANT US TO GO LAY IT TO REST?
CORRECT!
NO WAY.
I AGREE WITH YAKO...
I CAN'T COMMUNICATE WITH GHOSTS...
BUT YOU HAVE.
Twice.
...
TH-THAT WAS ME, BUT IT WASN'T ME.
RETREAT
BESIDES, I HAVE TENNIS PRACTICE AND HOMEWORK.
WITH ALL THAT I HAVEN'T GOTTEN MUCH SLEEP LATELY...
RETREAT
ZWOOP
ZWOOP
WELL, THEN...
SHOOP

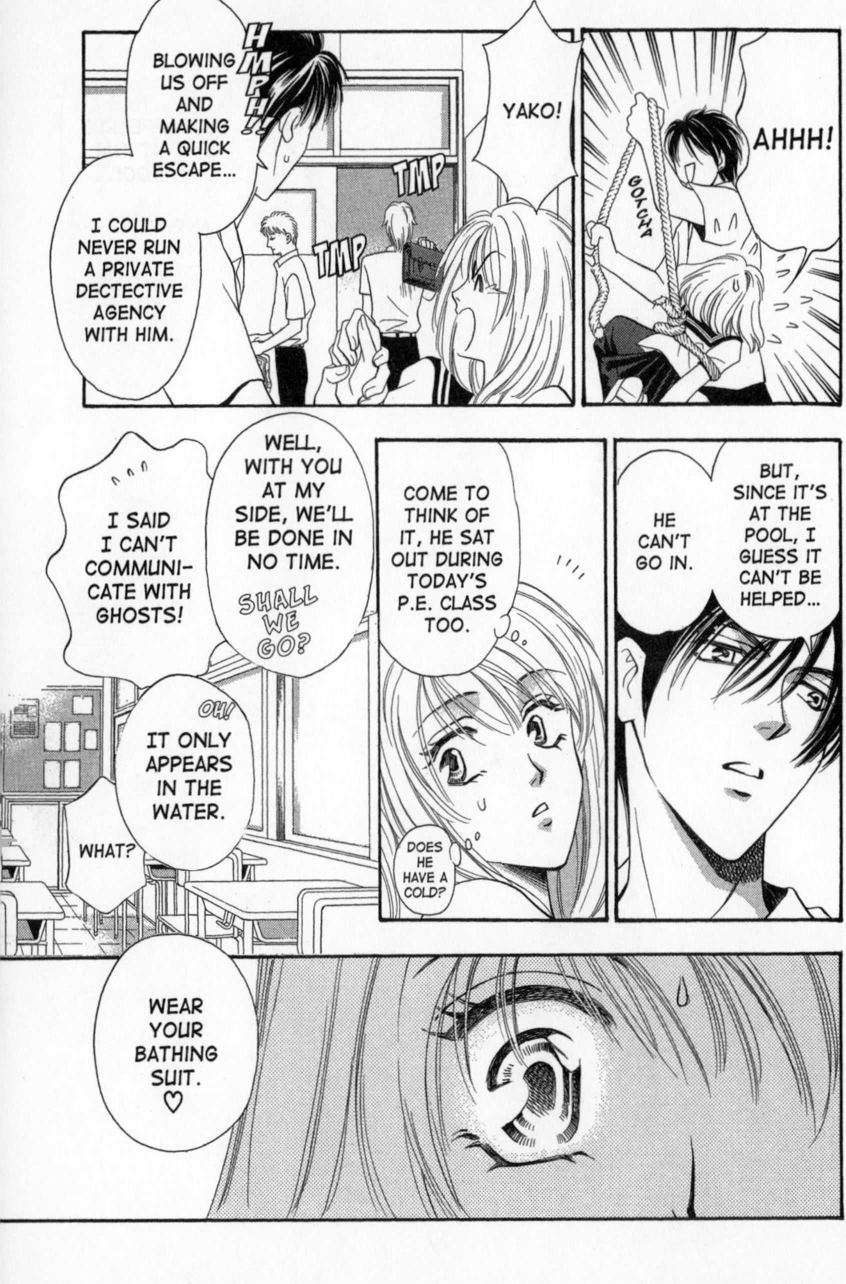
BLOWING US OFF AND MAKING A QUICK ESCAPE...
HMPH!!
I COULD NEVER RUN A PRIVATE DECTECTIVE AGENCY WITH HIM.
TMP
TMP
YAKO!
AHHH!
GOTCHA
I SAID I CAN'T COMMUNI-CATE WITH GHOSTS!
WELL, WITH YOU AT MY SIDE, WE'LL BE DONE IN NO TIME.
SHALL WE GO?
COME TO THINK OF IT, HE SAT OUT DURING TODAY'S P.E. CLASS TOO.
DOES HE HAVE A COLD?
HE CAN'T GO IN.
BUT, SINCE IT'S AT THE POOL, I GUESS IT CAN'T BE HELPED...
OH!
IT ONLY APPEARS IN THE WATER.
WHAT?
WEAR YOUR BATHING SUIT. ♡

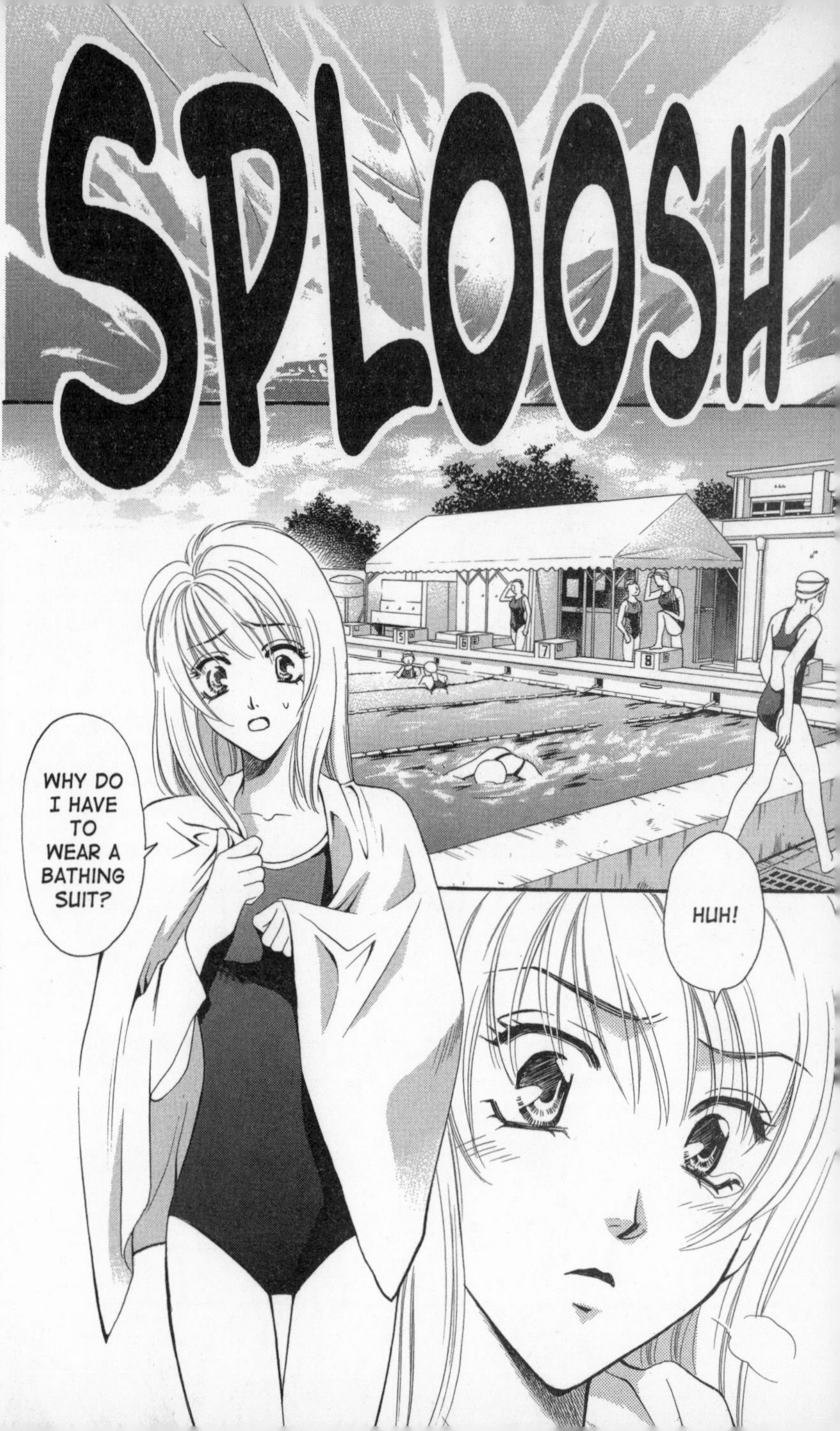
SPLOSH
WHY DO I HAVE TO WEAR A BATHING SUIT?
HUH!

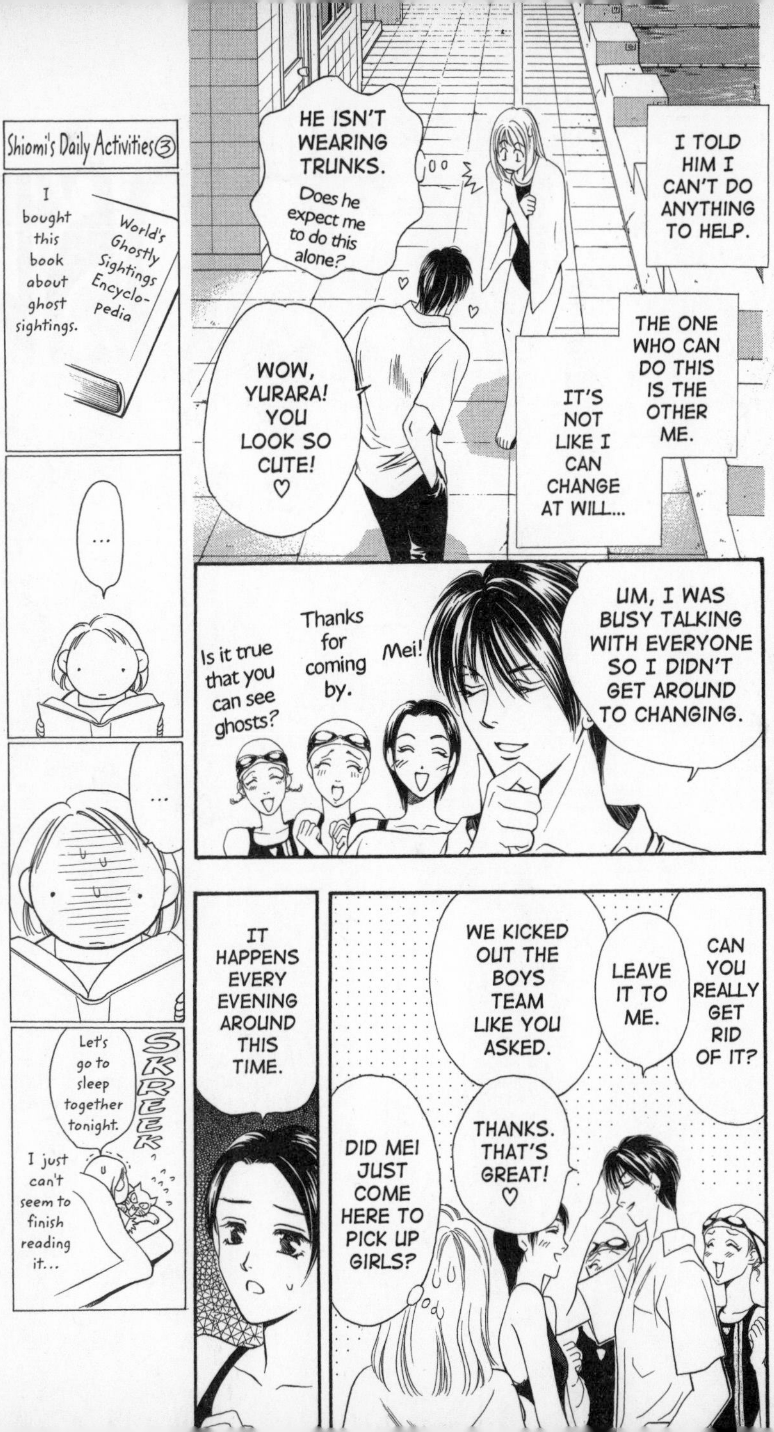
I TOLD HIM I CAN'T DO ANYTHING TO HELP.
THE ONE WHO CAN DO THIS IS THE OTHER ME.
IT'S NOT LIKE I CAN CHANGE AT WILL...
HE ISN'T WEARING TRUNKS.
Does he expect me to do this alone?
WOW, YURARA! YOU LOOK SO CUTE! ♡
UM, I WAS BUSY TALKING WITH EVERYONE SO I DIDN'T GET AROUND TO CHANGING.
Mei!
Thanks for coming by.
Is it true that you can see ghosts?
CAN YOU REALLY GET RID OF IT?
LEAVE IT TO ME.
WE KICKED OUT THE BOYS TEAM LIKE YOU ASKED.
THANKS. THAT'S GREAT! ♡
DID MEI JUST COME HERE TO PICK UP GIRLS?
IT HAPPENS EVERY EVENING AROUND THIS TIME.
Shiomi's Daily Activities ③
I bought this book about ghost sightings.
World's Ghostly Sightings Encyclopedia
...
...
Let's go to sleep together tonight.
SKREEK
I just can't seem to finish reading it...

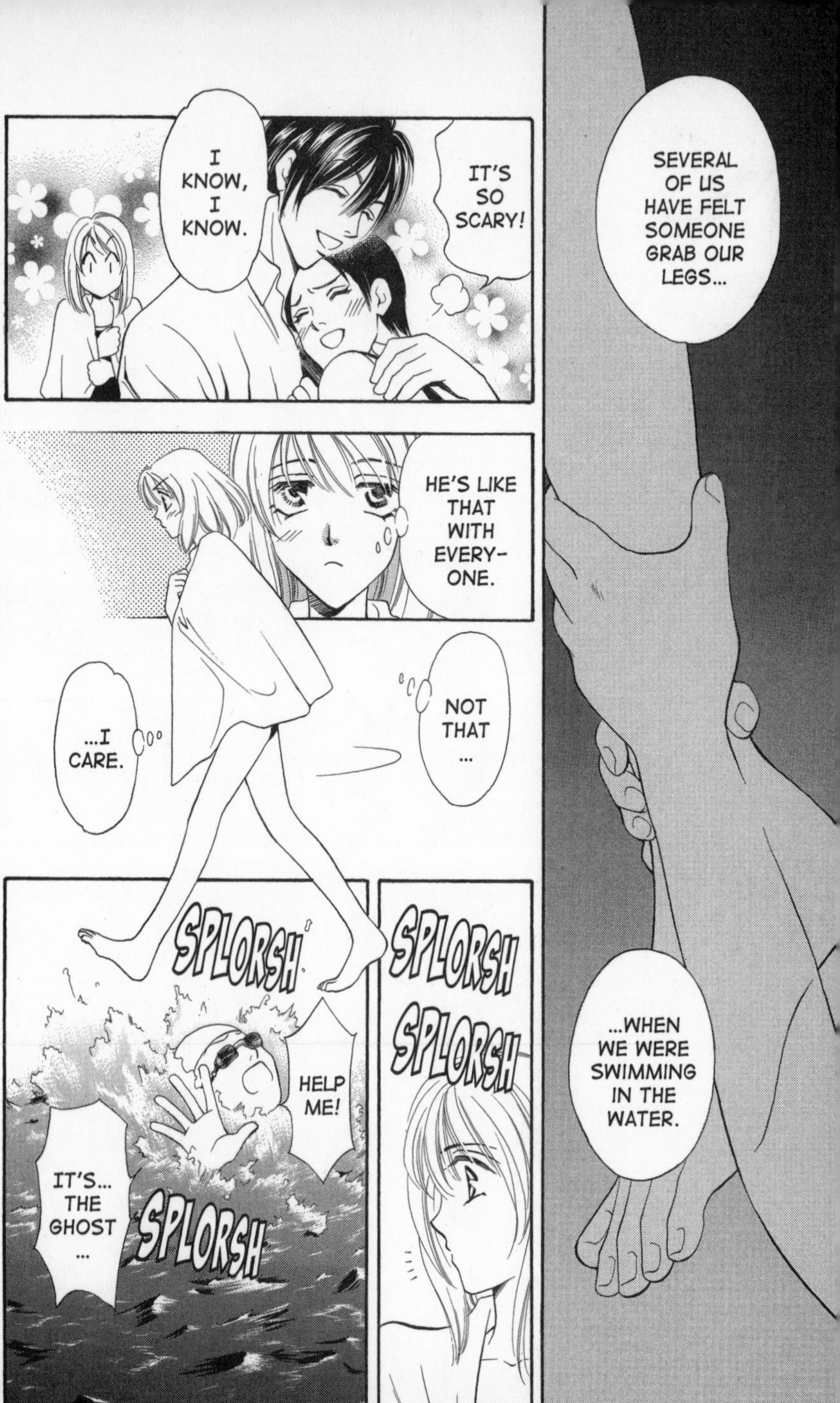
SEVERAL OF US HAVE FELT SOMEONE GRAB OUR LEGS...
...WHEN WE WERE SWIMMING IN THE WATER.
IT'S SO SCARY!
I KNOW, I KNOW.
HE'S LIKE THAT WITH EVERY-ONE.
NOT THAT...
...I CARE.
SPLORSH
SPLORSH
SPLORSH
SPLORSH
HELP ME!
IT'S... THE GHOST...
SPLORSH

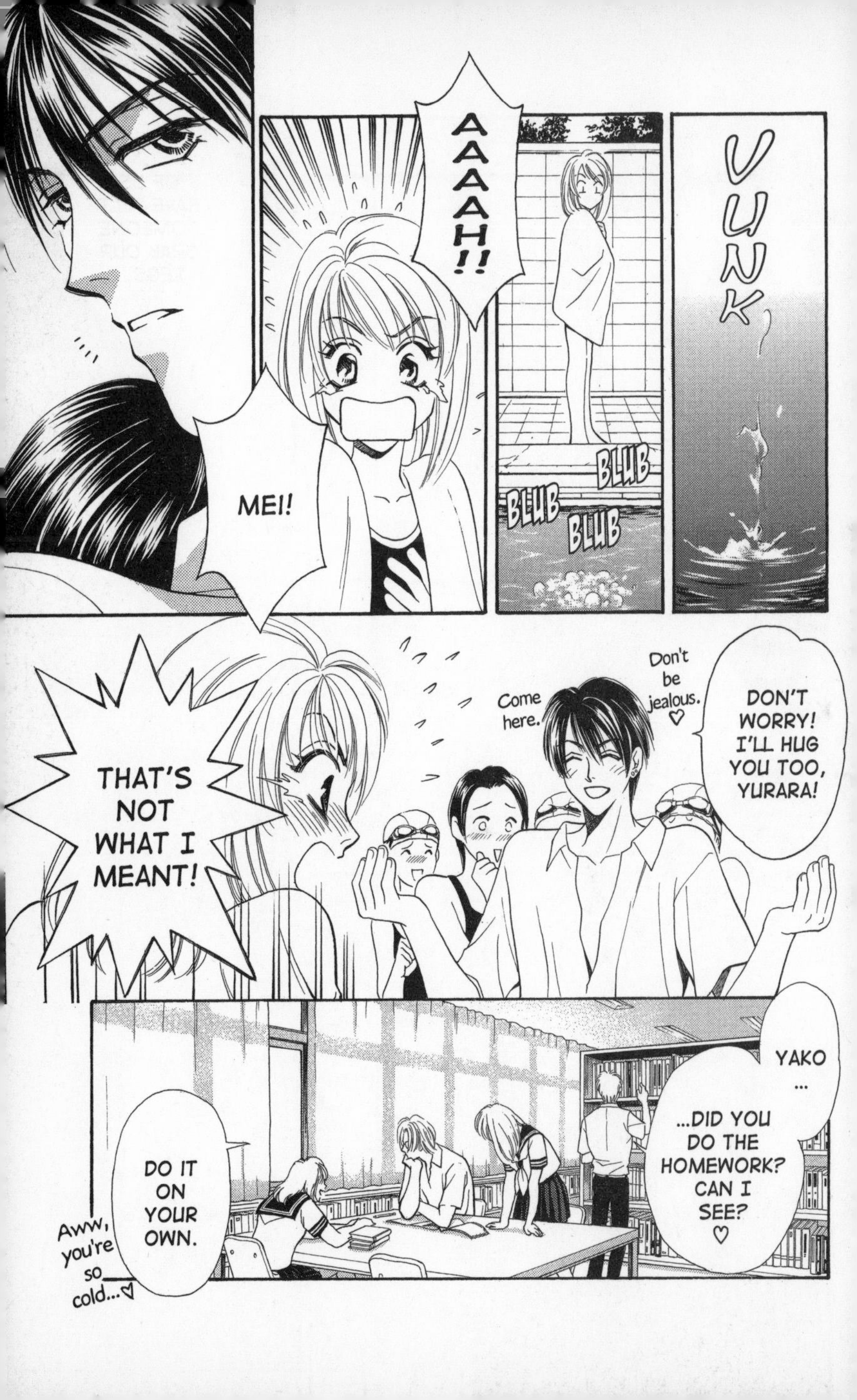
VUNK
BLUB BLUB BLUB
AAAAH!!
MEI!
DON'T WORRY! I'LL HUG YOU TOO, YURARA!
Don't be jealous. ♡
Come here.
THAT'S NOT WHAT I MEANT!
YAKO ...
...DID YOU DO THE HOMEWORK? CAN I SEE? ♡
DO IT ON YOUR OWN.
Aww, you're so cold...♡

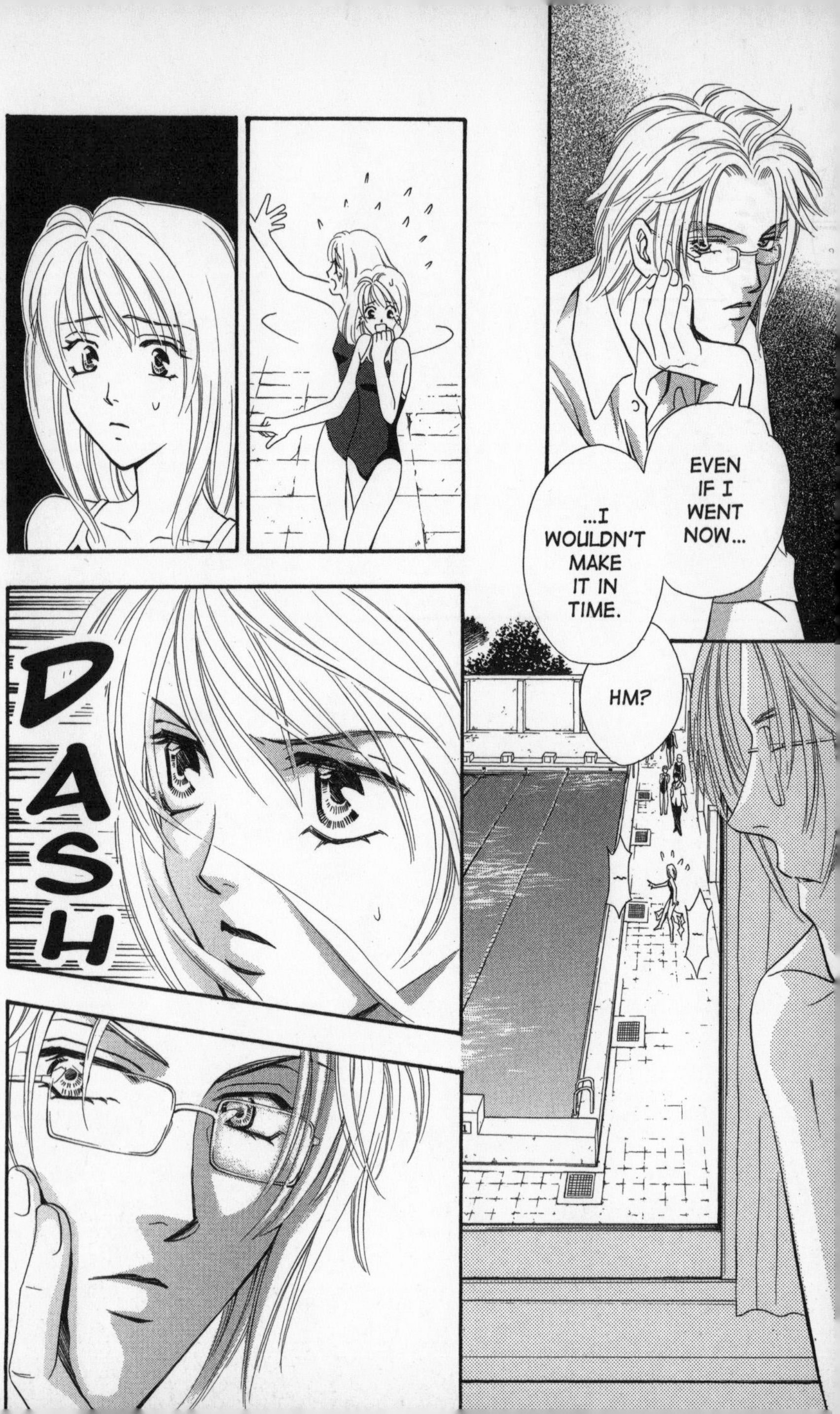
EVEN IF I WENT NOW...
...I WOULDN'T MAKE IT IN TIME.
HM?
DASH

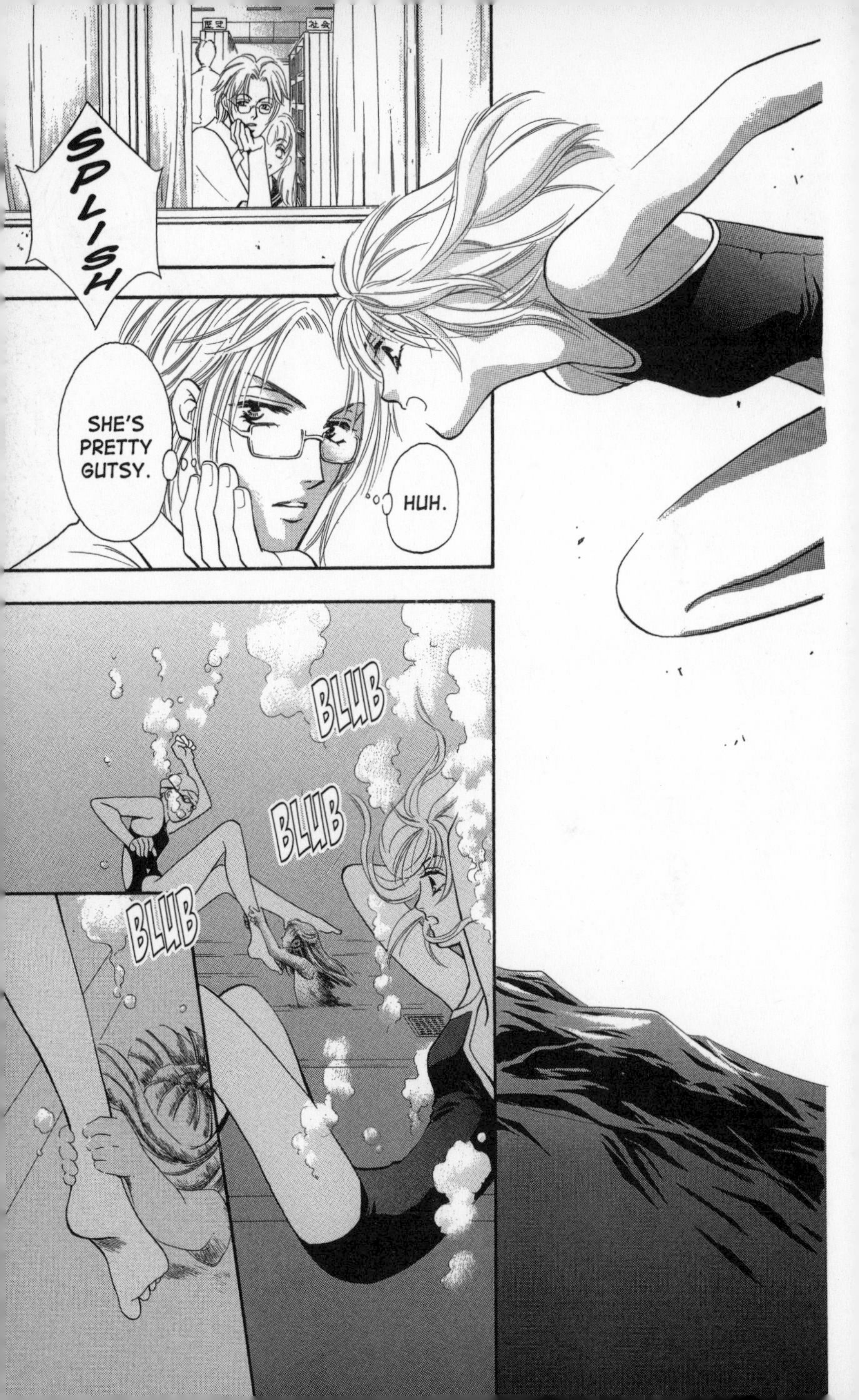
SPLISH
HUH.
SHE'S PRETTY GUTSY.
BLUB
BLUB
BLUB

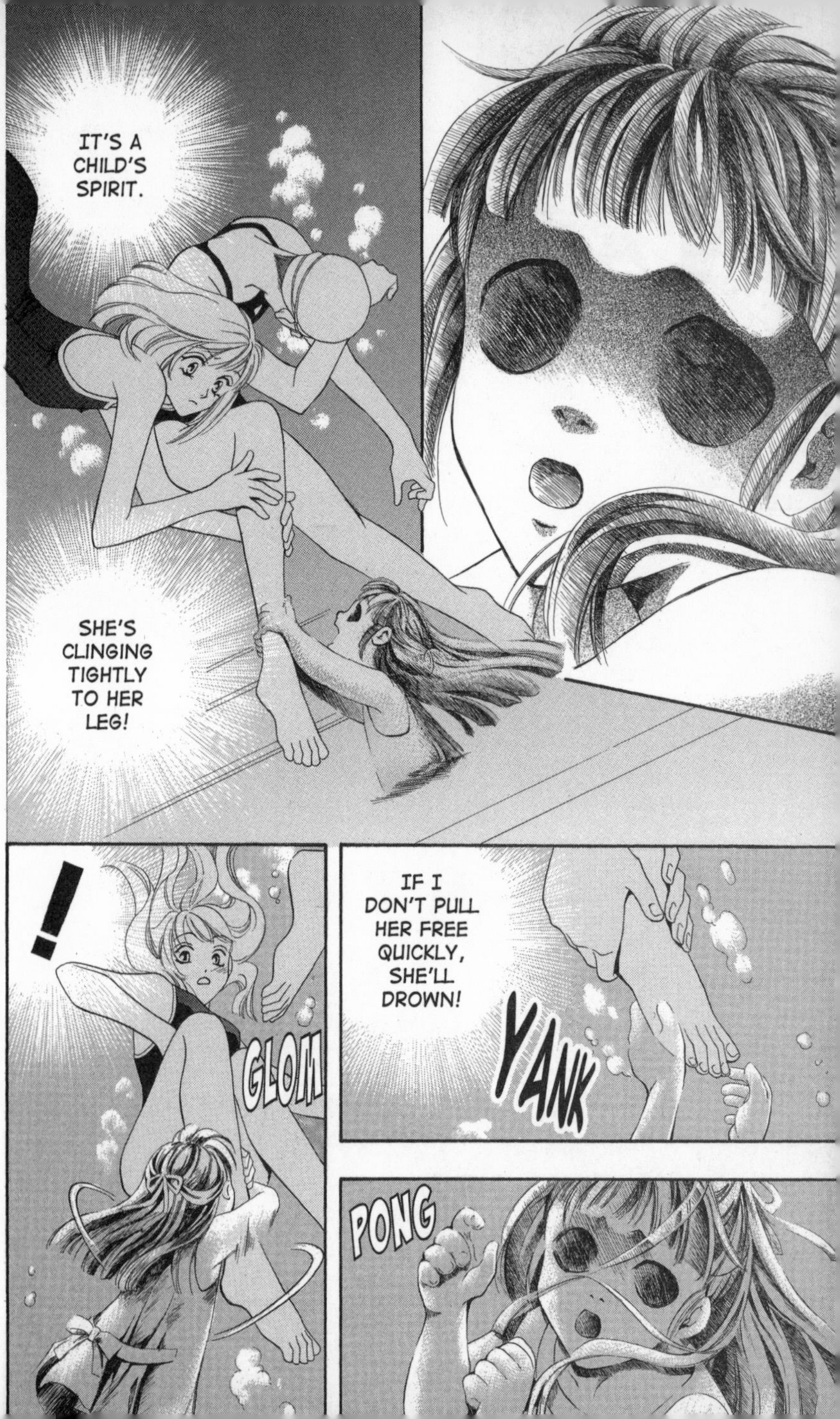
IT'S A CHILD'S SPIRIT.
SHE'S CLINGING TIGHTLY TO HER LEG!
IF I DON'T PULL HER FREE QUICKLY, SHE'LL DROWN!
YANK
PONG
!
GLOM

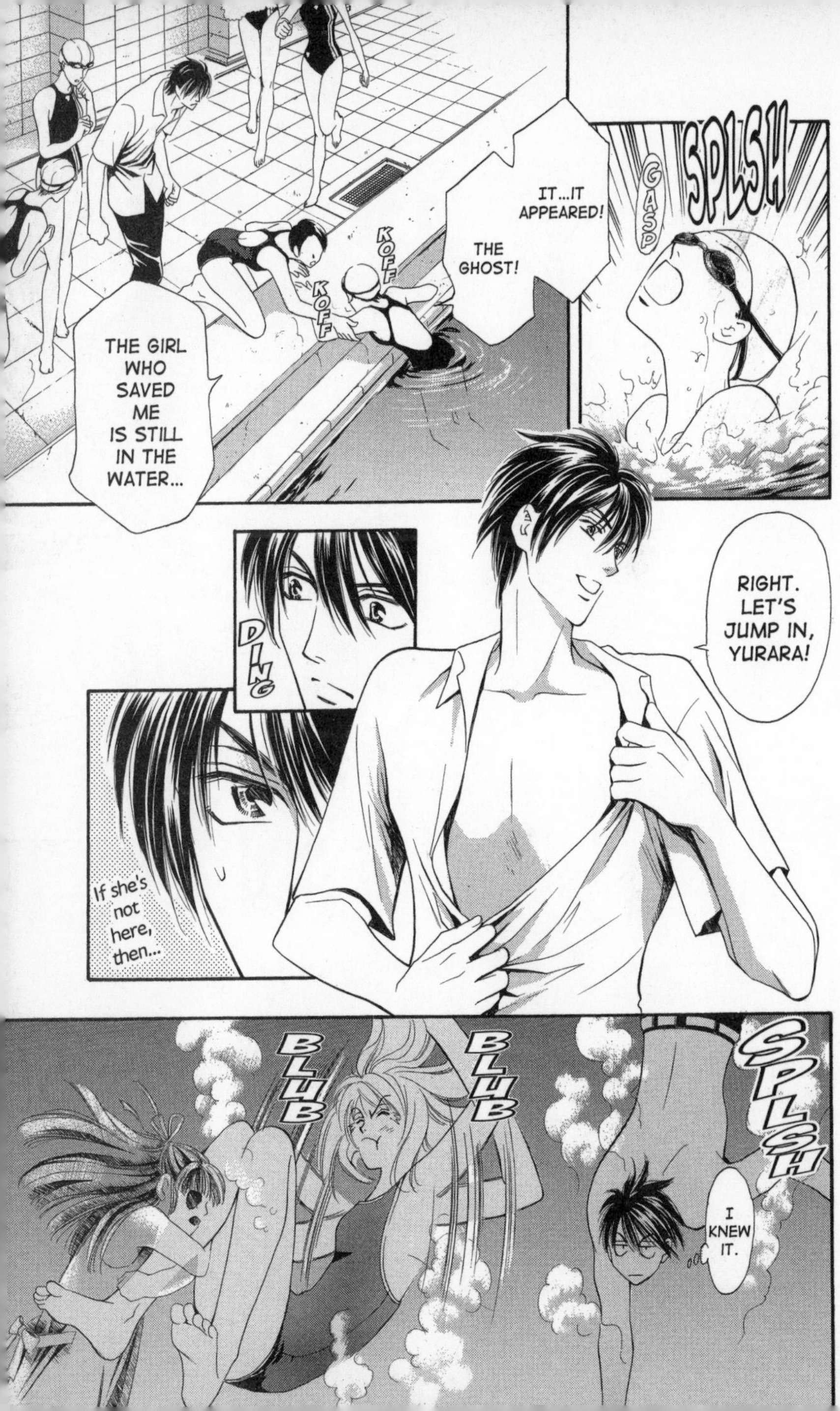
SPLSH
GASP
IT...IT APPEARED!
THE GHOST!
KOFF
KOFF
THE GIRL WHO SAVED ME IS STILL IN THE WATER...
RIGHT. LET'S JUMP IN, YURARA!
DING
If she's not here, then...
SPLSH
I KNEW IT.
BLUB
BLUB

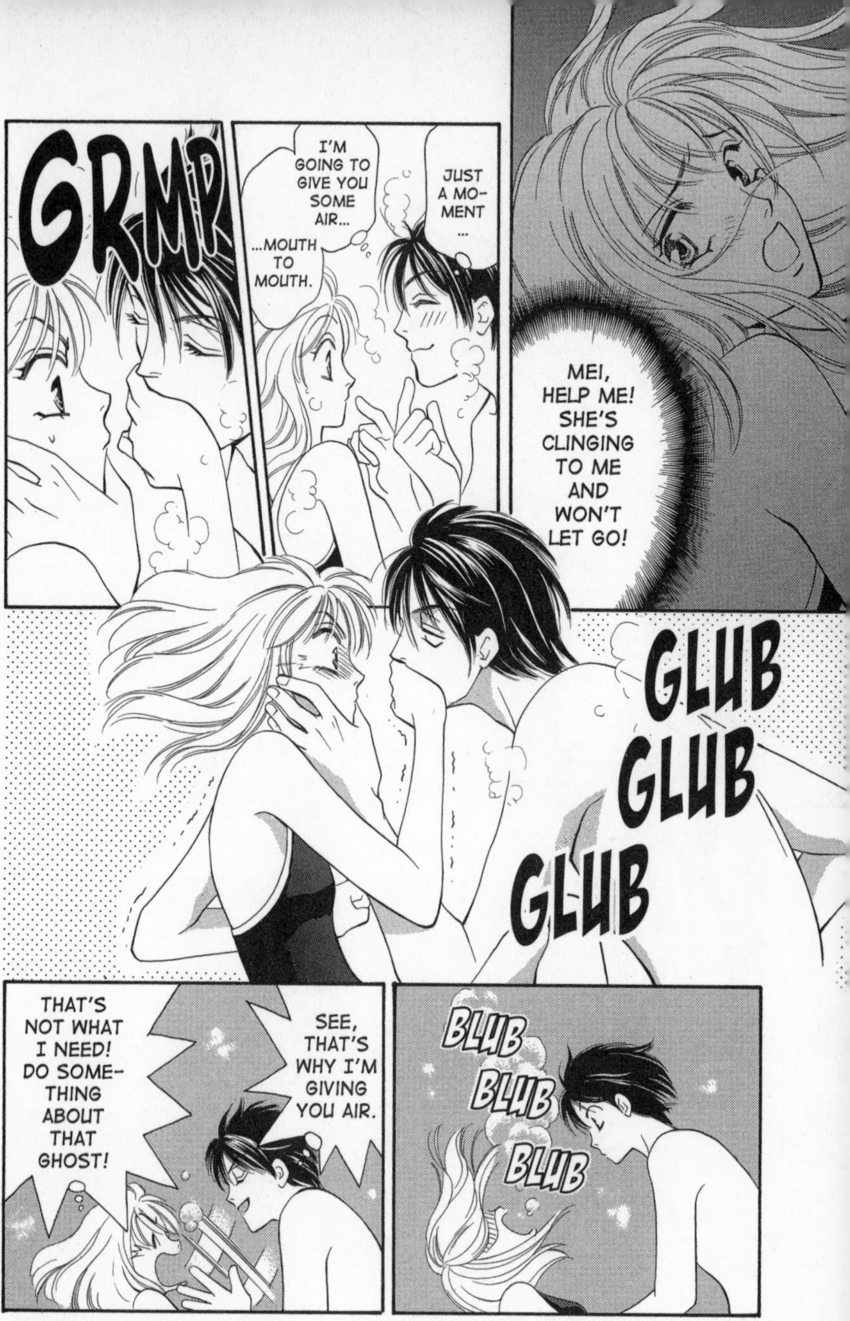
MEI, HELP ME! SHE'S CLINGING TO ME AND WON'T LET GO!
JUST A MO-MENT ...
I'M GOING TO GIVE YOU SOME AIR...
...MOUTH TO MOUTH.
GRMP
GLUB GLUB GLUB
BLUB BLUB BLUB
SEE, THAT'S WHY I'M GIVING YOU AIR.
THAT'S NOT WHAT I NEED! DO SOME-THING ABOUT THAT GHOST!

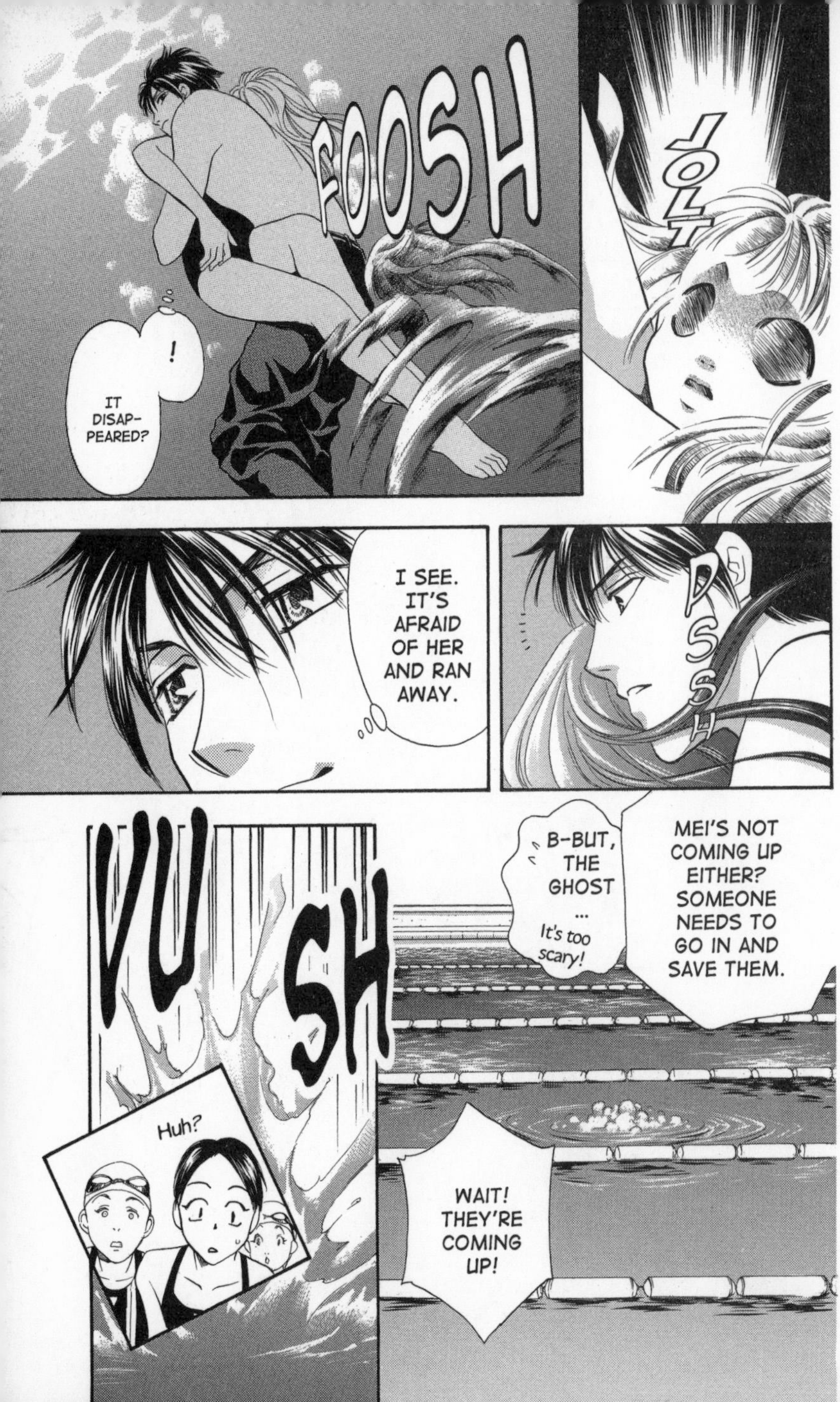
JOLT
FOOSH
!
IT DISAP-PEARED?
PSSH
I SEE. IT'S AFRAID OF HER AND RAN AWAY.
MEI'S NOT COMING UP EITHER? SOMEONE NEEDS TO GO IN AND SAVE THEM.
B-BUT, THE GHOST ...
It's too scary!
WAIT! THEY'RE COMING UP!
VUSH
Huh?

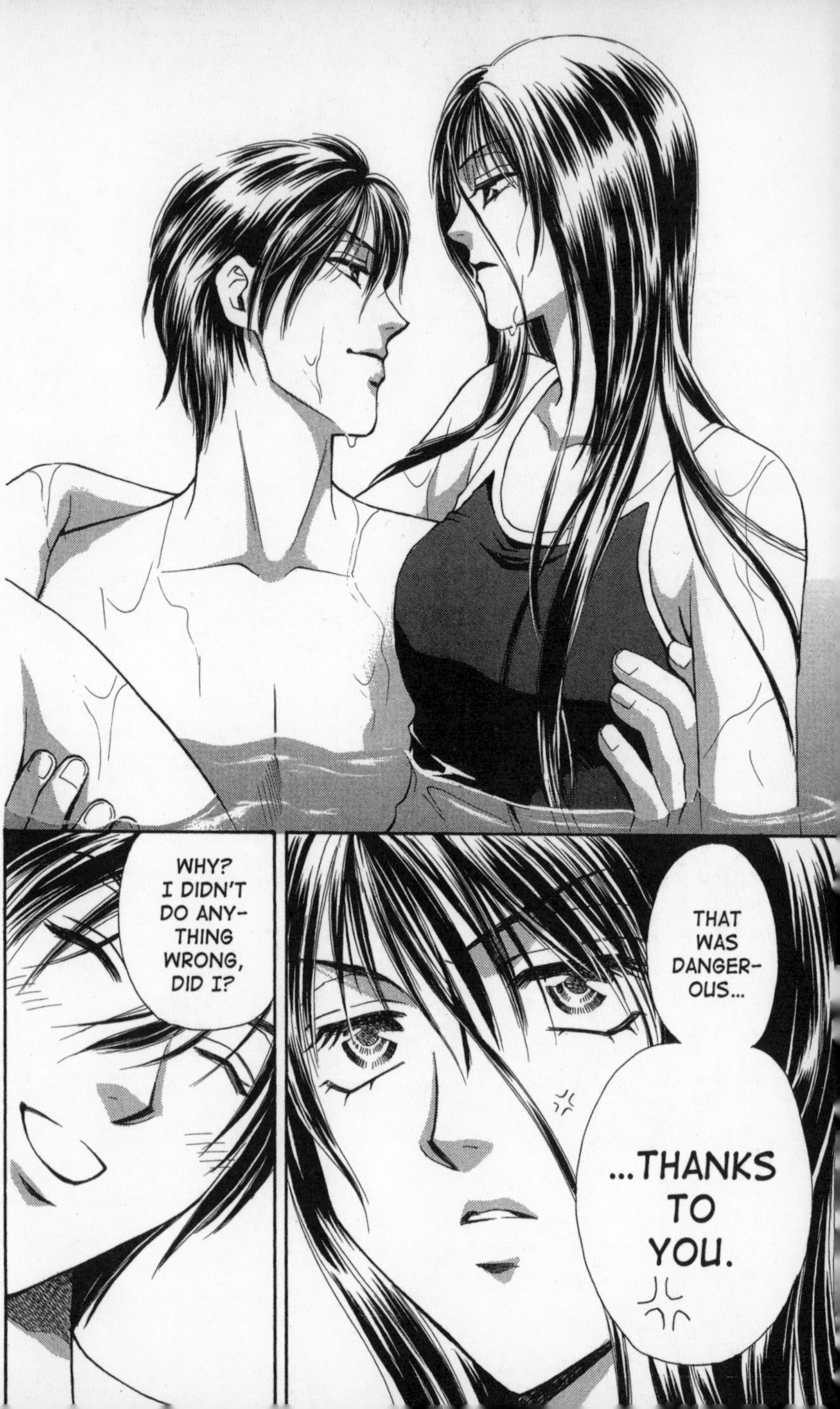
THAT WAS DANGEROUS...
...THANKS TO YOU.
WHY? I DIDN'T DO ANYTHING WRONG, DID I?

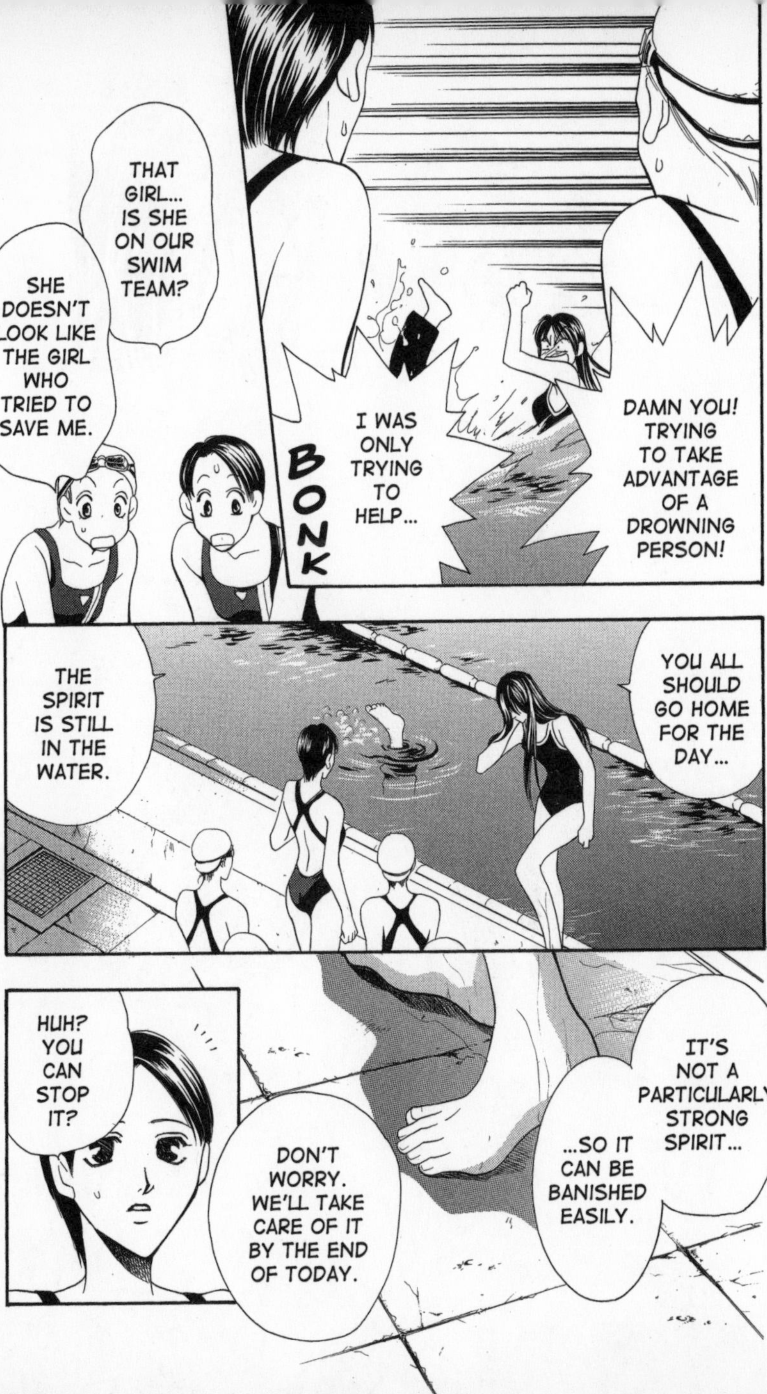

DAMN YOU! TRYING TO TAKE ADVANTAGE OF A DROWNING PERSON!
I WAS ONLY TRYING TO HELP...
BONK
THAT GIRL... IS SHE ON OUR SWIM TEAM?
SHE DOESN'T LOOK LIKE THE GIRL WHO TRIED TO SAVE ME.
YOU ALL SHOULD GO HOME FOR THE DAY...
THE SPIRIT IS STILL IN THE WATER.
IT'S NOT A PARTICULARLY STRONG SPIRIT...
...SO IT CAN BE BANISHED EASILY.
DON'T WORRY. WE'LL TAKE CARE OF IT BY THE END OF TODAY.
HUH? YOU CAN STOP IT?

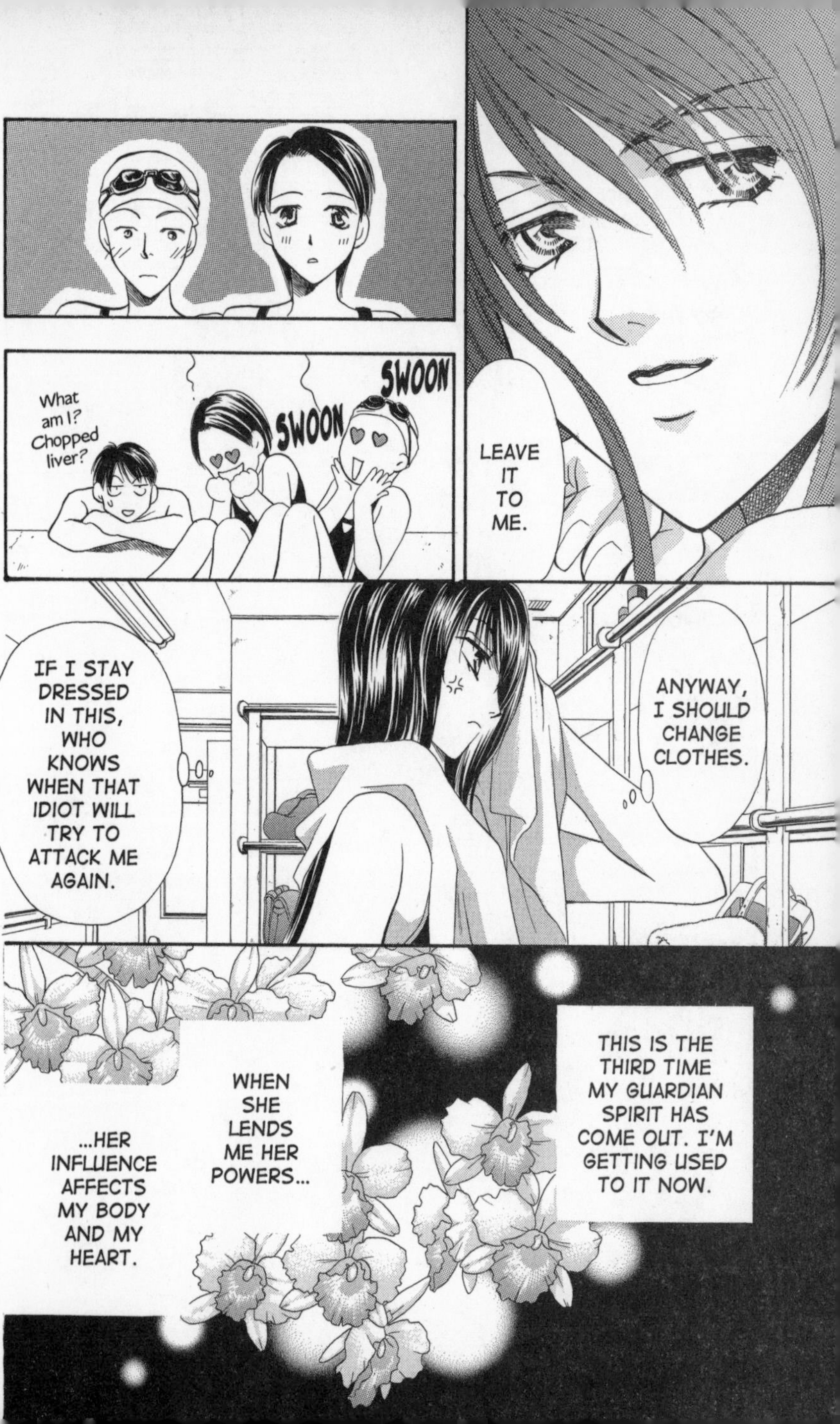

LEAVE IT TO ME.
SWOON
SWOON
What am I? Chopped liver?
ANYWAY, I SHOULD CHANGE CLOTHES.
IF I STAY DRESSED IN THIS, WHO KNOWS WHEN THAT IDIOT WILL TRY TO ATTACK ME AGAIN.
THIS IS THE THIRD TIME MY GUARDIAN SPIRIT HAS COME OUT. I'M GETTING USED TO IT NOW.
WHEN SHE LENDS ME HER POWERS...
...HER INFLUENCE AFFECTS MY BODY AND MY HEART.

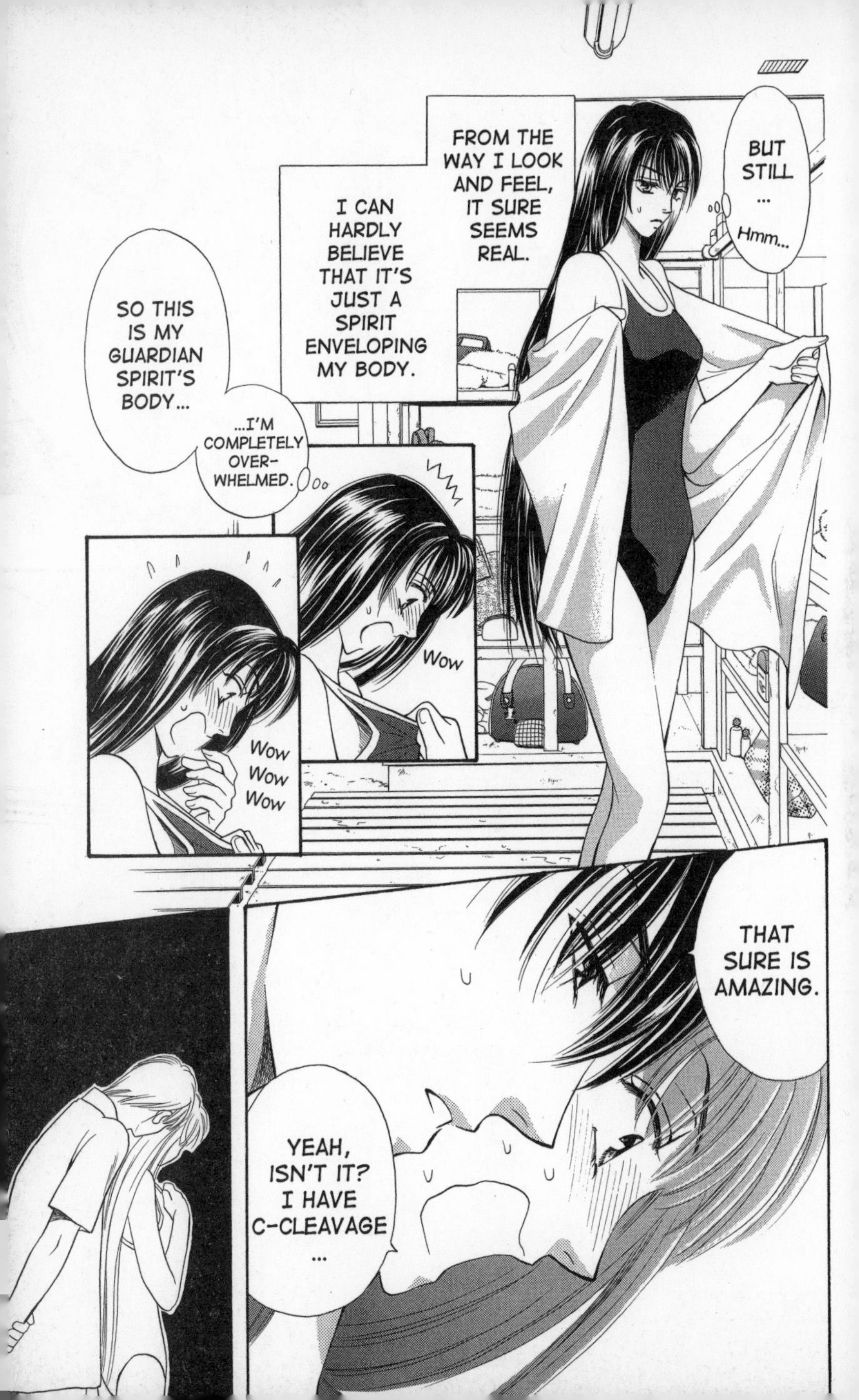
BUT STILL ...
Hmm...
FROM THE WAY I LOOK AND FEEL, IT SURE SEEMS REAL.
I CAN HARDLY BELIEVE THAT IT'S JUST A SPIRIT ENVELOPING MY BODY.
SO THIS IS MY GUARDIAN SPIRIT'S BODY...
...I'M COMPLETELY OVER-WHELMED.
Wow
Wow Wow Wow
THAT SURE IS AMAZING.
YEAH, ISN'T IT? I HAVE C-CLEAVAGE ...

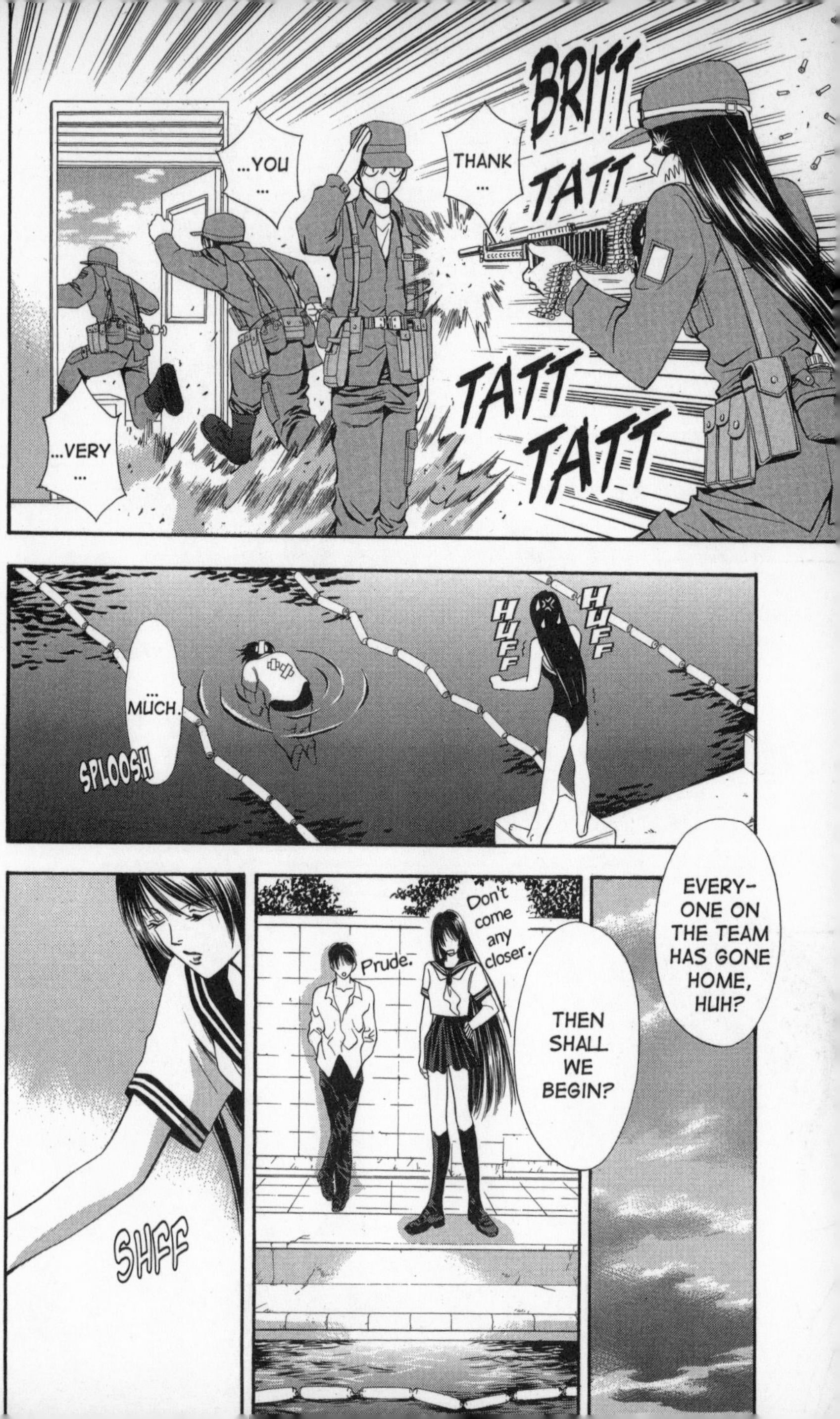
BRITT
TATT
THANK ...
...YOU ...
TATT
TATT
...VERY ...
HUFF
HUFF
... MUCH.
SPLOOSH
EVERY-ONE ON THE TEAM HAS GONE HOME, HUH?
THEN SHALL WE BEGIN?
Don't come any closer.
Prude.
SHFF

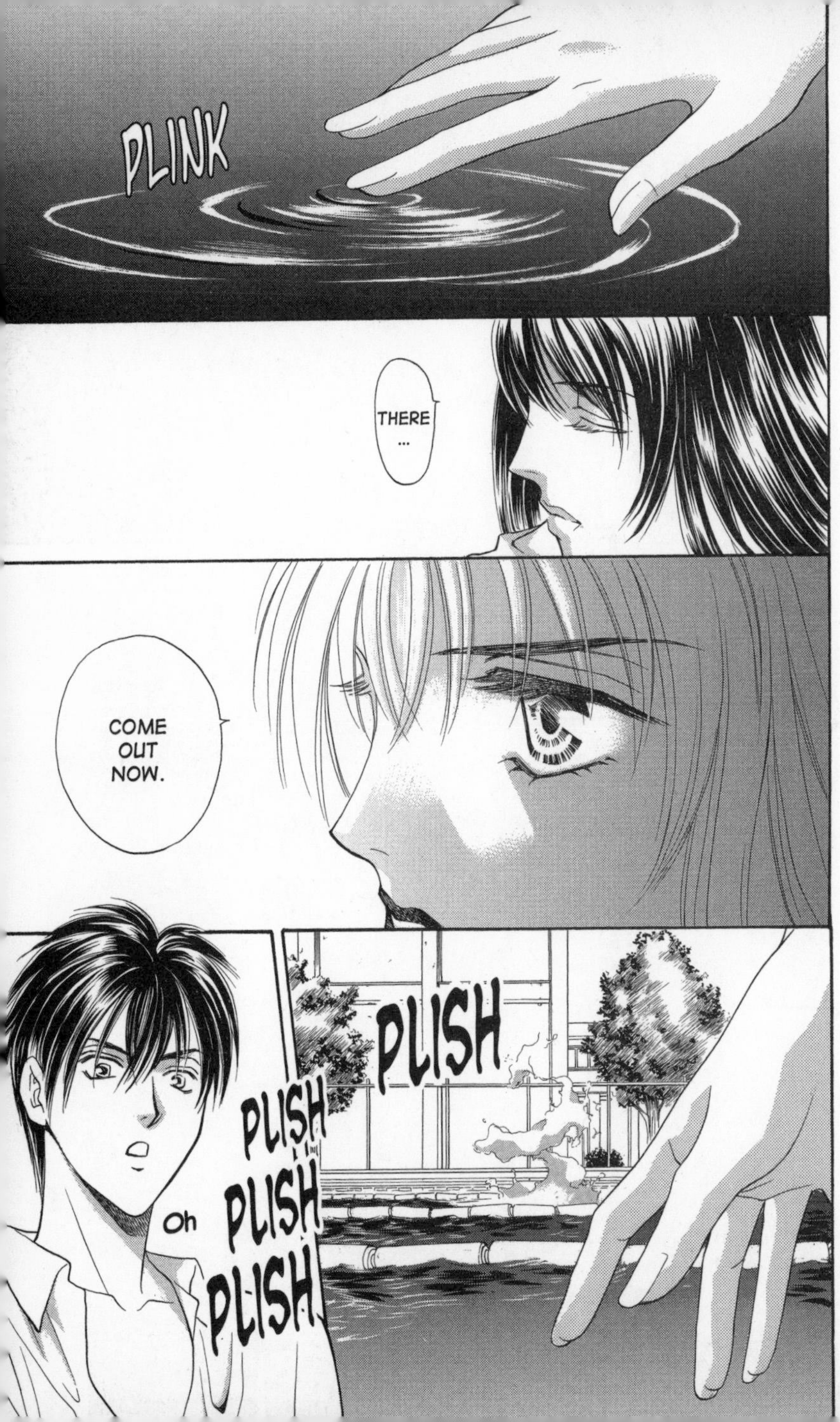
PLINK
THERE ...
COME OUT NOW.
PLISH
PLISH
PLISH
PLISH
Oh

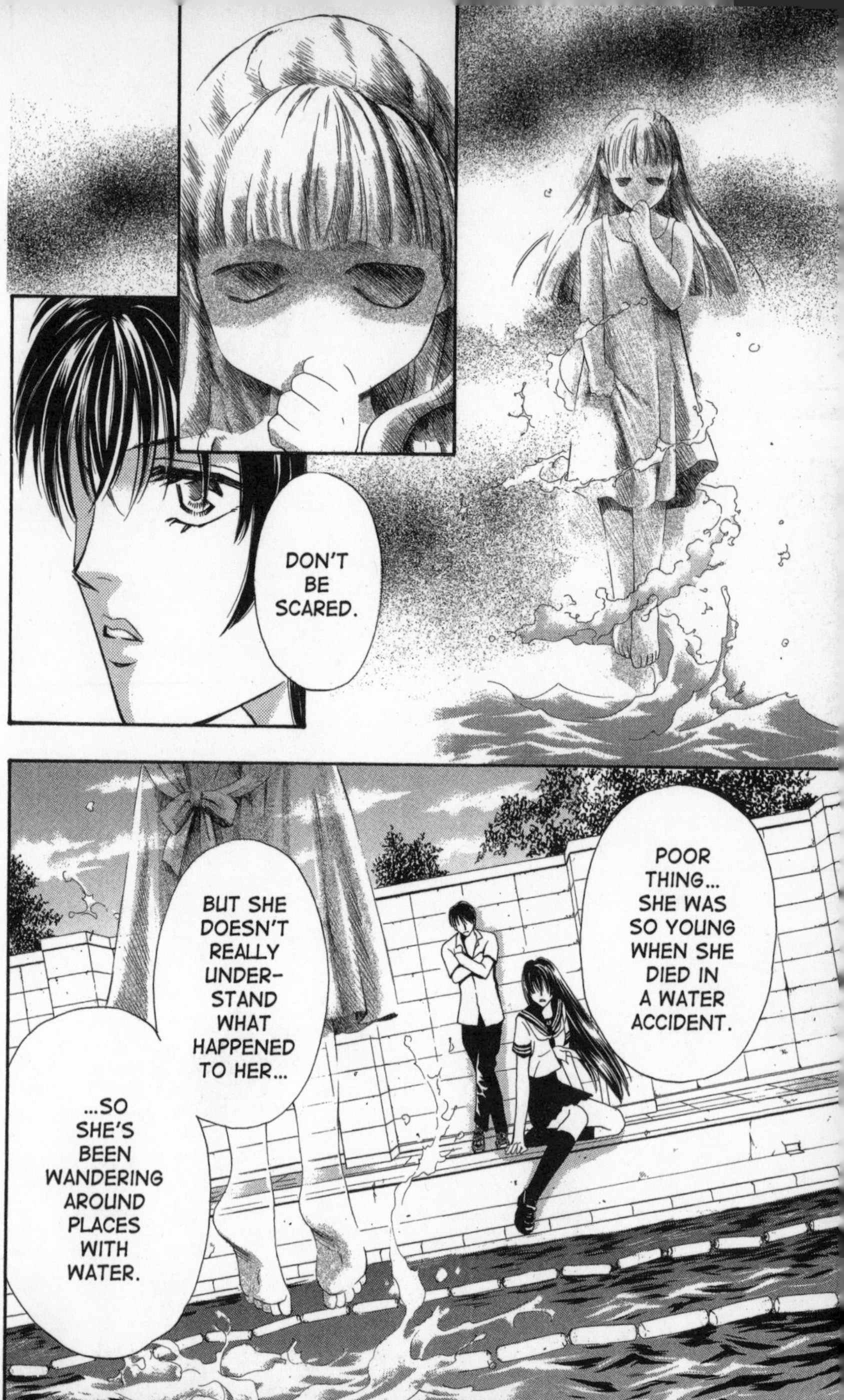
DON'T BE SCARED.
POOR THING... SHE WAS SO YOUNG WHEN SHE DIED IN A WATER ACCIDENT.
BUT SHE DOESN'T REALLY UNDER-STAND WHAT HAPPENED TO HER...
...SO SHE'S BEEN WANDERING AROUND PLACES WITH WATER.

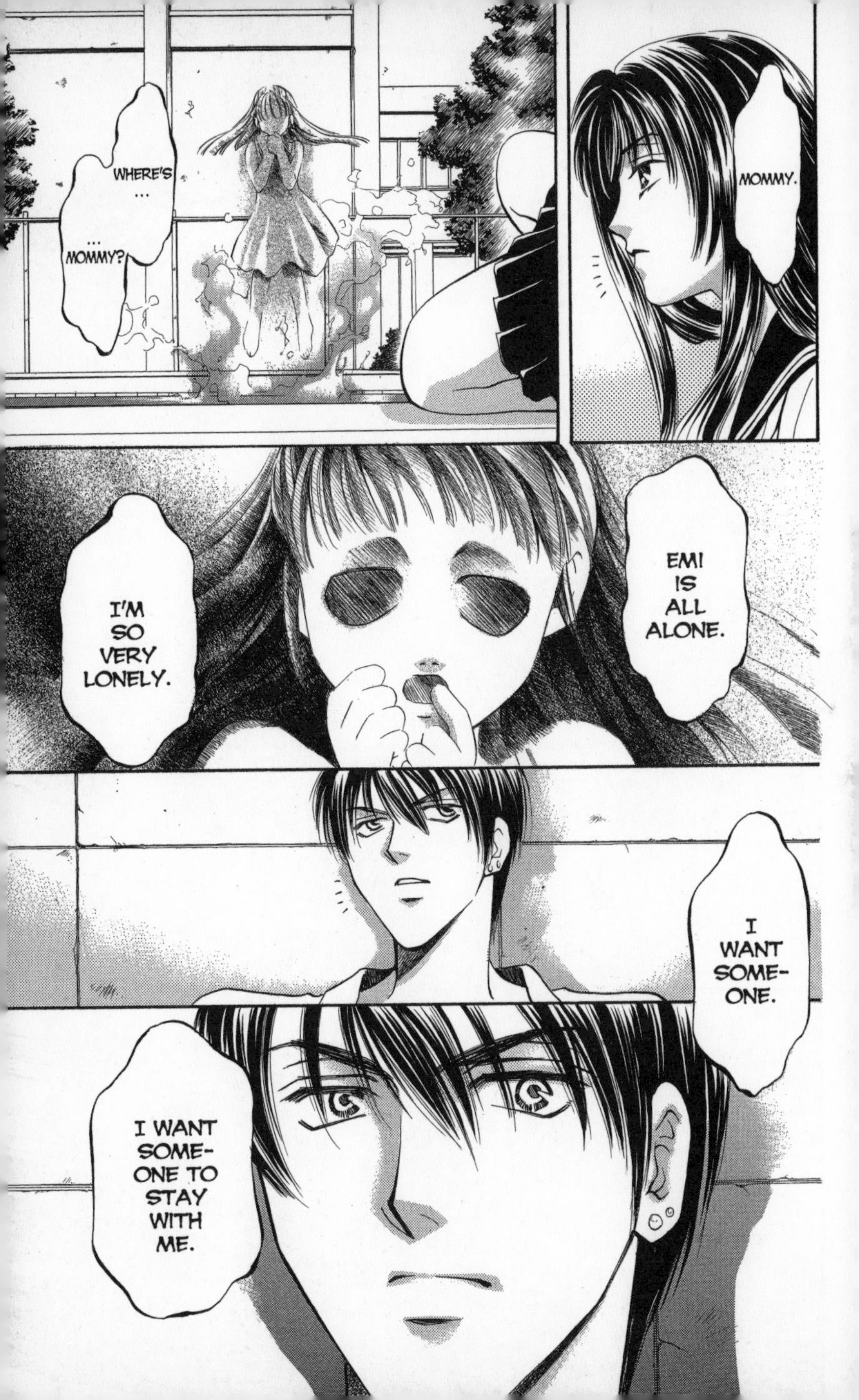
MOMMY.
WHERE'S ... ... MOMMY?
EMI IS ALL ALONE.
I'M SO VERY LONELY.
I WANT SOME-ONE.
I WANT SOME-ONE TO STAY WITH ME.

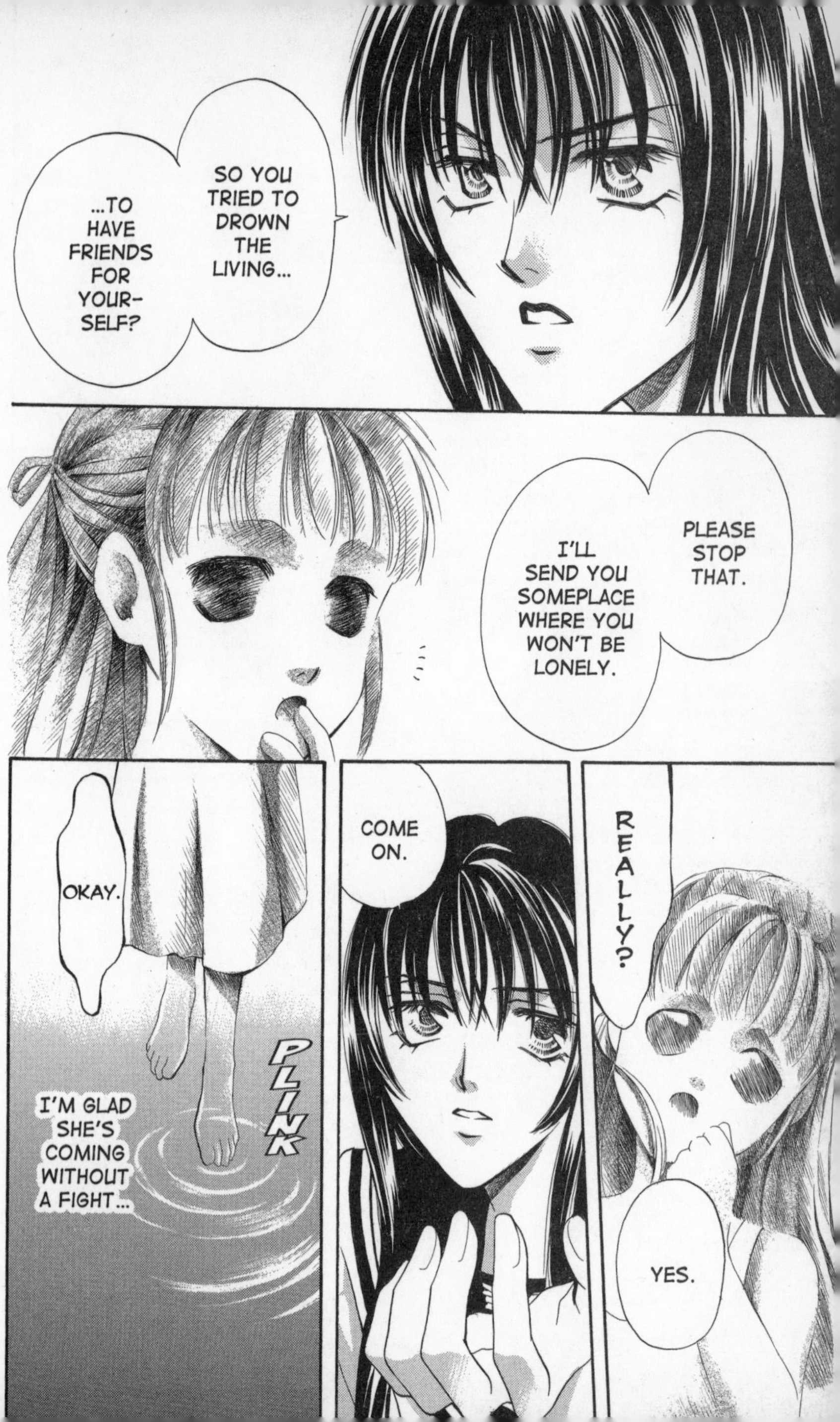
SO YOU TRIED TO DROWN THE LIVING...
...TO HAVE FRIENDS FOR YOUR-SELF?
PLEASE STOP THAT.
I'LL SEND YOU SOMEPLACE WHERE YOU WON'T BE LONELY.
REALLY?
YES.
COME ON.
OKAY.
PLINK
I'M GLAD SHE'S COMING WITHOUT A FIGHT...

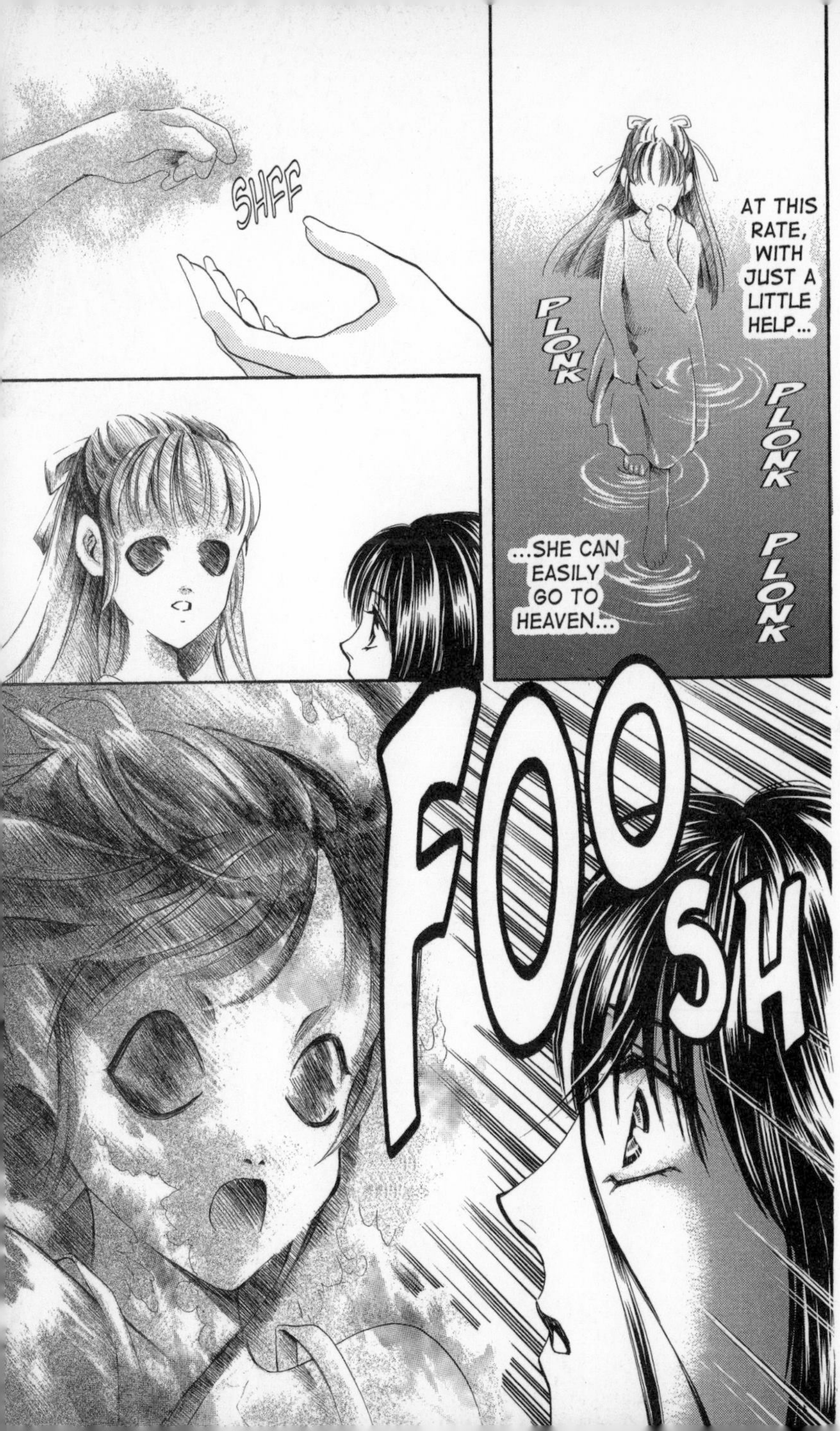
AT THIS RATE, WITH JUST A LITTLE HELP...
PLONK
PLONK
PLONK
PLONK
...SHE CAN EASILY GO TO HEAVEN...
SHFF
FOOSH

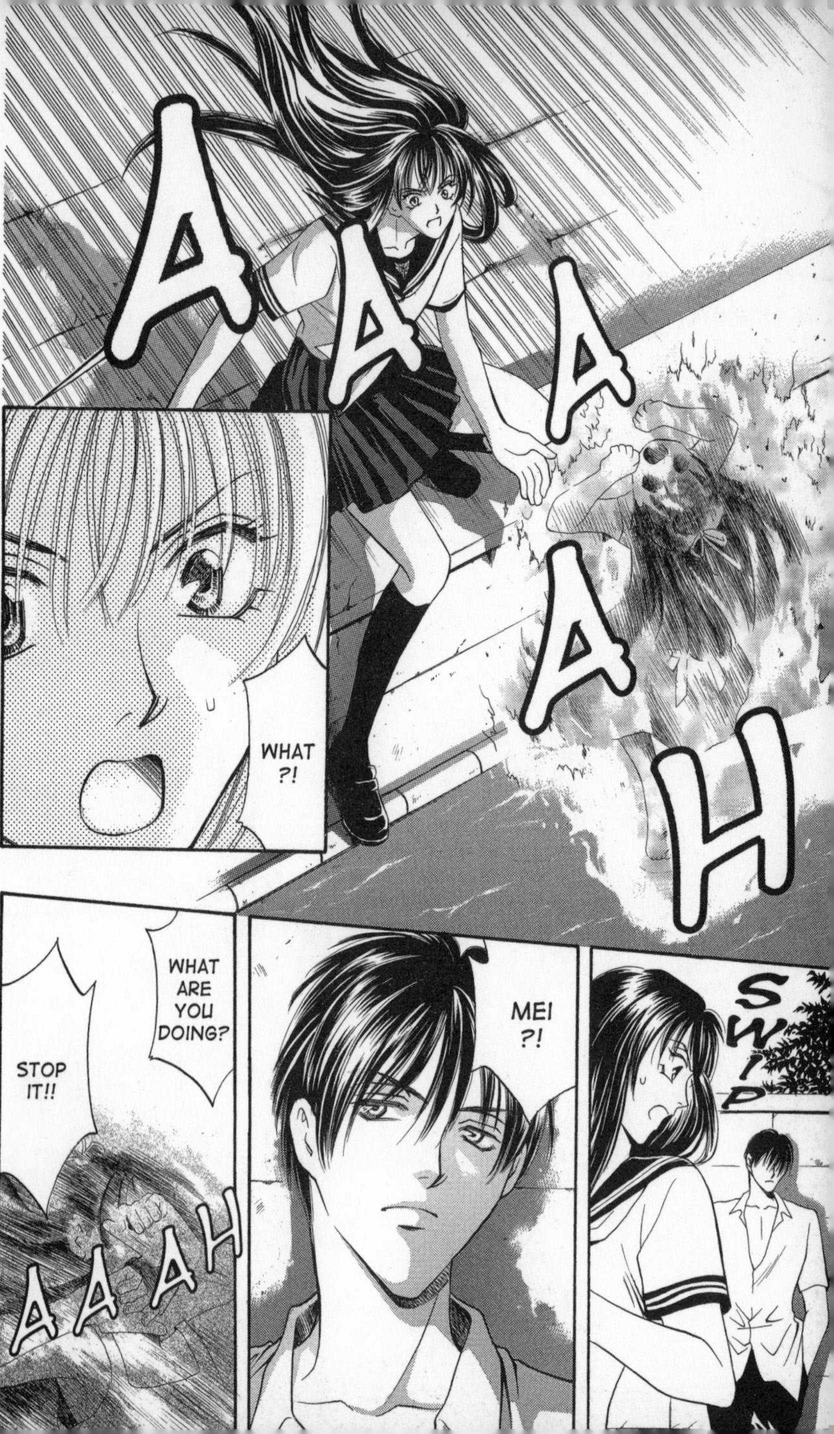
AAAAH
WHAT ?!
SWIP
MEI ?!
WHAT ARE YOU DOING?
STOP IT!!
AAAH

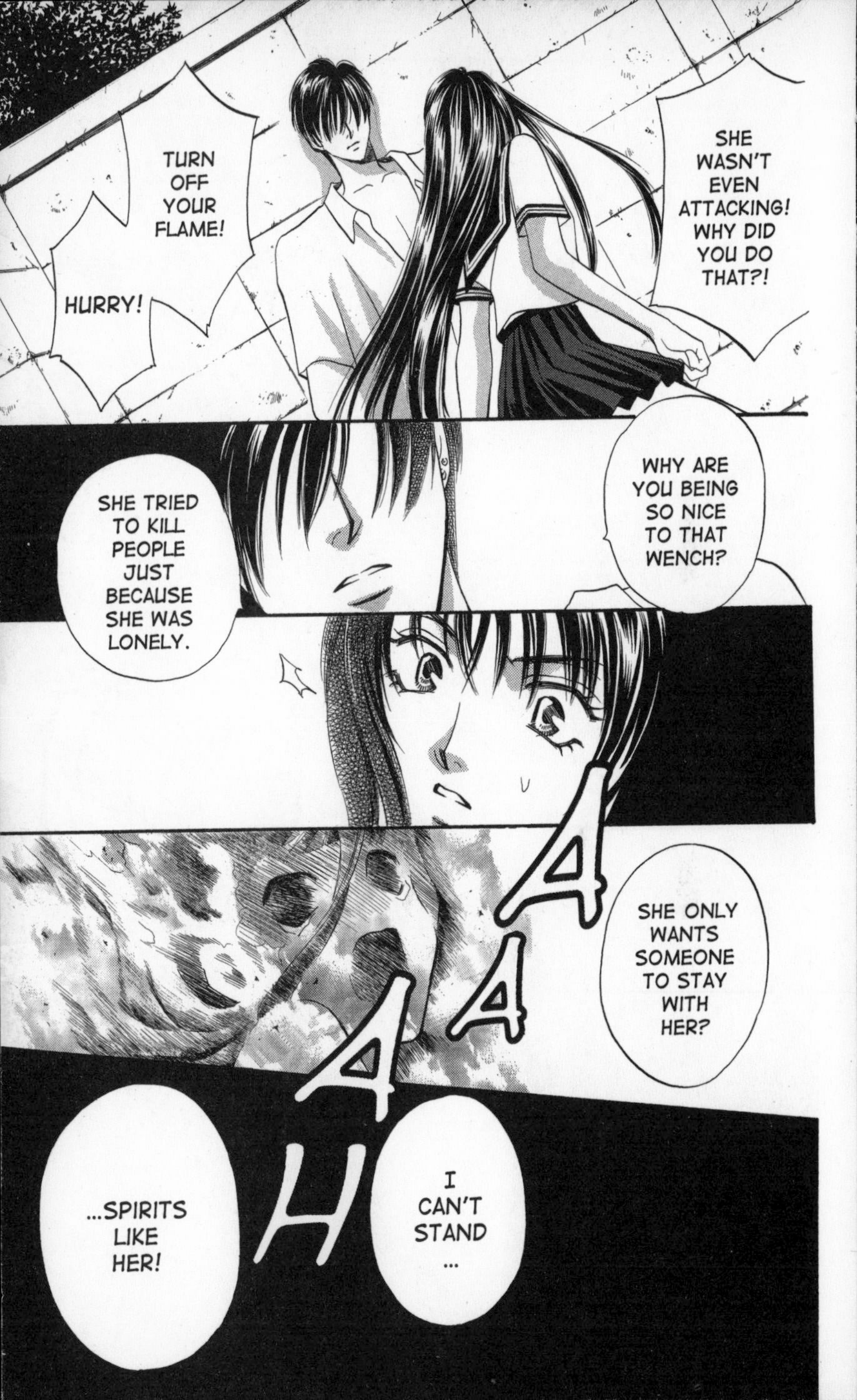
SHE WASN'T EVEN ATTACKING! WHY DID YOU DO THAT?!
TURN OFF YOUR FLAME! HURRY!
WHY ARE YOU BEING SO NICE TO THAT WENCH?
SHE TRIED TO KILL PEOPLE JUST BECAUSE SHE WAS LONELY.
SHE ONLY WANTS SOMEONE TO STAY WITH HER?
AAAAH
I CAN'T STAND ...
...SPIRITS LIKE HER!

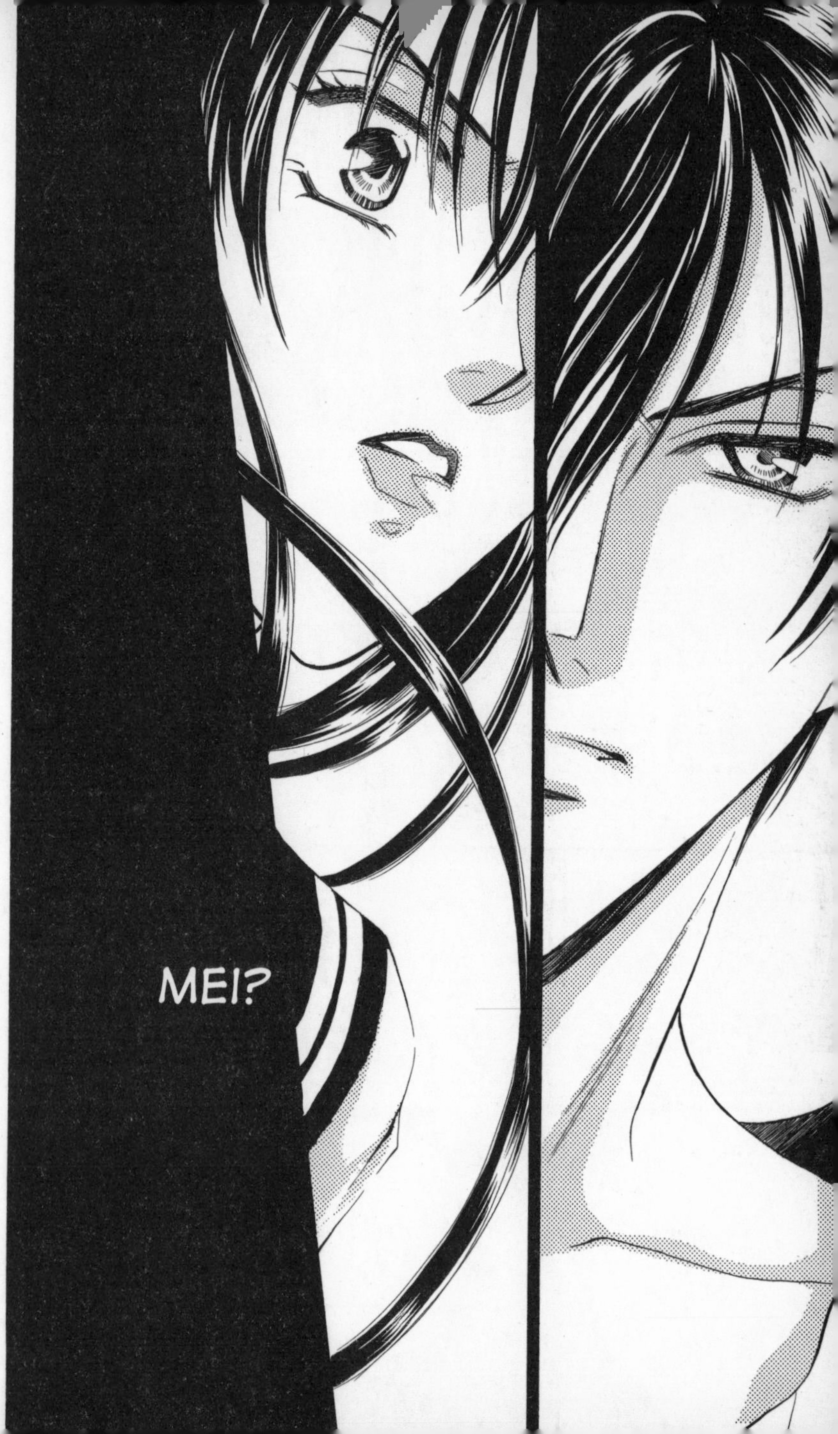
MEI?

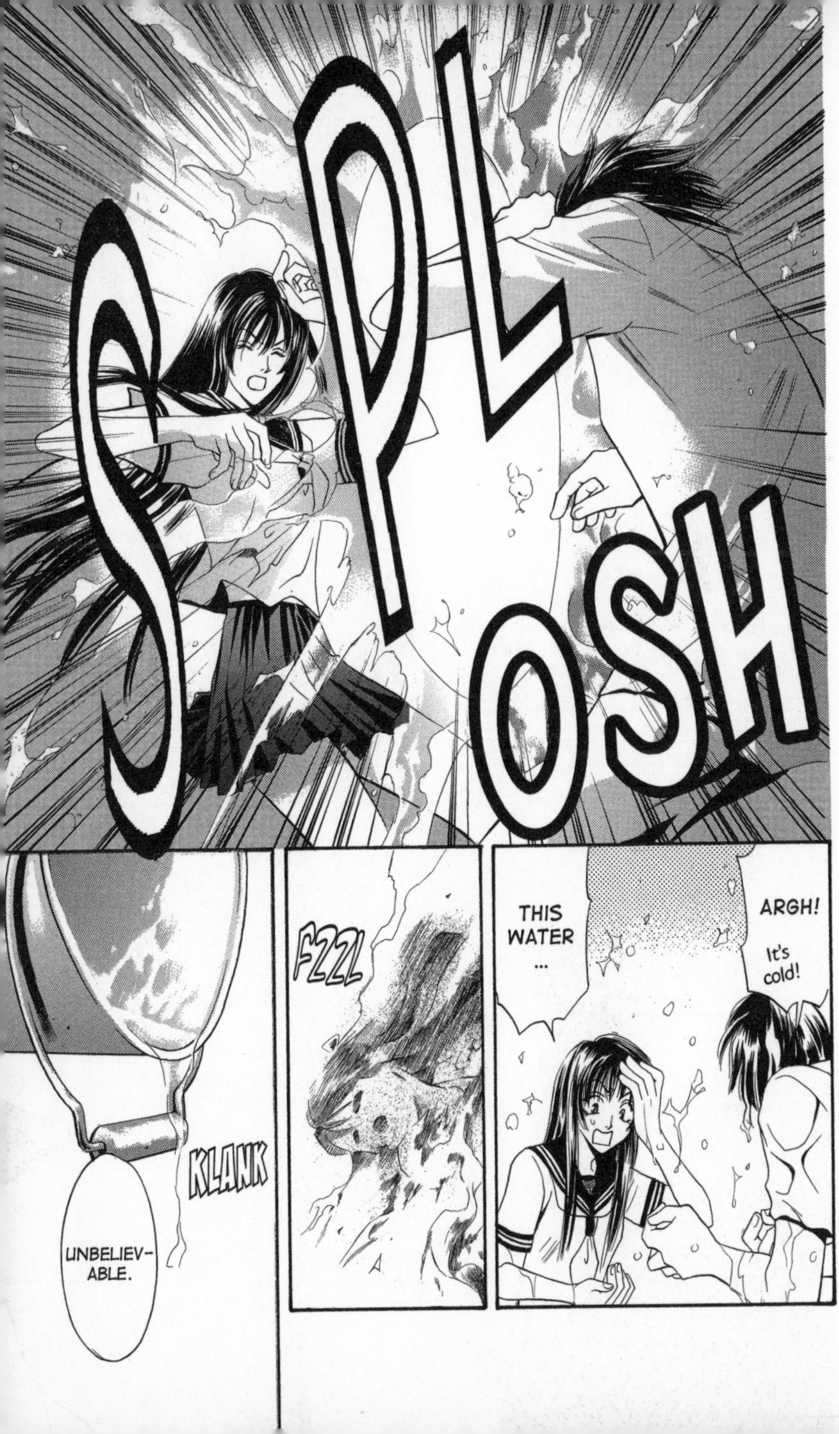
SPLOSH
ARGH!
It's cold!
THIS WATER ...
FZZL
KLANK
UNBELIEV-ABLE.

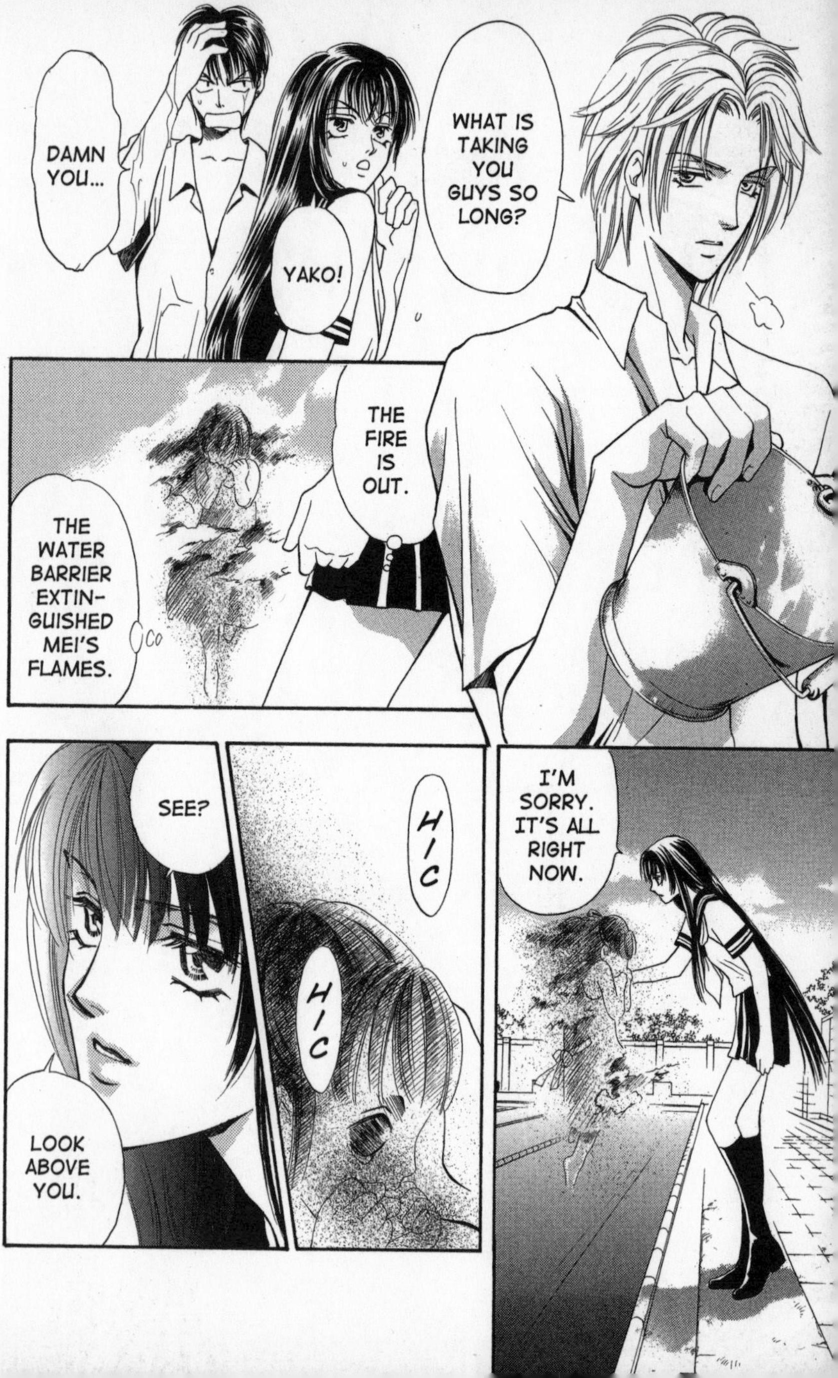
WHAT IS TAKING YOU GUYS SO LONG?
YAKO!
DAMN YOU...
THE FIRE IS OUT.
THE WATER BARRIER EXTIN-GUISHED MEI'S FLAMES.
I'M SORRY. IT'S ALL RIGHT NOW.
HIC
HIC
SEE?
LOOK ABOVE YOU.

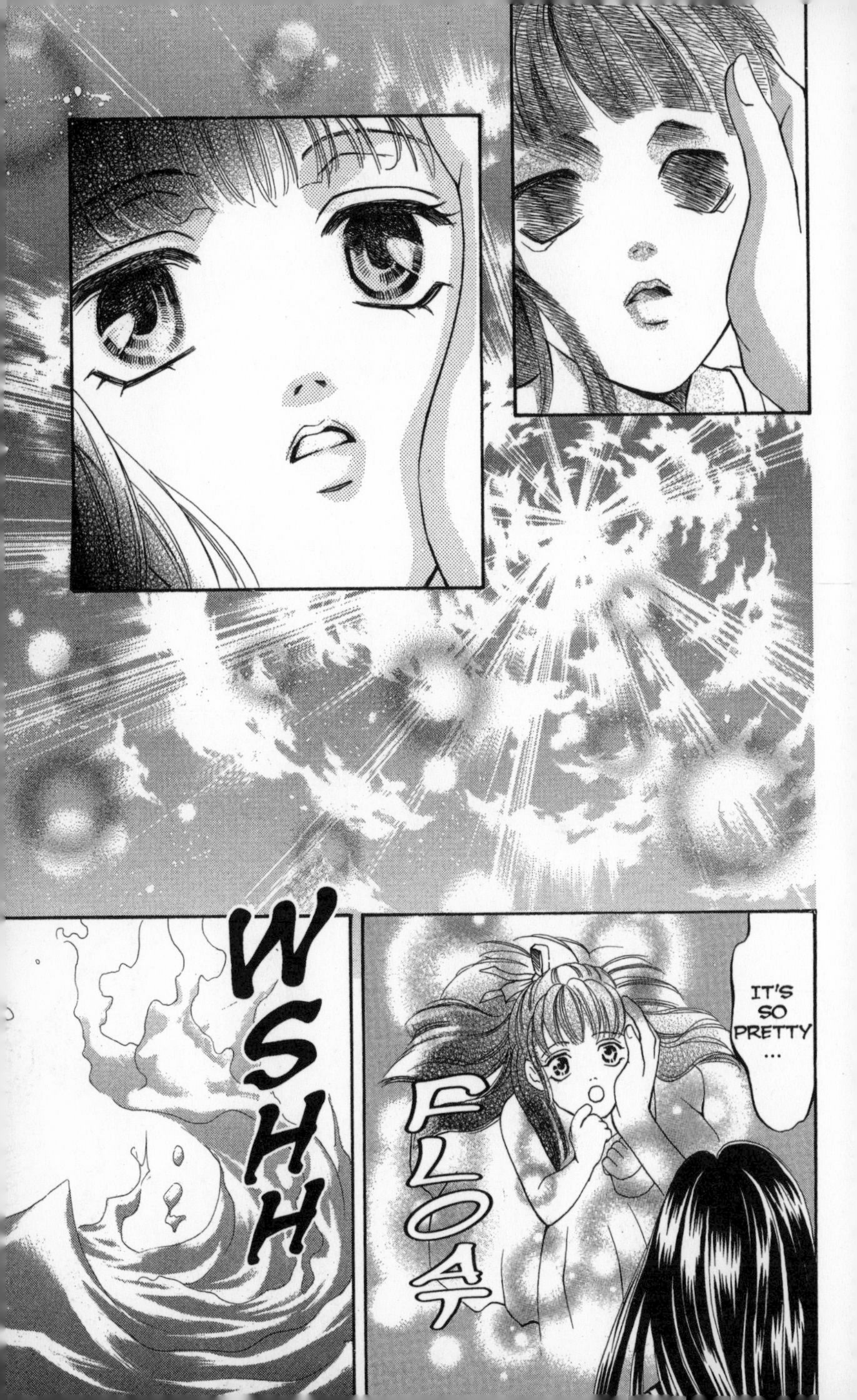
IT'S SO PRETTY ...
FLOAT
WSHH

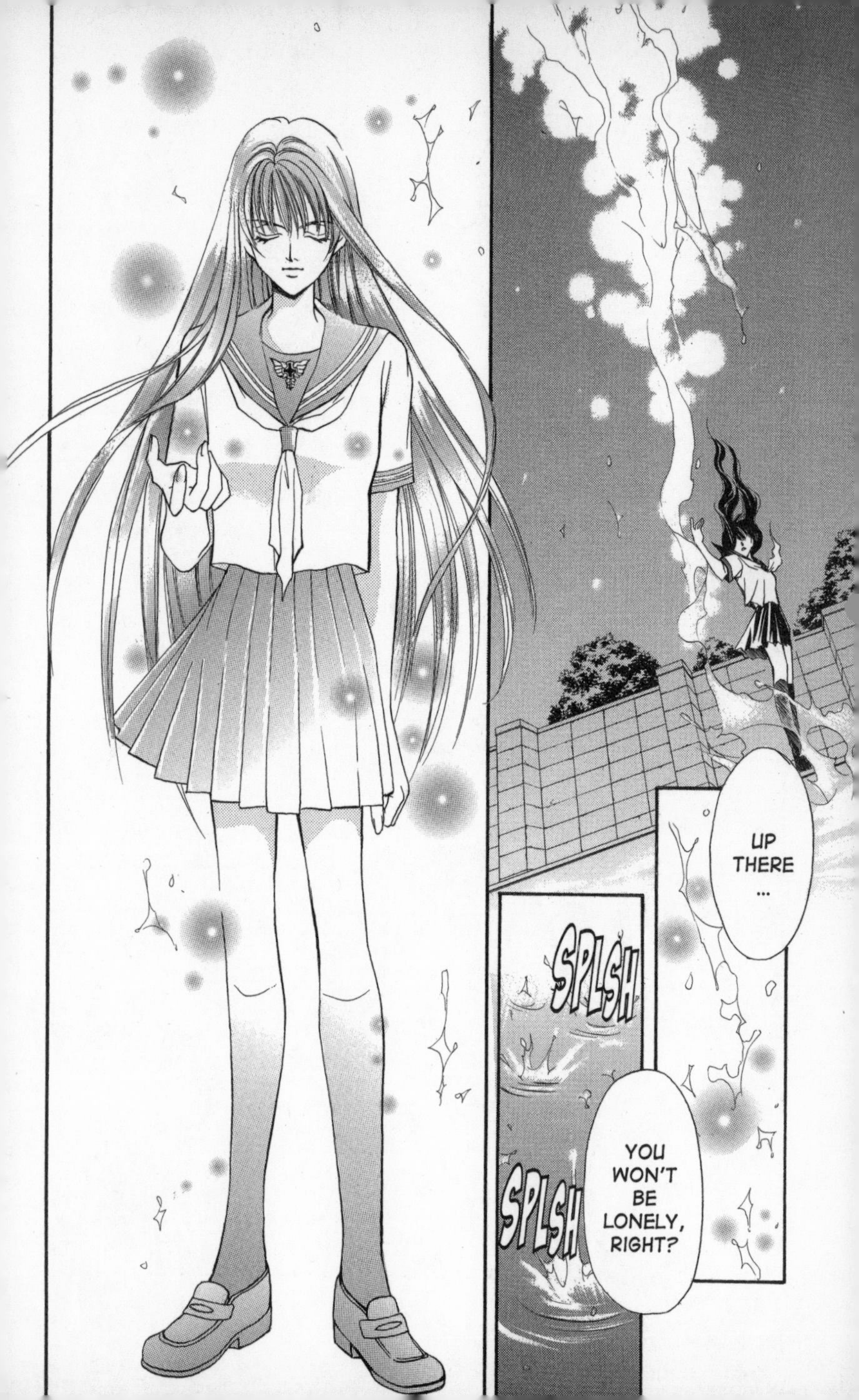
UP THERE ...
SPLSH
YOU WON'T BE LONELY, RIGHT?
SPLSH

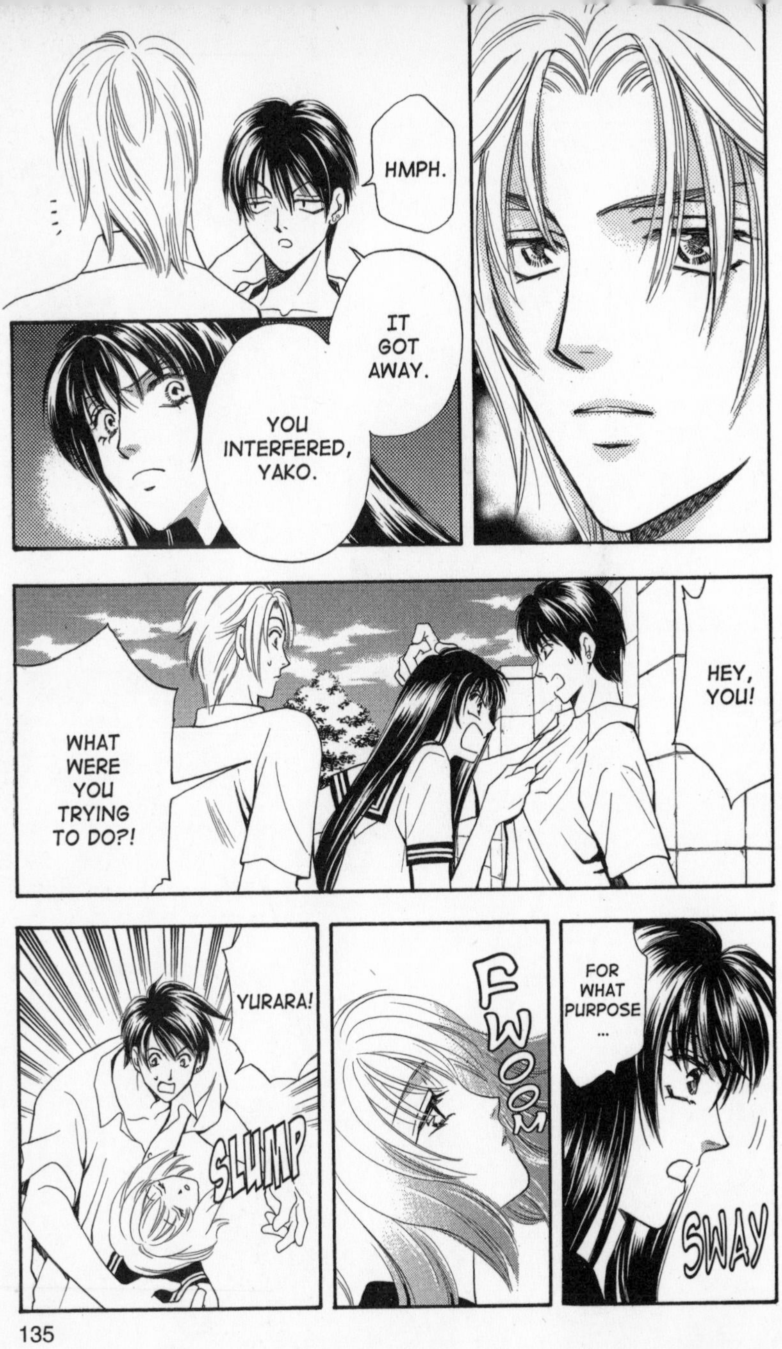
HMPH.
IT GOT AWAY.
YOU INTERFERED, YAKO.
HEY, YOU!
WHAT WERE YOU TRYING TO DO?!
FOR WHAT PURPOSE ...
SWAY
FWOOM
YURARA!
SLUMP

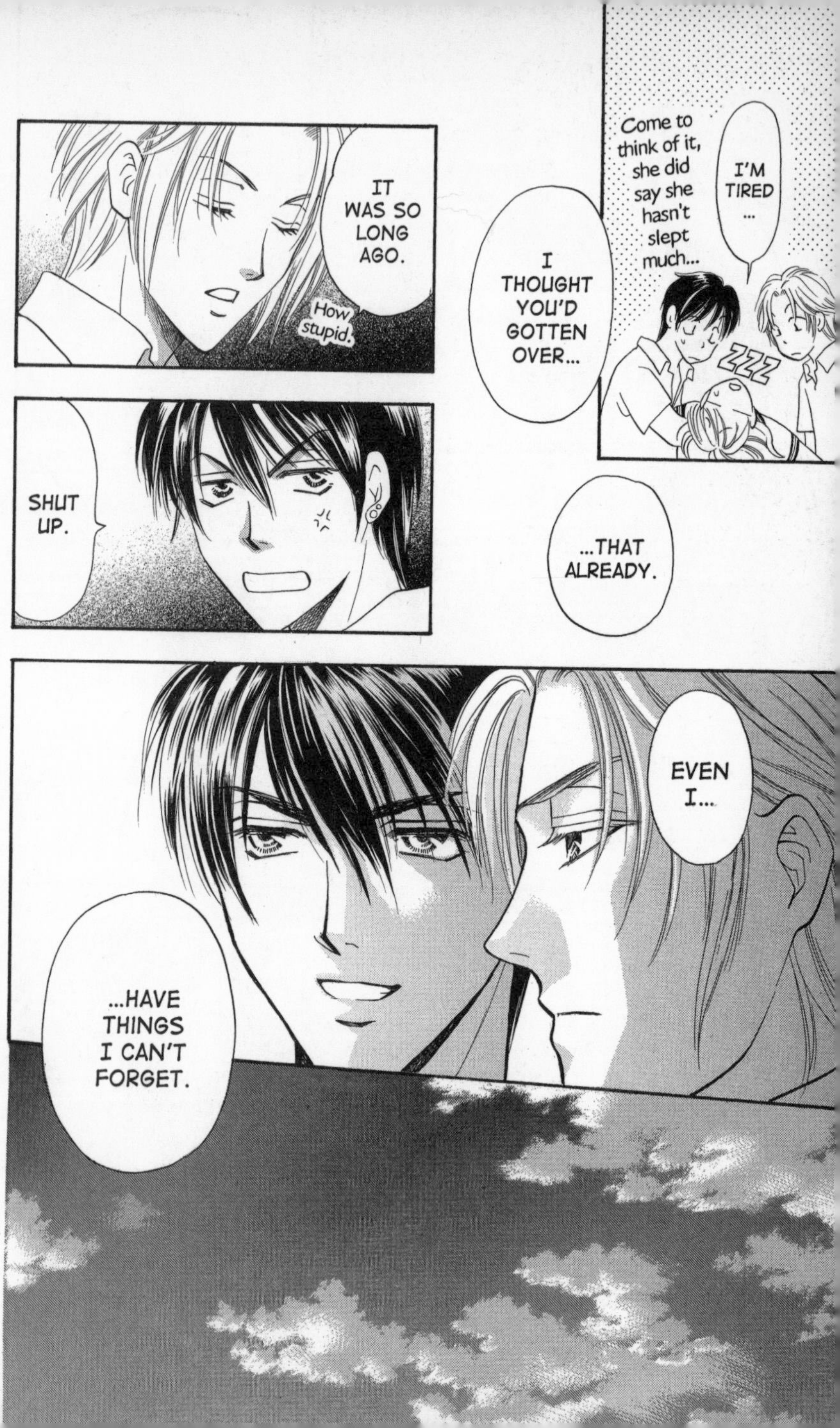
I'M TIRED...
Come to think of it, she did say she hasn't slept much...
ZZZ
I THOUGHT YOU'D GOTTEN OVER...
...THAT ALREADY.
IT WAS SO LONG AGO.
How stupid.
SHUT UP.
EVEN I...
...HAVE THINGS I CAN'T FORGET.

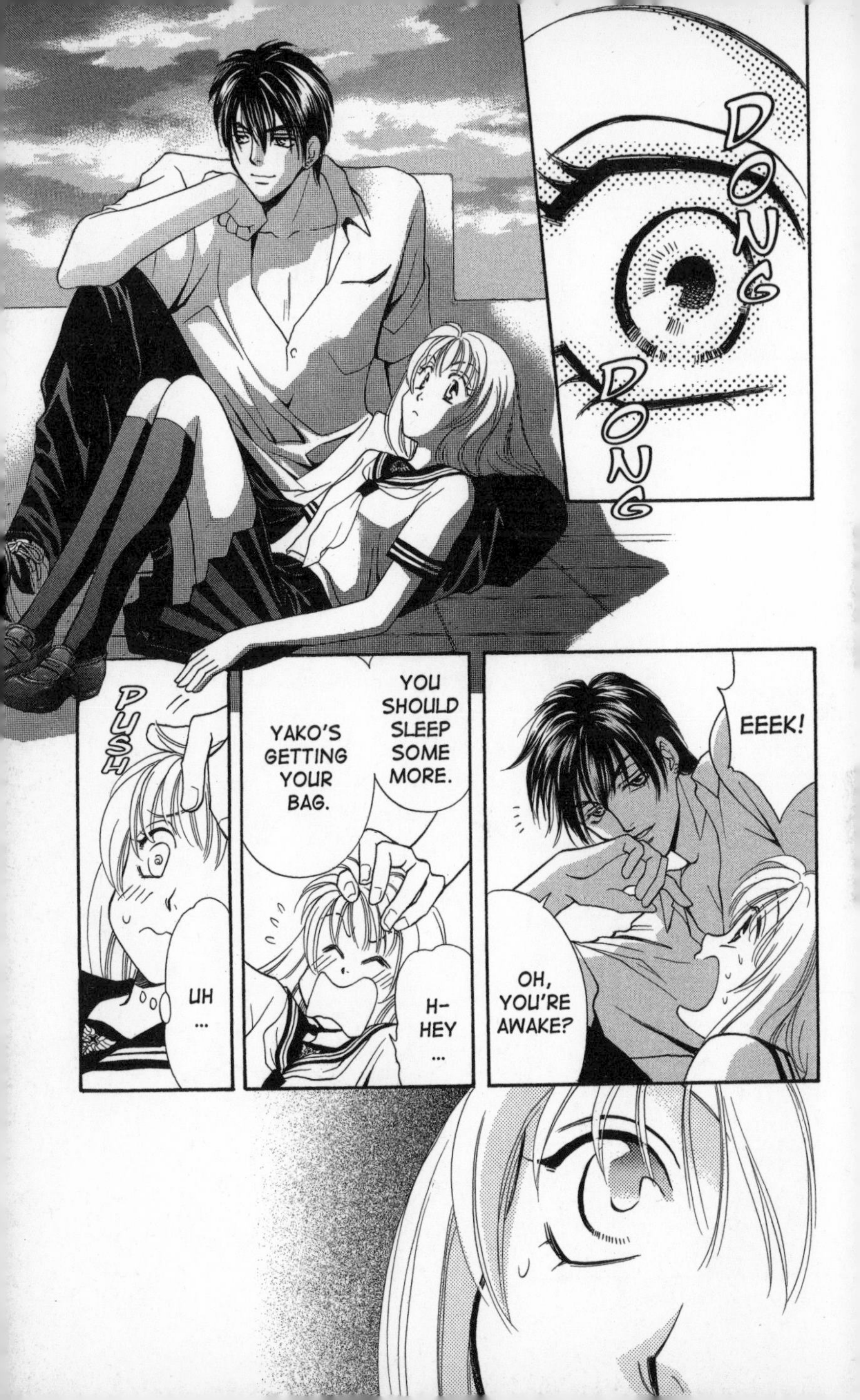
DONG
DONG
EEEK!
OH, YOU'RE AWAKE?
YOU SHOULD SLEEP SOME MORE.
YAKO'S GETTING YOUR BAG.
H-HEY ...
PUSH
UH ...

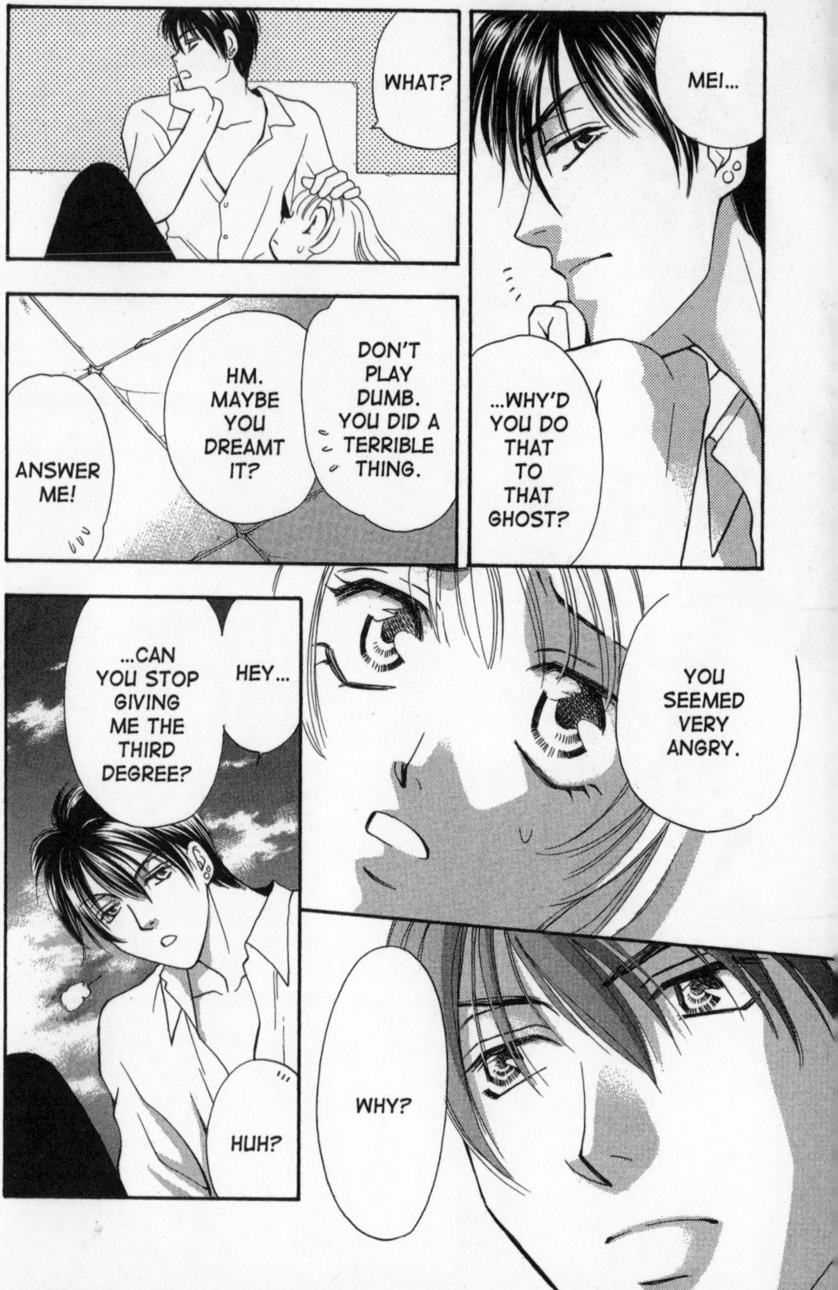
MEI...
...WHY'D YOU DO THAT TO THAT GHOST?
WHAT?
DON'T PLAY DUMB. YOU DID A TERRIBLE THING.
HM. MAYBE YOU DREAMT IT?
ANSWER ME!
YOU SEEMED VERY ANGRY.
WHY?
HEY...
...CAN YOU STOP GIVING ME THE THIRD DEGREE?
HUH?

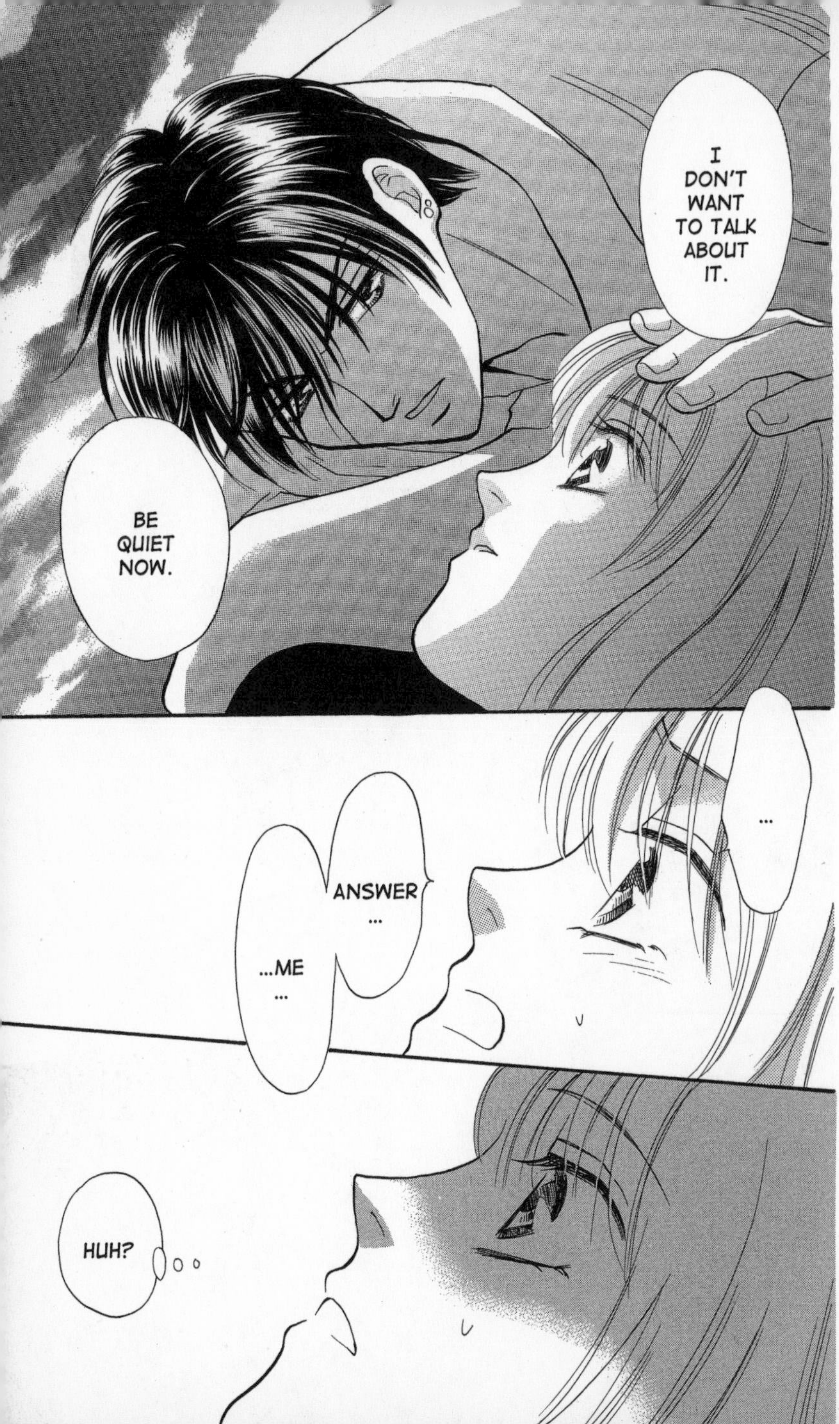
I DON'T WANT TO TALK ABOUT IT.
BE QUIET NOW.
...
ANSWER ...
...ME ...
HUH?

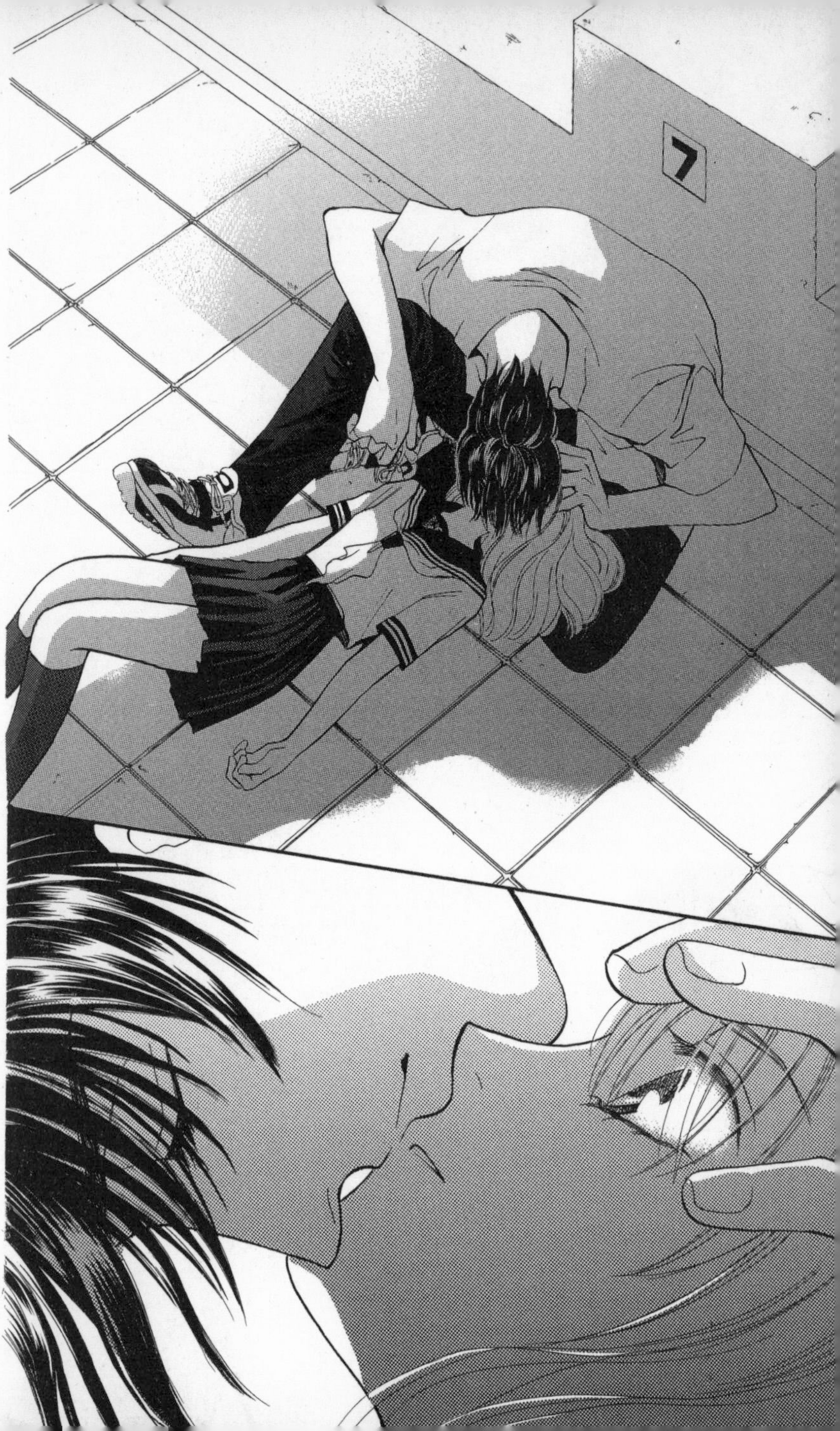
7

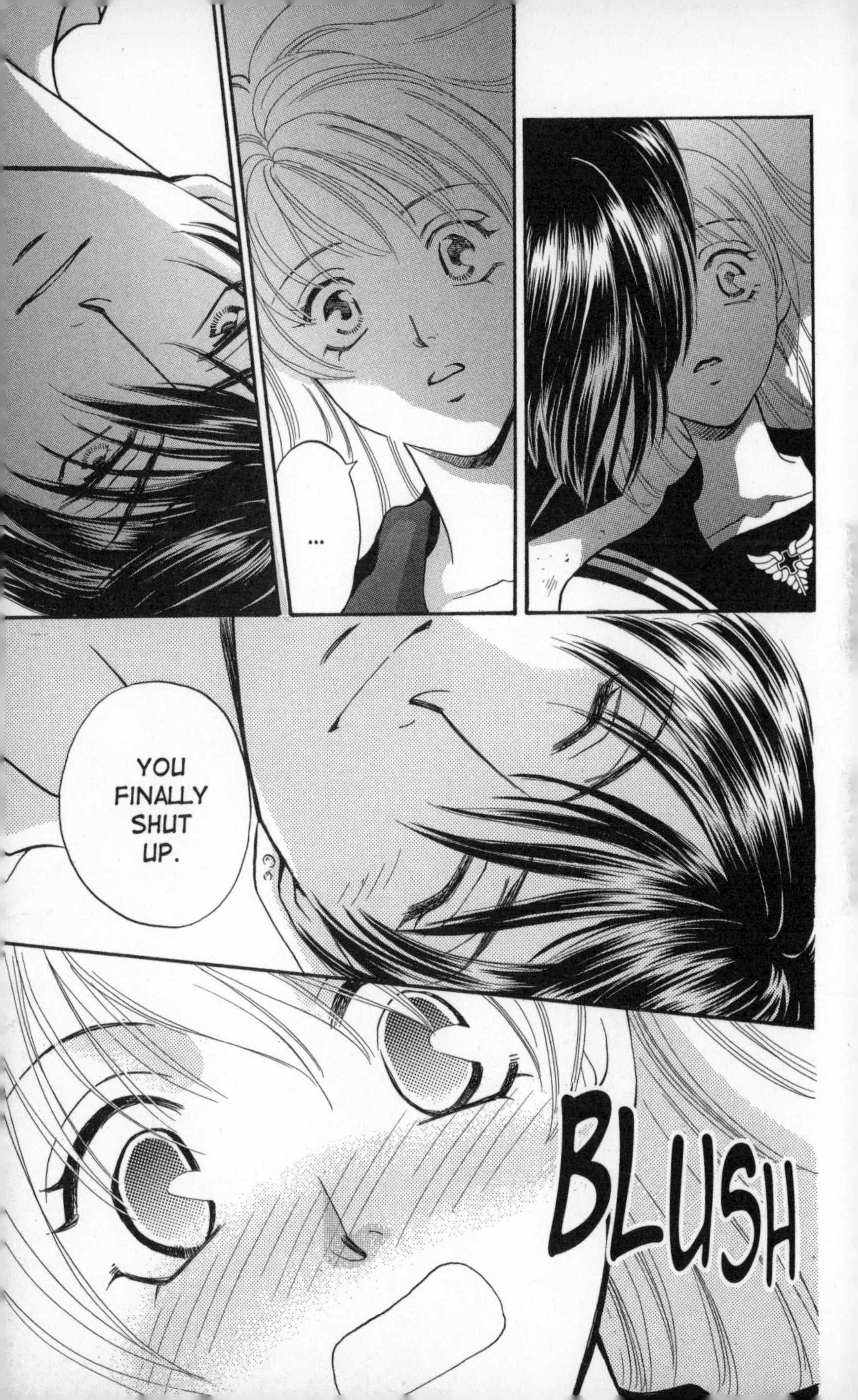
...
YOU FINALLY SHUT UP.
BLUSH

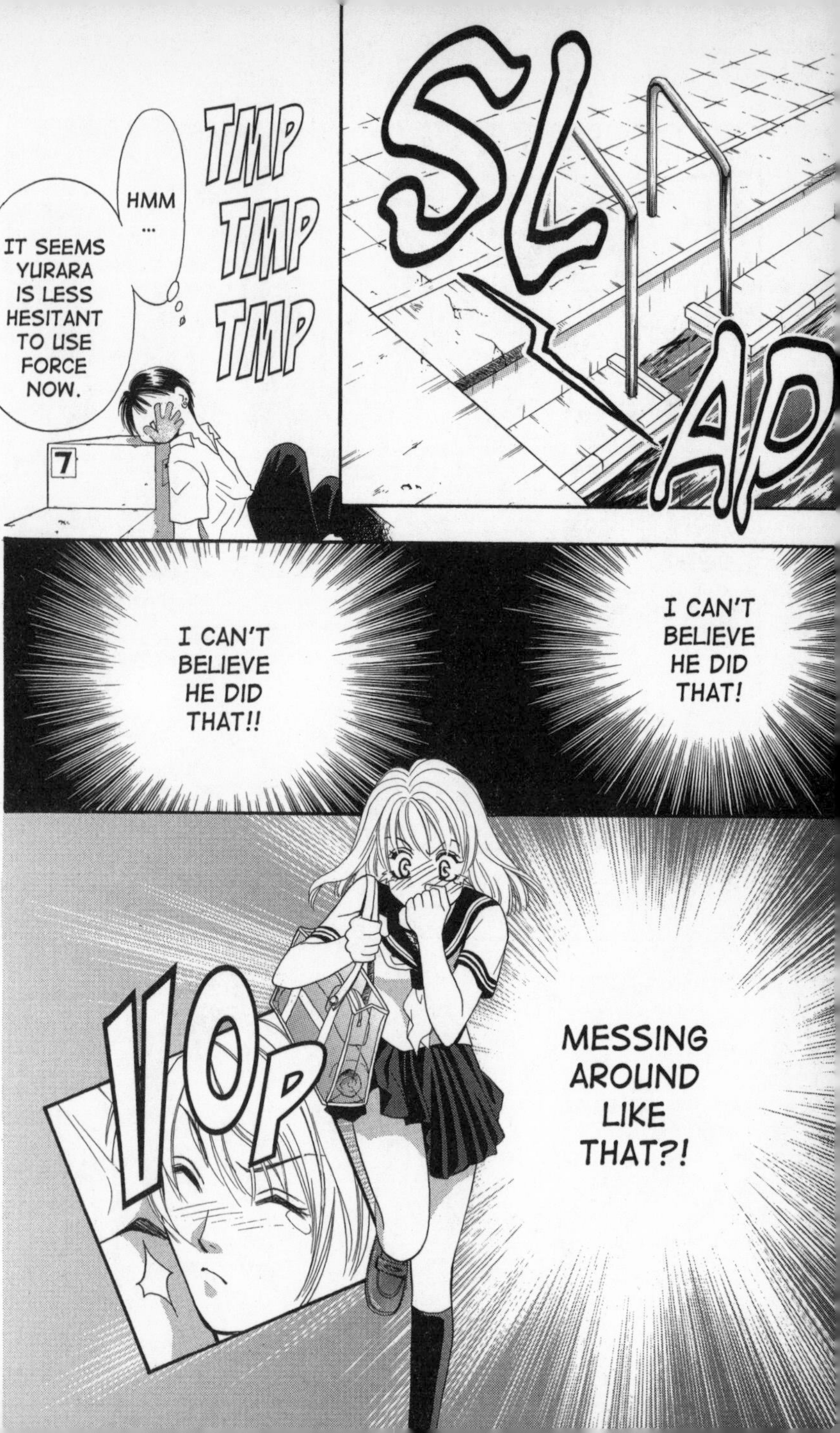

SLAP
TMP TMP TMP
HMM ...
IT SEEMS YURARA IS LESS HESITANT TO USE FORCE NOW.
7
I CAN'T BELIEVE HE DID THAT!
I CAN'T BELIEVE HE DID THAT!!
MESSING AROUND LIKE THAT?!
VOP

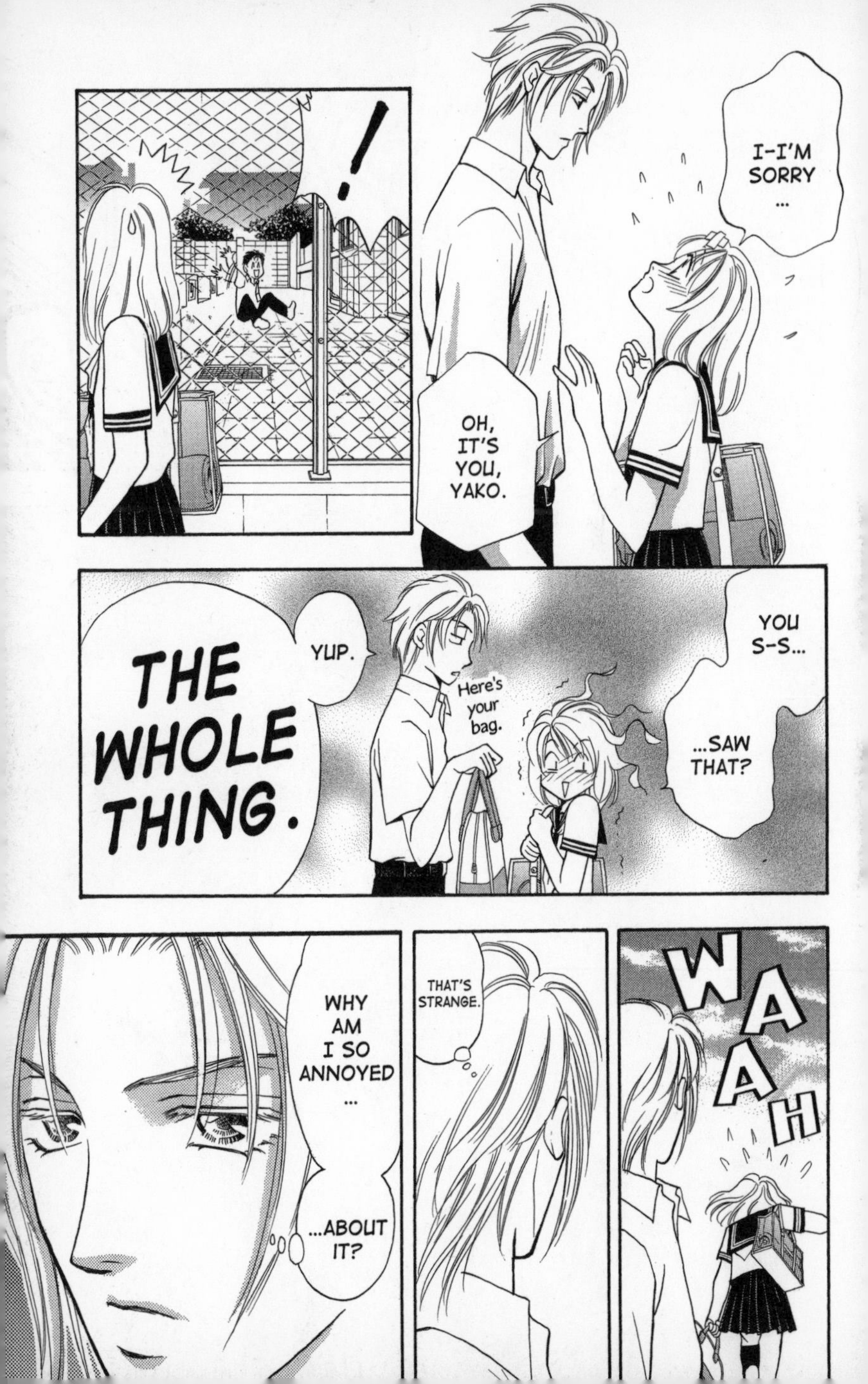
I-I'M SORRY ...
OH, IT'S YOU, YAKO.
!
YOU S-S...
...SAW THAT?
Here's your bag.
YUP.
THE WHOLE THING.
WAAH
THAT'S STRANGE.
WHY AM I SO ANNOYED ...
...ABOUT IT?

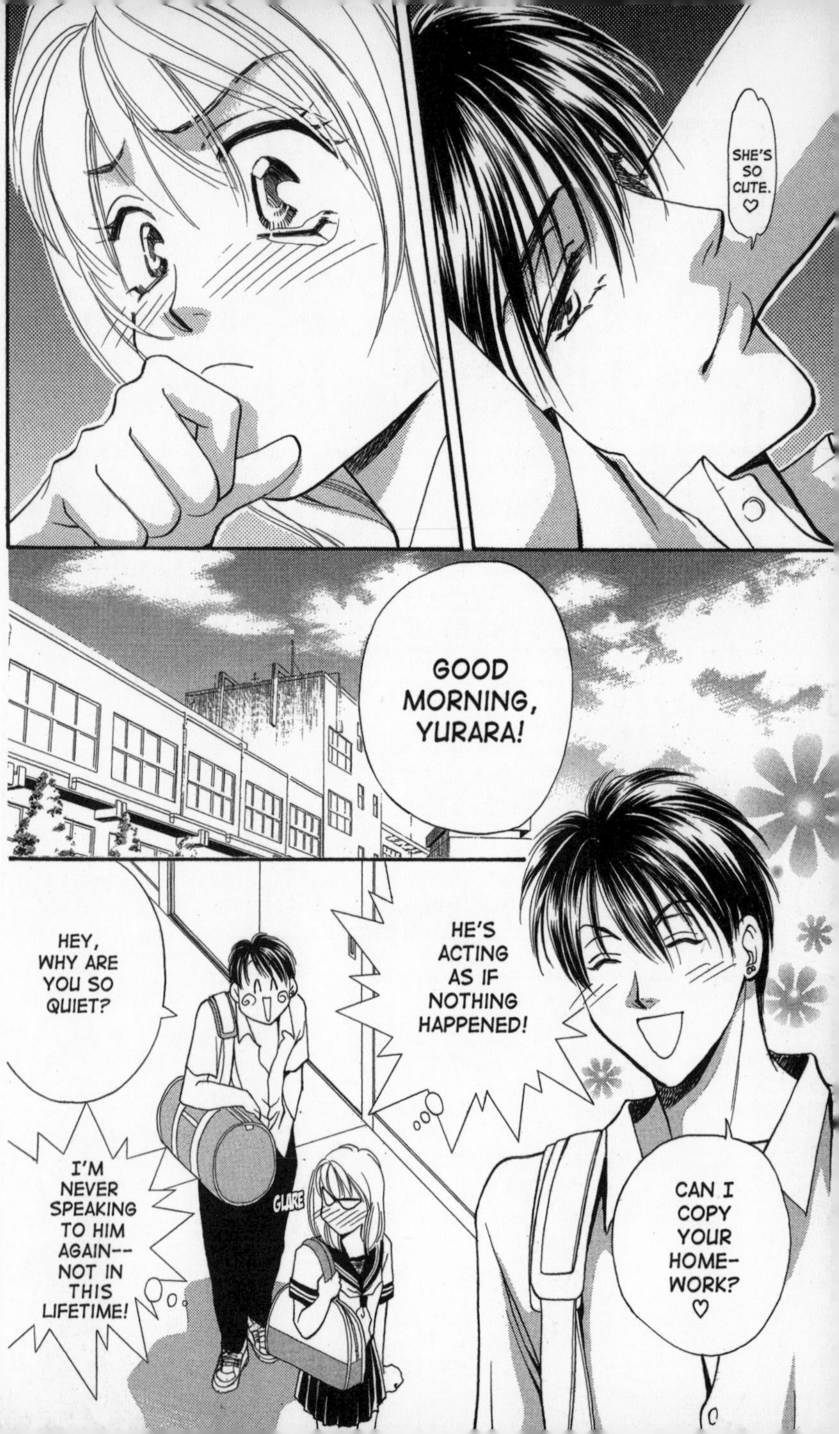
SHE'S SO CUTE. ♡
GOOD MORNING, YURARA!
CAN I COPY YOUR HOME-WORK? ♡
HE'S ACTING AS IF NOTHING HAPPENED!
HEY, WHY ARE YOU SO QUIET?
GLARE
I'M NEVER SPEAKING TO HIM AGAIN-- NOT IN THIS LIFETIME!

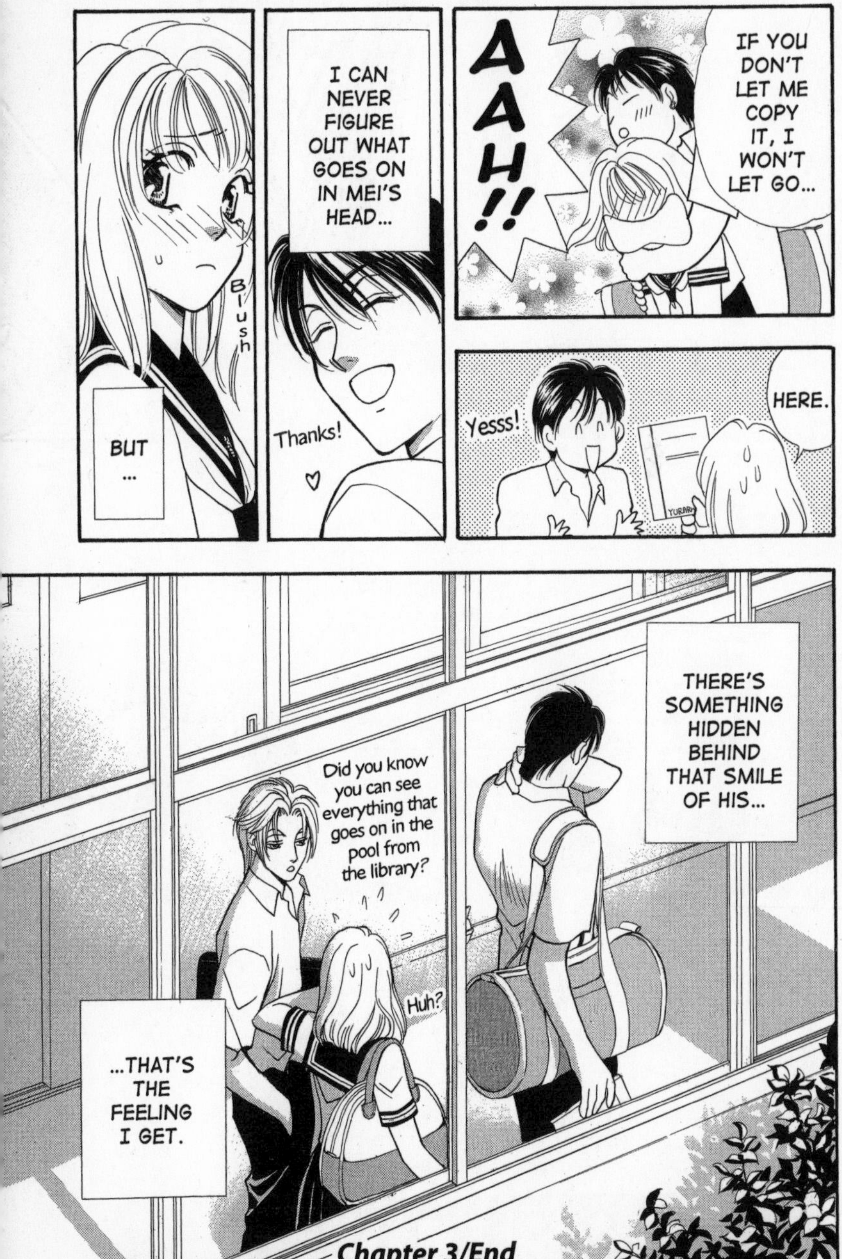
IF YOU DON'T LET ME COPY IT, I WON'T LET GO...
AAH!!
HERE.
Yesss!
I CAN NEVER FIGURE OUT WHAT GOES ON IN MEI'S HEAD...
Thanks!
Blush
BUT ...
THERE'S SOMETHING HIDDEN BEHIND THAT SMILE OF HIS...
Did you know you can see everything that goes on in the pool from the library?
Huh?
...THAT'S THE FEELING I GET.
Chapter 3/End

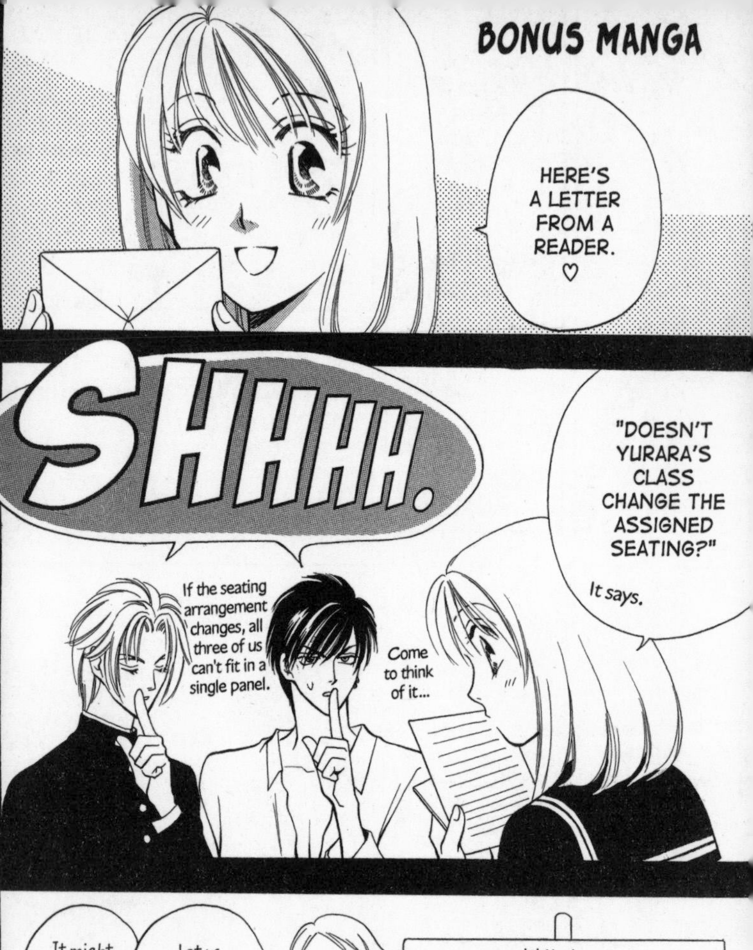
BONUS MANGA
HERE'S A LETTER FROM A READER. ♡
"DOESN'T YURARA'S CLASS CHANGE THE ASSIGNED SEATING?"
It says.
Come to think of it...
If the seating arrangement changes, all three of us can't fit in a single panel.
SHHHH.
Write to:
Chika Shiomi
c/o Yurara Editor
VIZ Media
P.O. Box 77010
San Francisco, CA 94107
Let us hear your thoughts. ♡
Check out my homepage too.
It might take a while, but I'll try to reply.
(Japanese site)
http://www.katch.ne.jp/~shiomi/

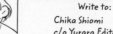

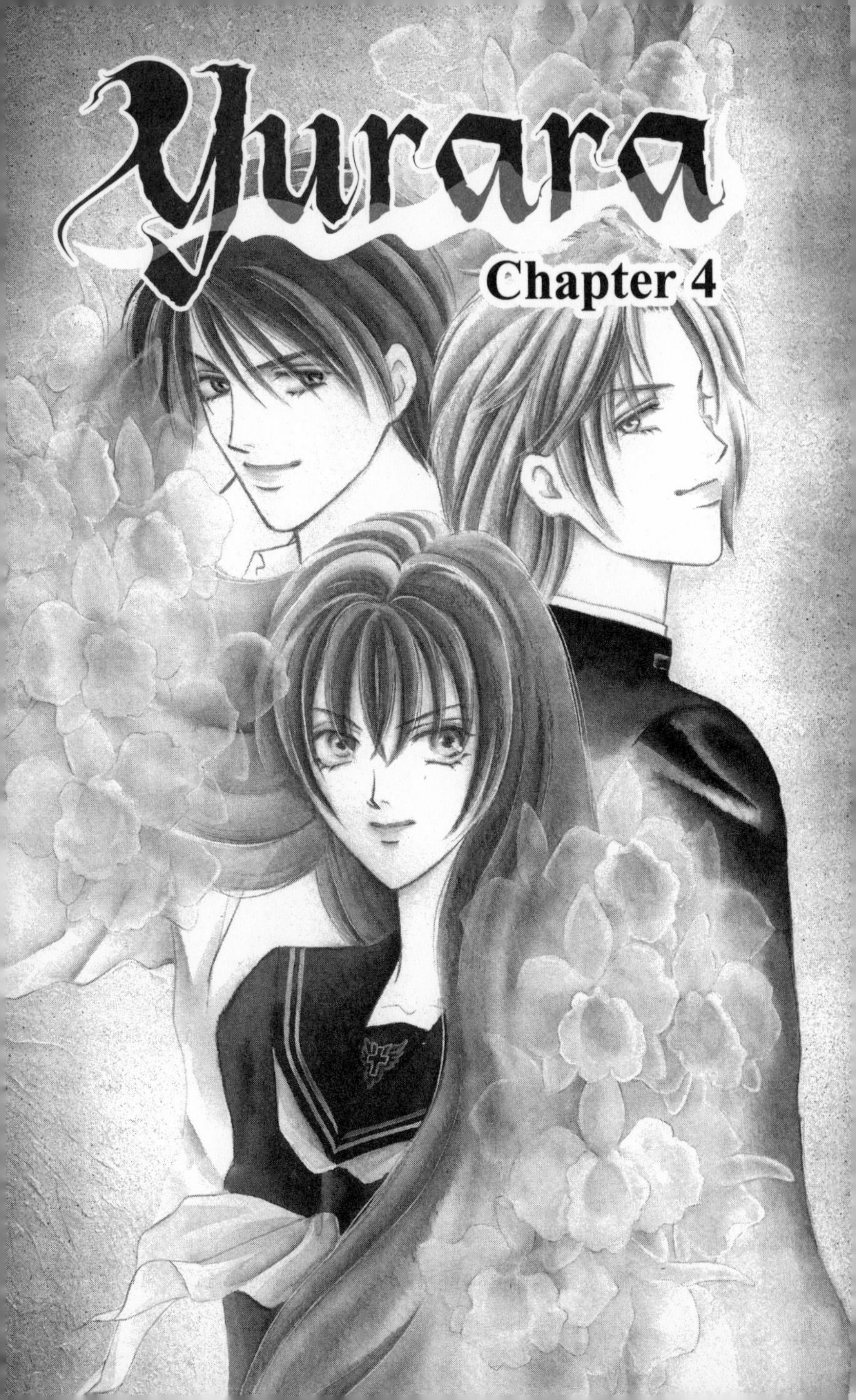
Yurara
Chapter 4

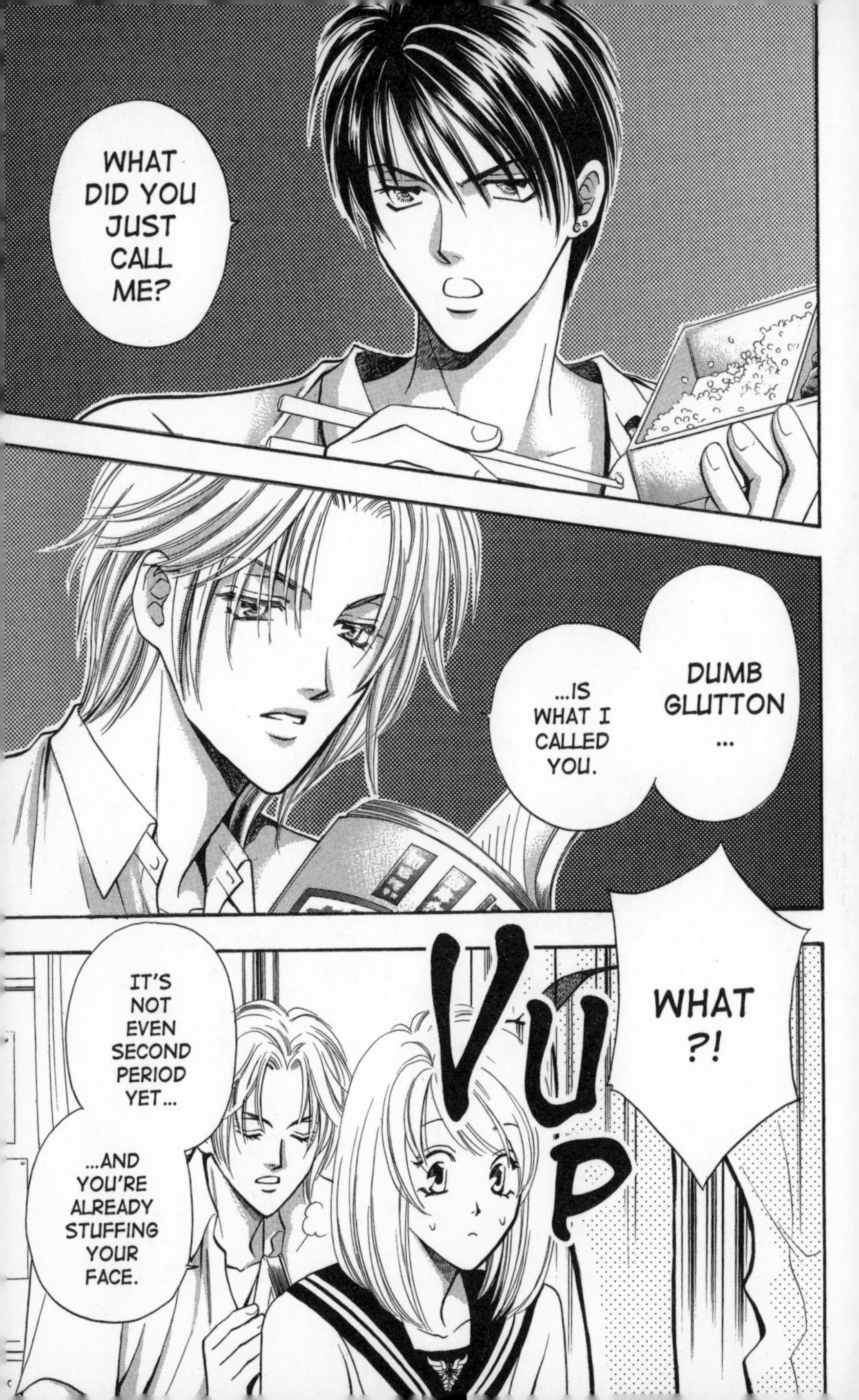
WHAT DID YOU JUST CALL ME?
DUMB GLUTTON ...
...IS WHAT I CALLED YOU.
WHAT ?!
VUP
IT'S NOT EVEN SECOND PERIOD YET...
...AND YOU'RE ALREADY STUFFING YOUR FACE.

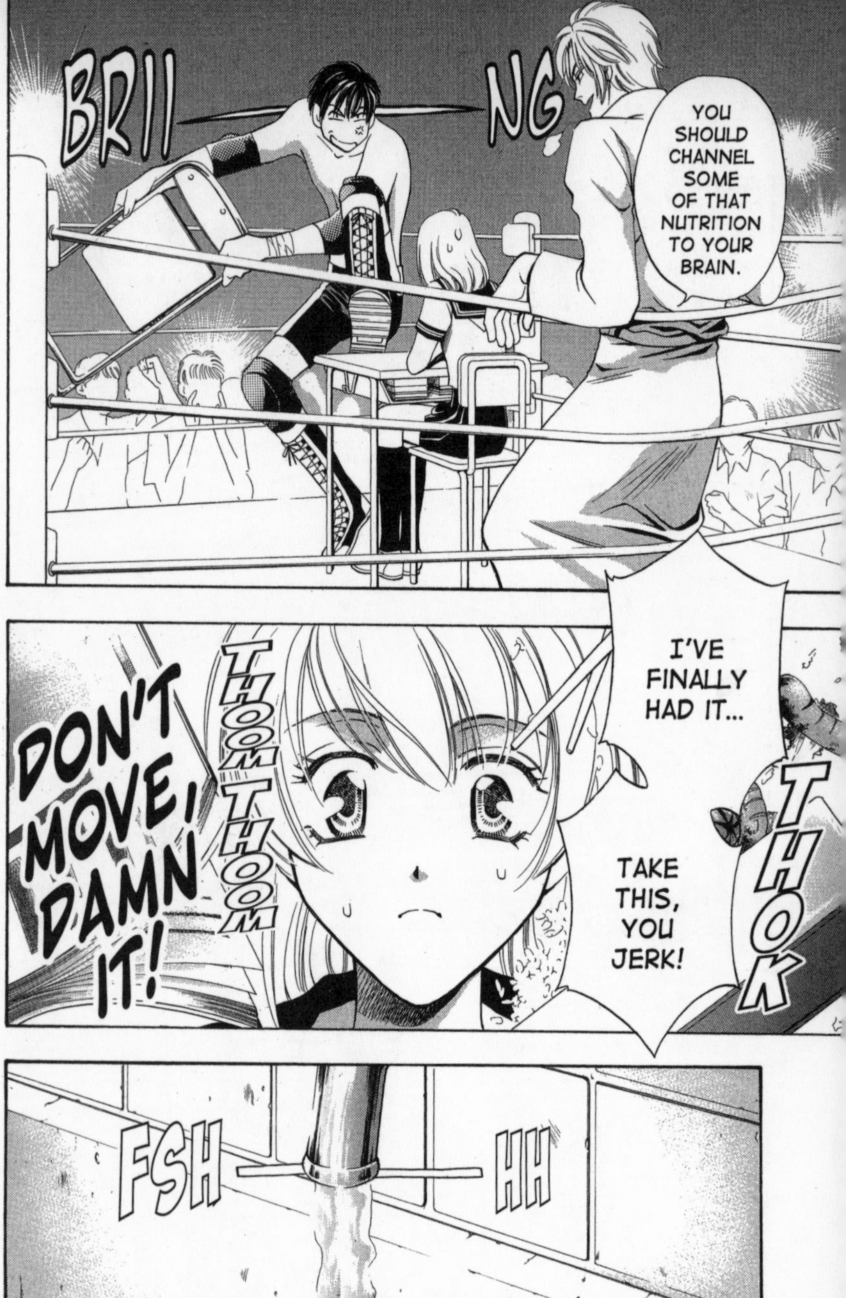
YOU SHOULD CHANNEL SOME OF THAT NUTRITION TO YOUR BRAIN.
BRIING
THOK
I'VE FINALLY HAD IT...
TAKE THIS, YOU JERK!
THOOM THOOM
DON'T MOVE, DAMN IT!
FSHHH

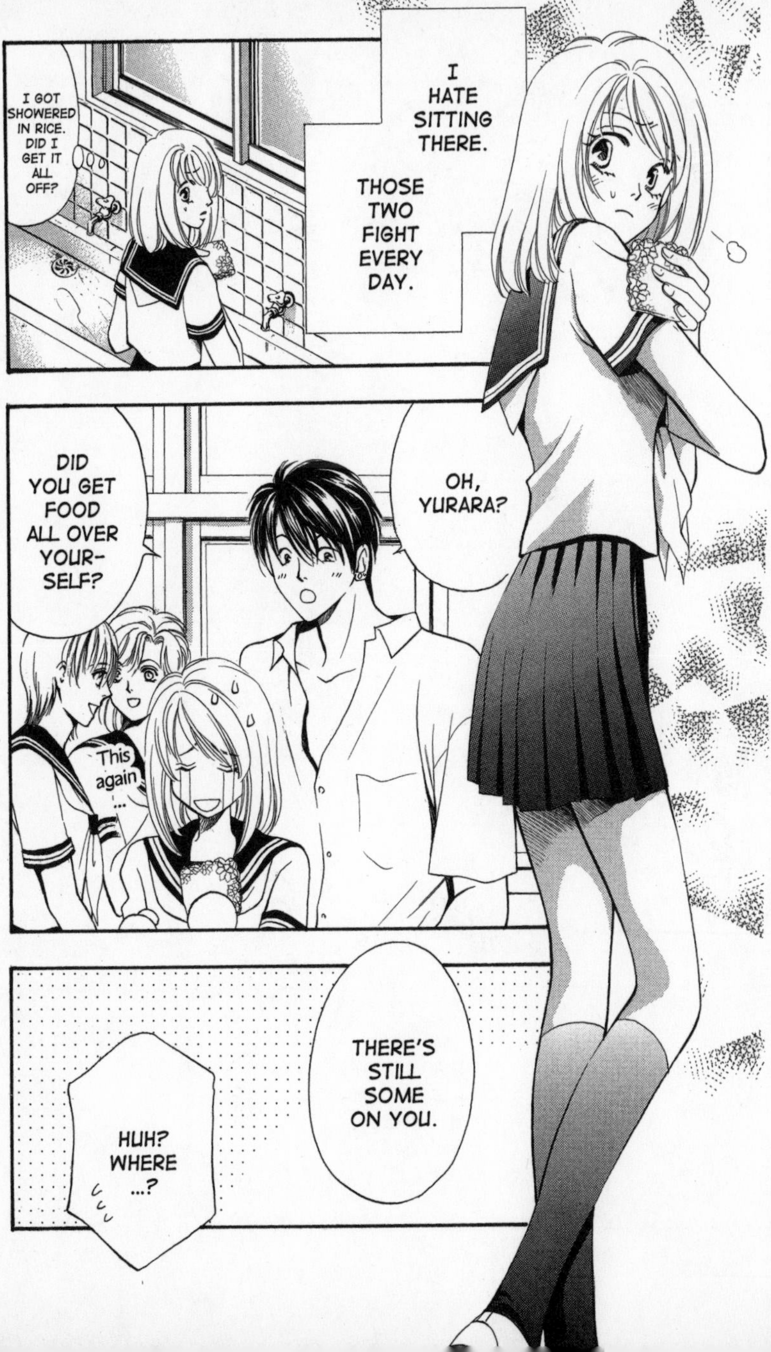
I HATE SITTING THERE.
THOSE TWO FIGHT EVERY DAY.
I GOT SHOWERED IN RICE. DID I GET IT ALL OFF?
OH, YURARA?
DID YOU GET FOOD ALL OVER YOURSELF?
This again...
THERE'S STILL SOME ON YOU.
HUH? WHERE ...?

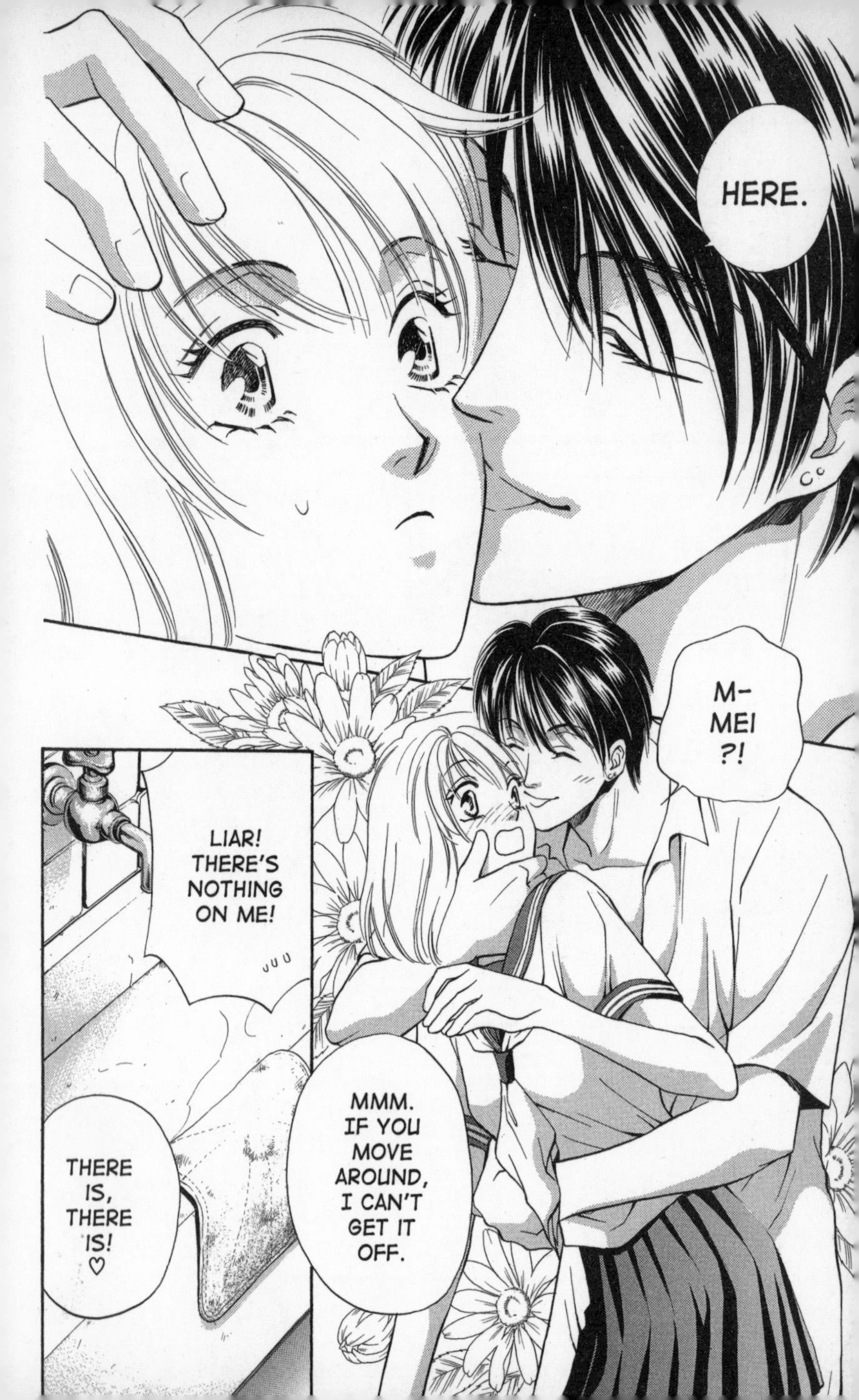
HERE.
M-MEI ?!
MMM. IF YOU MOVE AROUND, I CAN'T GET IT OFF.
LIAR! THERE'S NOTHING ON ME!
THERE IS, THERE IS! ♡

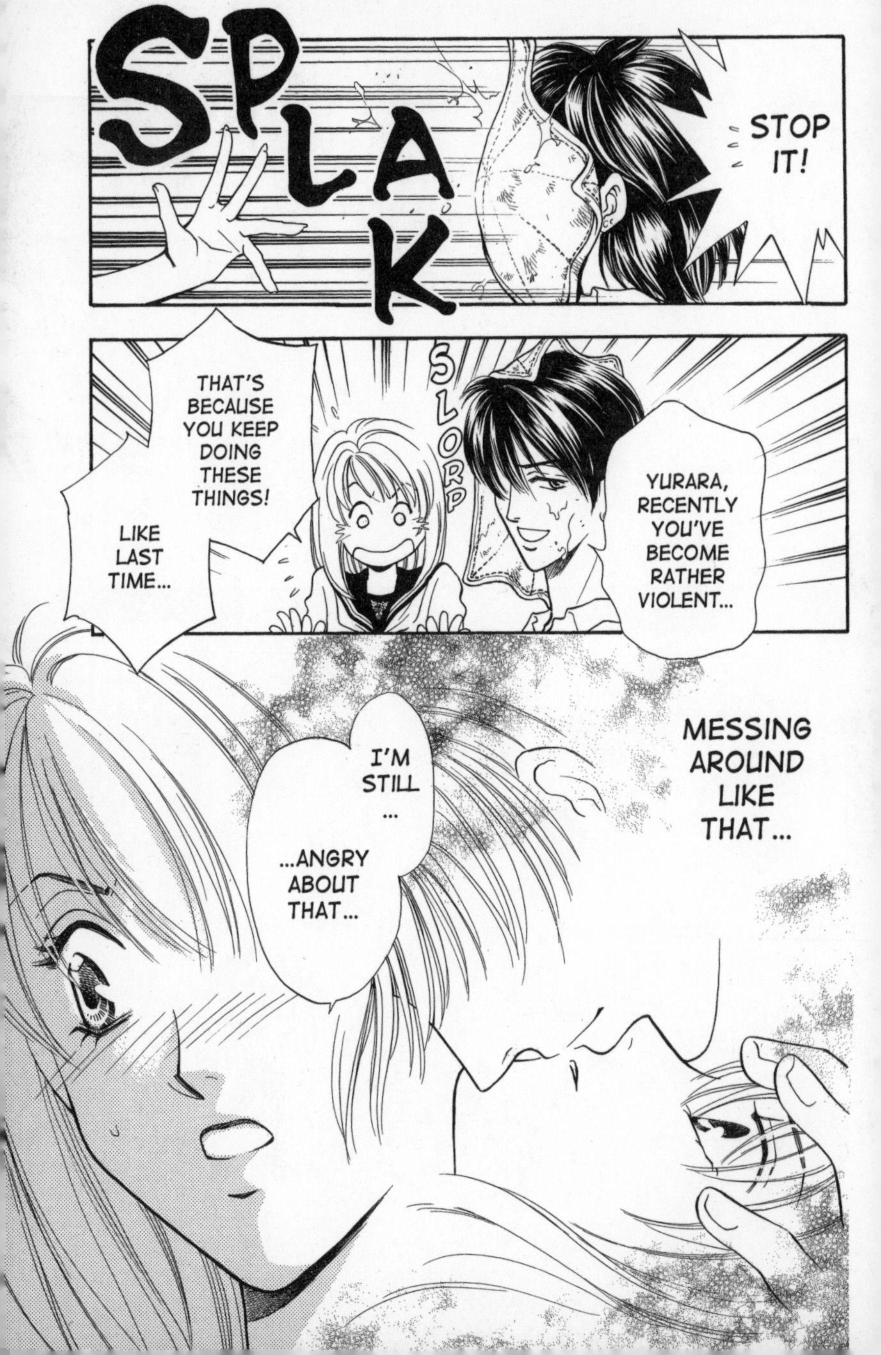
SPLAK
STOP IT!
YURARA, RECENTLY YOU'VE BECOME RATHER VIOLENT...
SLORP
THAT'S BECAUSE YOU KEEP DOING THESE THINGS!
LIKE LAST TIME...
MESSING AROUND LIKE THAT...
I'M STILL ...
...ANGRY ABOUT THAT...

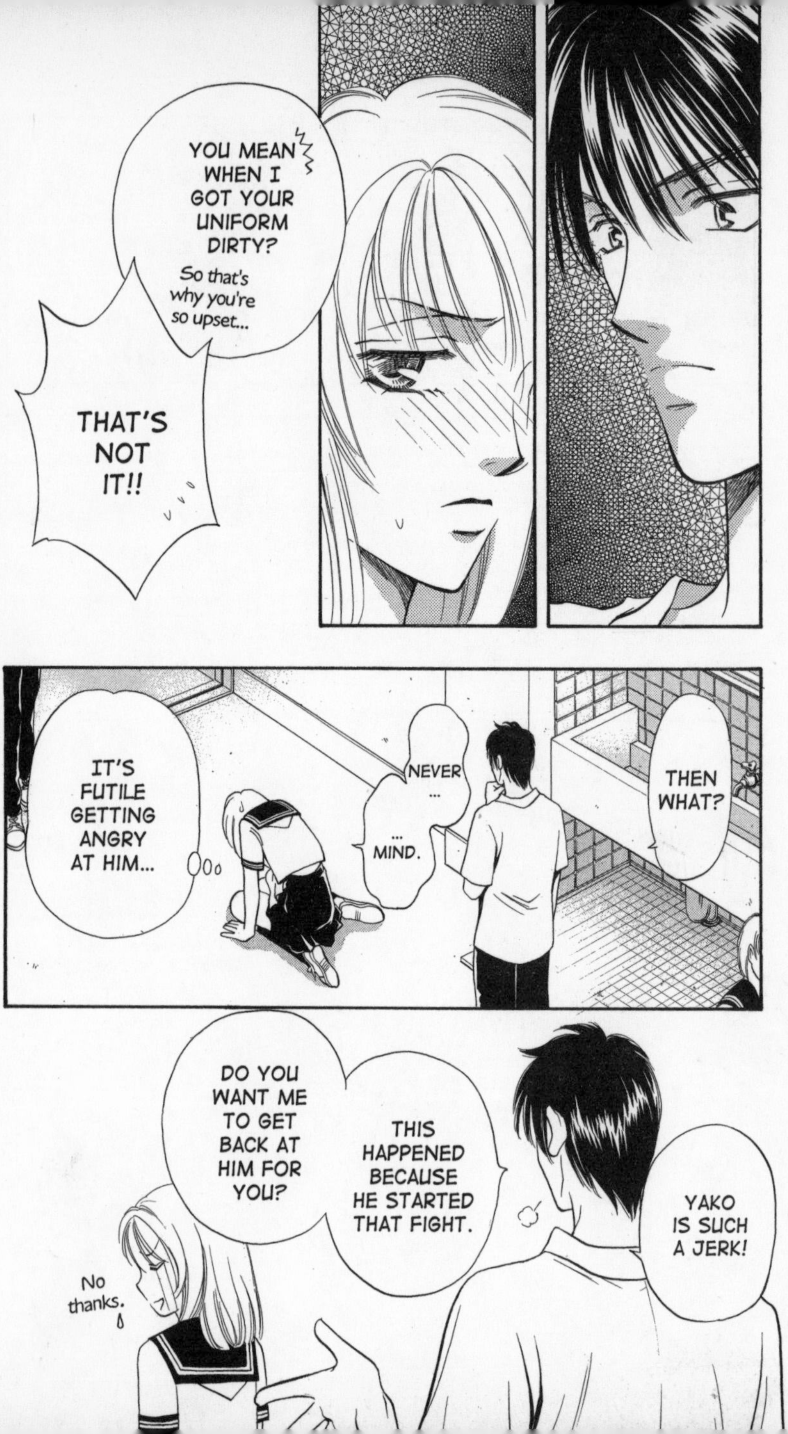
YOU MEAN WHEN I GOT YOUR UNIFORM DIRTY?
So that's why you're so upset...
THAT'S NOT IT!!
THEN WHAT?
NEVER...
...MIND.
IT'S FUTILE GETTING ANGRY AT HIM...
YAKO IS SUCH A JERK!
THIS HAPPENED BECAUSE HE STARTED THAT FIGHT.
DO YOU WANT ME TO GET BACK AT HIM FOR YOU?
No thanks.

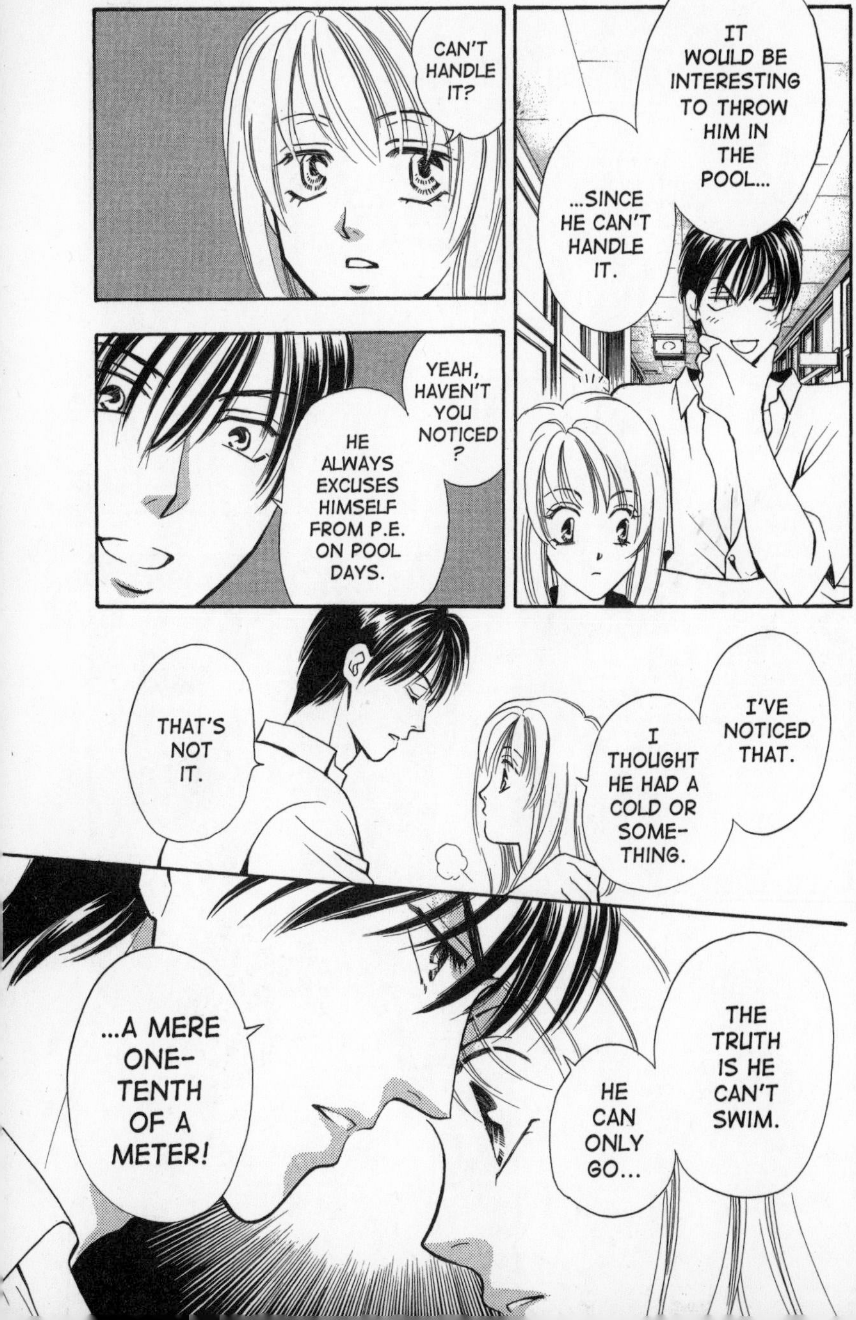
IT WOULD BE INTERESTING TO THROW HIM IN THE POOL...
...SINCE HE CAN'T HANDLE IT.
CAN'T HANDLE IT?
YEAH, HAVEN'T YOU NOTICED?
HE ALWAYS EXCUSES HIMSELF FROM P.E. ON POOL DAYS.
I'VE NOTICED THAT.
I THOUGHT HE HAD A COLD OR SOME-THING.
THAT'S NOT IT.
THE TRUTH IS HE CAN'T SWIM.
HE CAN ONLY GO...
...A MERE ONE-TENTH OF A METER!

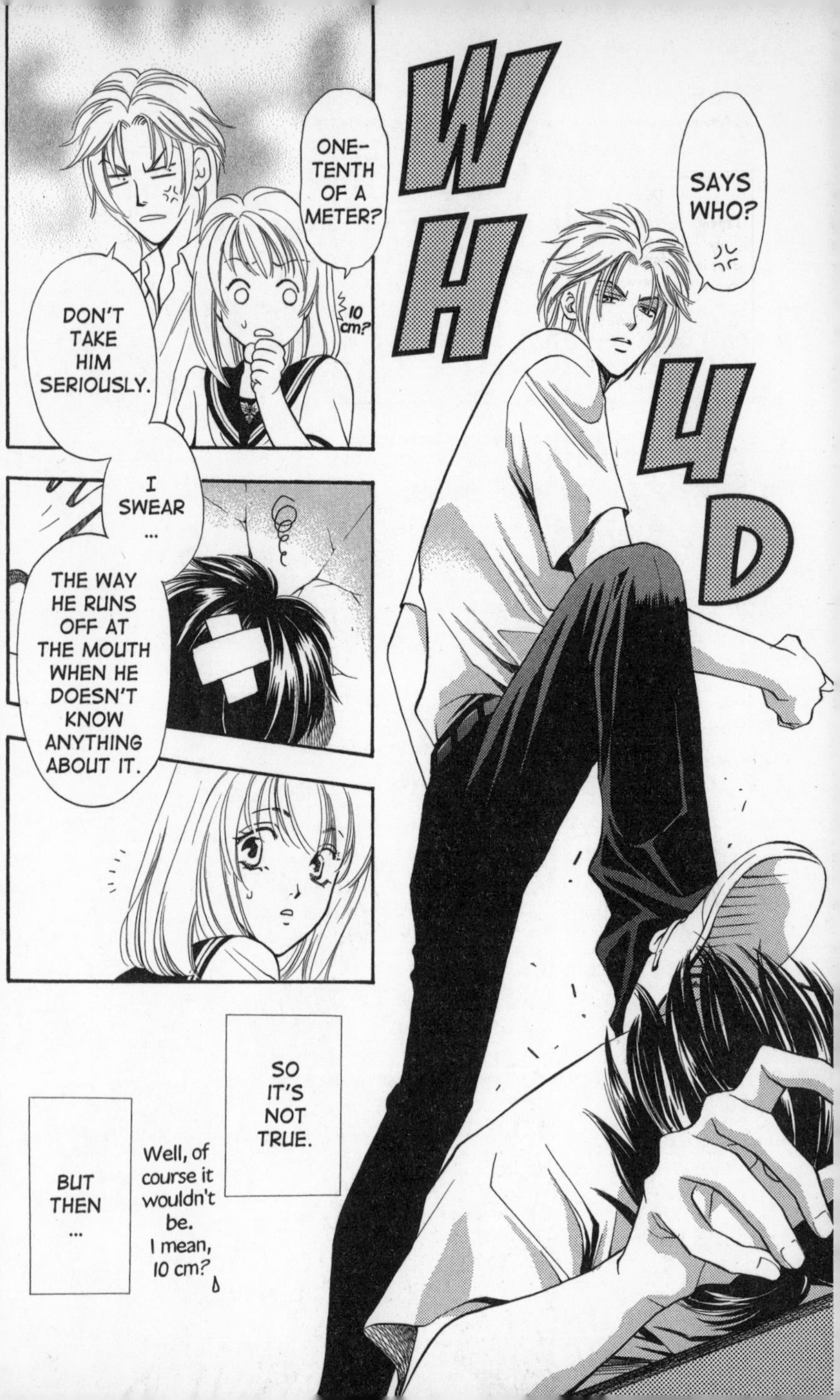
WHUD
SAYS WHO?
ONE-TENTH OF A METER?
10 cm?
DON'T TAKE HIM SERIOUSLY.
I SWEAR ...
THE WAY HE RUNS OFF AT THE MOUTH WHEN HE DOESN'T KNOW ANYTHING ABOUT IT.
SO IT'S NOT TRUE.
Well, of course it wouldn't be. I mean, 10 cm?
BUT THEN ...

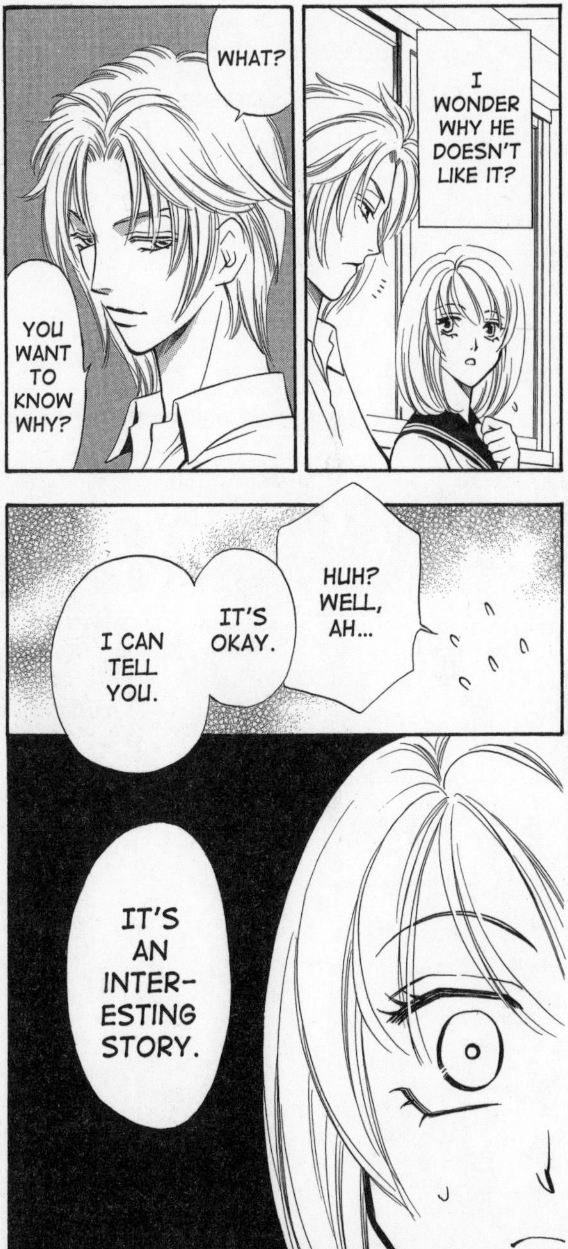
I WONDER WHY HE DOESN'T LIKE IT?
WHAT?
YOU WANT TO KNOW WHY?
HUH? WELL, AH...
IT'S OKAY.
I CAN TELL YOU.
IT'S AN INTER-ESTING STORY.

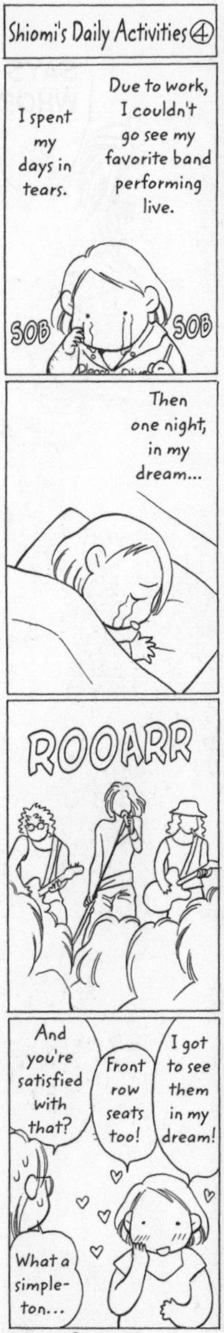
Shiomi's Daily Activities ④
Due to work, I couldn't go see my favorite band performing live.
I spent my days in tears.
SOB
SOB
Then one night, in my dream...
ROOARR
I got to see them in my dream!
Front row seats too!
And you're satisfied with that?
What a simple-ton...
It was Guns N' Roses.

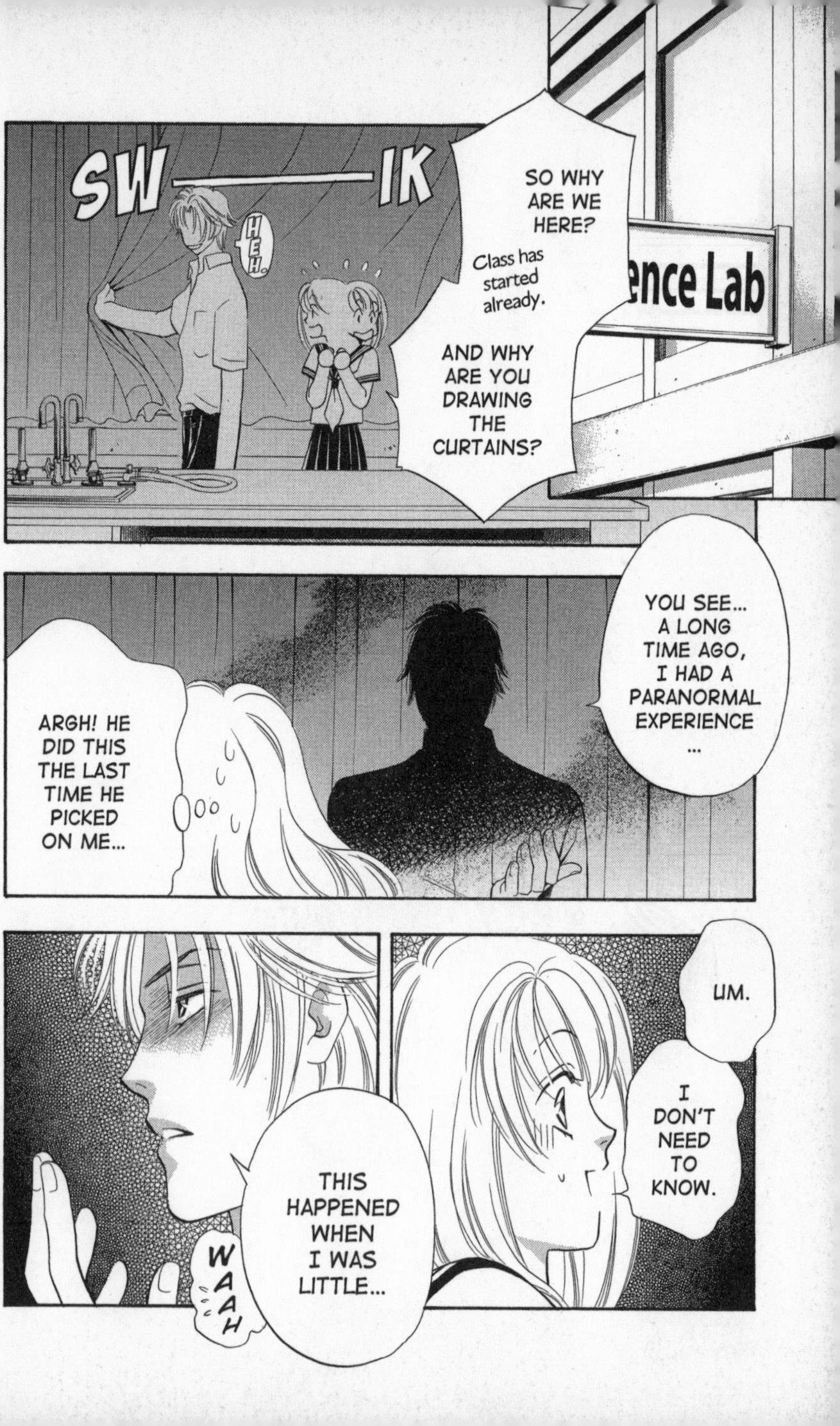
ence Lab
SO WHY ARE WE HERE?
Class has started already.
AND WHY ARE YOU DRAWING THE CURTAINS?
SW—IK
HEH.
YOU SEE... A LONG TIME AGO, I HAD A PARANORMAL EXPERIENCE ...
ARGH! HE DID THIS THE LAST TIME HE PICKED ON ME...
UM.
I DON'T NEED TO KNOW.
THIS HAPPENED WHEN I WAS LITTLE...
WAAH

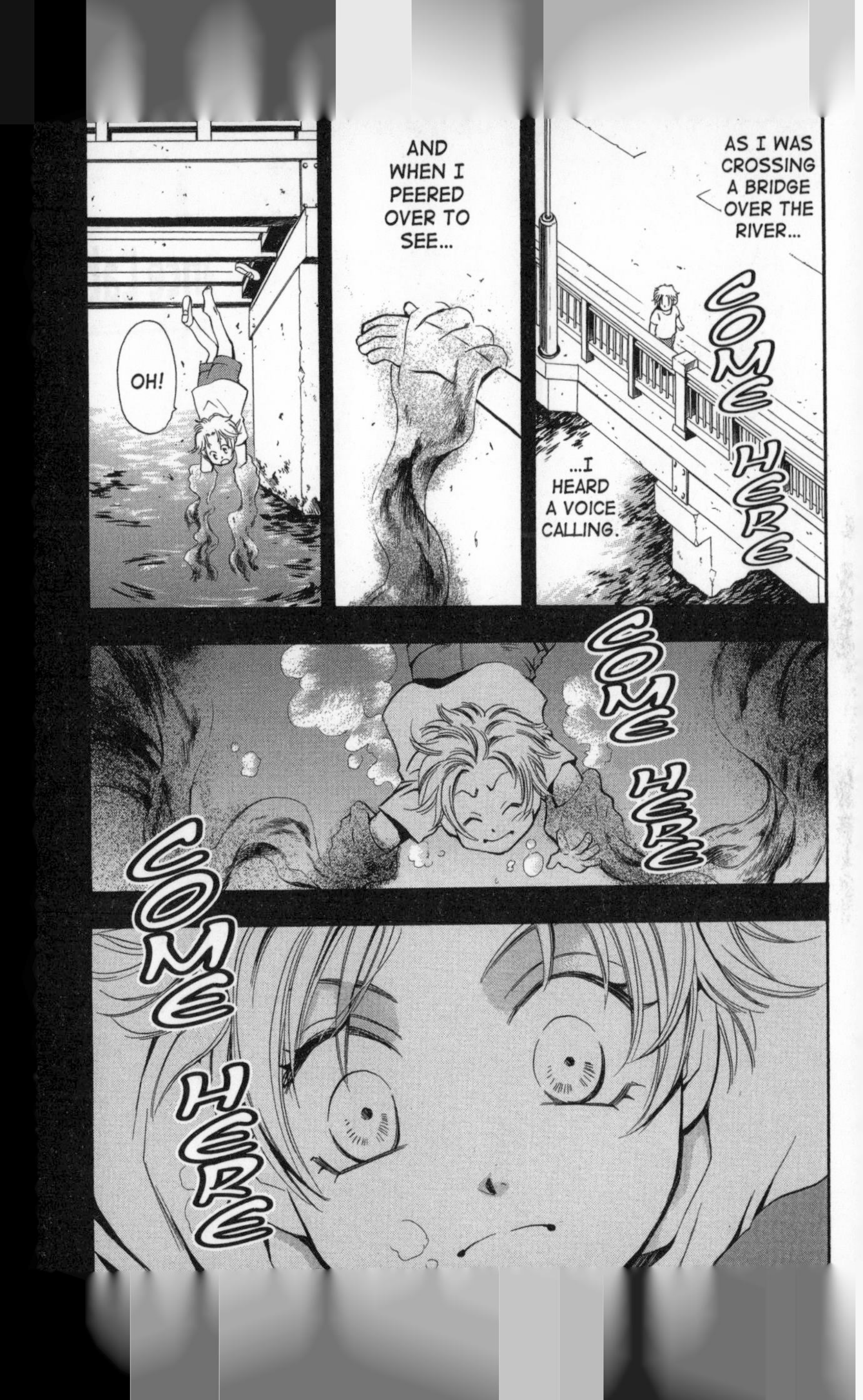
AS I WAS CROSSING A BRIDGE OVER THE RIVER...
COME HERE
...I HEARD A VOICE CALLING.
AND WHEN I PEERED OVER TO SEE...
OH!
COME HERE
COME HERE

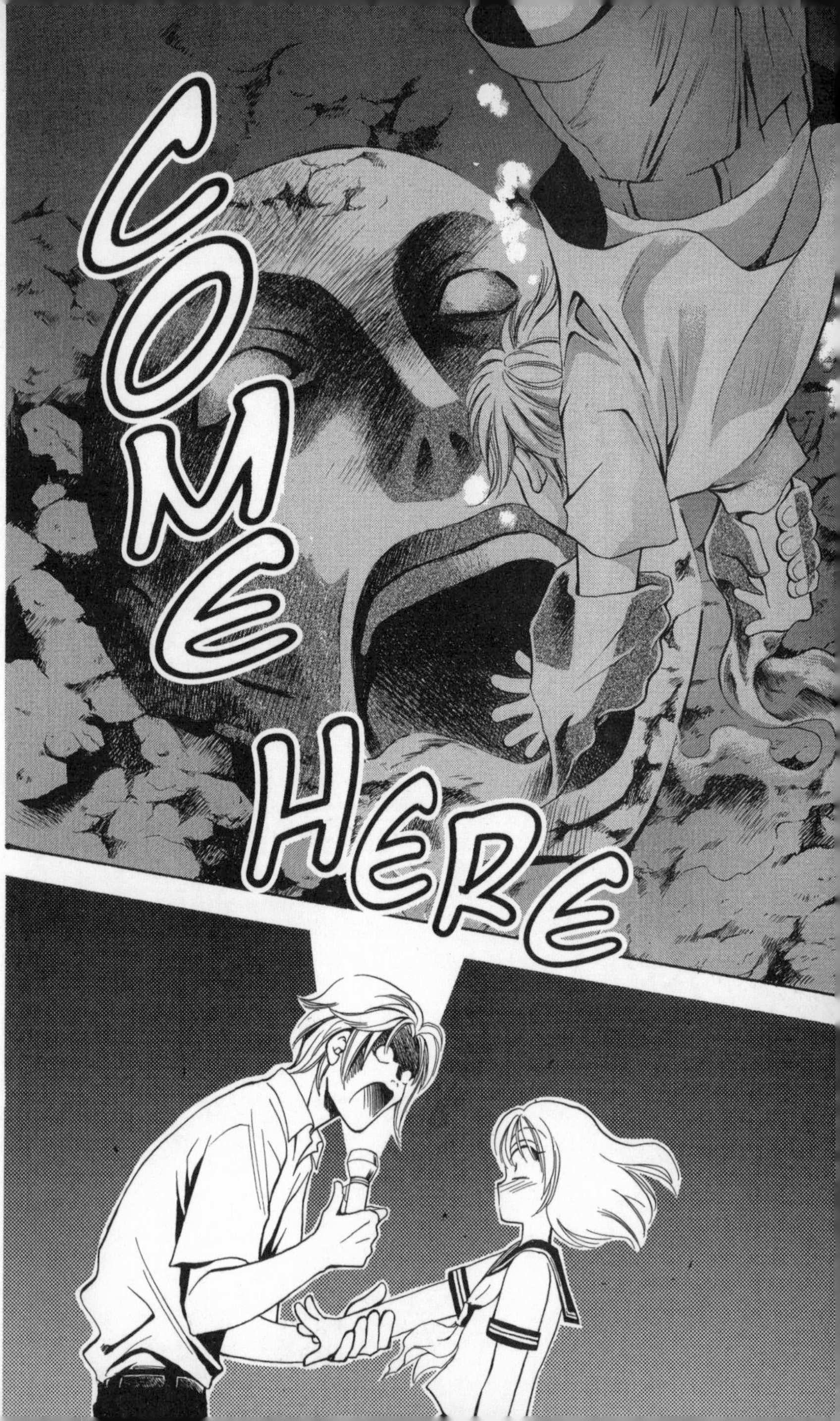
COME HERE

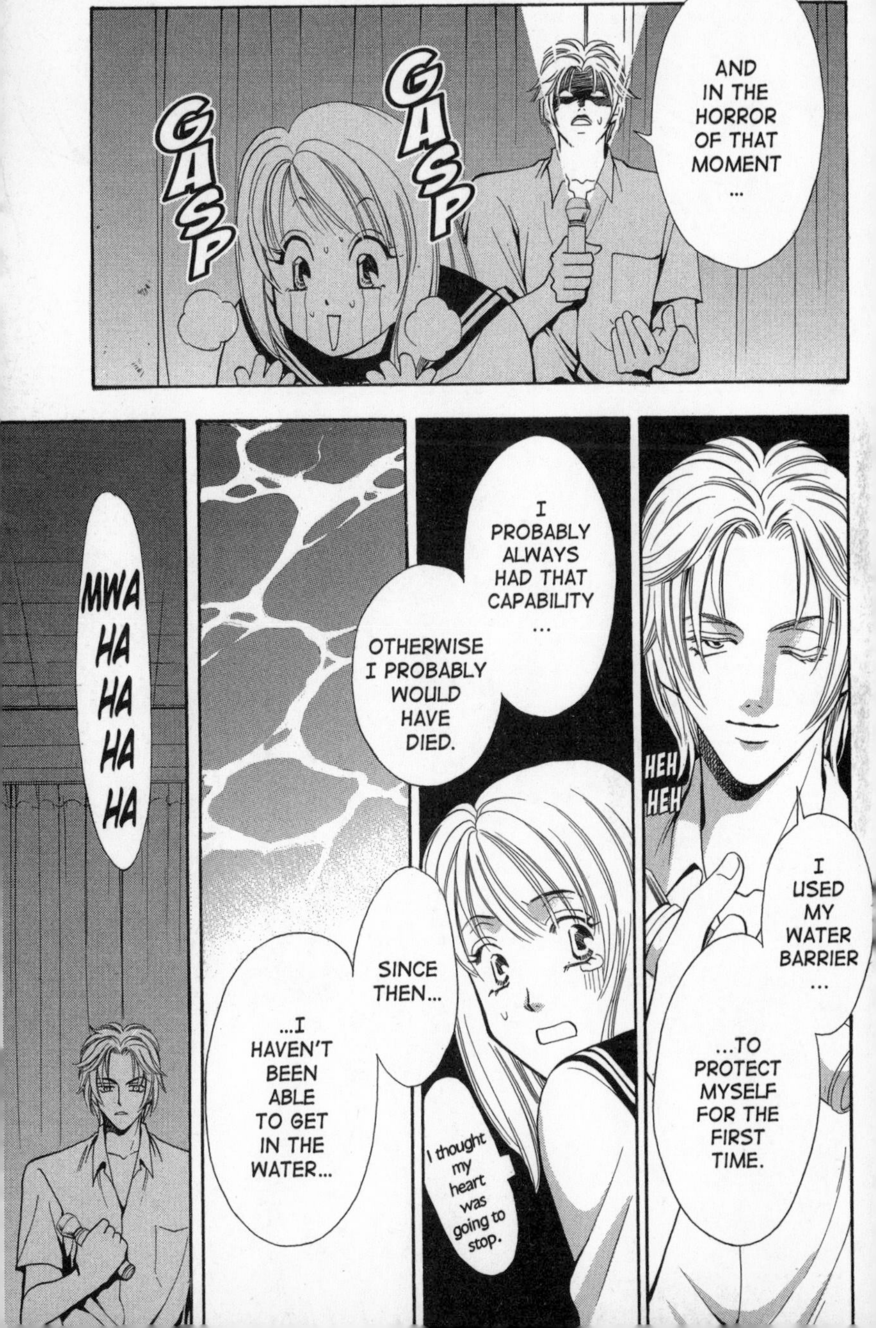
AND IN THE HORROR OF THAT MOMENT ...
GASP
GASP
I USED MY WATER BARRIER ...
...TO PROTECT MYSELF FOR THE FIRST TIME.
HEH HEH
I PROBABLY ALWAYS HAD THAT CAPABILITY ...
OTHERWISE I PROBABLY WOULD HAVE DIED.
SINCE THEN...
...I HAVEN'T BEEN ABLE TO GET IN THE WATER...
I thought my heart was going to stop.
MWA HA HA HA HA HA

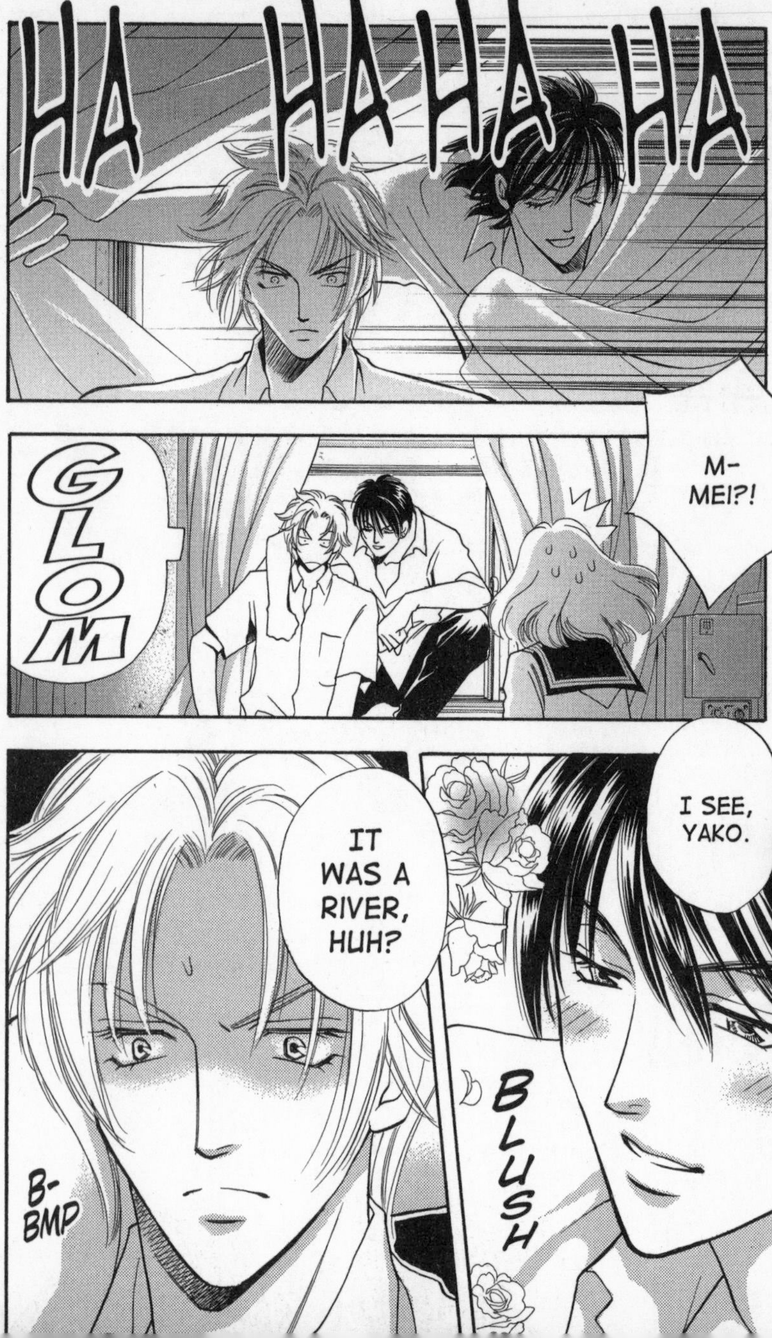
HA HA HA HA HA
M-MEI?!
GLOM
I SEE, YAKO.
BLUSH
IT WAS A RIVER, HUH?
B-BMP

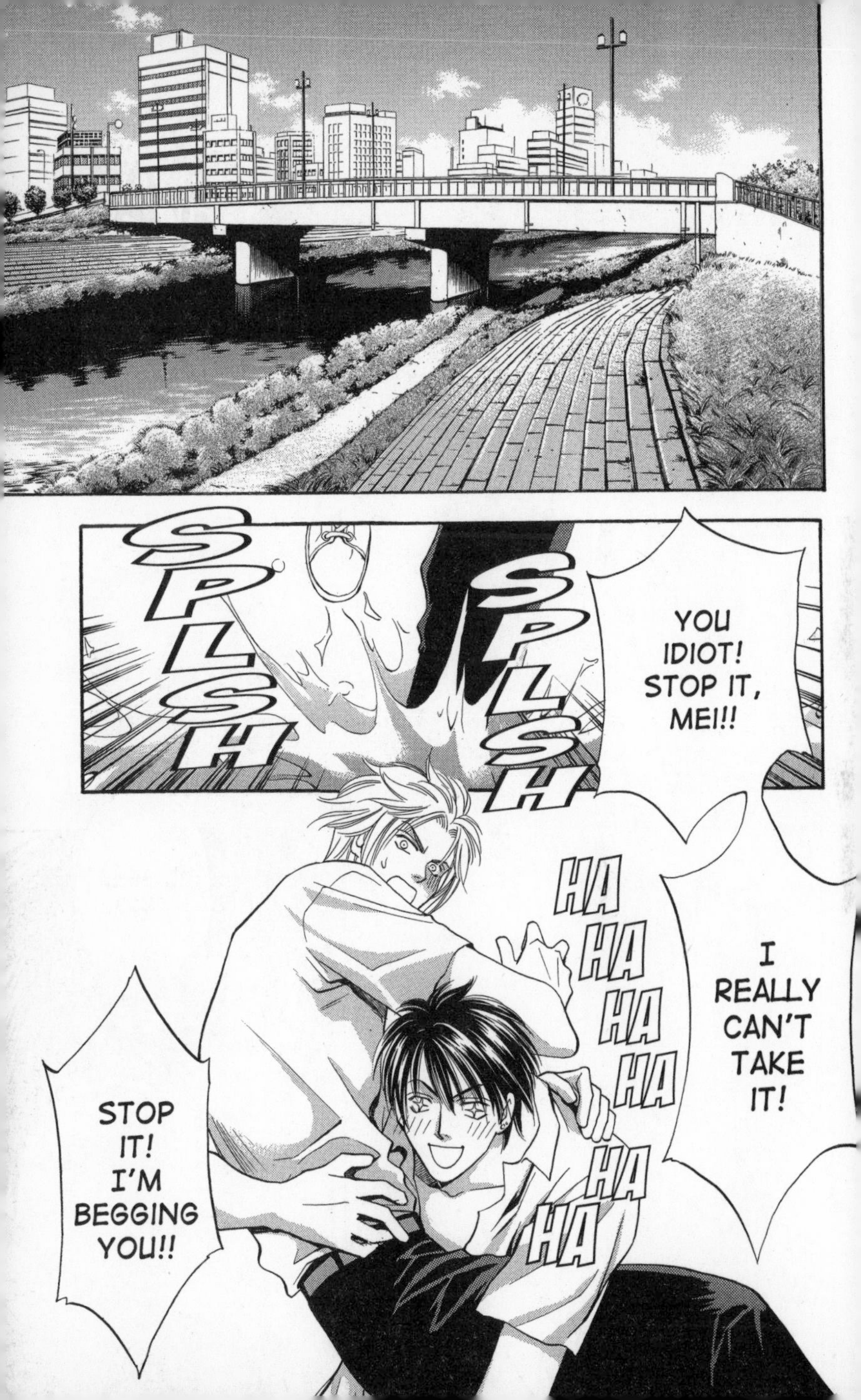
YOU IDIOT! STOP IT, MEI!!
SPLSH
SPLSH
I REALLY CAN'T TAKE IT!
HA HA HA HA HA HA HA
STOP IT! I'M BEGGING YOU!!

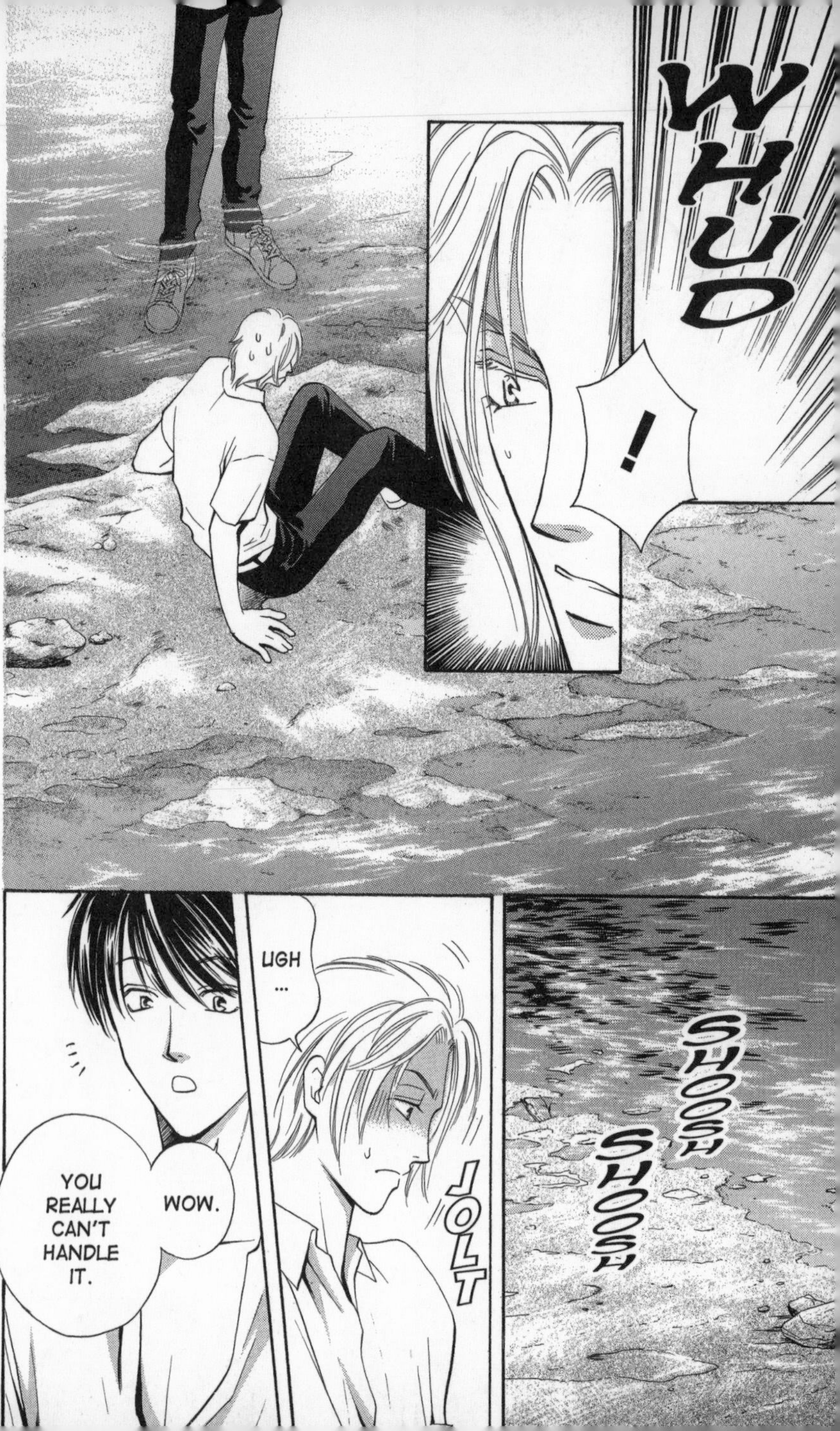
WHUD
!
SHOOSH
SHOOSH
UGH ...
JOLT
WOW.
YOU REALLY CAN'T HANDLE IT.

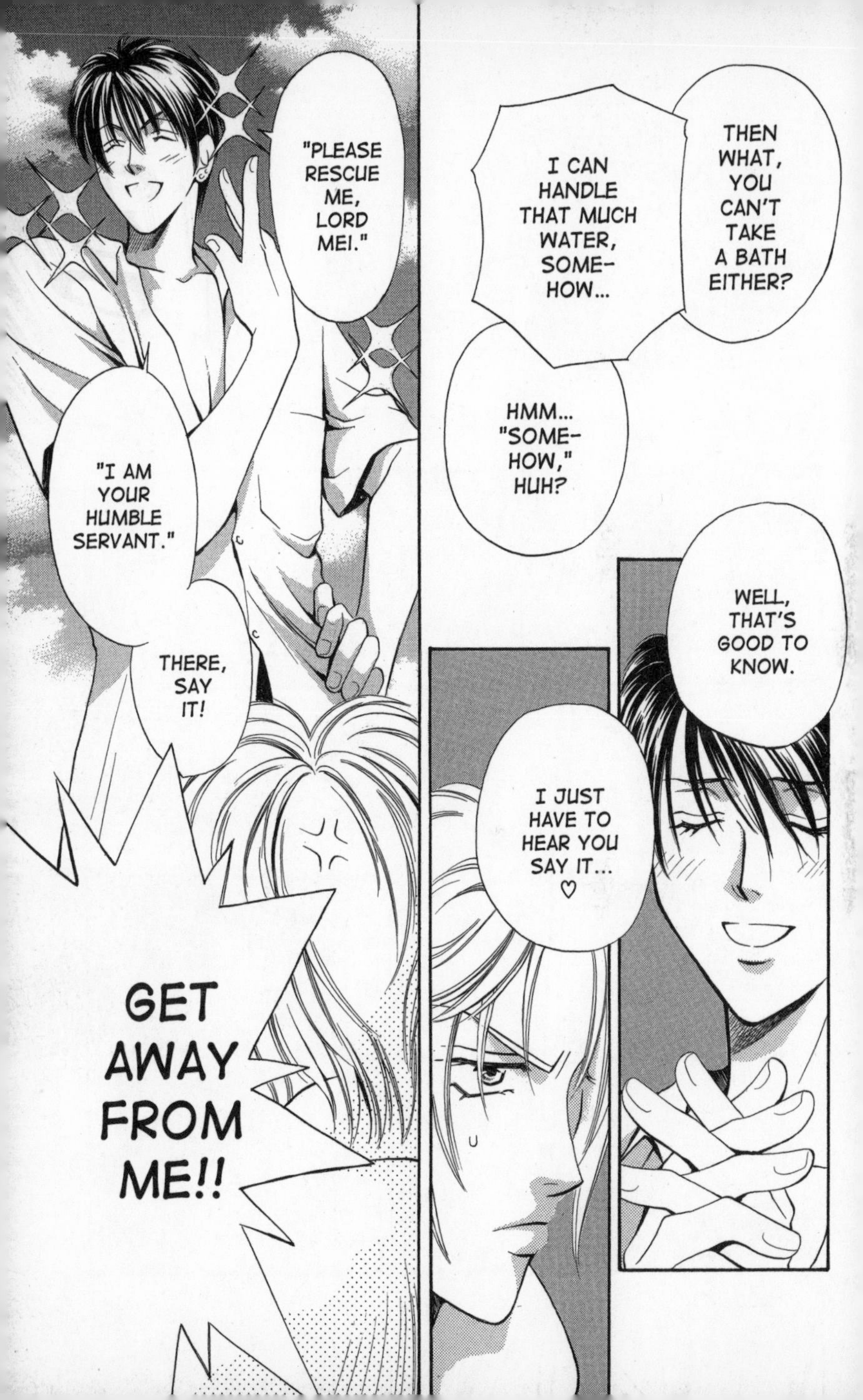
THEN WHAT, YOU CAN'T TAKE A BATH EITHER?
I CAN HANDLE THAT MUCH WATER, SOME-HOW...
HMM... "SOME-HOW," HUH?
WELL, THAT'S GOOD TO KNOW.
I JUST HAVE TO HEAR YOU SAY IT... ♡
"PLEASE RESCUE ME, LORD MEI."
"I AM YOUR HUMBLE SERVANT."
THERE, SAY IT!
GET AWAY FROM ME!!

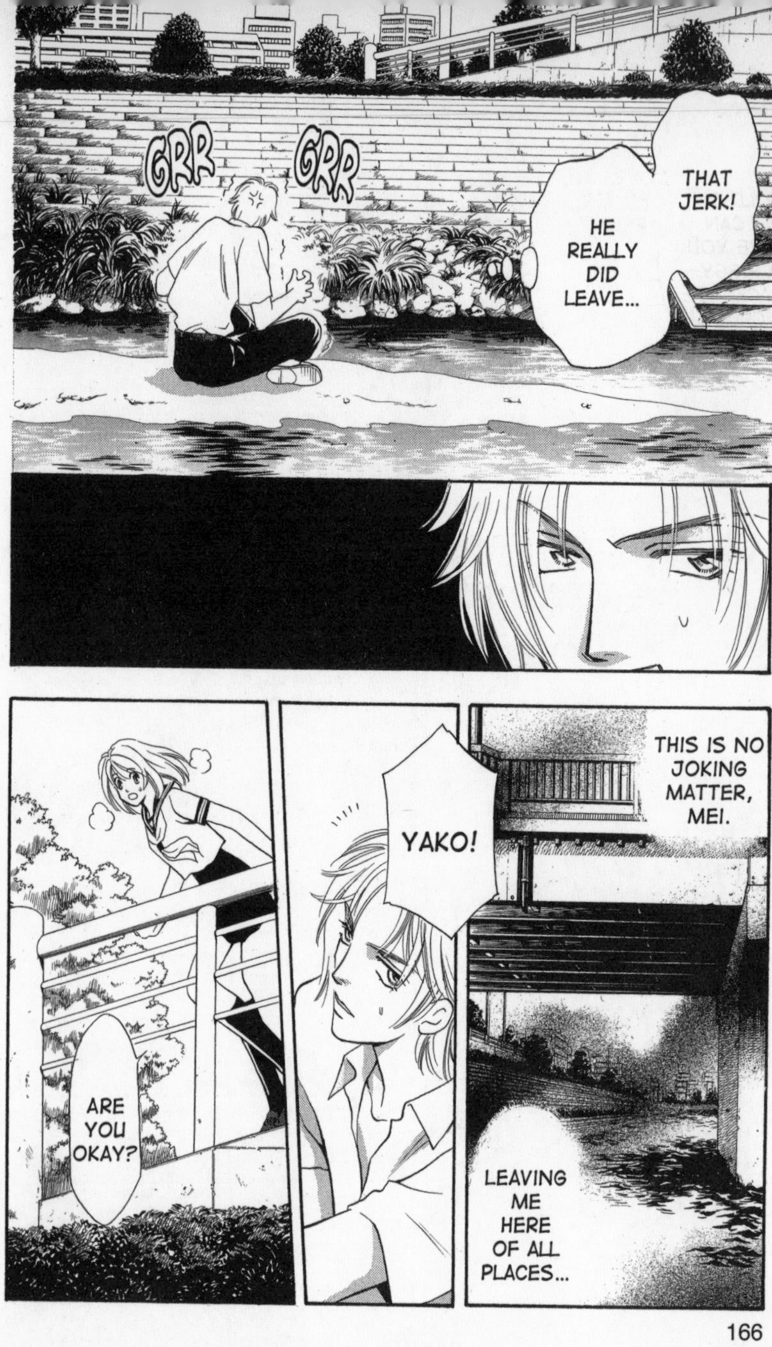
THAT JERK!
HE REALLY DID LEAVE...
GRR
GRR
THIS IS NO JOKING MATTER, MEI.
LEAVING ME HERE OF ALL PLACES...
YAKO!
ARE YOU OKAY?

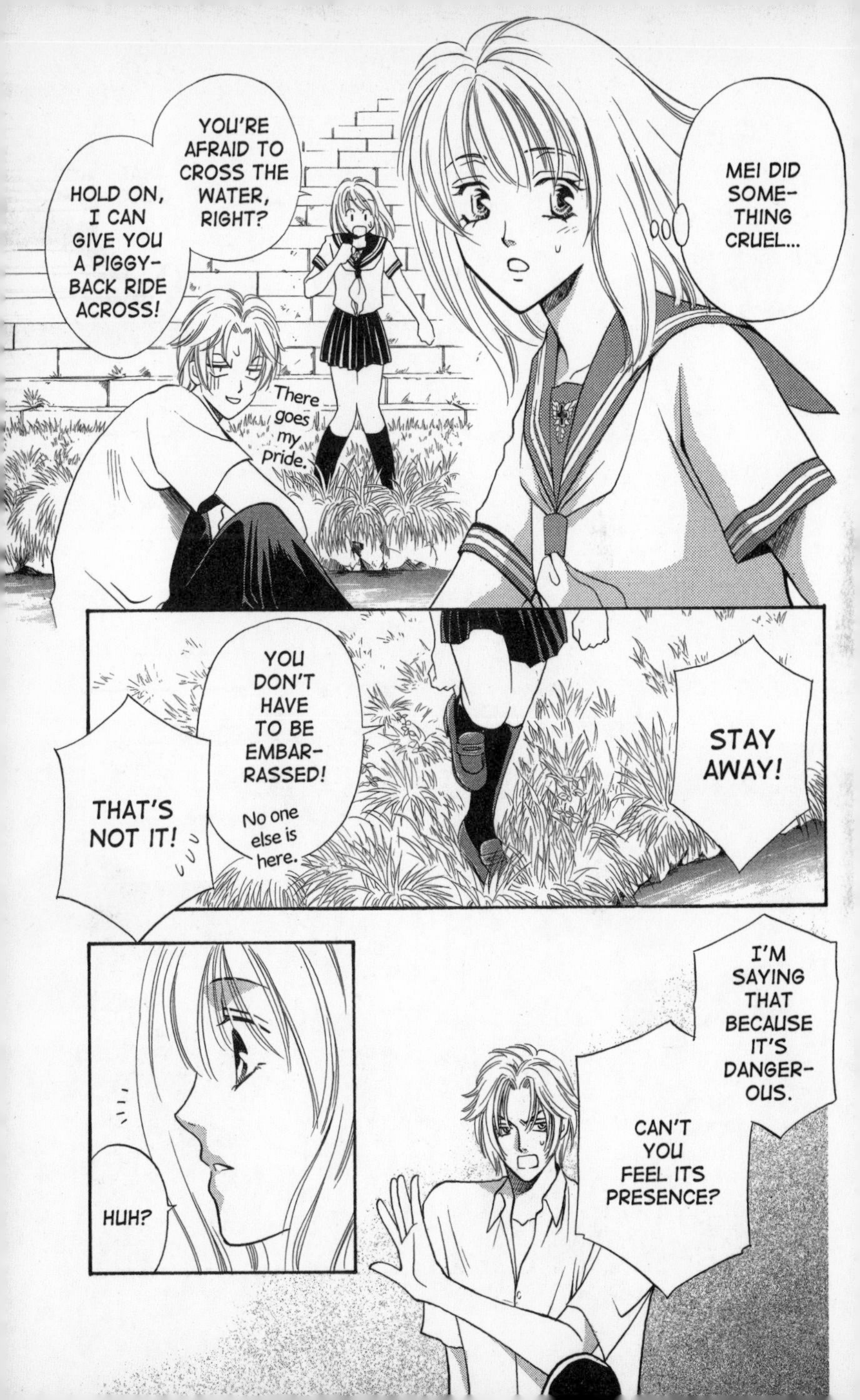
MEI DID SOMETHING CRUEL...
YOU'RE AFRAID TO CROSS THE WATER, RIGHT?
HOLD ON, I CAN GIVE YOU A PIGGY-BACK RIDE ACROSS!
There goes my pride.
STAY AWAY!
YOU DON'T HAVE TO BE EMBARRASSED!
No one else is here.
THAT'S NOT IT!
I'M SAYING THAT BECAUSE IT'S DANGEROUS.
CAN'T YOU FEEL ITS PRESENCE?
HUH?

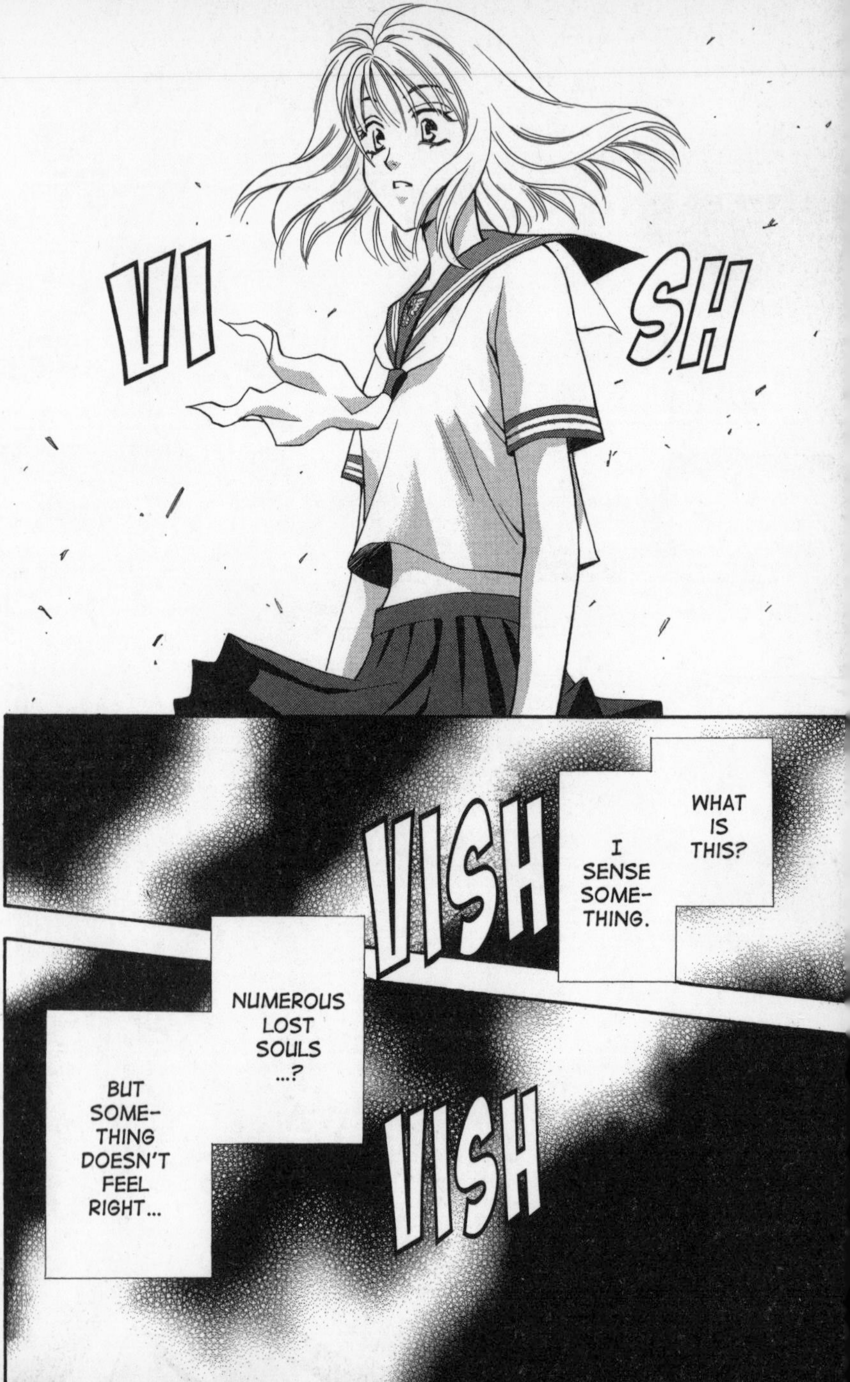

VI SH
WHAT IS THIS?
I SENSE SOME-THING.
VISH
NUMEROUS LOST SOULS ...?
BUT SOME-THING DOESN'T FEEL RIGHT...
VISH

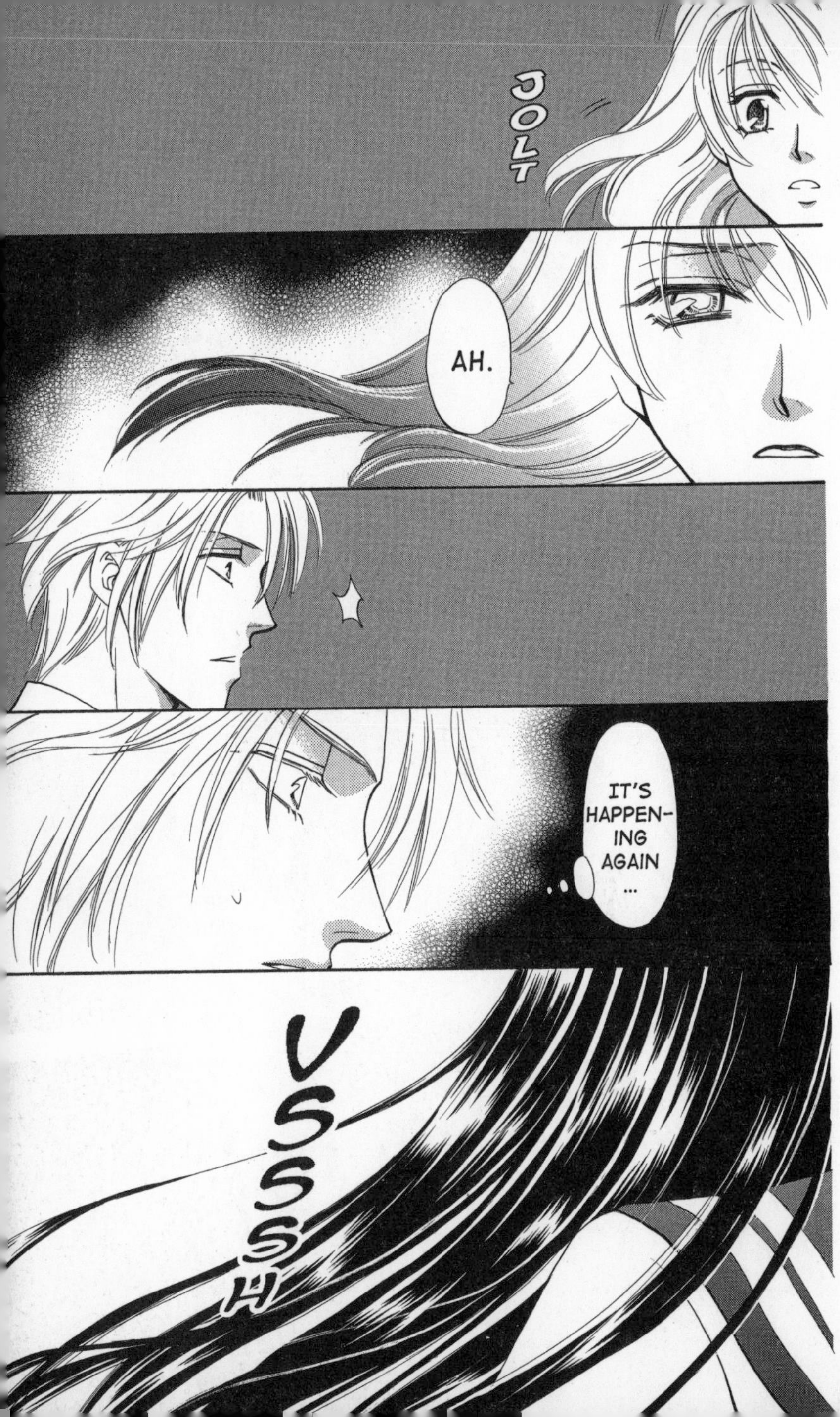
JOLT
AH.
IT'S HAPPENING AGAIN ...
VSSSH

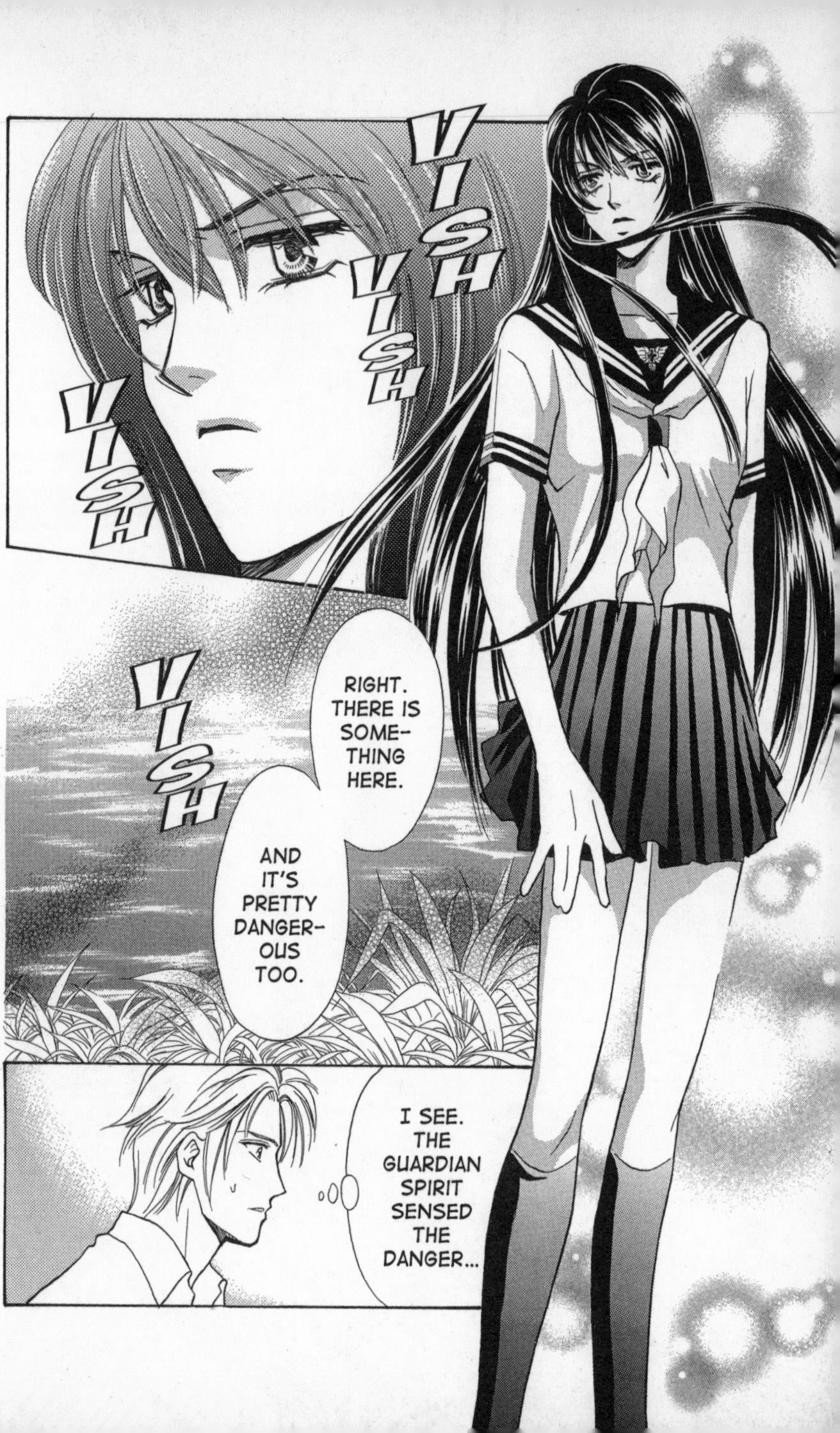
VISH
VISH
VISH
VISH
RIGHT. THERE IS SOME-THING HERE.
AND IT'S PRETTY DANGER-OUS TOO.
I SEE. THE GUARDIAN SPIRIT SENSED THE DANGER...

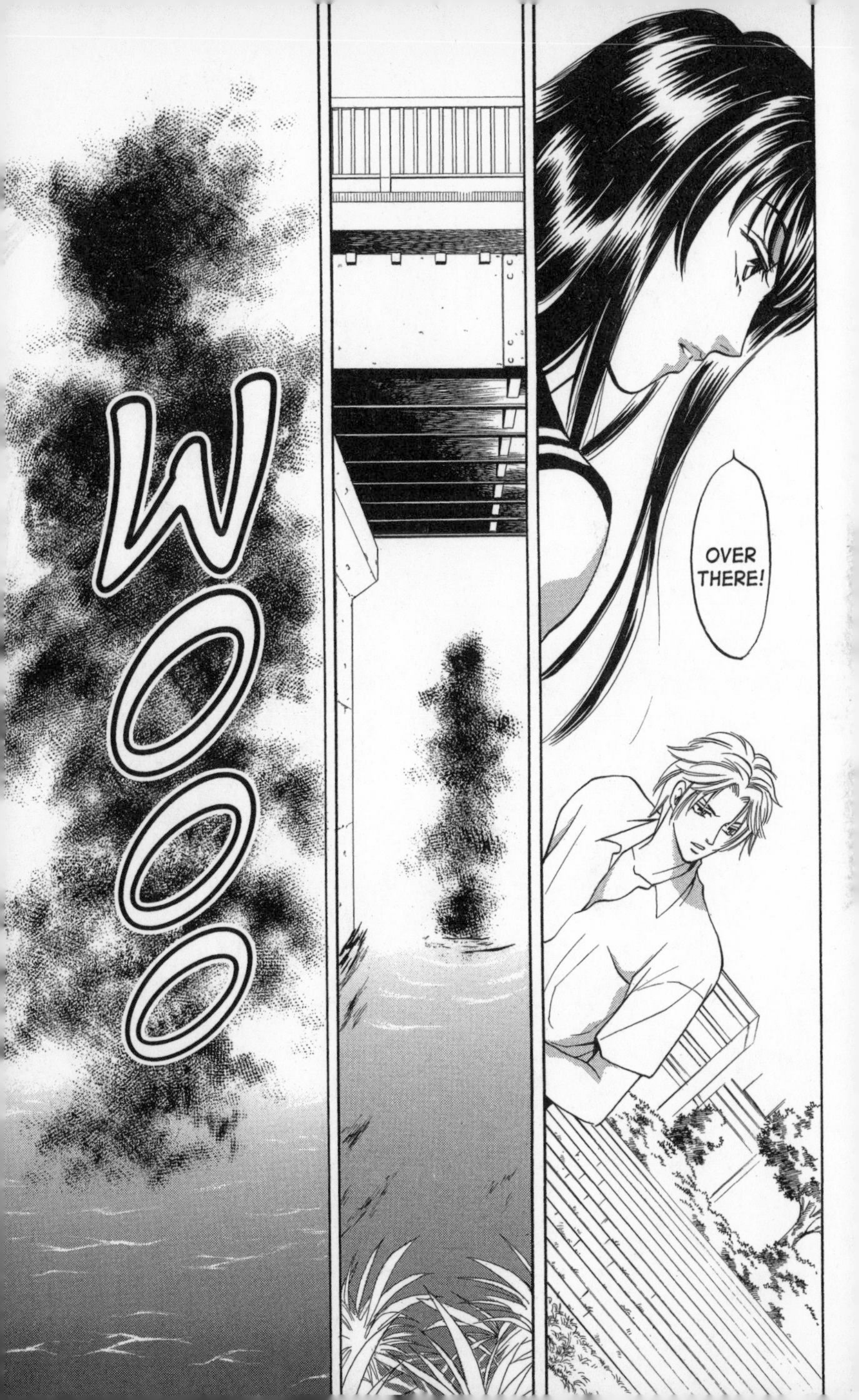
OVER THERE!
WOOOO

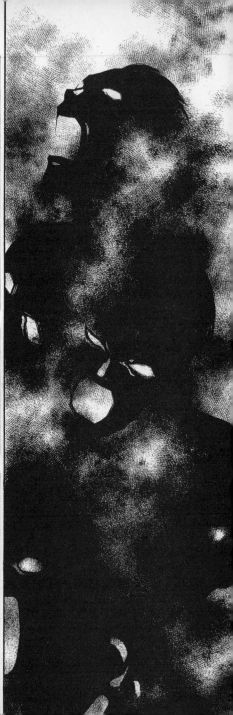

WHY ARE THERE SO MANY...?

ALL THOSE EVIL SPIRITS ARE JOINED TOGETHER.

THIS WILL BE DIFFICULT.

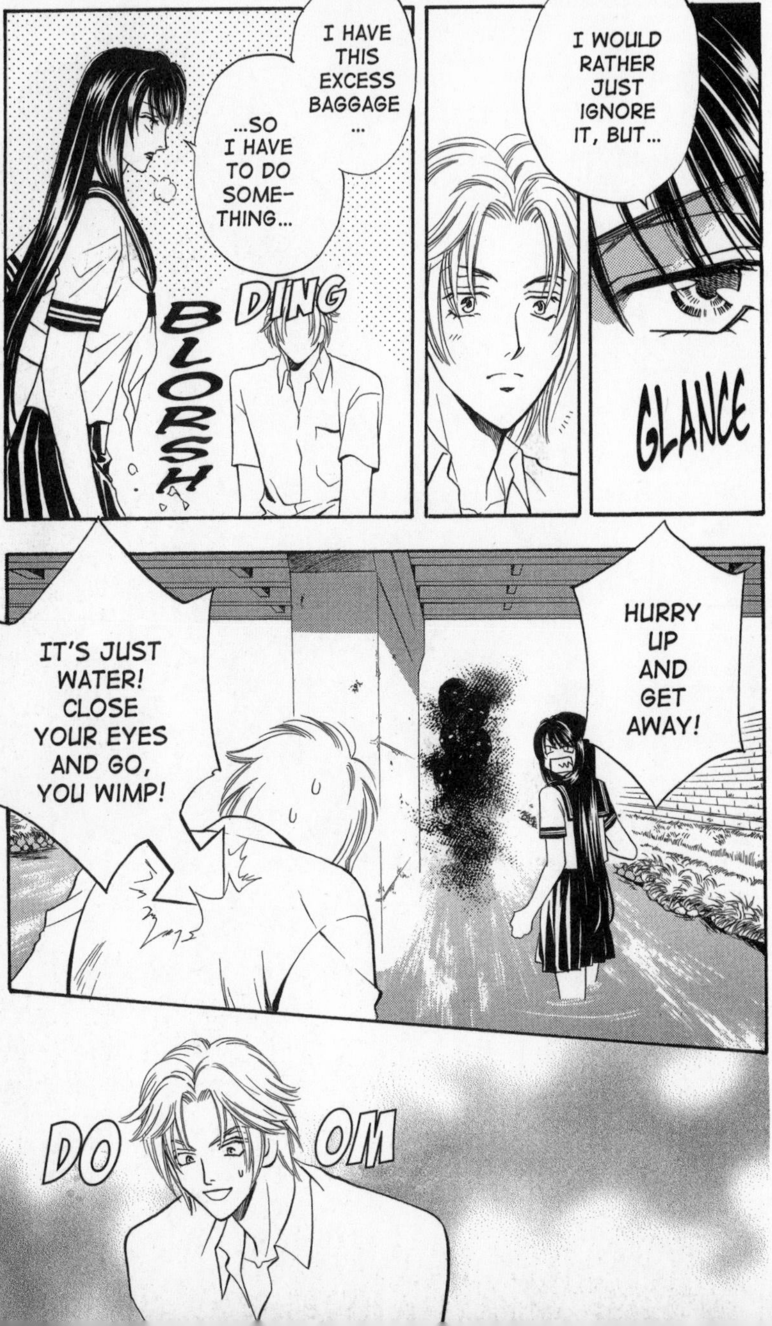
I WOULD RATHER JUST IGNORE IT, BUT...
GLANCE
I HAVE THIS EXCESS BAGGAGE ...
...SO I HAVE TO DO SOME-THING...
DING
BLORSH
HURRY UP AND GET AWAY!
IT'S JUST WATER! CLOSE YOUR EYES AND GO, YOU WIMP!
DO OM

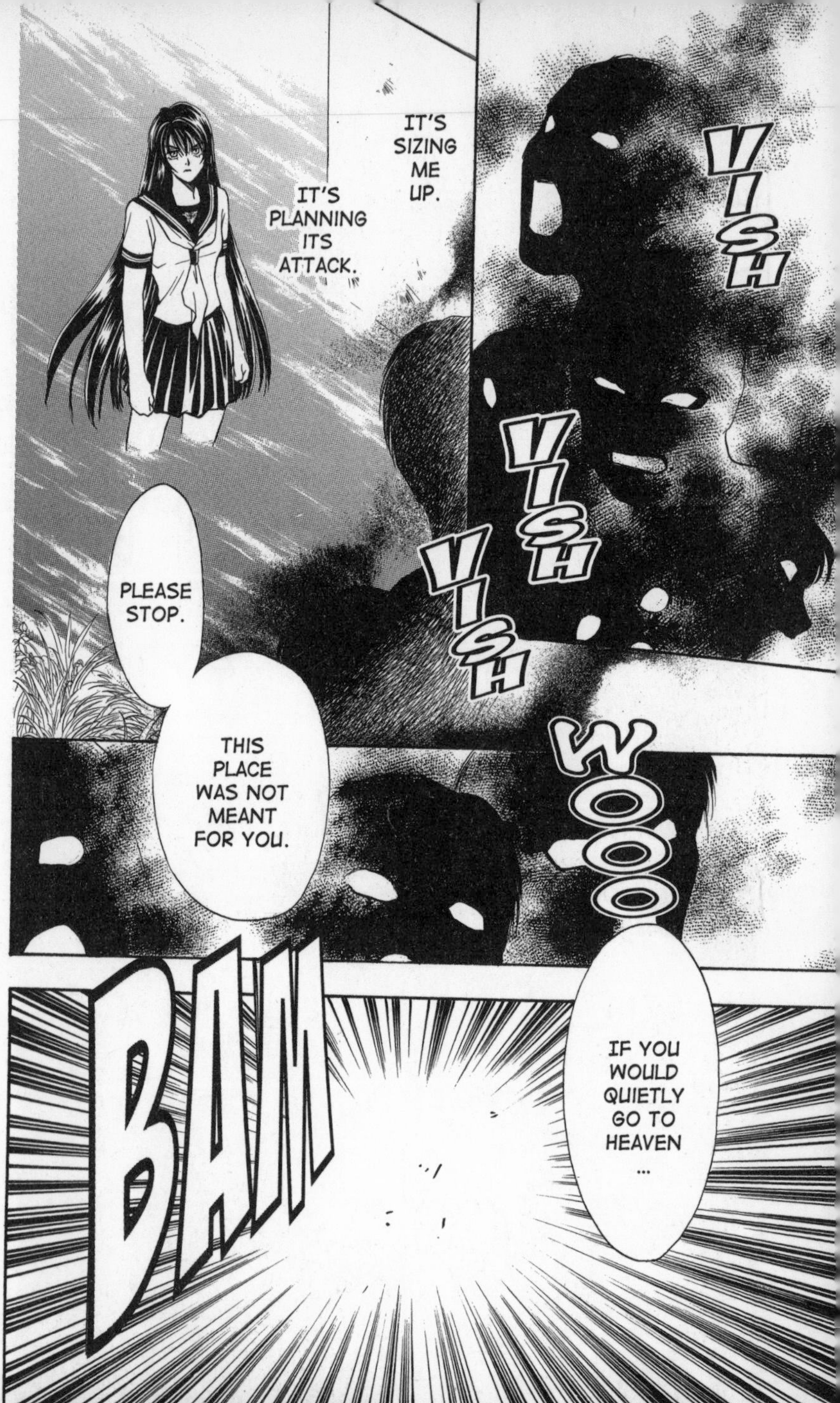
VISH
VISH
VISH
IT'S SIZING ME UP.
IT'S PLANNING ITS ATTACK.
PLEASE STOP.
WOOO
THIS PLACE WAS NOT MEANT FOR YOU.
IF YOU WOULD QUIETLY GO TO HEAVEN ...
BAM

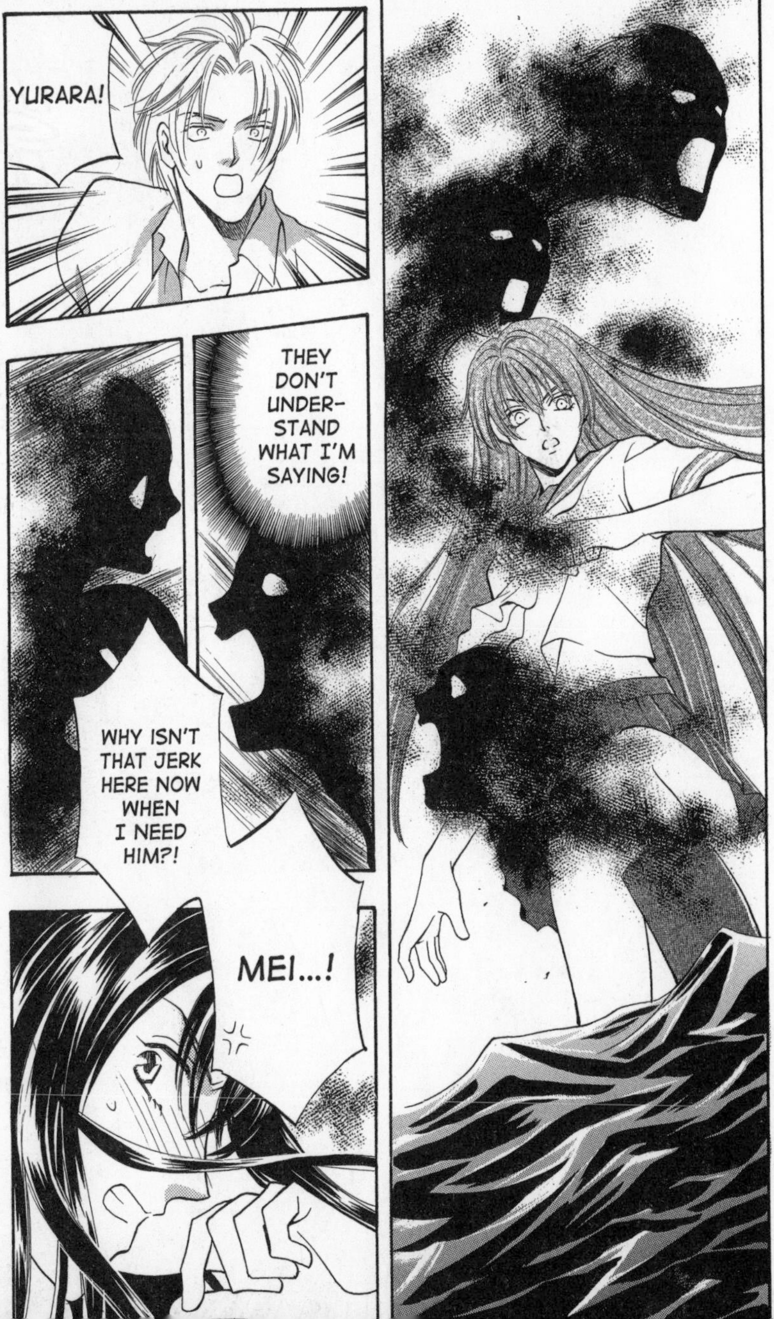
YURARA!
THEY DON'T UNDER-STAND WHAT I'M SAYING!
WHY ISN'T THAT JERK HERE NOW WHEN I NEED HIM?!
MEI...!

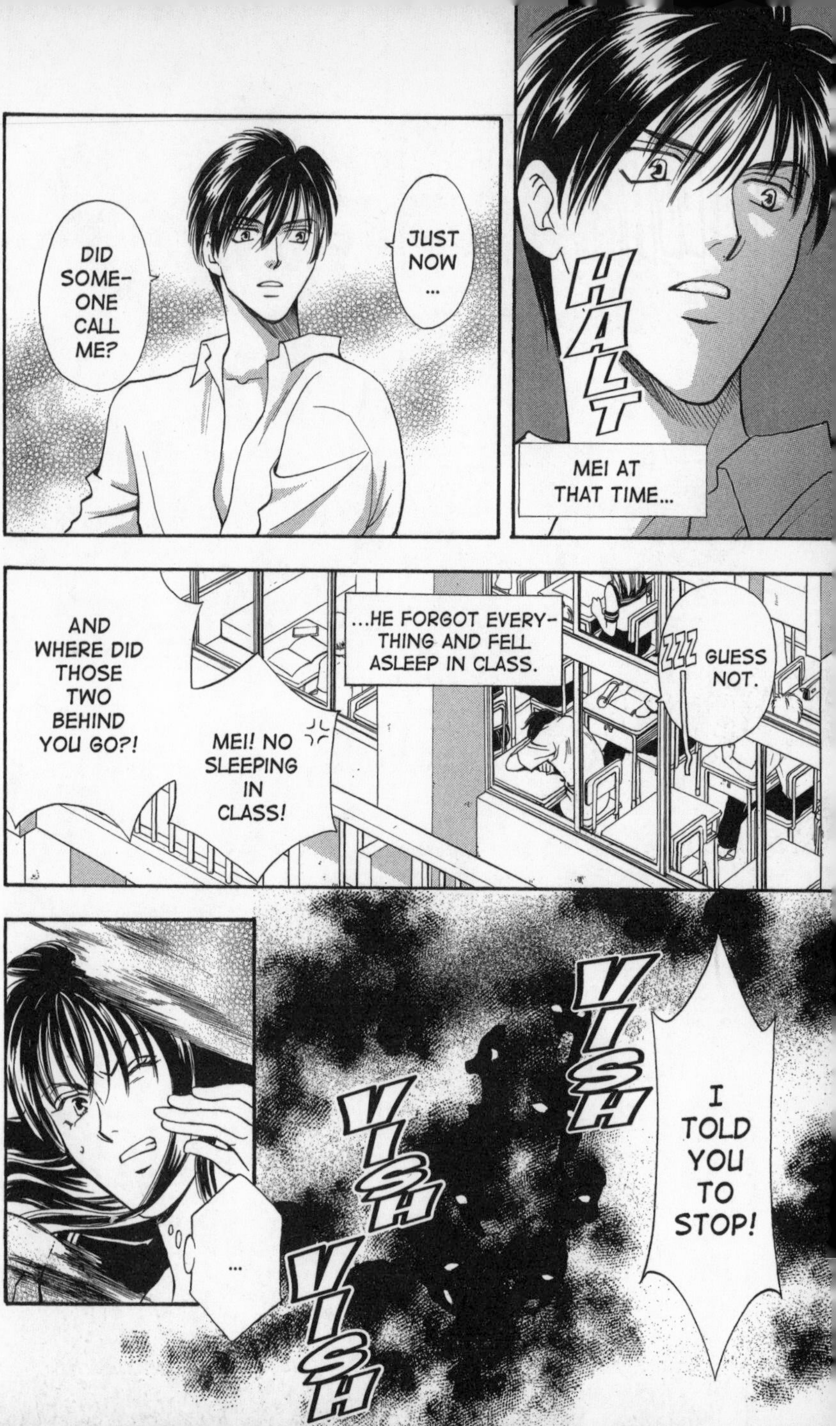
HALT
MEI AT THAT TIME...
JUST NOW ...
DID SOMEONE CALL ME?
GUESS NOT.
ZZZ
...HE FORGOT EVERYTHING AND FELL ASLEEP IN CLASS.
MEI! NO SLEEPING IN CLASS!
AND WHERE DID THOSE TWO BEHIND YOU GO?!
I TOLD YOU TO STOP!
VISH
VISH
VISH
...

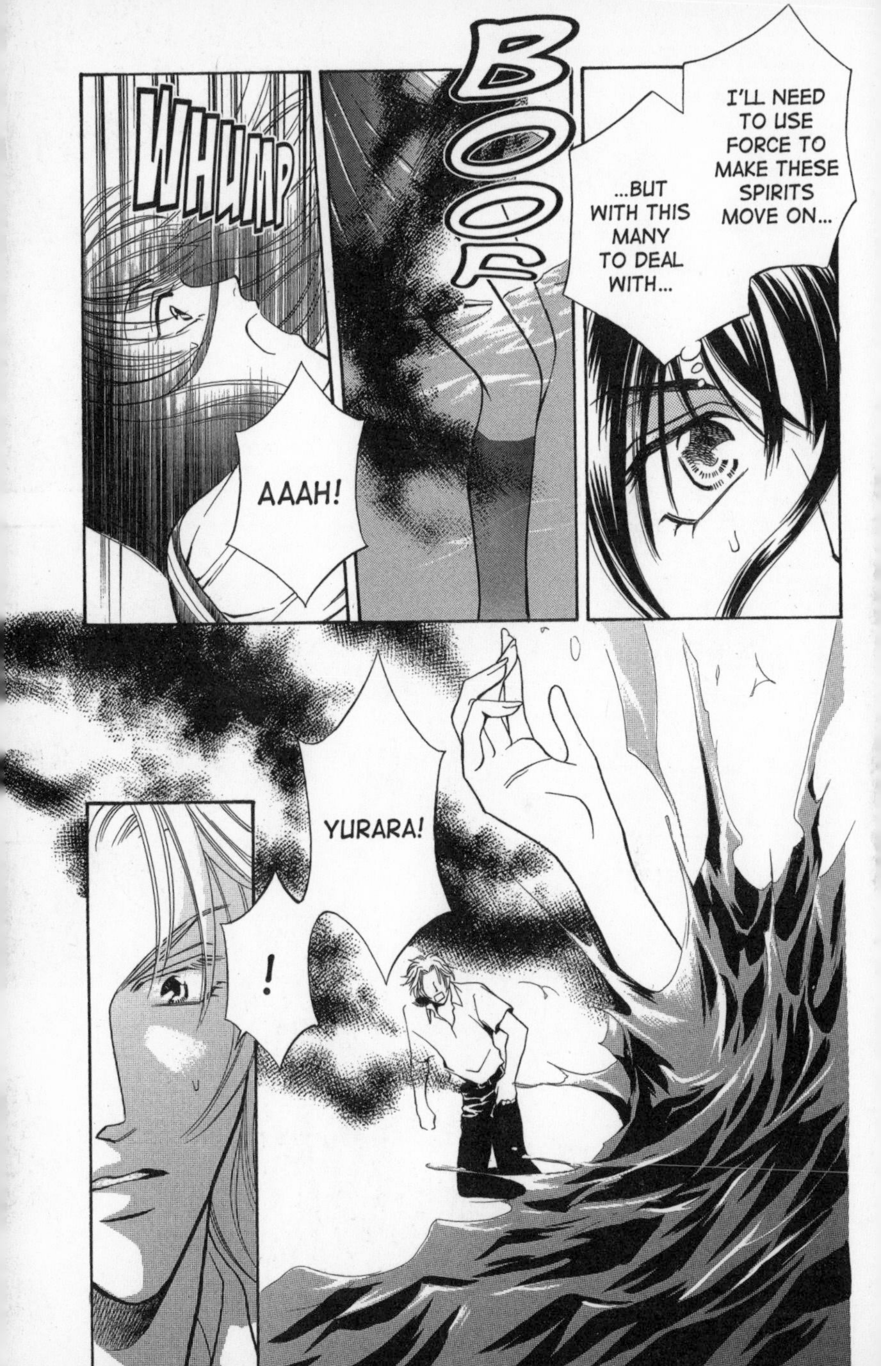
I'LL NEED TO USE FORCE TO MAKE THESE SPIRITS MOVE ON...
...BUT WITH THIS MANY TO DEAL WITH...
BOOOF
WHUMP
AAAH!
YURARA!
!

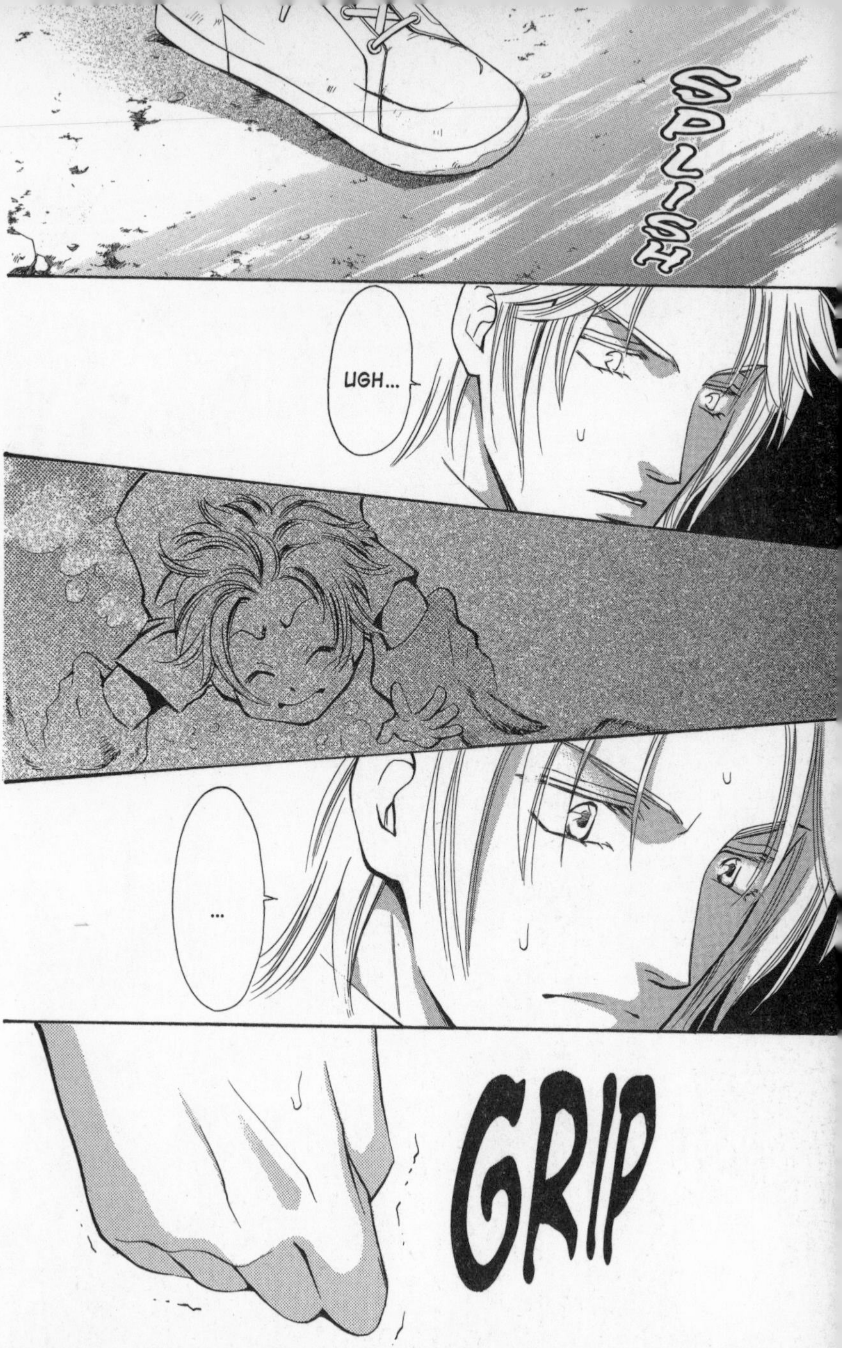
SPLISH
UGH...
...
GRIP

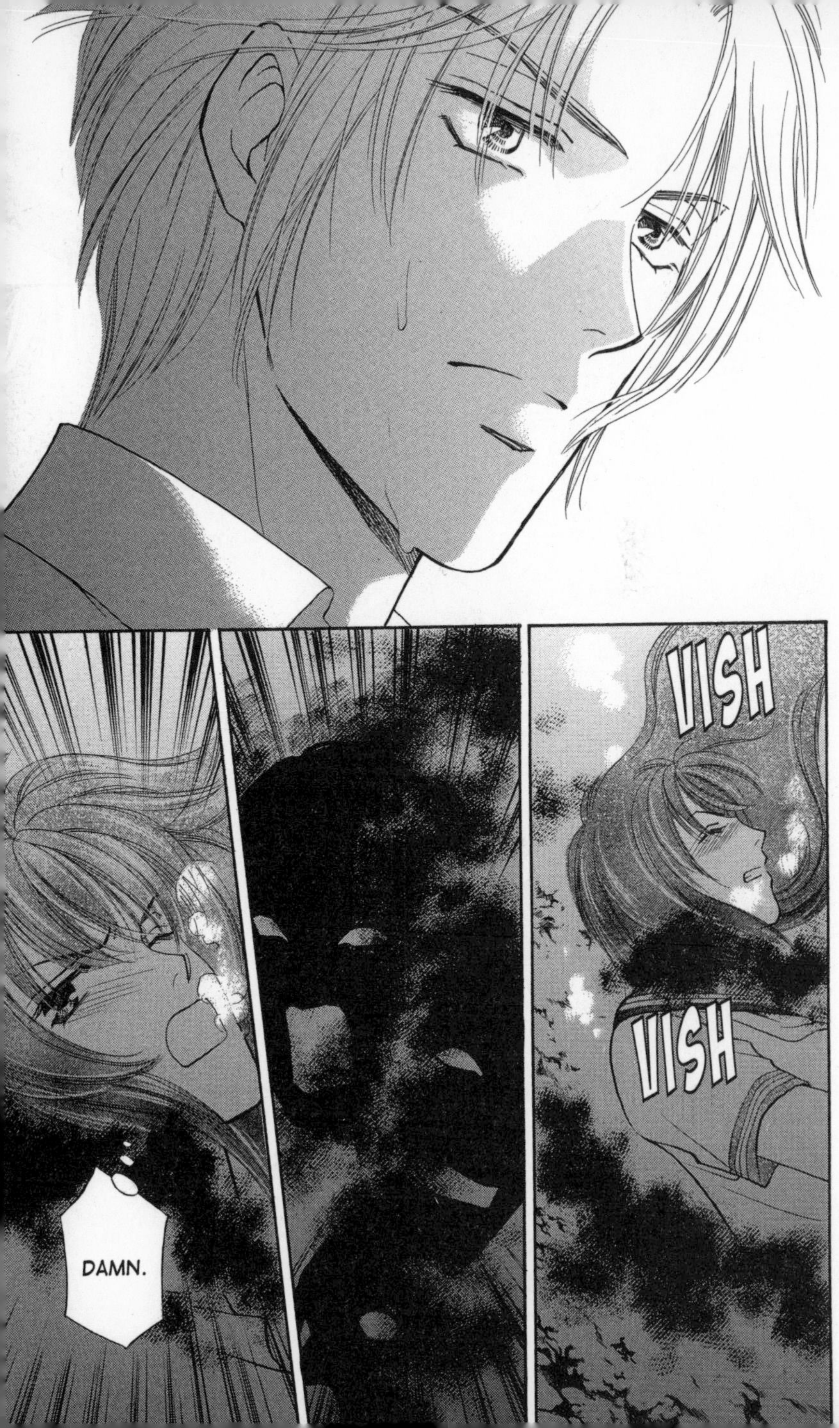
VISH
VISH
DAMN.

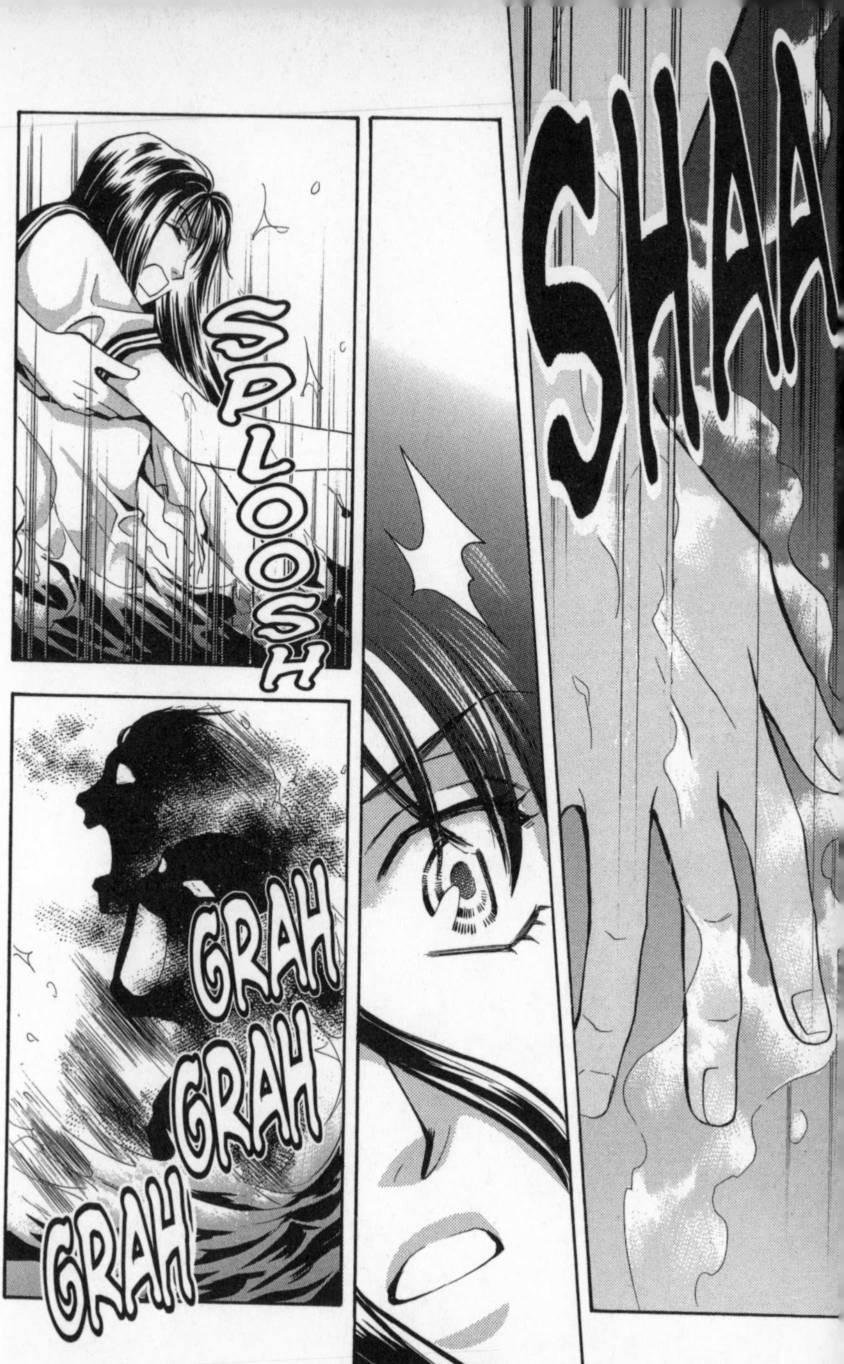
SHAA
SPLOOSH
GRAH
GRAH
GRAH

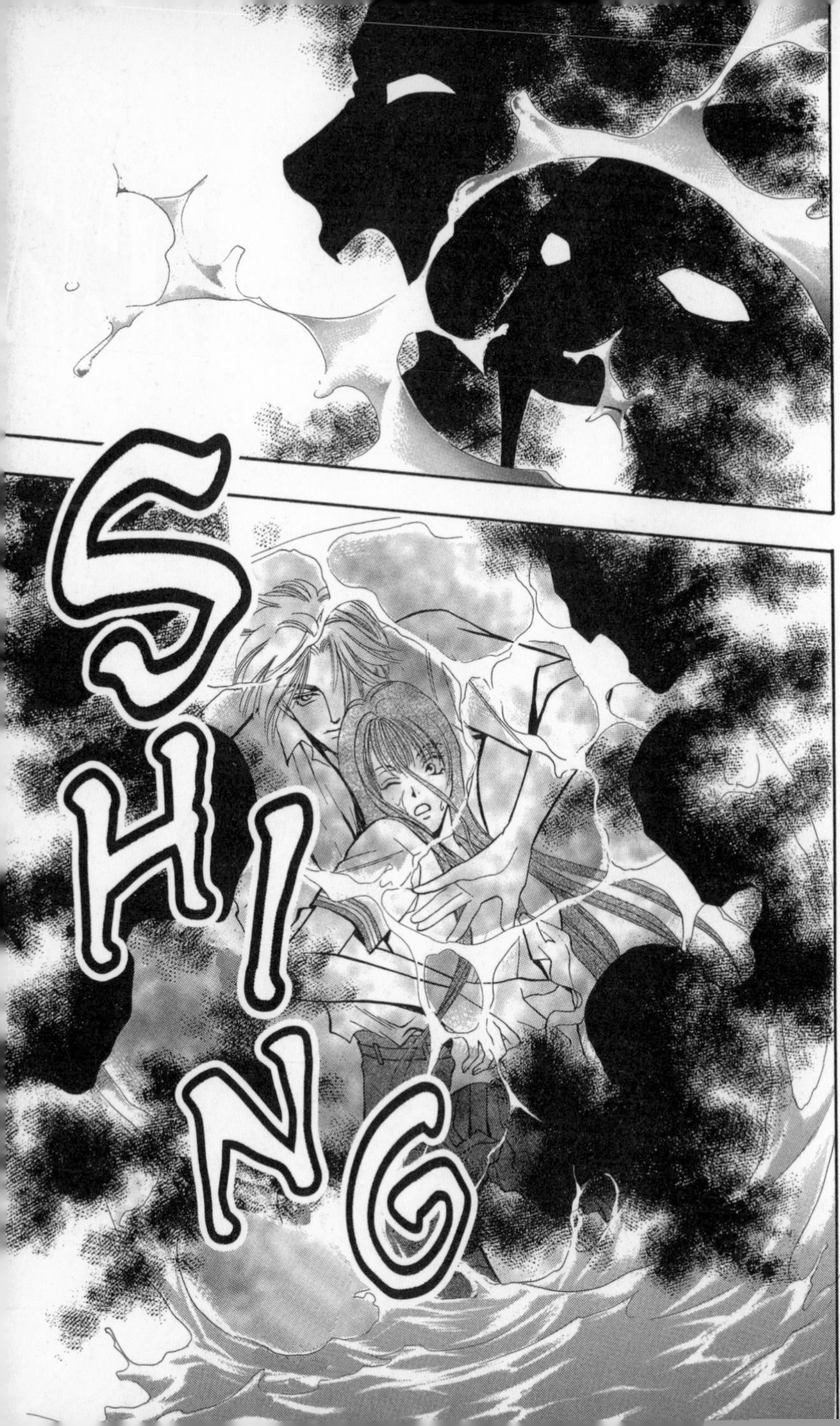
SHING

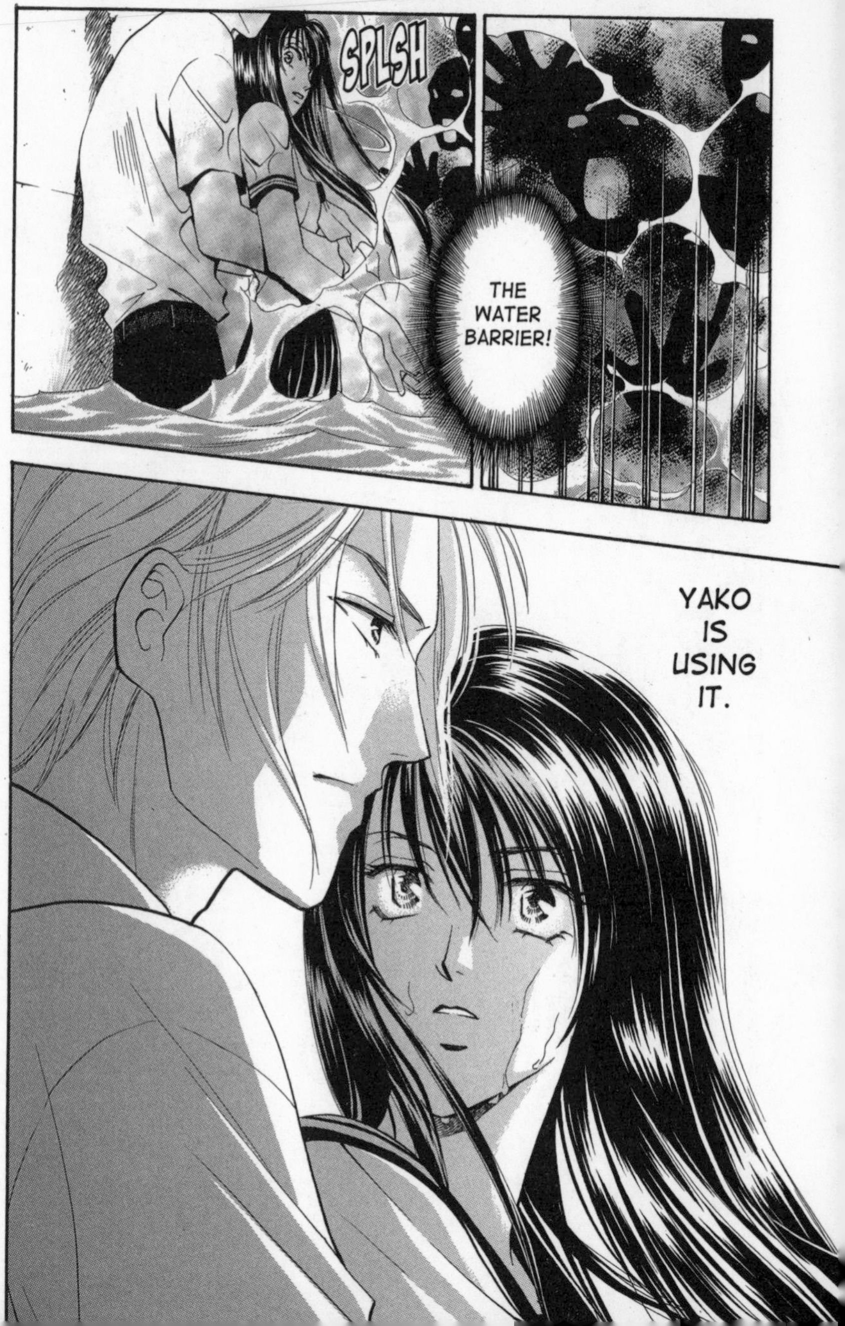
SPLSH
THE WATER BARRIER!
YAKO IS USING IT.

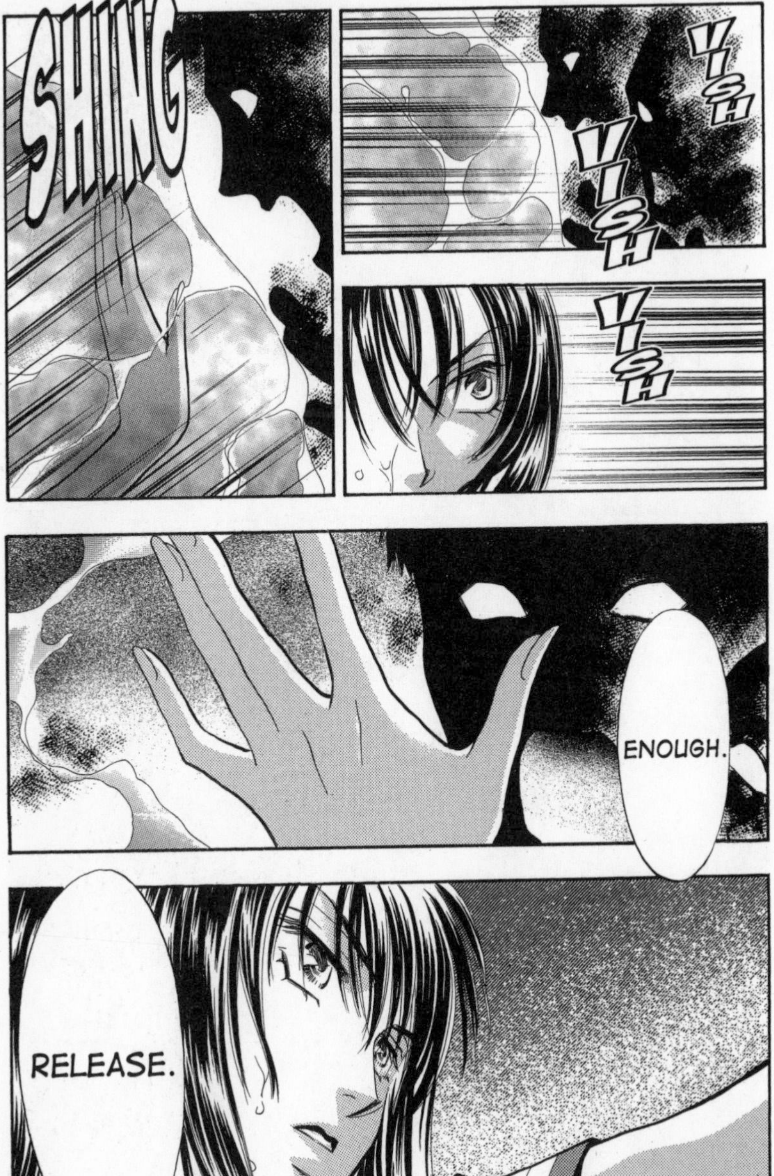
VISH
VISH
VISH
SHING
ENOUGH.
RELEASE.

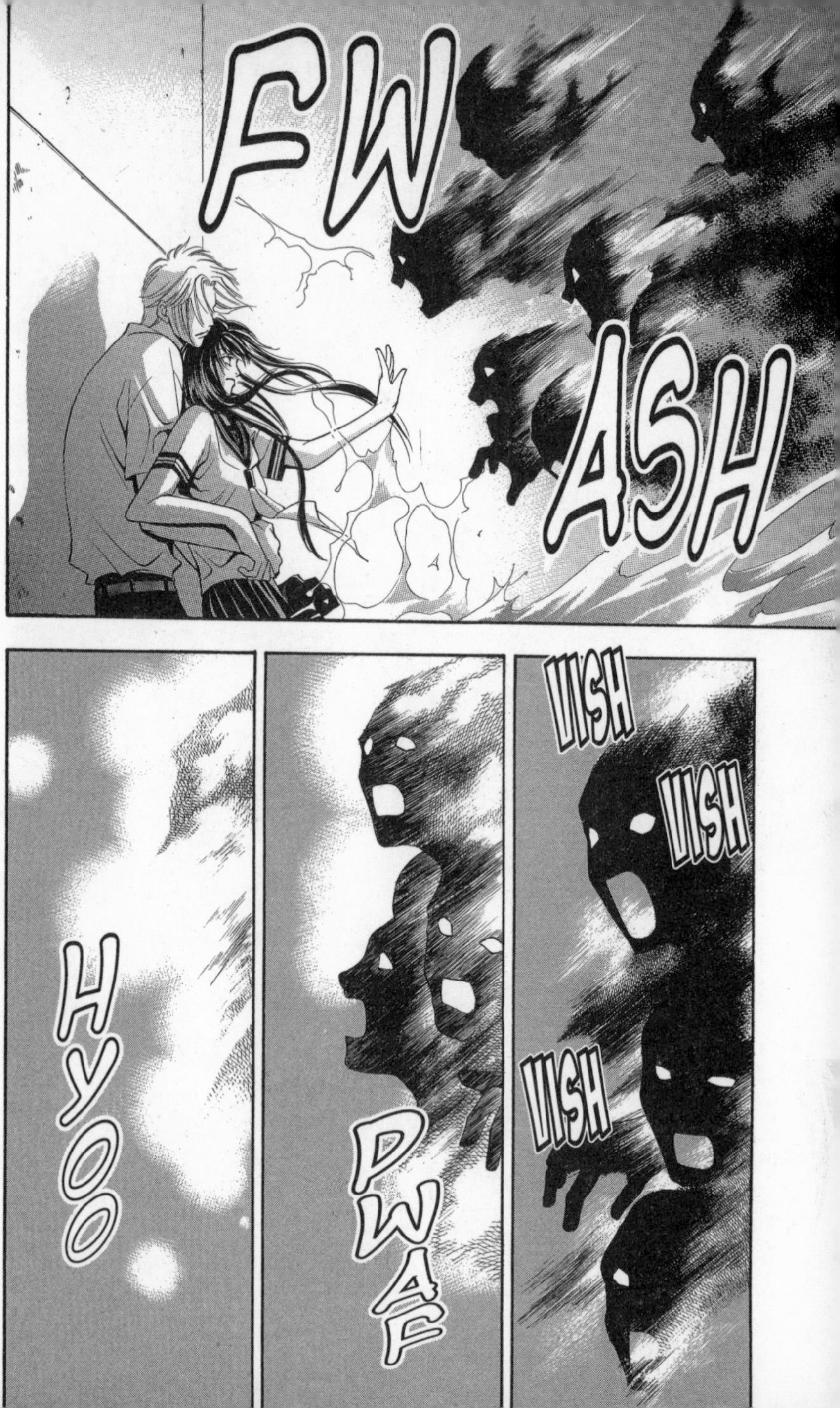
FW
ASH
VISH
VISH
VISH
DWAF
HYOO

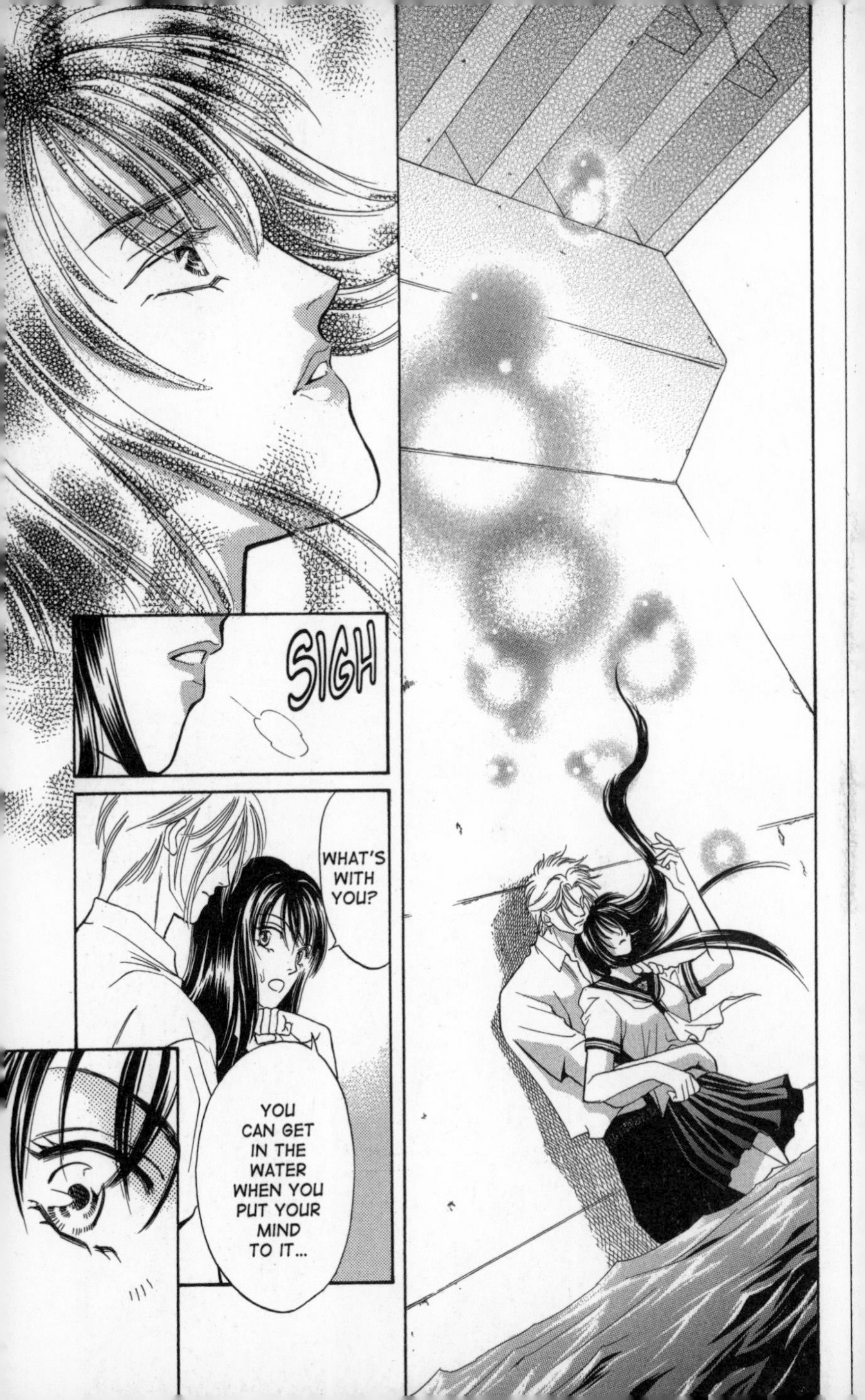
SIGH
WHAT'S WITH YOU?
YOU CAN GET IN THE WATER WHEN YOU PUT YOUR MIND TO IT...

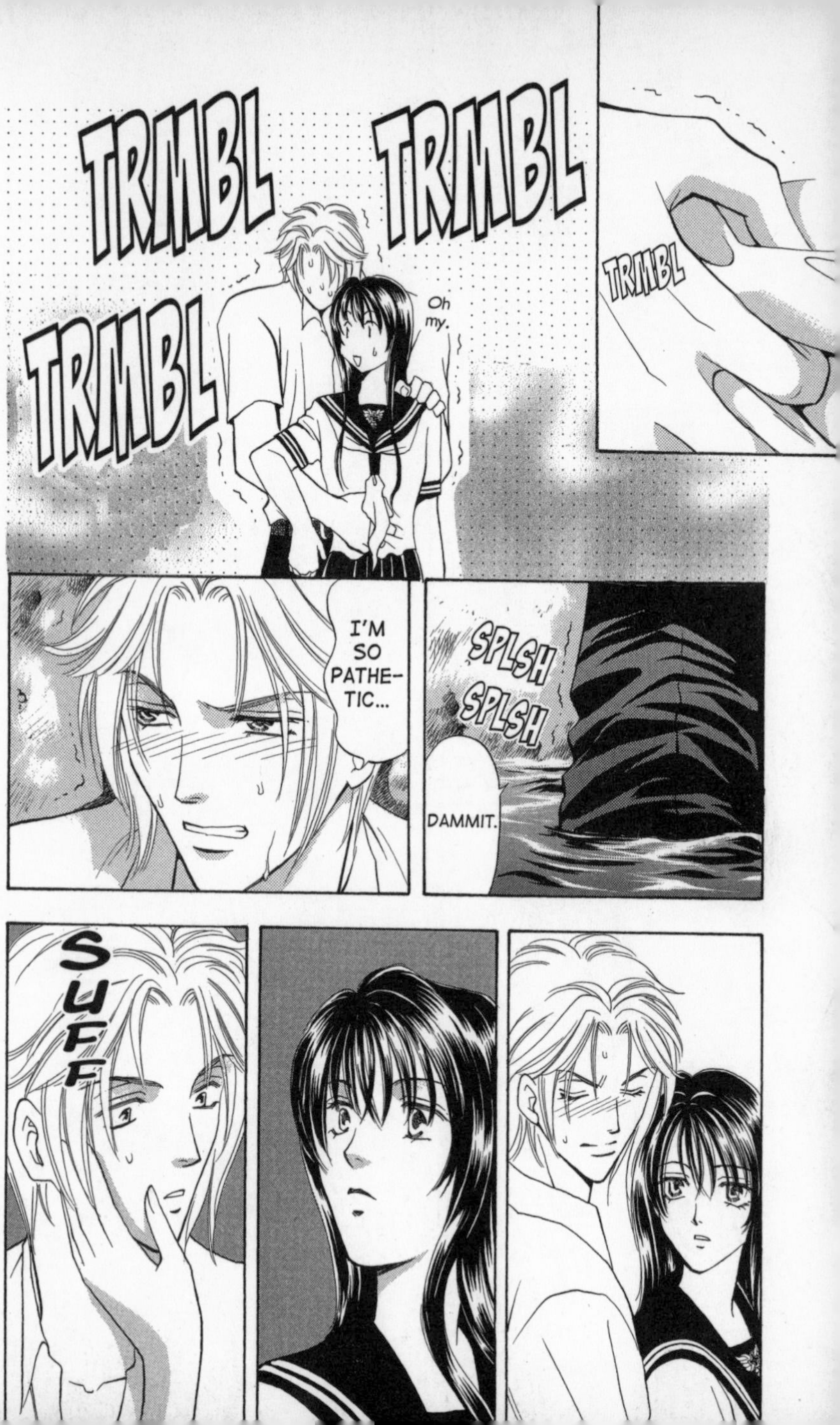
TRMBL
TRMBL
TRMBL
Oh my.
TRMBL
SPLSH SPLSH
DAMMIT.
I'M SO PATHETIC...
SUFF

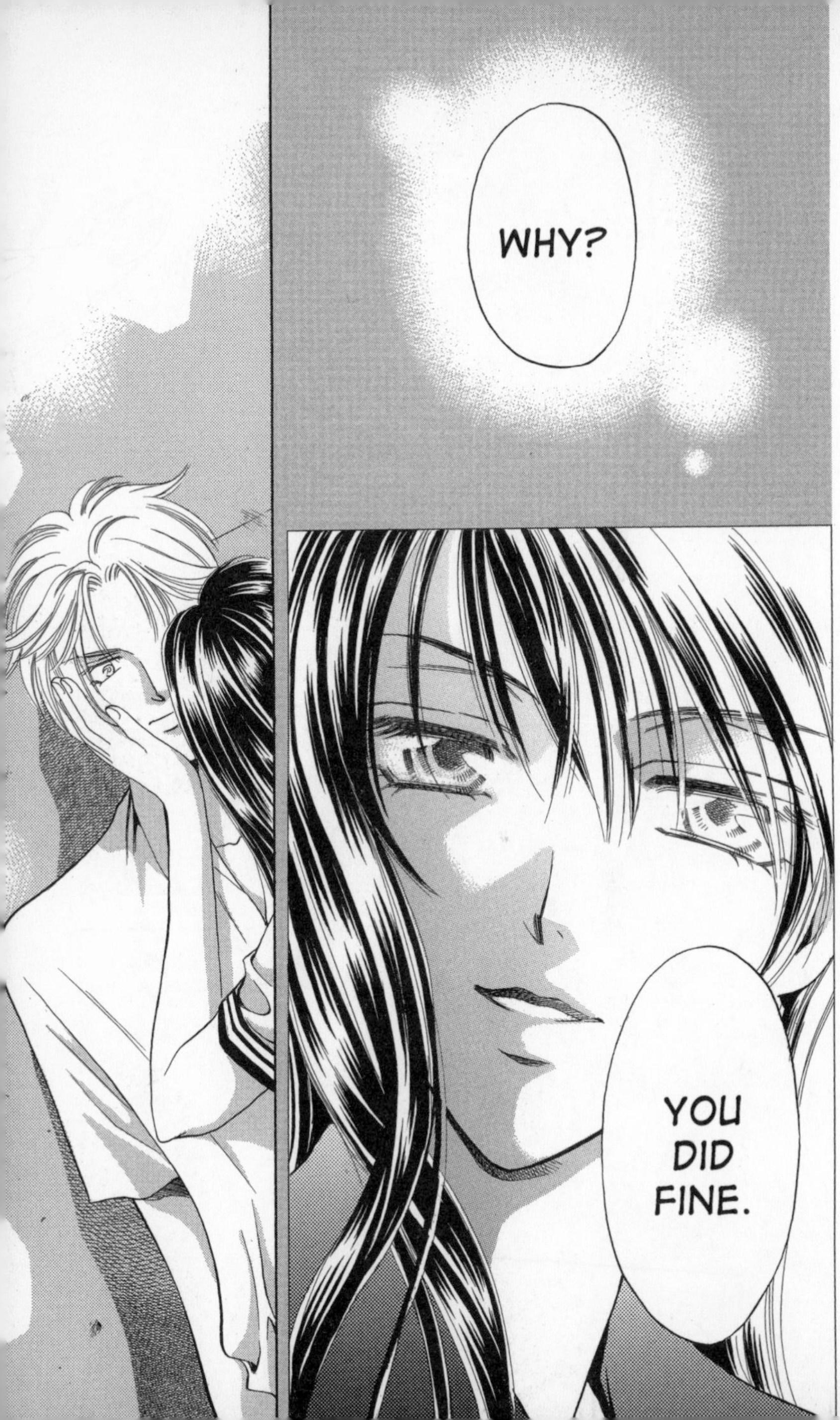
WHY?
YOU DID FINE.

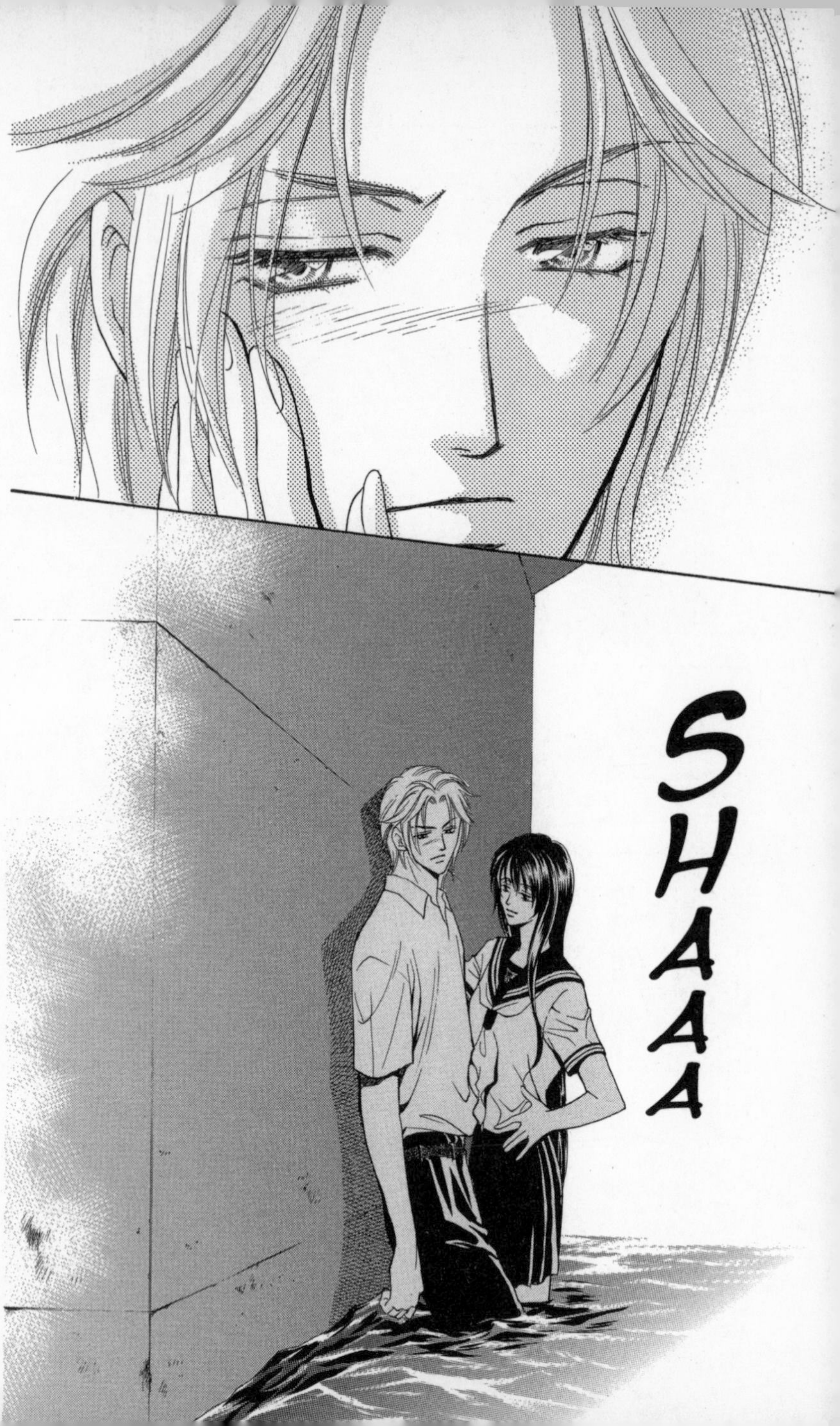
SHAAA

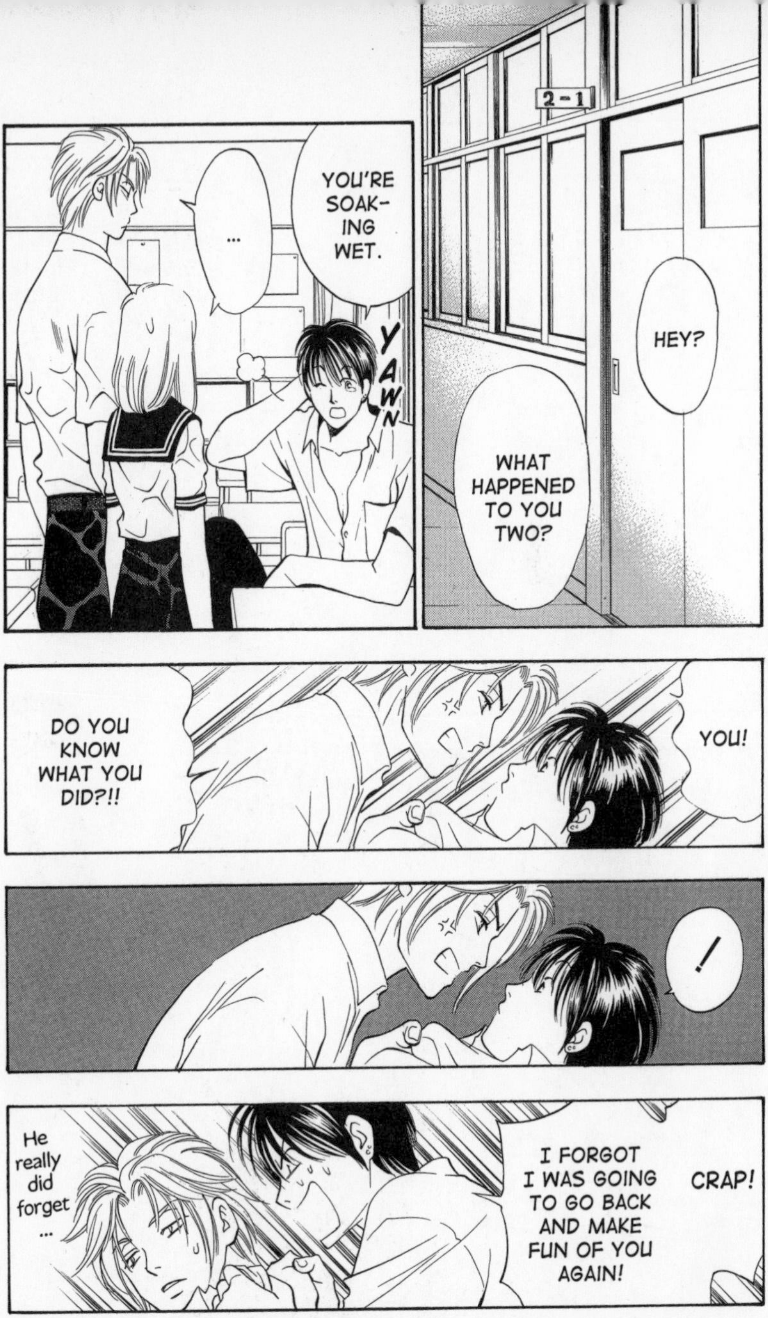
2-1
HEY?
WHAT HAPPENED TO YOU TWO?
YOU'RE SOAK-ING WET.
YAWN
...
YOU!
DO YOU KNOW WHAT YOU DID?!!
!
CRAP!
I FORGOT I WAS GOING TO GO BACK AND MAKE FUN OF YOU AGAIN!
He really did forget ...

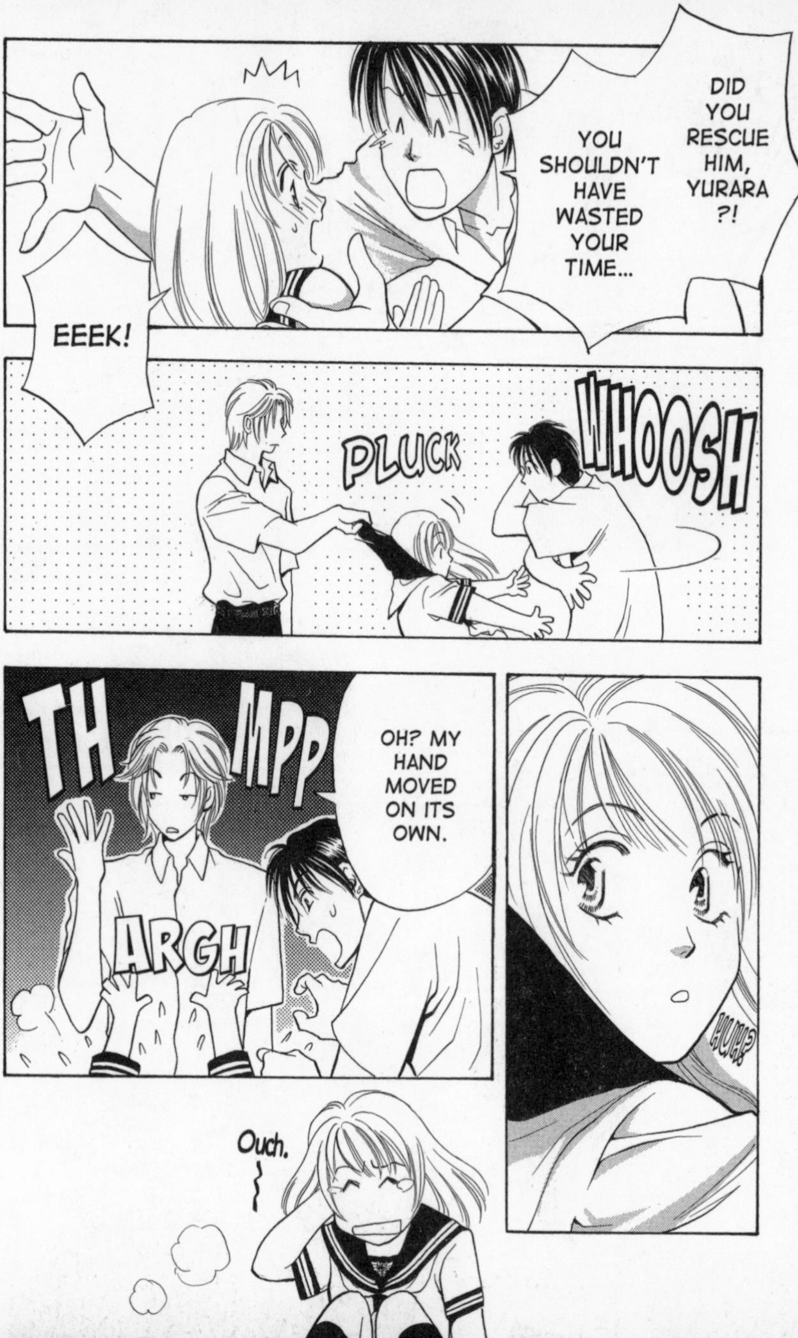

DID YOU RESCUE HIM, YURARA ?!
YOU SHOULDN'T HAVE WASTED YOUR TIME...
EEEK!
WHOOSH
PLUCK
HUH?
OH? MY HAND MOVED ON ITS OWN.
THMPP
ARGH
Ouch.

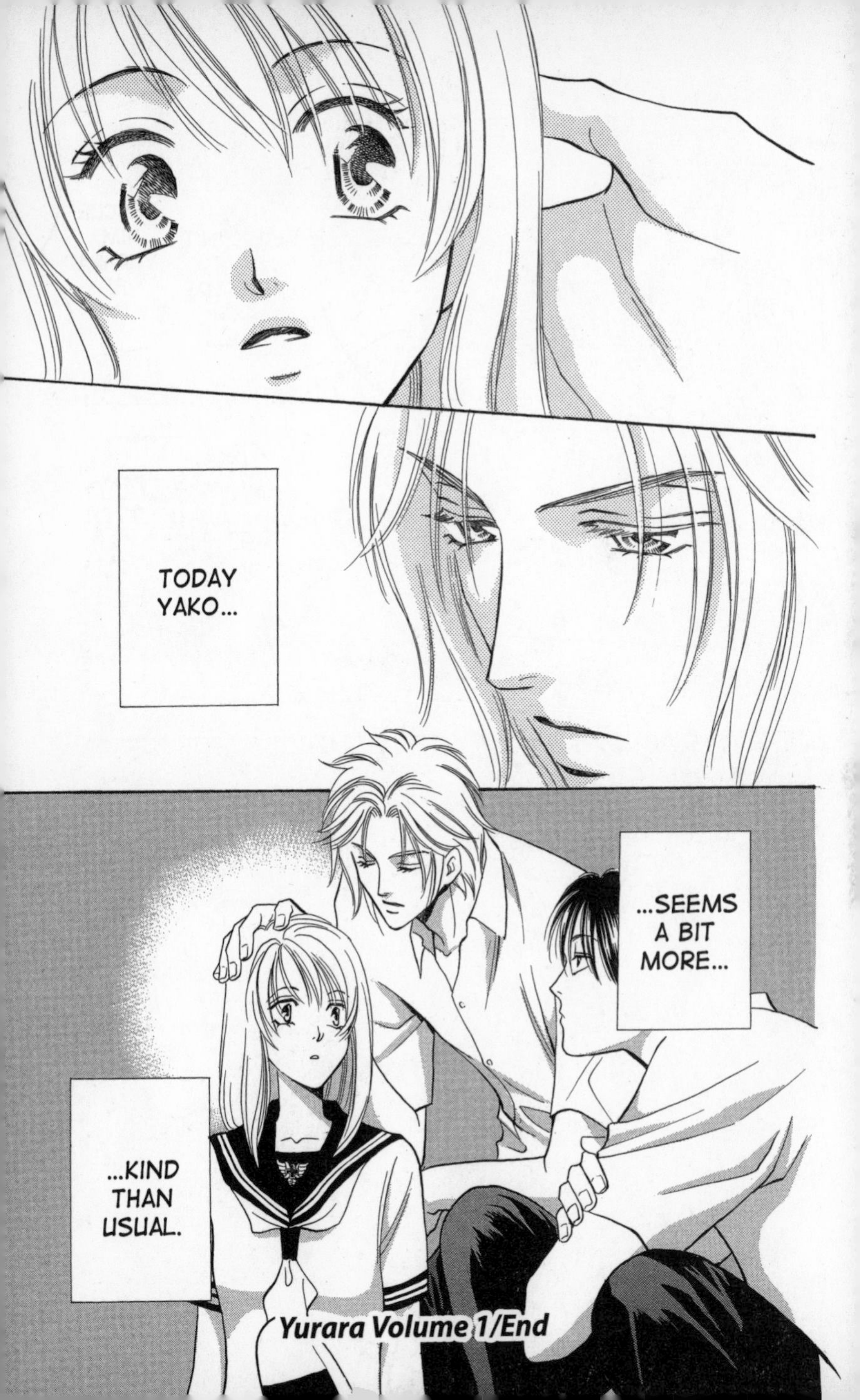
TODAY YAKO...
...SEEMS A BIT MORE...
...KIND THAN USUAL.
Yurara Volume 1/End

Chika Shiomi lives in the Aichi Prefecture
of Japan. She debuted with the manga
Todokeru Toki o Sugitemo (Even If the
Time for Deliverance Passes), and her work
is currently running in two magazines,
Bessatsu Hana to Yume and *Mystery Bonita*.
She loves reading manga, traveling, and
listening to music by Aerosmith, Hyde, and
Guns N' Roses. Her favorite artists include
Michelangelo, Hokusai, Bernini, and Gustav
Klimt.

Yurara

Vol. 1
The Shojo Beat Manga Edition

STORY & ART BY
CHIKA SHIOMI

English Adaptation/Heidi Vivolo
Translation/JN Productions
Touch-up Art & Lettering/Freeman Wong
Design/Izumi Hirayama
Editor/Nancy Thistlethwaite

Editor in Chief, Books/Alvin Lu
Editor in Chief, Magazines/Marc Weidenbaum
VP, Publishing Licensing/Rika Inouye
VP, Sales & Product Marketing/Gonzalo Ferreyra
VP, Creative/Linda Espinosa
Publisher/Hyoe Narita

Printed in Canada

Published by VIZ Media, LLC
P.O. Box 77064
San Francisco, CA 94107

Shojo Beat Manga Edition
10 9 8 7 6 5 4 3
First printing, June 2007
Third printing, November 2008

store.viz.com

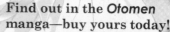

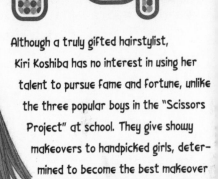